A WHOLE LANGUAGE APPROACH TO READING

Gordon S. Anderson
University of Dayton

UNIVERSITY
PRESS OF
AMERICA

LANHAM • NEW YORK • LONDON

All University Press of America books are produced on acid-free
paper which exceeds the minimum standards set by the National
Historical Publications and Records Commission.

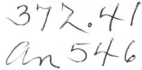

REFERENCES CITED

"An Alternative Theoretical Model" in Language and Thinking in School by Smith, E.B., Goodman, K.S. and Meredith, R. Copyright 1976, Pp. 21-25. Reprinted by permission from CBS College Publishing.

"Oral Language Development" in The Psychology of Reading by Eleanor Gibson and Levin, Harry. Copyright 1975, Pp. 27-30. Reprinted by permission from The MIT Press.

"Phase I Functions" in Learning How to Mean: Explorations in the Development of Language, Series: Explorations in Language Study edited by Peter Doughty and Geoffrey Thorton by M.A.K. Halliday. Copyright 1975, Pp. 31-37. Reprinted by Permission from Edward Arnold (Publishers) Ltd., London.

"The Functional Basis of Language" in Explorations in The Functions of Language, Series: Explorations in Language Study edited by Peter Doughty and Geoffrey Thorton by M.A.K. Halliday. Copyright 1973, Pp. 38-42. Reprinted by permission from Edward Arnold (Publishers) Ltd., London.

"Taxonomic-Gray Comprehensive Model of Reading"; Psychometric-Holmes Substrata Model of Reading; Psychological-Skinner, Staats and Gagne' Models of Reading" by Joanna Williams in "Learning to Read: A Review of Theories and Models" Reading Research Quarterly, Vol. 8, Winter 1973. Pp. 55-56; 58-59. Reprinted with permission of Joanna Williams and the International Reading Association.

"The Reading Process" in Proceedings of Western Learning Symposium in Reading by Kenneth Goodman. Copyright 1975. Pp 65-71. Reprinted by permission from Sixth Western Symposium on Learning and Reading, Western Washington State College.

"Second Generation Miscue" and "Fourth Generation Miscue" in Findings of Research in Miscue Analysis: Classroom Implications. Edited by P. David Allen by William D. Page. Figure 4:2 on page 100 and Figure 4:3 on page 101. Reprinted with the permission of the National Council of Teacher of English.

"Treasures Under the Sea" in Scott Foresman Readers. Pp 107-108. Reprinted with the permission of Scott Foresman Company.

"An Informal Reading Inventory" by Betts,·Emmett and
Welch, Carolyn. Pp. 119-126. Reprinted with the
permission of American Book Company.

Dedication

To my wife Grace, and children,
Lisa, Rachel and David for their
patience and understanding while
the book was written.

ACKNOWLEDGEMENTS

I wish to express my gratitude to many people who have provided support, encouragement and assistance in the process of completing the book.

I wish to thank Dr. Simon Chavez, Chairperson of Elementary Education Department, University of Dayton for his encouragement.

To Dr. Ellis Joseph, Dean of the School of Education, University of Dayton for his support throughout the project.

To Dr. John Geiger, Chairperson of the Department of Teacher Education, University of Dayton for his consultation and advice in getting the book published.

I would like to thank all students and teachers who have contributed comments and teaching procedures that have strengthened and made the book practical.

I want to thank the following who typed the rough drafts of the manuscript: Mary, Lidia, Anita, Regina, Shirley, and Helen.

Appreciation is expressed to Irene Terry who typed the final manuscript.

Finally, my thanks to to Lisa who did the illustrations for the book.

TABLE OF CONTENTS

ILLUSTRATIONS

Figure

PREFACE

There are many textbooks available about methods for teaching reading. One wonders why there is a need for another book on reading methods. However, over the past two decades and now in the 1980's we have available a vast body of knowledge about the language learning process and the comprehension process. Traditional theories and practices of teaching reading and learning to read have been questioned, found inconsistent with new insight and inadequate for learning and applying language. The study of language learning by psycholinguists, sociolinguists and reading educators has produced new theories and generated different teaching and learning practices as well as verified some traditional instructional activities.

This book is based on a socio-psycholinguistic theory of the language learning process. The theory is translated into practical classroom application. Knowledge of the language learning process has produced substantial evidence that reading can be learned more efficiently and effectively than formerly thought.

Chapter I provides an overview of oral and written language development and identifies language processes, language systems and cultural setting. A socio-psycholinguistic model of language learning and a teaching-learning model based on socio-psycholinguistic principles are described. An explanation of teaching competencies is included. Competencies are identified as knowledge, teaching and affective for each chapter beginning with Chapter II.

Chapter II considers oral language development. Knowledge of oral language development is essential for teachers to expand the child's use of oral language and upon which to build literacy. Teachers need to develop insight about how oral language develops, why the child learns oral language, the functions and uses of oral language, implications for learning written language, and similarities and differences in purposes and learning of oral and written language.

Chapter III examines the reading process from various models of the process. The models of the reading process described are whole language and skills models. The whole language model is based on socio-psycholinguistic research, particularly the theories of Kenneth Goodman, Frank Smith and M.A.K. Halliday. The

orientation of this book is the whole language model.
The basic premise is that for teachers to be effective
in developing student's reading abilities they need to
be knowledgeable about how the reading process operates
from a socio-psycholinguistic perspective.

Chapter IV describes evaluation procedures enabling teachers to assess student's reading development.
Each evaluation procedure is related to and consistent
with the socio-psycholinguistic (whole language) nature
of the reading process. The evaluation techniques involve teachers in systematic observation and recording
observable reading behaviors as students read in connected, whole language texts.

Chapter V reviews the socio-psycholinguistic
nature of the reading process from a whole language
perspective. The components of a whole language model
of the reading process are identified and described.
The focus is on direct teacher intervention in student's
reading development. Examples of reading strategy lessons are given related to a miscue analysis of student's
reading strengths and weaknesses. The components of
the reading instruction are identified from a whole language model and a skill model. However, all examples
of strategy lessons are based on a whole language model.
The teacher must know the components of the process
whether instruction is related to a skills or a whole
language model. Also, teachers should understand the
interrelatedness of the components. From a whole language perspective the components include language cues
and learning strategies. These cues and strategies are
described and an explanation given about how they operate interdependently during the reading process.

Chapter VI describes the socio-psycholinguistic
nature of reading and whole-language reading approaches,
methods, and materials. Chapter V on reading instruction and Chapter VI on reading approaches are similar
yet different. The distinction is made between reading
instruction and real reading, even though the teacher
is instrumental in planning, organizing and providing
the conditions for learning. However, in Chapter V the
teacher's role is that of direct intervention in the
student's reading development by planning specific lessons involving the development of certain language cues
and strategies related always to comprehension. In
Chapter VI, although the teacher provides conditions for
the learning situation, the student learns to read in
more general and real reading situations, always interacting with whole, connected text for the purpose of

understanding text. A comparison between a skills reading program and a whole language program is described. The chapter is devoted to explaining and providing examples of various whole language reading approaches, including integrating, speaking, writing, listening, art, music, and other curriculum areas. Each whole language approach is related to a socio-psycholinguistic model of the reading process. In practice reading instruction and "real" reading blend together.

Chapter VII explains procedures for organizing a whole language classroom. The goals of the classroom are identified and various school-wide and classroom organizational plans are described. The focus is on encouraging and providing procedures for teachers to evolve from a traditional classroom organization to an integrated language-content classroom consistent with the goals identified for a whole language classroom. The chapter integrates the whole language model of language learning based on socio-psycholinguistic knowledge of the reading process with components of classroom organization. The components teachers must deal with, include: scheduling time, space, use of personnel, evaluation methods and materials (approaches and instruction) and grouping. Learning centers and thematic units are described as significant organizational procedures to effectively integrate language and content learning. In actual classroom practice the information in Chapters V, VI, and VII functions simultaneously.

It is hoped that the theory and practical ideas presented in this book will help educators to re-examine existing beliefs and practices (skill-centered) that are counter-productive to oral and written language learning of students.

CHAPTER I

A WHOLE LANGUAGE MODEL OF TEACHING AND LEARNING

Teaching and learning are complex processes involving a teacher and a group of learners in the school situation. Obviously, all teaching and learning does not occur only in the school setting. The preschool child has made significant process in developing cognitive, social, psychomotor, linguistic and affective abilities. The child has developed physically, mentally, socially and emotionally in his/her own unique and personal manner. The child has inherited individual characteristics and is influenced by environmental stimuli and experiences. Each individual child assimilates and accommodates incoming stimuli and experiences in his or her own way to construct meaning and understanding of the world.

The preschool child has accomplished a tremendous amount of language and cognitive learning. Persons in the child's environment, hopefully, provide support, encouragement, and experiences enabling the human organism to develop in an optimal fashion.

Among the many learning accomplishments a child makes, perhaps, language learning is one of the most phenomenal achievements. The child at age six has basically internalized the adult language model. The child within his or her linguistic environment is able to comprehend the spoken language of language users and has the ability to communicate needs, wishes, ideas and desires to others in her or his environment. Communication is largely accomplished and learned by the child without any direct teaching or instruction. Significant language users are necessary in the child's environment. There needs to be interaction between language users and the child in a socially meaningful experiential context. It is truly a remarkable achievement that a child learns to "language" and to "mean" within a relatively short period of time without formal instruction or training.

All learning progresses along a continuim or in stages of growth and development. Children have already learned how to learn many things in life before they arrive at school. As was briefly mentioned earlier, most children have already closely approximated the adult language model at school entrance. The child can comprehend oral communication of others in her and his

1

linguistic environment and is able to orally communicate effectively in her or his language contexts. Children have been exposed to written language as well as oral language. They have usually been read to numerous times, and have an intuitive, or perhaps, a real understanding that "squiggles" on a page have something to do with language and meaning. Children have observed parents and older siblings reading print materials such as newspapers, magazines, the TV Guide, the Bible, cookbooks, telephone directories, and many other print materials. Most children are aware of print in their environment such as television, food products, signs and other print. Children have observed people in their environment encoding language although, not as frequently as speaking, listening and reading. Children observe parents writing shopping lists, letters, writing bills, writing in checkbooks, and older siblings writing homework assignments, to mention only a few writing tasks. Therefore, children come to school with a foundation in all communication processes.

Recent research findings from sociolinguistics and psycholinguistics have provided knowledge of the language learning process. Sociolinguistics, language used in social contexts, has investigated the relationship between the use and development of language in social situations. Psycholinguistics, the study of human learning and linguistics, has contributed insight into how learning and language are interrelated. Sociopsycholinguistics is a study of how humans learn and use language in social situational contexts within a cultural setting.

Learning language is a complex human process. The child learns and uses thoughts and language in many social situations. Essentially, learning language involves a language user (one who has learned and uses language) providing language learning situations and conditions so the learner can construct her/his language. The learner needs exposure to language in socially contextual situations in which she/he samples linguistic stimuli, tests hypothesis and constructs language. Language learning is enhanced when language is experientially-based. The learner learns language developmentally and holistically in meaningful experienced-based situations. Not all the complexity of learning language is completely understood. However, we do know more about the conditions necessary for language learning to take place.

Language Processes

The Language Processes humans use to communicate are speaking, listening, reading and writing. There is no particular sequence as to how humans learn and use each language process. In a broad sense, all language processes are interacting and learned interdependently. However, speaking and listening processes appear to develop earlier from birth and writing and reading develop later. Nevertheless, at an earlier age than once thought, reading and writing abilities emerge. Speaking and writing are referred to as productive language processes and listening and reading as receptive processes. Figure 1:1 shows the relationships of the oral and written language processes:

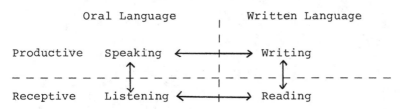

Communication with Speaker/Author

Language Processes

Figure 1:1

There are similar developmental stages, although, at different ages for oral language and written language development. The dotted lines in the diagram above illustrates the close interrelationships among the four language processes. Even though children learn to talk and understand talk before they learn to read and write, oral language provides a base for the development of written language. At a relatively early stage language processes become integrated in the life of the child. Before school age children have been immersed in oral and written language and have developed mastery of oral language and to some extent written language. School language programs need to build upon the development in oral and written language by integrating the language processes. In other words, the receptive processes, listening and reading are enhanced through speaking and writing. So too, listening and reading are developed through opportunities to speak and write in meaningful situations.

Language Systems

The language processes use much the same language elements or systems of language cues. The only difference is that speaking and listening use the sound system (phonemic) and reading and writing use the print (graphemic) system. Oral and written language processes use the morphological, syntactic, and semantic cueing systems. Figure 1:2 illustrates the language elements common to oral and written language:

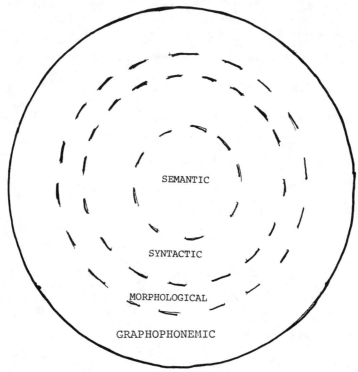

SEMANTIC

SYNTACTIC

MORPHOLOGICAL

GRAPHOPHONEMIC

LANGUAGE SYSTEMS

FIGURE 1:2

The dotted lines indicate the interrelationship of language elements within the language systems as children develop oral and written language competence.

4

The language system is superimposed upon the language processes in Figure 1:3 to illustrate the common features of oral and written language:

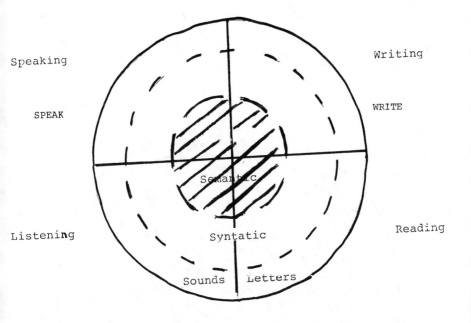

Speaking

SPEAK

Listening

Writing

WRITE

Reading

Semantic

Syntatic

Sounds | Letters

THE LANGUAGE ARTS AND

LANGUAGE SYSTEMS

FIGURE 1:3

Whole Language and Whole Child in the Culture

Language learning occurs in a cultural setting and in a variety of social situational contexts. A child learns the oral language code within the culture of the society. The written language code is learned related to the extent that the society uses written language. The language system for oral and written language will be directly related to the linguistic code accepted in the culture. The semantic element (meanings), syntactic (grammar), morphemic (unit of meanings) and graphophonemic (print-sound elements) are unique to the linguistic code within the culture.

5

The child is exposed to the linguistic code in the home, community and school. Within each of these settings are social situational contexts in which language is used for communication of meaning. The whole child is immersed in use and development of language processes and language systems in the culture.

Figure 1:4 illustrates the interrelationship of language processes, language systems and culture impacting upon the child:

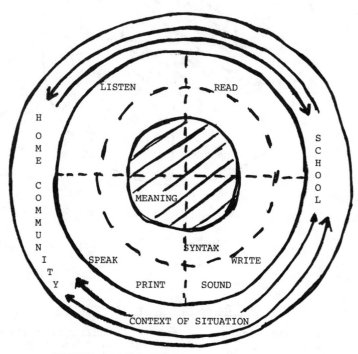

CULTURE - WHOLE LANGUAGE AND WHOLE CHILD

FIGURE 1:4

The system of language is learned and used by the child within the culture of the home and community in meaningful social situational contexts. Unfortunately, the school does not always provide meaningful situations and purposes for oral and written language to be learned and used. There are significant conditions available that contribute to the child's oral and written language learning in the home and community, and to some extent, in the school. These conditions are: (1) role models or language users available to support language learning; (2) language use serves a purpose; (3) language is used in meaningful social contexts; and, (4) language is kept whole. When learning to talk and listen, the systems of language, phonemic, morphemic, syntactic, and semantic are integrated. The child gradually learns and uses the language cues to construct meaning, representing experiences symbolically with language.

The productive language processes, writing and reading, and the elements of written language, graphic, morphemic, syntactic, and semantic are also integrated in the home and community environment. The child learns to construct meaning from print in meaningful context in the home and community. However, in school, the child usually faces a conflict in language learning. In reading and writing the language systems are frequently isolated, the language processes are fragmented, immediate language role models are not available, isolated language cues are not purposeful and language is not learned/used in meaningful social situational contexts. In school, language is often used by the teacher, to talk about language, or language rules. Thus, learning written language is often abstract, non-purposeful, de-contextualized and fragmented.

A Socio-Psycholinguistic Model of Language Learning

A socio-psycholinguistic view of language learning considers the learner within a culture learning and using language to represent thinking in social situational contexts in home, community and school settings. During the language learning process the learner is engaged in transactions with other language users.

Figure 1:5 illustrates factors involved in the development of language processes and the language system within a socio-psycholinguistic perspective.

The model shows the interrelationships in the language process. Language learning involves a transaction between speaker and listener and writer and reader.

7

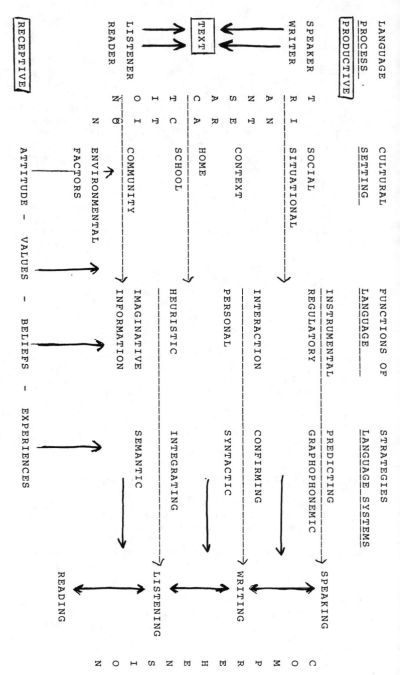

SOCIO-PSYCHOLINGUISTIC MODEL OF LANGUAGE LEARNING

FIGURE 1:5

The text is the message encoded by the speaker/writer and acted upon or decoded by the listener/reader. During any transaction context of culture influences the communication of the message. Although speaker/writer and listener/reader reside in the same linguistic cultural society, there are differences in language systems, experiential background, ideational, interpersonal and textural attributes each brings to the communication. The setting and social situational context influences how language is used differently in the home, community, and school environment.

The early development of oral and written language involves language users learning the language system related to experiences and at the same time learning the functions of language. The child entering school learning to read and write has an easier task than the young child learning oral languages because she/he already know the uses of language and the language systems. Written language is used for similar purposes as oral language. The developing writer and reader need to learn an alternative language system (graphemic) although the graphomorphemic system of written language is closely related to oral language. The learner's focus is on meaning. The culture and context in home, community and later at school provide the framework for the learner to construct a system of meaning related to thinking, experiences and functions of language. The phonemic/graphemic, morphemic and syntactic elements develop so that the child can produce/receive meaning and develop the functions of language. The child samples and selects the units of language from his/her linguistic--experiential environment and eventually is able to produce and receive more complex structures. According to Halliday (1973), the separate functions of language merge into macro-functions called ideational, interpersonal and textual. An elaboration of Halliday's language functions is given in Chapter II.

The early development of syntactic structures in oral language enables the child to communicate experiences with others in context in complex ways. The early development of written language appears to take place in a similar way. However, the child uses an oral language base upon which to develop facility in writing and reading. The beginning and later stages of writing and reading may be learned and used for separate functions but as the writer and reader develop he/she can communicate in larger units to communicate ideas (ideational) with others (interpersonal) in a context (textual) of situations.

9

Oral and written language is a symbolic system representing experiences and concepts organized into cognitive structures or a schema. The child constructs an interrelated network of concepts with labels for concepts. The language uses (phonemic, graphemic, morphemic, syntax, and semantics) are organized in a coherent form enabling language users to communicate propositions (ideas) within accepted linguistic structure in the culture.

The language learner needs to learn the arbitrary sequences of the phonemic, graphemic, morphemic, syntax and semantic systems as they function related to experiences in order to produce/receive oral and written language. During the process the learner samples from language, selects the language cues and predicts (develops hypothesis), tests predictions (confirms or disconfirms) self-corrects and integrates meaning. The process involves risk-taking and miscue-making. Miscues by the speaker/listener and writer/reader are evidence of developmental stages the learner is going through at any given time as she/he moves closer toward the conventional use of language accepted in the culture. As Goodman (1968) has stated, miscues made by readers are not random. There is considerable evidence that children go through stages of inventing spellings in writing that indicate a developmental process, according to Read (1972). During oral language development children overgeneralize language rules and in a sense, "miscue," on certain conventional pronunciations, i.e., "goed" for "went," "comed" for "came," and others. Eventually overgeneralized words become more precise and conform to conventional usage.

It is important for teachers to be aware of the conditions that need to be present for language learning. The text provides the message for language transactions to occur. The text is influenced by the culture and social situational settings in which language is used in the home, community and school. The language systems, strategies and functions of language are learned within the text related to experiences in social contexts and become operational to express thoughts, concepts, and attitudes with other language users. There must be a textual setting for without text there can be no real communication of ideas. Thoughts and concepts become organized into complex schemata related to the language systems, functions of language, learning strategies, experiences, and attitudes. The development of schemata allows language users to organize propositions related to experiences.

Finally, the language learner's purpose and goal is always focused on meaning. The end result in language learning is the communication of meaning or making experiences comprehensible. There can be no other reason for communication. Instructional programs in the school setting need to consider the interrelationships between how language processes are learned and used in social-cultural settings, and how language functions and the learning strategies operate within the communication process.

A Teaching-Learning Model Related to Communication Abilities

In the teaching-learning interaction process the teacher brings his/her knowledge, skills, attitudes, values, interests, experiences and personality to the interaction. The teacher is responsible for developing his/her knowledge, teaching skills and affective behavior so that each child has the opportunity to develop as a unique individual and is able to function effectively in the society. The teacher has a responsibility to understand and respect the uniqueness and individuality of each child and to provide learning opportunities which relate to natural growth patterns. (See Figure 1:6, Page 12)

Thus, the teacher and learner interact in the development of language processes in which the teacher is responsible for knowledge of the communication process; is able to assess and monitor all language performance; and facilitates language learning by providing conditions conducive to promoting higher levels of language proficiency. The teacher must be cognizant of the need to consider the child's growth in linguistic, cognitive, psychomotor and affective behaviors. Conditions and instructional approaches for learning to speak, listen, read and write should be natural and related to real needs within the school setting. A Teacher-Learning Model to develop Communication Abilities is given in Figure 1:7, on Page 13.

Since teachers, like the parents, have responsibility for facilitating the child's learning and development, it is essential that teachers are knowledgeable about language and competent. Teaching and learning involve complex interaction between a teacher and a learner or a group of learners. Both the teacher and the individual learner and a group of individual learners possess a body of knowledge, skills and affective behaviors. The teacher's role includes: a

11

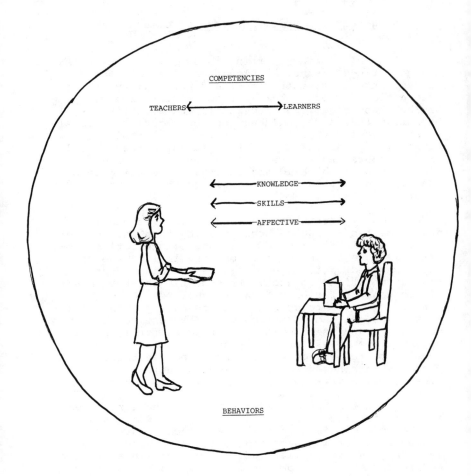

TEACHER AND LEARNER COMPETENCIES

FIGURE 1:6

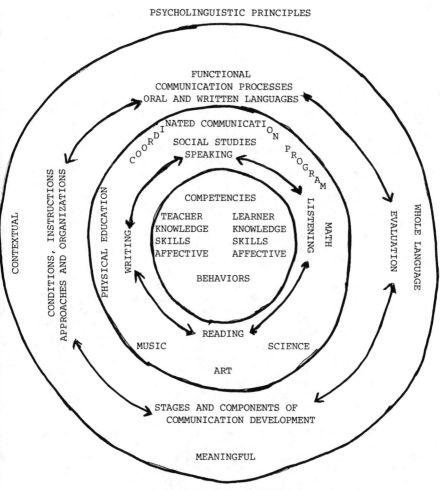

PSYCHOLINGUISTIC PRINCIPLES

FUNCTIONAL
COMMUNICATION PROCESSES
ORAL AND WRITTEN LANGUAGES

COORDINATED COMMUNICATION PROGRAM

SOCIAL STUDIES
SPEAKING

CONTEXTUAL

CONDITIONS, INSTRUCTIONS
APPROACHES AND ORGANIZATIONS

PHYSICAL EDUCATION

WRITING

COMPETENCIES

TEACHER   LEARNER
KNOWLEDGE   KNOWLEDGE
SKILLS   SKILLS
AFFECTIVE   AFFECTIVE

BEHAVIORS

LISTENING

MATH

EVALUATION

WHOLE LANGUAGE

READING

MUSIC   SCIENCE

ART

STAGES AND COMPONENTS OF
COMMUNICATION DEVELOPMENT

MEANINGFUL

SOCIOLINGUISTIC PRINCIPLES
A TEACHING-LEARNING MODEL TO DEVELOP
COMMUNICATION ABILITIES

FIGURE 1:7

knowledge of the communication process which relates to
reality; application of knowledge; developing teaching
competence; and a person with a positive attitude toward learners. The learner's role includes his or her
uniqueness and individuality as a person possessing
knowledge, language, learning strategies and affective
behavior. The teacher is responsible for continuously

13

identifying the learner's experiential knowledge background, developing language strategies and abilities, and to provide conditions to enhance self-concept and positive self-image.

To develop the teacher's role and responsibility, a systematic, yet humanistic approach is necessary to train teachers. The teachers preparation program described is competency-based. The teacher's knowledge, teaching strategies and affective behaviors will be identified for each component of the teaching-learning process. The competencies identified are not all inclusive and are selected primarily based on the author's experiences. The identified competencies have been experimented with and tested in pre-service and in-service reading and language arts courses since 1970. The competencies have not been empirically tested or proven to be the only valid competencies. Rather, the competencies described have been subjectively evaluated and utilized by hundreds of students who have been enrolled in the author's courses.

A competency-based program risks the isolation and fragmentation of teaching-learning behaviors and frequently avoids, or considers in a limited way, affective behaviors. An attempt is made to integrate components of the teaching-learning model so that teaching and learning language is meaningful and natural. As children learn to communicate effectively in whole, meaningful, comprehensible situations, so do teachers become more effective if prepared in a program which focuses on the integration of learning in a purposeful and functional setting.

The assumption is made that there is no distinct difference in language learning for any child, although there will be differences in rate at which children learn, i.e. differences in affect, emotional characteristics, mental traits, social maturity and physioneurological differences within individual learners and a group of learners. However, the basic language processes it is believed are essentially the same for all humans, except for persons with severe impairment in cognitive physical, mental, psychomotor and/or affective behavior. It is further assumed that evaluative techniques are basically similar and are appropriate for application with all learners. The stages and components of communication or oral and written language development, it is assumed, are similar for all children, except those children with extreme handicaps. Finally, the conditions and instructional approaches,

14

although varied for an individual child or group of children, are similar and are different in the degree to which certain conditions and instructional approaches are planned and organized.

A further supposition is made that the training and preparation of teachers, whether at pre-service or in-service level, is basically similar, except with regard to experiential background and teaching maturity. The pre-service and in-service teacher needs to develop similar knowledge teaching strategies and affective behaviors, although, the rate at which competencies can be assimilated or accommodated and applied will differ on the basis of experience, uniqueness and individuality. Therefore, the competencies are similar for pre-service and in-service, however, generally a higher degree of proficiency should be expected with teachers at the in-service level.

Summary

This chapter has briefly described the accomplishment of preschool children in oral and written language learning. Children come to the school situation with substantial language learning strengths upon which the school needs to build and extend.

A whole language model of learning described the complexity of understanding how language is learned and used as a communication tool. The language processes, speaking, listening, reading, and writing were identified as interrelated and interdependent processes. Each productive and receptive language process is reinforced and strengthened by other processes. The preschool child is immersed in oral and written language. The school needs to also integrate the language process so that each develops naturally.

The language system for language learning and use was identified and related to the language processes. Each language process uses the same language system, except oral language (speaking and listening) uses the phonemic element while written language uses the graphic element. Both oral and written language processes have a syntactic and semantic system.

Next, the language processes, language system and culture were described. The child develops oral and written language in a cultural setting within the contexts of situations in the home, community, and the school. The home and community provide a meaningful setting in which language is learned and functions related to socially situational contexts and experiences in the environment. Oral and written language are learned and used by the child in whole, connected language under certain conditions: access to language role models and language users; language is used purposefully; language is meaningful; language is whole and intact. By contrast, language learning in school frequently does not provide the same conditions.

A socio-psycholinguistic model of language learning was designed and described to illustrate the interrelationships of processes, context, functions, language systems, and provide a framework for teachers to understand the language learning process.

In Chapter II, a description is given or oral language development and implications for learning to read and write.

Reading References

Halliday, M.A.K. Exploration in the Functions of Language. New York: Elsevier, 1973.

CHAPTER 2

DEVELOPMENT OF ORAL LANGUAGE

Knowledge Competencies

1. How does oral language develop?
2. In what ways does spoken language provide the basis for reading and writing?
3. What are the similarities and differences in oral and written language development?
4. What are the functions of language?

It is hypothesized that oral and written language development are alternative linguistic systems which have a common function to communicate meaning. Each linguistic process, speaking, listening, reading, writing, is related directly to other processes. Oral language has traditionally been accepted as the primary mode of communication and written language as a secondary process. Studies concerning early humans communication substantiate the hypothesis that historically oral language evolved earlier than written language. Possibly even before human learned a linguistic system for communication, paralinguistic techniques were utilized, such as grunts, gestures, facial expressions and the like, to communicate. In most cultures humans learn oral language first and written language is developed at a latter stage. However, there is some evidence that a child learns written language parallel to spoken language, at least at the onset of using grammatical structures, usually at about eighteen months when the child is beginning to combine words into holophrases, or two or more words into a structure.

The English Language

Language is an activity and a behavior. Language involves organized noises while writing uses organized marks, both produced by muscles. Language is a completely organized system. Speech is commonly thought to be a primarily language phenomena. Both speech and writing are organized according to habits and behaviors. However, the writing system does not directly reflect the speech system. Speech is usually more informal including fragments of sound sequences which convey meaning to a listener, while the writing system is generally more formal in style. Language is conventional in that similar language users share an agreed upon behavior, or usage, which has been established. Language learning involves unconscious habit by the proficient language user. Language involves emotional overtones concerning the "correctness" of usage among language users and language involves rationalizations or preferences once a conventional usage is established.

There persists a controversy and confusion concern- the relationship of thought and language. Piaget's formulation of sensory-motor development demonstrates that the rudiments of intelligent behavior evolve before language develops. Regarding the relationship between intelligence and language, Piaget (1967) stated:

> Intelligence actually appears well before language, that is to say, well before internal thought, which presupposes the use of verbal signs (internalized language). It is an entirely practical intelligence based on the manipulation of objects; in place of words and concepts it uses percepts and movements organized into "action scheme." For example, to grab a stick in order to draw up a remote object is an act of intelligence (and a fairly late developing one at that: about eighteen months). Here, an instrument, the means to an end, and is co-ordinated with a pre-established goal...(p.11)

On the other hand, Vygotsky (1962) stated:

> Inner speech is not the interior aspect of external speech--it is a function in itself. It still remains speech, i.e., thought connected with words. But while in external speech thought is embodied in words, in inner speech words die as they bring forth thought. Inner speech is to a large extent thinking in pure meanings. It is a dynamic, shifting, unstable thing, fluttering between word and thought, the two more or less stable, more or less firmly delineated components of verbal thought. It's true nature and place can be understood only after examining the next plane of verbal thought, the one still more inward than inner speech.

Whether language develops before thought or thought is essential before language or if both thought and language develop simultaneously, it might be said that language is a device for human interaction. A device for expression of thoughts.

The English language has been said to be copious, haphazard and without order. Moreover, that English does not have the order and rules of Latin. However, linguistic studies indicate that English as other languages has its own order and logic. English utilizes syntactic or grammatical structures to provide order and logic to the language system. Words function related to the syntactic ordering of word structures to convey meaning.

Finally, many things go into the making up of a language. There is no single system but three systems that go together. There is the speech system which includes all varieties of English ideolect and dialect and socially useful or not socially useful language conventions. The writing system is made up of twenty-six letters in various sequences which is arbitrary and standardized. And there are other world systems, including how language might be used, such as school textbook language. Therefore, the English language is not a simple thing but a complex of systems.

The teacher has a formidable task in facilitating children's language development. The teacher's responsibility is to help each child develop increased competence in talking and to provide learning experiences and conditions for alternative forms of language, reading and writing, to develop in natural, meaningful and functional ways.

How and Why Children Learn Language: A Model

Considerable research into language development and language acquisition has been accomplished, particularly during the 1960's, 1970's and now in the 1980's. Linguistics, psycholinguistics, and sociolinguistics have provided new insight into language learning and language acquisition.

Studies by Piaget (1971), Brown (1970), Menyuk (1977), Dale (1976), Halliday (1973), Vygotsky (1962), and others, each from their own perspective, have traced the development of a child's oral language development from birth through at least five or six years of age. Chomsky (1969) has identified language learning characteristics of children at elementary school age.

All investigations of child language learning have concluded that the "normal" child of five or six years of age has achieved a phenomenal mastery of his

or her native language systems. There are different
theories how oral language is internalized and used
automatically by five or six years of age. Yet the
fact remains, the "normal" child with appropriate language stimulation, encouragement and language models
learns and uses language.

There are also different points of view or philosophies why a child learns language. For what purpose,
function or need does a child learn language? Smith,
Goodman, and Meredith (1976) contended that language
learning is not a natural organic part of growing up.
They point out that children who grow up isolated from
human society do not develop language. Furthermore,
human beings have a capacity to produce a great variety
of sounds. Smith (1971) also stated that language is
not learned just for the sake of learning. There is no
intrinsic need for a child to learn language. Possibly,
a child learns language because it is there. It is
available and used naturally in the child's environment.
Perhaps, also as Lenneberg (1966) states, the child is
predisposed to learn language. There is an innate
capacity, or as McNeill (1966) points out, a language
acquisition device (LAD) which biologically predisposes
human beings to learn language.

Two human qualities may explain the development
of language. One is the innate capacity of the human
mind to imagine and use symbols and, second, the human's
need to communicate. Thus, humans have the capacity to
think symbolically and to produce sound symbols making
it possible to learn language. The need to communicate
makes it necessary to learn language according to Smith,
Goodman, and Meredith (1975).

A sociolinguistic perspective of language learning emphasizes the social function and uses of language.
Language is learned to enable the very young child to
fulfill personal needs, to control his or her own and
others behaviors, to develop his or her personality,
attitudes and values and to interact with self and
others. Language becomes the socializing agent so that
the child can communicate in purposeful and meaningful
ways with significant others in his or her environment.
A sociolinguistic point of view regarding language
learning focuses on the contextual situation in which
the child interacts with others in the environment. The
child in a particular cultural context is exposed to a
language, in varied situational contexts and uses language related to real experiences. Many experiences in
repetitive context associated with language enables a

child to eventually develop phonological, morphological, syntactic and semantic systems which are internalized and used by the child to communicate with others. Halliday (1973), identified various "models" or functions of language which the child develops and internalizes over a period of time within contextual situations in interaction with others in his or her linguistic and experiential environment. These "models" or functions will be described in a later section of this chapter.

Smith, Goodman, and Meredith (1975) have proposed a theoretical model of how children learn language. The model identifies six stages of language learning including significant characteristics related to each level of development. However, each stage is not discrete but overlaps with the preceeding and following stages in language learning. It is suggested that all children progress through each language development stage, although at different rates. See Figure 2:1 on Page 22.

The Random Stage

There is a pre-linguistic stage from approximately birth to six months characterized by babbling and experimenting with sounds which is not considered language, but rather as sounds as a part of a reaction to discomfort such as when hungry, wet, in pain, cold, hot, or frightened. As adults respond to a child's noise, the child acquires a generalized ability to use sounds as an attention-getting signal. There is no selection process at the pre-linguistic stage, but rather the child produces a random assortment of sounds. Toward the end of the random stage, the child appears to engage in some intentional imitative behavior. She or he acquires control over certain sounds which eventually leads to the child's ability to make sounds at will. The phonological development of the child will be described in this chapter.

The Unitary Stage

As the child learns to discriminate and produce more distinct sound features and is continuously exposed to a language model in many varied and repetitious language-experience contexts, he or she eventually develops units of language. The units of language begin to serve a communication function, although the units may not be appropriate adult words in the language, but bundles of sounds which may or may not approximate the

21

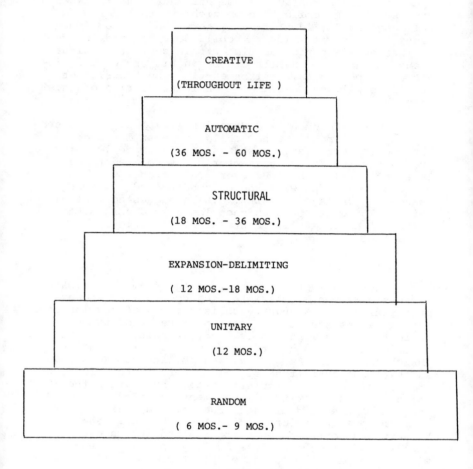

STAGES OF LANGUAGE DEVELOPMENT

FIGURE 2:1

22

language being learned. The first words are usually thought to be developed by a child at about twelve months. However, Halliday (1975), has observed that intelligible "words," bundles of sounds are communicated with meaning as early as six to nine months.

During the unitary stage, the following character-istics have been observed. Each utterence at the begin-ning of the stage was often limited to a single syllable. A particular syllable was the child's approximation of a feature of language associated with the situation. Brown and Bellugi (1970) studied a boy and a girl learn-ing to talk who repeated statements of their mother in a kind of "telegraphic" language. The utterances pro-duced were two to four morphemes in length. However, one syllable "words" or approximations of words, or bundles of sounds articulated in certain situation con-texts actually conveyed a whole meaning, even though the child was physically and intellectually able to use holophrases. The speech of a child at this stage and evolving into the next level, has a grammatical consis-tency, although devoid of inflection markers such as -ed, -ing, -s, and function words (is, are, was, were, the).

The Stage of Expansion and Delimiting

During this stage the child's language expands from one to two syllable utterances and begins to approximate adult speech. The child expands his or her language so that minor features are included. At the unitary stage in the context of eating the child may only say, "eat" or some other approximation of the word eat. At a later stage the child may expand the utter-ances to, "wanna eat" and later to, "I want to eat." Also, the child begins to delimit or become more pre-cise in the use of language. The child's utterances become more precise in expressing more particular needs, wishes, and feelings. The child strives for more effective communication and learns precise limits within which adults will accept utterances as appropriate.

Brown and Bellugi (1970) in their study report mothers tended to repeat and expand utterances appro-priate to the situation. For example, when the child said, "Baby high chair." The mother responded, "Baby is in the high chair."

23

Stage of Structural Awareness

The child prior to this stage has acquired a larger vocabulary of language utterances and has learned how language is used in specific situations. During this stage the child is developing the ability to generalize and generate language patterns and order in situations she or he experiences. The child begins to notice common elements in similar utterances. The child develops the use of negatives and experiments with negatives. The child becomes aware of very common patterns in the structure of utterances such as: subject-verb-object as in, "I see you," pattern. Also there is increased awareness of less common language patterns.

Prior to this stage the child's speech is reasonably grammatical in that it retains the exact surface structure of the adult speech model. However, as the child becomes aware of the deep structure of language she or he begins to construct her or his own utterances according to half-defined rules. The child's language goes through a stage of being ungrammatical by adult norms. The child begins to overgeneralize grammatical rules and produces utterances such as: "I brunged the toy home." The child is regularizing irregular forms or structures using her or his knowledge of language rules and patterns by testing generalizations.

At this stage words or phrases begin to take on meaning and the child develops awareness of the interchangeability of words. The child becomes aware of the element of meaning contributed by each word or phrase to the complete meaning of sentences. This is a very complex process in that every word in an utterance has contextual meaning, not only lexical or dictionary meaning. A child must encounter a word or phrase in many utterances before she or he begins to know the limits of the lexical meaning of words.

The Automatic Stage

The "average" child has reached the automatic stage of language by the time she or he begins kindergarten at age five. The basic grammar of her or his language, home and community, is deeply embedded in her or him. It is constantly reinforced by the language she or he hears and uses at home and play. The child is greatly increasing her or his conceptualization and greatly increasing the quantity of effectiveness of language. The child's language has reached a point at

24

which she or he has automatic control over it and it is
adequate to meet the communicative needs common to persons of her or his age in the immediate society.

The Creative Stage

As language develops the child literally invents
her or his own. However, the need for effectiveness in
communication is so strong that the child is constantly
pushed in the direction of the language of her or his
community. The child's language conforms to the language of her or his community. Language becomes for
the most part, a vast collection of cliches and almost
everyday communication is carried on with trite expressions. This conformity reflects the manner in which language has become automatic to repetitive situations.

However trite and systematic, language never becomes completely static and unchanging. Humans, individually and socially, never lose the ability to
create language. Children pass into a stage of creative
manipulation of language. It is possibly due to the
child's increasing ability to conceptualize and think
in metaphors and abstractions. Children push language
beyond conventional limits. It is related to the need
children have to test all adult limits. Children have
needs and interests not shared with adults. Children
develop sub-dialects and teenagers particularly tend to
create language. The teenager must have language
uniquely her or his own and uniquely express life as he
or she sees it. Terms are invented which are generally
negative adult terms, i.e., "crazy," "mad," "tough,"
"bad," which become positive in teen language.

Elements of Language

It should be useful for teachers to acquire an
understanding concerning how the child develops various
elements or components which are integrated into a language system. It is evident that most children are linguistically mature at approximately age five or six.
The child has made considerable progress in phonological,
morphological, semantic, and grammatical development.
Oral and written language and communication is dependent
upon the child's development in these language elements.
Gibson and Levin (1975) have outlined the oral language
development of the phonological, morphological, semantic,
and grammatical process most children master to a degree
by the time they are five or six years of age. See
Figure 2:2 on Page 26.

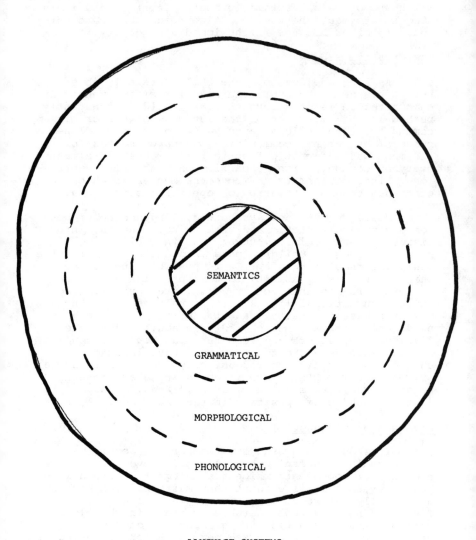

SEMANTICS

GRAMMATICAL

MORPHOLOGICAL

PHONOLOGICAL

LANGUAGE SYSTEMS

FIGURE 2:2

Phonological Development

The child's mastery of the sound system in perception and production is very good when children normally start to read. The phonological system of language by and large is set and the child possesses a notion of distinct features.

Jakobson (1968) has provided a powerful theory of phonological development, at least in its productive aspects. The keystone to Jakobson's theory is the notion of <u>distinctive features</u>. Briefly, distinctive features are a set of contrasts or features applied to phonemes. Phonemes are the smallest units of language or sound units. Every phoneme is characterized by a pattern of presence or absence of those features. A segment of sound has phonemic function in the language if it differs from all other sounds by at least one distinctive feature. For example, "b" and "p" have the same values on all features except one, voicing. In general, phonemes that share many features are more confusable than sounds that have few features in common.

At eleven months, according to Jakobson, children babble less, as though attending to speech sounds around them without interruption of their own vocalization. At first, children produce contrasts in sound which represent extremes of a feature, and further sound contrasts successfully define other features. The early sounds which a child produces have features common to many languages, hence the claim for the interlanguage universality of the sequences which children exhibit.

In summary, the acquisition of the sound system of a language can best be understood by a theory of distinctive features. Significant sounds in a language are unique bundles of a reasonably small inventory of features. Development involves the abstraction and use of the set of features. This development is hierarchial, which means that a general feature such as consonant-vowels is used first, then is differentiated into another feature contrast, like oral-nasal, which is further differentiated and so forth. The school-aged child has mastered some distinctions more reliably than others. The vowel-consonant feature appears early. Within the consonants, those that are most easily identified appear earlier than those less easily identified sounds. Likewise, easily produced sounds, in terms of motor articulatory gestures involved, are mastered earlier than sounds made by more complex motor articulations.

27

Morphological Development

Compared to language that conjugate verbs elaborately or mark those cases of nouns and their adjectival modifiers, English has a reasonably simple system of inflectional morphology, according to Gibson and Levin (1975). They go on to describe the morphological development of children based on several research studies.

Besides the simple system of inflectional morphemes, English has a more elaborate system of derivational morphemes, which are sounds and spellings that derive one part of speech from another: "happy-happiness," "relax-relaxation," etc.

Research studies provide information about children's knowledge of morphological rules at age five or six, when they usually start to read. For morphemes that are spelled "s", the child knows the phonological rules that yield the allomorphemes "s" and "z". For "iz" the child uses the base form alone as its plural or possessive or third person singular. Since "iz" follow sibilants (e.g., "glasses" or "churches"), children are prepared to take a word ending in a sibilant as the inflected form.

Vocabulary Development

Gibson and Levin (1975) described the vocabulary development of children. The major increase in a child's vocabulary size occurs around two and a half to three years of age. This is the structural stage of language development. At this time children's utterances become longer and grammatically more complex. The child begins talking in more complicated sentences which means he or she is using more words.

Several vocabulary studies classified words according to their part of speech. It was found that children around the age of two utter words that are preponderantly classified as nouns, roughly 60%. This figure may be misleading since children at this age are emitting one or two word utterances which usually reflect objects or events immediately available to the child in his or her surroundings.

After this noun-ful period, only about 20% of a child's conversation will consist of nouns. The change is also understandable in terms of the grammatical constraints of sentences. As language matures from one or two word sentences to adult-like sentences, nouns have

specific and limited functions in the sentences. The
sentences require articles, verbs, adjectives, prepositions, adverbs, etc., which inevitably reduce the overall proportion of nouns.

Grammatical Development

A summary of Gibson and Levin (1975) findings in
grammatical development indicated that around the first
year children say single understandable words, then
around eighteen months put two words together and gradually there is evidence of more two than one word utterances. Occasionally there will appear a three word
group and then the size of sentences will explode.
During the period of single word utterances, known as
the holophrasic period, the word functions as a phrase
or a sentence. Two word utterances arrange themselves
into a neat and simple pattern. One class has fewer
words and usually precedes the larger class.

Children are not just putting words together but
are trying to say things meaningful to them. One theory
of language development emphasizes the primacy of the
semantic component or meaning in the production and comprehension of language. Before language, from birth,
children attend to and differentiate their world. The
process is one of perceptual and cognitive learning in
which the child extracts distinctive features and in-
variates from experiences, group objects, and events
that share features and classify on the basis of similar and different features. Before the child speaks,
the child is semantically wise. The task of language
acquisition is to relate language to her or his existing
perceptions and cognitions.

More important the child indicates agent-action-
object relationships, which are the most pervasive yet
simple relationships in language. Several studies of
children's grammatical development indicate that by the
time a child is five or six years of age, she or he
appears to control the bulk of adult-like grammar.

Semantic Development

Gibson and Levin (1975), have described how children acquire meanings of words from several investigations. The result of those studies will be summarized
here. They have stated that the semantic knowledge of
children is prior to grammar and is reflected in grammar.

The meaning of a word may be defined by a bundle of semantic features which differentiate that word from others. Semantic features can be thought of as similar to phonological features. The concept of semantic features is considerably less developed than that of phonological distinctive features. At this time the study of meaning using a semantic feature strategy is gaining currency and appears to be very promising.

Most of the following from Gibson and Levin (1975) is based upon the work of E. Clark (1973) concerning the development of word meanings. For the child the meaning of a word involves only a few features, so that the development of meaning involves the differentiation of more specific features. Gibson and Levin differed with Clark's belief that when a child initially learns the meaning of a word he or she learns matrix of semantic features which define that word. More likely, the word "dog" is first an attribute of the object being named. The object "dog" has an infinite number of characteristics or features, and the child has no basis for choosing some group of these features to serve as a criteria for "dog." The word "dog" is simply another characteristic of a familiar object. If, however, the child extends the word "dog" to a cow and learns the error, he or she has a basis for abstracting the semantic features which distinguish a dog from a cow. Features are contrastive. Features are not an arbitrary choice of characteristics than can be assigned or an object, but a set of characteristics that permit contrast between the meaning of objects, events, or relationships.

Gibson and Levin (1975) have stated that semantic features are derived from perceptual abstractions: abstractions, because if four-leggedness is a feature of defining the category animal, we ignore whether the legs are long as a giraffe's or as short as a basset hound's. whether they move like a gaited horse's or like a running dog's. Semantic features are themselves abstractions. "Animate" is an inference based on growth, breathing, animate motion (compared to rigid motion, for example, etc.). Several investigations concluded that word meanings occur from the concrete to the abstract, Anglin (1970) and Clark (1973), and that word meanings start with the general features and develop in a general-to-specific fashion.

The Functions of Language

It has been previously discussed that a child
develops and learns language because of a biological,
innate predisposition to learn language. A child learns
to communicate using language because of the need to
verbally interact with significant others in his or her
environment. Related to the assumption that a child
develops language to communicate with others, to understand what others mean, and to communicate meaning to
others, is the concept that a child learns language as
a functional approach. For the child to participate
fully in his or her environment there is a need to learn
language to function effectively and in a meaningful
way. Language is the vehicle which enables the child to
fulfill needs, wants, and desires. Language permits the
socialization of the child in the social culture and
setting, to learn appropriate and inappropriate behavior
through understanding the language of others in his or
her environment, and in producing his or her own language to develop his or her appropriate role in the environment. Language provides the means for the child
to more fully develop his or her personality, self-
concept, attributes, values and interests. The use of
language allows the child to express his or her individuality and to further develop uniqueness as an individual within the context of the culture in which the
child lives. Learning to use language enables the child
to interact in meaningful ways with others in his or her
environment. Language functions for the child to explore and describe his or her environment, to develop
concepts, to integrate experiences with language, to
discover and interpret the world. A child uses language
to imagine, to create and build his or her own world,
to fantasize, pretend and participate in make-believe.
Finally, language serves a meaningful purpose for the
child to learn language to describe his or her interpretation of the environment, to represent symbolically
ideas and knowledge of the world. It may be said that
language is learned in order for the child to function
effectively and fully in his or her surroundings.

In addition to understanding the language characteristics at various stages of language development and
how various language elements are learned and integrated
into a communicative whole, we need to know more about
the nature of language learning related to the function
which language serves as the child is growing and developing. The development of language should be understood concerning the psychological, physiological,

sociological and affective aspects. In this section the focus will be primarily on the sociological implications of the nature of language and language learning.

From a sociolinguistic perspective, Halliday (1973), states, "that a functional approach to language means that, first of all, investigating how language is used; trying to find out what are the purposes that language serves us and how we are able to achieve these purposes through speaking, listening, reading and writing. It means seeking to explain the nature of language in functional terms."

Halliday (1973) described relevant "models" of language considered from the point of view of the child. In effect, about the child's image of language. What is the "model" of language that he internalizes as a result of his own experiences? This, Halliday asserts, will help us decide what is relevant to the teacher, since the teacher's view of language must at least encompass all the child knows language to be. The child knows what language is because he knows what language does. The child has used language in many ways--for satisfaction of material and intellectual needs, for mediation of personal relationships, the expression of feelings, and so on. Language in all these uses has come within his or her own direct experience. She or he is subconsciously aware that language has many functions that affect him or her personally.

According to Halliday (1973), the normal child has internalized a "model" of language which is highly complex by the age of five. There is sufficient evidence available that the child by age five or six has achieved a stage of automaticity in language use and has almost fully approximated the phonology, morphology, syntax, and semantic adult language model, commensurate with the child's experiential development. Halliday states that, "teachers need to be cognizant concerning the "models" of language the normal child is endowed with by the time she or he comes to school; the assumption being that if the teacher's own "received" conception of language is in some way less rich or less diversified it will be irrelevant to the educational task. Much of the child's difficulty with language in school arises because she or he is required to accept a stereotype of language which is contrary to insight the child has gained from experience. Traditional first "reading and writing" tasks are a case in point, they fail to coincide with the child's own convictions about the nature and uses of language."

32

Halliday (1973; 1975) identified a set of basic functions of language by which the child learns how to mean; and the meaning potential he or she can do with language. The child's learning of his first language in the period extending roughly from six to eighteen months of age is investigated. The approach Halliday used is through semantics. The learning of language is interpreted as the learning of a system of meanings. A child who is learning his or her first language is learning how to mean; in this perspective, the linguistic system is to be seen as semantic potential. It is a range of possible meanings; together with the means whereby those meanings are realized, or expressed. Language is regarded as social behavior potential--what the speaker "can do." The concept of what the speaker "can mean"--the linguistic potential of how the speaker is able to construct his language--sentences, words, phrases--to what he or she can say. The potential of language is a meaning potential. The meaning potential is the linguistic realization of the behavior potential--"can mean" is "can do" when translated into language. The meaning potential in turn is realized in the language system as lexicogrammatical potential--what the speaker "can say."

The language "models" or function identified by Halliday (1973) include the following:

(1) Instrumental   (5) Heuristic

(2) Regulatory   (6) Imaginative

(3) Interactional   (7) Informational

(4) Personal

Halliday has said that the child develops ability to utilize the seven functions in a developmental, progressive way, in stages over a period of time. Observing one particular child from approximately six months to eighteen months, Halliday suggested that the child made use of all functions during this period of time. During the early stages of language learning each "model" is used separately by the child and at later stages, when a lexicogrammatical, or grammatical structure is accomplished, the functions are generally integrated and employed together. The adult language integrates all the functions in various and complex ways so that each basic function learned and used separately by the very young child is hardly distinguishable in adult communication.

33

Halliday (1973) described each of the basic learning functions or "models" in the following manner. (See
Figure 2:3 below.)

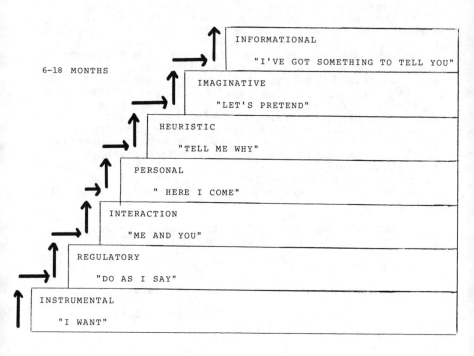

6-18 MONTHS

INFORMATIONAL

"I'VE GOT SOMETHING TO TELL YOU"

IMAGINATIVE

"LET'S PRETEND"

HEURISTIC

"TELL ME WHY"

PERSONAL

" HERE I COME"

INTERACTION

"ME AND YOU"

REGULATORY

"DO AS I SAY"

INSTRUMENTAL

"I WANT"

HALLIDAY'S "LANGUAGE MODELS"

FIGURE 2:3

34

(1) Instrumental. The simplest of the child's models
of language and first to evolve is the instrumental
model. The child becomes aware that language is used
as a means to get things done. Language serves the
function of "I want," the satisfaction of material
needs, of enabling him or her to obtain the goods and
services that he or she wants. It is likely to include
a general expression of desire, some element meaning
simply, "I want the object there (present in the context)," as well as perhaps other expressions relating to
specific desires, response to questions, "Do you
want...?" and so on.

(2) Regulatory. Closely related to the instrumental
model is the regulatory model of language. It is the
function of language as controlling the behavior or
others, something which the child recognizes very easily
because language is used on him this way; language is
used to control his own behavior and he soon learns that
he or she can turn the tables and use it to control
others. The regulatory is the "do as I tell" function
of language. The difference between the regulatory and
the instrumental is that in the instrumental the focus
is on the goods or services required, and it does not
matter who provides them, whereas regulatory utterances
are directed toward a particular individual, and it is
the behavior of that individual that is to be influenced.
Typically therefore this function includes meanings such
as, again a generalized request, "Do that," meaning
"Do what you have been doing (in context)," "Do that
again"; as well as specific demands particularly in the
form of suggestions "Let's do...," such as "Let's go
for a walk," "Let's sing a song" and so forth.

(3) Interactional. Closely related to the regulatory
function of language is its function in social interaction. The third model postulated as forming part of
the child's image of language is the interactional model.
This refers to the use of language in the interaction
between self and others. The closest of the child's
personal relationships usually with mother, is partly,
and in time, largely mediated through language. Aside
from a child's experiences of language to maintain per-
manent relationships, the neighborhood and activities
of the peer group provide context for complex and rap-
idly changing demands on individual linguistic resources.

    Language is used to define and consolidate the
group, to include and exclude, to improve status and to
contest status, and humor, ridicule, deception, per-
suasion and so forth are brought into play. This is the

35

"me and you" function of language.

(4) Personal. This is the language to express the child's own uniqueness. It refers to the child's awareness of language as a form of individuality. The child becomes aware of self and in particular higher stages of that process, the development of personality in which language plays an essential role. The shaping of self through interaction with others is very much a language-mediated process. The child is able to offer someone else that which is unique to self, to make public his or her own individuality; in turn this reinforces and creates this individuality. This includes expression of personal feelings, of participation, and withdrawal, of interest, pleasure, disgust, and so forth. Halliday calls this the "here I come" function of language.

(5) Heuristic. The other side is the child's growing understanding of the environment--since environment is first of all, the non-self--that which is separated out in the course of establishing where he or she begins and ends. Once the boundary between the child and his or her environment is beginning to be recognized, then the child can turn toward the exploration of the environment. This is the heuristic function of language, the "tell me why" function, that which later on develops into the whole range of questioning forms that the young child uses. At a very early stage in language development, in its most elementary form the heuristic use of language is the demand for a name, which is the child's way of categorizing the objects of the physical world; but it soon expands into a variety of more specific meanings.

(6) Imaginative. This is the function of language whereby the child creates an environment of his or her own. As well as moving into, taking over and exploring the universe which he or she can find around, the child also uses language for creating a universe of his or her own, a world initially of pure sound, but which gradually turns into one of story and make-believe and let's pretend, and ultimately into the realm of poetry and imaginative writing. Language in the imaginative function is not necessarily "about" anything at all; it does not have to be a make-believe copy of the world of experiences, occupied by people, things and events. Halliday calls it the "let's pretend" function of language.

(7) _Informational_. (representational) - Language in addition to other uses is a means of communication about something, of expressing propositions. The child is aware that he or she can convey a message in language--a message which has specific reference to the processes, persons, objects, abstractions, qualities, states and relations to the real world around. This is the only model of language that many adults have; and a very inadequate model it is from the point of view of the child. It is not the earliest function to come into use and does not become a dominant function until a much later stage in development toward maturity. This is the "I've got something to tell you" function. The idea that language can be used as a means of communicating information to someone who does not already possess the information is a very sophisticated one which depends on the internalization of a whole complex set of linguistic concepts that the young do not possess.

Smith (1977) proposed "that the uses to which language is put lie at the heart of language comprehension and learning and that the uses of language must therefore be constant concern for language teachers." He adds three additional uses of language to the seven language functions identified by Halliday (1973). The three other functions are:

(1) Divertive (Enjoy this) which includes puns, jokes, riddles and so forth.

(2) Authoritative (How it must be) which is language used for contractual purposes, for example, statutes, laws, regulations, agreements, and contracts.

(3) Perpetuating (How it was) which includes records, histories, diaries, notes, scores, etc.

Smith (1977) discussed tentative observations relevant to the study of language and to practice of language instruction including questions requiring further reflection and research with respect to implications for education.

Briefly, Smith, observed "that even a tenfold categorization of language functions and uses oversimplifies all the varied uses of language. He points out that language generates a number of uses related only to itself, for example, language used to talk about language, or metalanguage. Much of school language is metalanguage in which teachers frequently use terms with children such as sounds, letters, phonics,

parts of speech, sentences, punctuation, phrases, definitions, and so forth." (p. 641.) He further comments,
"...skill in one use of language need not generalize to
skill in others, for example, interactional or divertive.
Children arriving at school find little supportive interactional language to which they are highly tuned and a
good deal of representational or informational which is
largely foreign to them. Also, language is not usually
employed for just one use at a time as the functions
become merged into a smaller number of "macrofunctions"
and "megafunctions" with the development of grammar."

Halliday (1973) explained that during the course
of maturation is a process possibly called "functional
reduction"--the original functional range of a child's
language is a set of discrete functional components
each with its own meaning potential. This is gradually
replaced by a more highly coded and abstract, but sim-
pler functional system. In early language development
of the very young child each function, e.g., "instrumental," "regulatory," "interactional," and so forth, are
used separately to communicate meaning. As the child
acquires a grammar or syntactic system the child is
able to integrate various functions or uses in more
complex ways. There is immense diversity in adult's
uses of language--immense in the kind of activity language plays a part. The diversity of usage is reduced
in internal organization of the adult language system,
in the grammar, to a small set of functional components.
These are called "Macro-functions" to distinguish them
from functions of the child's emergent language system,
"instrumental," "regulatory," etc. These "macro-
functions" are highly social uses of language. The in-
numerable social purposes for which adults use language
are not represented directly, one by one, in the form
of functional components in the language system, as
those of the child. With the very young child, "function" equals "use." There is no grammar, no intermediate level of internal organization in language,
only content and expression. With adults there are
only three or four functions or "macro-functions."

Halliday (1973) identified and described macro-
functions which are integrated into the adult language
system and have their beginning in the several language
functions of the very young child. These macro-functions
are the ideational, interpersonal, and textual. (See
Figure 2:4 on Page 39.) The ideational element is present in all adult language uses. The ideational use is
the potential for expressing content in terms of the
speaker's experiences and the speech community. It is

38

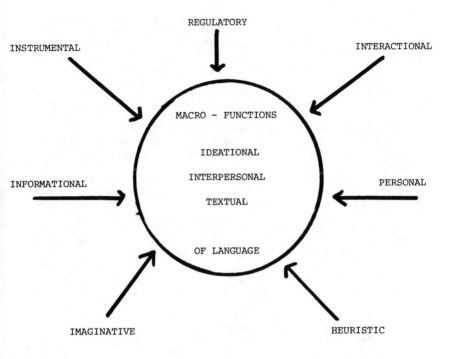

INSTRUMENTAL

REGULATORY

INTERACTIONAL

MACRO - FUNCTIONS

IDEATIONAL

INFORMATIONAL

INTERPERSONAL

TEXTUAL

PERSONAL

OF LANGUAGE

IMAGINATIVE

HEURISTIC

HALLIDAY'S LANGUAGE MODELS: MACRO-FUNCTIONS

FIGURE 2:4

a major component of meaning in the language system,
basic to more or less all the uses of language and represent categories of our interpretation of experience.
The ideational function encodes our experience in the
form of content and specifies available opinions in
meaning, also determining the nature of structural
realizations.   The clause is a structural unit, one by
which we express a particular range of ideational meanings, our experience of processes including the exter-
nal world, concrete and abstract, the process of our
consciousness, seeing, thinking, liking, talking, etc.

According to Halliday (1973), "For the child, the
use of language to inform, to express ideas is just one
instance of language use, one function among many.   The

ideational component in the very young child does not
appear to be found in the informational function which
seems to be found in a combination of the personal and
heuristic functions. Language for the child is a means
of organizing and storing experiences. The beginnings
of grammar, a level of lexicogrammatical organization,
or a "linguistic form," utterances having more than one
function. It appears that much of the initial impetus
to learning formal patterns (distinct from spontaneous
modes of expression characteristic of the first few
months) was the need to impose order on environment and
define his or her person in relation to and distinct
from it. Until a grammar has developed, the young child
is unable to express ideas or communicate experiences
that had not been shared. The ideational element, as
it evolves, becomes crucial to the use of all language
in all functions the child has learned to control which
gives clue to its status as a macrofunction. Whatever
specific use one is making of language, sooner or later
one finds it necessary to refer explicitly to categories of one's experiences of the world. All, or nearly
all, utterances come to have an ideational component.
At the same time they have something else.

Halliday (1973) identified the interpersonal use
of language as another macro-function. There are non-
ideational elements in the adult language system. They
are grouped together as a single "macro-function" in
grammar, covering a whole range of particular uses of
language. This is the macro-function referred to as
"interpersonal." It includes all uses of language to
express social and personal relations, including all
the forms of the speaker's intrusion into the speech
situation and the speech act. The young child also
uses language interpersonally, interacting with other
people, controlling their behavior (regulatory) and expressing his or her own personality (personal), attitudes, feelings, but these uses are specific and differentiated. Later on these functions are generalized in
a single functional component of the grammatical system at a more abstract level. In the clause, the interpersonal element is represented by mood and modality.
The selection by the speaker of a particular role in
the speech situation of the choice of roles for the
addressee (mood) and expression of judgement and predictions (modality). In adult language an integrated
"interpersonl" component provides meaning potential for
interpersonal as present in all uses of language, just
as the "ideational" provides resources for the representation of experiences.

These two macro-functions, ideational and interpersonal, together determine a large part of the meaning potential incorporated in grammar of every language.
This is seen clearly in the grammar of the clause which
has ideational aspect, mood, including modality.

Also, a third macro-function, the "textual," which
fills the requirement that language should be operation-
ally relevant, it should have a texture, in real contexts of situation, distinguishing a living message from
a mere entry in a grammar of dictionary. A prerequisite
to effective language operation is the "textual" function. Language becomes text, related to itself, to its
contexts of use. Without the textual component meaning
we should be unable to make any use of language at all
(Halliday (1973).

Halliday (1973), discussed the seven basic language "models" or language functions, enumerated and
described previously, provided some significant thoughts
for teachers of language which seems applicable to children learning to read and write. He states, "For the
child, all language is doing something--in other words
it has meaning. It has meaning in a very broad sense,
including a range of functions. Halliday cites the
work of Bernstein who has shown that educational failure is often in a very general and rather deep sense,
language failure. The child who does not succeed in
school may be the one who is not using language in ways
required by the school. In simple terms this may mean
that the child cannot read or write or express himself
or herself adequately in speech. But these are extremes
of linguistic success. It is likely that underlying
the failure to master these skills is a deeper problem,
a fundamental mismatch between the child's linguistic
capabilities and the demands made on them." Halliday
suggested, "This is not a lack of words or vocabulary
or a problem in grammar. Rather, a child who has only
a "restricted code" suffers a limitation in respect of
the rest of the linguistic models, e. g., instrumental,
regulatory, personal, etc." He suggested, "some of the
functions of language have developed one-sidedly. The
"restriction" is a restriction on the range of the uses
of language. In particular, the child may not make use
of his or her linguistic resources in two functions
which are most crucial to success in school; the personal
and heuristic functions. These functions, it may be recalled, provide the impetus for the development of the
"ideational" functional component when a grammar is
achieved."

Halliday (1973), continued, "educational failure may be attributed to linguistic failures--it is a limitation on the child's control over relevant functions of language in their adaptation to certain specific demands. The failure may be in language or failure in the use of language. The implication for a teacher is that his or her own model of language should at least not fall short of that of the child. If the teacher's image of language is narrower and less rich than that already present in the minds of those he or she is teaching (or which needs to be present, if they are to succeed), it will be irrelevant to him or her as a teacher."

Halliday (1973), stated, "that a minimum requirement for an educationally relevant approach to language is that it takes account of the child's own linguistic experience, defining the experience in terms of its richest potential and noting where there may be differences of orientation which could cause certain children difficulties in school. This is one component. The other component of relevance is the relevance to the experience the child will have later on: the linguistic demands society will eventually make on him or her, and in the intermediate stage, demands on language the school is going to make and which must be met to succeed in the classroom."

Finally, Halliday (1973), stated, "language serves a wide range of human needs, what is common to every use of language is that it is meaningful, contextualized and in the broadest sense, social. This is clear to the child in day-to-day experiences. The child is surrounded by language, not in the form of grammar, dictionaries, or randomly chosen words and sentences of undirected monologues. What the child encounters is "text" or language in use; sequences of language articulated each within itself and with the situation in which it occurs. Such sequences are purposeful, though varied in purpose and have social significance. The child's awareness of language cannot be isolated from awareness of its language function and be educationally relevant."

What Teachers Should Know About Language Learning

The preceding sections have described some theoretical models of oral language learning, the elements of language which are learned and the child's learning of "models" or functions of language learning. It is postulated that an understanding of oral language development and learning will have implications for teachers to assist children to learn to read and write in more effective and efficient ways.

Goodman (1974) stated, "all children have immense resources when they enter school. By understanding and respecting and building on the language competencies of kids we can make literacy an extension of the natural language learning of children. Teachers must know and understand kids, their language and the reading process in order to bring this about."

Fillion, Smith and Swain (1976) suggested "universal statements" about language that are relevant for the teacher who teaches language. Concerning the nature of language, teachers need to understand that natural language is never independent of function. Language without a function is meaningless. Third, language is initially based on an individual's reality but it also constitutes its own reality. Fourth, the four general language skills, speaking, listening, reading, and writing are largely independent. A lack of skill in one does not necessarily reflect a lack of skill in another. Each skill appears to develop through practice of that skill, although the development of one skill will increase the potential of the individual for development in other skills. Fifth, comprehension always exceeds production. Sixth, comprehension entails an understanding of both content and function. It requires experience in the function of language. Seventh, all dialects can potentially convey the same meanings and serve the same function.

Concerning language learning, the following universal statements are suggested for examination. First. the processes of language learning are not directly observable or manipulative like meaning itself. Language learning takes place at the deeper levels of an individual's prior knowledge and cognitive processes. Second, language is not learned independently of meaning or function. Third, meaning and function are learned as language is learned, largely through the efforts to make sense of the linguistic environment and to produce language which accomplishes one's intentions. Fourth, skill in some functions of language does not mean that all functions have been mastered. Language is needed for a variety of purposes. Fifth, language used for a function that has not been mastered will not contribute to learning. Sixth, motivation and persistence are both necessary for language learning. Seventh, individuals learn the language and functions of individuals with whom they wish to identify. Fillion, Smith, and Swain

(1976), conclude by stating several "universals" concerning language in school. First, in its meanings, functions, and forms, the language of instruction differs from much out-of-school language. Second, teachers and students speak different languages. Third, children set the norms for children's language in school. Fourth, demands for unfamiliar language use inhibit spontaneous speech or writing. Fifth, education is in large part a matter of learning school language. Finally, no specific statements about language instruction are universally valid.

Higginbotham (1972), in a review of psycholinguistic research and language learning, suggested several conclusions pertinent to elementary education which have emerged:

1. The period from ages two to twelve are the productive years for language learning. The pre-school years are the most critical for language acquisition but development continues throughout the elementary grades.

2. The implicit knowledge of the linguistic system acquired as the child learns to speak the language can facilitate his acquisition of other language skills.

3. All languages share the same potential for expression, but people differ in the uses they make of language and therefore vary in the potential they extract from language.

4. Children habituated in a restricted communication code may be impeded in some aspect of school learning.

Based on the above suggested conclusions, Higginbotham (1972) concluded, ". . . that an important beginning has been made in developing a theory of language instruction based on our growing knowledge of language as it develops and functions for the child. This new perspective calls into serious question prescriptive approaches which have no significant effect on language behavior and enrichment programs whose vague and general goals have little relevance for the development of individual children. What is wanted is an approach which builds on the considerable linguistic knowledge the child already possesses. . . ." She states further, ". . . the greatest challenge in the new theory of language instruction may be that posed for teacher education.

44

Psycholinguistics theory can have an appreciable impact on the classroom only if teachers have the knowledge and the training which will enable them to: describe and assess the child's language capabilities; make human and rational judgements about his or her most salient needs; and provide communication experiences which will develop new patterns and functions while still maintaining those already established in the home environment."

Loban (1969) discussed the importance of teacher knowledge about language abilities children already possess. He stated, "it will be difficult for a teacher to decide what language to improve and develop language abilities of children, without insight into language learning processes. Teachers need information for intelligent planning for the development of reading, writing, speaking and listening based on the child's oral language development. A child's language forms the basis of a developmental program in speaking, listening, reading, and writing. The teacher needs to know at what stage the child is."

Loban commented, "research investigations provide evidence that facility with oral language improves and relates to high achievement in reading, writing and listening. Pupils ranking high in silent reading comprehension and in oral reading interpretation prove to use fewer short oral utterances; those expert in silent reading show more verbal dexterity and flexibility with the syntax of spoken communication. This confirms what observant teachers point out from classroom experiences. Children, especially the less verbal children, need many oral experiences before they read or write."

Using oral language as a base for successful reading and writing depends on whether or not any transfer takes place. What is learned about speaking must have some valuable carry over to writing and reading, however, writing and reading have conventions and domains of their own. They cannot be acquired successfully without a base in oral language is the point.

O'Donnel (1974) raised several interesting ideas about language learning and language teaching which has implications for teacher's knowledge of how children learn and acquire language. He assumed that attention to children's language learning is motivated by the hope that knowledge of how children learn their native language will help us to understand how they learn other things and enable us to teach more effectively. O'Donnel states, "Although there is still much to learn about the language learning process, it is likely that the accumulated knowledge about children's language can be applied in devising teaching materials and strategies. However, there is little evidence or information about how teachers can apply knowledge of language development to aid in the classroom situation. The teacher who knows something about language development can avoid mistakes and provide some opportunities for learning that might otherwise be overlooked."

O'Donnel drew a distinction between learning language and learning about language. He said, "The child brings an impressive linguistic knowledge to the school which is learned without direct instruction or formal teaching as is listening comprehension. It seems to be a natural process requiring little deliberate effort on the part of the learner and little guidance on the part of an instructor. However, reading and writing, though based on the same grammatical system serve different purposes than speaking and listening, and appear to require much effort on the part of a learner and a teacher."

Similarities and Differences in Learning Oral and Written Language

Although speaking, listening, reading and writing involve different settings, they are based on similar language elements and linguistic structures, and are used for communication purposes. Language users employ certain language processes to produce utterances which are meaningful to others (speaking and writing) and receive communication which is meaningful from others (listening and reading). Communication is usually a two-way process to communicate meaning for some purpose. Oral language, speaking, usually learned first, makes use of immediate social situational contexts with other significant language users. Usually, first-hand experiences with objects, events create a close relationship between language and the particular experience. Spoken language also makes use of intonation, facial expressions and gestures which possibly enables a child to learn to speak and listen more easily. Speaking and listening occur in a spatial direction using sound. Oral language is not directly segmented into sounds but occurs in a fairly rapid, informal manner. Yet the listener and developing speaker is able to abstract significant features of sounds, differentiate sound features, and over a period of time the listener and speaker has approximated the adult language model, usually by ages five or six.

Reading and writing generally does not take place in a direct social situational context with significant others, except for interactional purposes when a parent, teacher or someone else in the child's environment interacts with the child such as reading to the child or writing an experience story with the child related to some experience. Reading and writing are not usually related to first hand experiences, however, reading may accompany an experience such as reading travel brochures while traveling to visit places of interest. Reading and writing are usually long-distance communication processes in which the two parties are not communicating directly to one another. There is not the direct interaction and feedback which is usually possible when oral language communication is learned and used for producing or receiving a message. Reading and writing make use of literary conventions such as capital letters, punctuation, letters, spaces, and a linear direction, left to right and top to bottom. Written language is segmented by spaces between letters, words, sentences, and paragraphs.

There are three basic understandings which teachers need to develop and maintain to enable each child to communicate effectively in each language process. The first is that communication should be meaningful and comprehensible. Speaking and listening develop in meaningful and contextualized situations in which the child knows what language can do and there is a communication need to learn and use language in relevant ways. Reading and writing though different in some aspects, have much in common with speaking and listening, and also need to develop in real, meaningful communication settings. Second, language is learned and used in whole communication context. Language does not need to be fractionated and broken down into separate, discrete language elements. Speaking and listening abilities develop when language is used by significant language users in holistic structures. The child is equipped with language learning strategies to abstract the essential sound, graphic, semantic, and syntactic elements presented in meaningful, contextualized, holistic language situations. The reading and writing processes can develop similar to speaking and listening using holistic language which is meaningful and relevant to the child. Reading and writing can be learned related to first-hand, contextual, experiential-based language approaches. Reading and writing, although used in different situations to communicate, are employed for similar functions. Learning to read and write should be as easy as learning to talk and listen because the

47

child already possesses an oral language base. A third basic understanding that teachers should know concerning language learning is that language is learned naturally. The more learning is made a natural process the easier the child will learn. Learning to talk and listen occurs naturally without artificial interferences or adult interruptions. Knowledge about oral language development, can be applied to written language learning. In a highly print-oriented society such as ours, children are exposed to a tremendous amount of written language. Most print is highly contextualized such as store signs, T.V. commercials, food labels on products and the like. Often, parents or significant others use oral language to relate to environmental print within the child's first-hand experience. This is a natural way for children to learn the relationship between oral and written language. Of course, reading to a child continuously reinforces the child's concept that print is an alternative language process to communicate meaning. Beginning reading and writing can be learned naturally when language processes are meaningful to the child.

Summary

A description was given of the nature of the English language and how and why children learn language.

A theoretical model and stages of oral language development was described identifying characteristics of children's language.

The development of the phonological, syntactic and semantic systems was described as children learn to use language.

Children learn the uses and functions of oral language early in their development. Teacher knowledge of language functions developed by children in oral language relates to learning the functions of written language.

Also presented was a description of the similarities and differences in oral and written language learning and implications for learning to read and write.

Teaching Competencies

1. Record the speech of a couple of 2-3 year old children. What analytical statements can be made about the sample speech? Bring the tape recording of the

children's speech to class for colleagues to listen to.

2. Report observed changes in the oral language development of children at different ages. If possible, listen to children of pre-school age and compare their language development with that of older children. What differences do you observe in phonological, morphological, syntactic, and semantic development. Share your findings with colleagues.

3. If possible, make a case study of the oral language development of one child (you may examine existing case studies). Explain how the evidence presented compares with ideas previously heard. Share findings with colleagues.

Affective Behaviors

1. Accepts individual differences in the language development of children.

2. Respects dialect and ideolect differences in phonology, syntax and semantic language elements in an individual child-spoken language.

3. Encourages and motivates each individual child's unique language growth.

4. Enables each child to develop and maintain a feeling of self-worth concerning his/her language experience and thinking.

5. Provides a learning environment in which each child's language is valued.

6. Provides a learning environment in which children are free to express themselves in a non-threatening atmosphere and risk-taking is encouraged.

7. Treats each child's language with dignity.

Questions to Investigate

1. Why is it important for teachers to be knowledgeable about children's oral language development?

2. Investigate and discuss various theories of oral language development. How are they similar and how are they different? Provide your rationale for accepting one particular language theory.

3. What key factors appear to enhance and influence children's language development? How do these factors differ for children from varied socio-economic and ethnic backgrounds?

4. What aspects of language in children's language development remain to be developed during school years from ages six to fourteen?

5. What are the instructional implications related to a teacher's knowledge about children's oral language development?

Reading References

Brown, Roger. "The First Sentence of Child and Chimpanzee." In Roger Brown, Psycholinguistics. New York: The Free Press, 1970, pp. 208-231.

Brown, Roger and Bellugi, Ursula. "The Three Processes in the Child's Acquisition of Syntax." In E.H. Lenneberg (ed.), New Directions in the Study of Language. Cambridge, Massachusetts: The MIT Press, 1964, pp. 131-161.

Clark, E. V. "What's in a Word? On the Child's Acquisition of Semantics in His First Language." In Moore, T. E. (ed.), Cognitive Development and the Acquisition of Language. New York: Academic Press, 1978.

Dale, Philip S. "Reading and Language Development: Some Comparisons and a Perspective." Southwestern Symposium on Learning Language and Reading, Western Washington State College, 1975.

Fillon, Bryan; Smith, Frank and Swain, Merrill. "Language Basics for Language Teachers: Toward a Set of Universal Considerations." Language Arts, Vol. 53, October 1976, pp. 740-745.

Gibson, Eleanor and Levin, Harry. The Psychology of Reading. Cambridge, Massachusetts: MIT Press, 1975.

Goodman, Kenneth S. "Effective Teachers of Reading Know Language and Children." Elementary English, Vol. 51, September 1974, pp. 823-829.

Goodman, Kenneth S. "Reading: The Key is in Children's Language." _Reading Teachers_, Vol. 25, 1972.

Halliday, M. A. K. _Explorations in the Functions of Language_. Elsevier: New York, 1973

Halliday, M. A. K. _Learning How to Mean: Explorations in the Development of Language_. Elsevier: New York, 1975.

Higginbotham, Dorothy C. "Psycholinguistic Research and Language Learning." _Elementary English_. Vol. 49, October 1972, pp. 811-818.

Lenneberg, Eric. "A Natural History of Language." _The Genesis of Language: A Psycholinguistic Approach_. Editors: Frank Smith and George A. Miller, The MIT Press: Cambridge, Massachusetts, 1966.

Loban, Walter. "Oral Language and Learning." _Oral Language and Reading_. Edited by James Walden, _National Council of Teachers of English_, 1969, pp. 101-112.

Lundsteen, Sara W. "On Developmental Relations Between Language Learning and Reading." _The Elementary School Journal_. Vol. 77, January 1977, pp. 192-204.

Mc Neill, David. "Developmental Psycholinguistics." _The Genesis of Language: A Psycholinguistic Approach_. Editors: Frank Smith and George A. Miller, The MIT Press: Cambridge, Massachusetts, 1966.

Menyuk, Paula. _The Acquisition and Development of Language_. Englewood Cliffs: Prentice-Hall, 1971.

O'Donnel, Roy C. "Language Learning and Language Teaching." _Elementary English_, Vol. 51, January 1974, pp. 115-118.

Piaget, Jean. _Six Psychological Studies_. New York: Vintage Boods, 1967.

Smith, E. B.; Goodman, K. S. and Meredith, R. _Language and Thinking in School_. New York: Holt, Rinehart and Winston, 1976.

Smith, Frank. "The Use of Language." <u>Language Arts</u>, Vol. 54, September 1977, pp. 638-639.

Vygotsky, Lev Semenovich. <u>Thought and Language</u>. Cambridge, Massachusetts: The MIT Press, 1962.

CHAPTER III

THE READING PROCESS

Knowledge Competencies

1. Identify and describe different theories and models of the reading process.
2. What is the relationship between oral and written language processes? What are implications for instructional practice in reading and writing?
3. What are the basic differences between skills, phonic and whole language reading models?
4. What do teachers need to know about the reading process from a whole language perspective that has implications for instruction?

More is known about oral language development, although exactly how humans develop language is still an elusive question requiring further investigation. Until only within the past twenty years, less was understood about the reading process, despite thousands of research studies conducted and reported concerning reading. The research reported about the reading process has been highly fragmentary, conflicting, and unconvincing. Most of the research related to the reading process has focused on what is assumed to be the components or elements of the reading process. Research investigations frequently involved subjects in experimentally controlled situations responding to isolated language elements which are considerably unlike the natural language process, into which they are embedded. Isolated bits of language such as visual discrimination of letters, syllables, words, nonsense words and sentences; auditory discrimination of isolated sounds, syllables, words, nonsense words and sentences, characterized many investigations about the reading process. Most of the research related to understanding the reading process has emphasized the graphological and phonological aspects often in isolation. Experimental techniques such as paired associate learning of letters, syllables and words and timed flashed letters, syllables and words have been frequently used. The result of such experiments are then extrapolated and related to procedures for reading instruction. It is interesting to note that many "so-called" reading tests are based on similar techniques to predict and evaluate the child's reading performance. It follows that many published materials for teaching reading, mirror the techniques used for research and tests used to assess

reading performances. Furthermore, most classroom instruction is highly similar to certain research techniques, test construction, and published material for
reading instruction.

Therefore, if research findings, test construction,
published material and reading instruction are largely
unrelated to what actually happens during the process
of reading, it is reasonable to assume that the inability and difficulty so many children have developing reading proficiency may be related to insufficient
and inadequate knowledge about the reading process.

Goodman (1969), discussed the emphasis on the
isolated elements of language, particularly the word,
which has characterized much research about the reading process and tests utilized to assess reading performance and instructional methods, stated, " . . .
that much of the research on language and the teaching
of language has been based on the assumption that words
are natural units of language and that words in print
correspond with words in speech. In reading, in particular, the focus on words has grown in great part
from the mistaken assumption that they are gestalts of
language."

Several theoretical models are described to familiarize teachers with different views of the reading
process. A basic premise is that reading instruction
will be ineffective if teachers do not have insight into what is now known about the reading process. Evaluation techniques, instructional approaches, conditions
for learning, organization of instruction and identifying difficulties some children experience, must be
directly related to sound, realistic based theory and
model of the reading process. Teachers must not continue to base reading practices on only one set of
materials, or a sequence of skills to organize instruction.

This chapter includes a description of several
theoretical models of the reading process. Then an
examination of the orthographic systems of written language will be given. Next, an exploration of how
learning to read is directly related to how children
learn oral language. Finally, a review of significant
ideas teachers need to know about the reading process,
and implications for instruction is described.

The Reading Process: Theories and Models

Williams (1973) identified and described several recent models which represent a wide variety of approaches. She categorizes them as follows: taxonomic, psychometric, psychological, linguistic, and transactional. Most models of the reading process can be categorized on the basis of letter-sound models, skills-models, and whole language models. The whole language or socio-psycholinguistic model will be described in more depth later in this chapter.

Skills Reading Model

Gray's Comprehensive Skill Model (1960). This model categorizes skills underlying reading into four classes; word perception (including pronunciation and meaning); comprehension; reaction to and evaluation of ideas of the author; assimilation of what is read through fusion of old ideas and information obtained through reading. In an elaboration of Gray's theory, Robinson added a fifth category, rate of reading, which is flexibly adapted to varying reading purposes. Robinson also treated the importance of differentiating reading skills from processes and from instructional procedures. Gray's model is a skills model. Some attention is given to the process of reading, although it is mainly a catalog of skills for various aspects of reading. The four aspects are: word perception, comprehension, reaction to and evaluation of ideas of an author, and assimilation of what is read through fusion of old ideas and information obtained through reading operate simultaneously. Reading is a "unitary act," word perception is at the center of the process, without it communication can not take place. Gray identifies three levels of comprehension or types of understanding including: literal comprehension with is a clear grasp of what is read (reading the lines); reaction or critical reading is using an inquiry attitude and making an emotional response to the content. The assimilation or fusion of ideas is explained as the exercise of critical judgement, creative thinking and combining information secured from reading with one's previous experience.

Holmes Substrata-Factor Theory (1953). This is a very complex model based on substrata analysis in which a variety of tests are chosen, which assess variables that on the basis of theory or past research seem to contribute to the variance in reading comprehension. Factors that turn out to account for most of the variance in the criterion are determined, and then these factors are again analyzed, leading to set of "sub-variable" e.g., those factors that make a significant contribution to variance of each first order factors. The goal is to determine the nature of the combinations of the hierarchial organized subsystems that form a working system for attaining speed and power of reading. There is an attempt to isolate the most significant elements from the combination of many elements that are involved in reading.

Reading according to the sub-strata factor theory is defined as an audio-visual verbal processing skill of symbolic reasoning sustained by the inter-facilitations of an intricate hierarchy of sub-strata factors that have been mobilized as a psychological working system and pressed into service in accordance with the purpose of the reader.

Three related models make up the sub-strata factor theory of reading: neurological, psychological, and statistical. The model identifies neurological sub-systems of brain cell assemblies containing various kinds of information; such as memories for shapes, sounds, meaning of words and word parts, memories for vicarious and experiential material, conceptualizations, meaningful relationships stored as substantive verbal units in phrases, idioms, sentences, etc.

The working system is a dynamic set of sub-abilities mobilized for the purpose of solving a particular problem. Neurologically, the working system is a nerve-net pattern in the brain that functionally links together various substrata factors mobilized into a workable communication system.

The problem was to find a method for specifically isolating the most significant elements from the combination of many elements. A statistical technique, multiple correlation, was needed to yield the substrata factors. From thirty-seven independent variables those which made a direct or indirect yet statistically significant and "independent contribution to the variance of criterion speed and/or power of reading was identified."

Goodman (1969) commented on Holmes' Substrata Factor Theory stated " . . . Holmes' substrata factor theory, is not a theory at all, but rather an artifact of manipulation of statistics generated by a set of reading tests." A diagram of the skills model is given below in Figure 3:1.

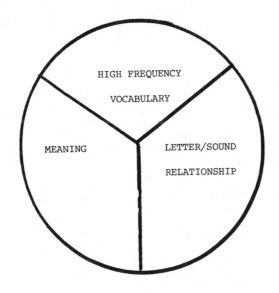

SKILLS MODEL

FIGURE 3:1

Diane De Fore (1981) conducted a study comparing
beginning readers who were taught to read with materials
and activities representing the skills model, letter-
sound model, and whole language model. She found certain characteristics of readers who had learned to read
from each model. Most conventional basal reader published programs are characteristic of the skills model.
These programs have a highly organized scope and sequence of skills introduced to beginning readers through
the teachers manual, workbooks, basal readers stories
and supplementary materials. The characteristics De
Ford identified were as follows:

Skills Approach

1. There is a high rate of omission and the reader
   shows little strategy to "attack words."
2. There is a strategy to omit words.

3. Readers have a higher rate of substitutions and substitutions have little graphic/sound similarity.
4. Readers produce fewer non-words. Substitutions are usually real words. The word substituted looks graphically the same but has a different meaning.
5. The controlled vocabulary imposed by the basal reader is applied by the child.

Letter-Sound Models

Williams (1973) described three behavioral models of the reading process developed by Skinner (1957), Staats (1970) and Gagne (1970). Skinner did not have a great deal to say about reading. In Verbal Behavior (1957), textual behavior is described as vocal verbal responses under the control of non-auditory reinforcement of reading activity; that is reinforcement based on the reader's interests. He talks about the appropriate units in instruction. He discusses the difference between the beginner, for whom the textual behavior is predominant, and the skilled reader, whose behavior in response to written verbal stimuli may be "nontextual," i.e., he responds directly as he would to any feature of the environment. (. . . this refers essentially to the dropping out of the decoding phase.) Skinner's formulation does not stress the nature of the written as a code: he compares textual behavior with echoic behavior and mimicry. "The automatic reinforcement of reading an "interesting" text, however, has merely the effect of increasing the probability of occurrence of such behavior; it does not differentially reinforce correct forms at the phonetic level."

Staats. Staats began with a behaviorist point of view of the reading process. Reading acquisition according to Staats, is "discrimination training where certain verbal responses are reinforced in the presence of certain visual "stimuli." The emphasis on the development of a system of reinforcers (tokens which could be exchanged for trinkets and edibles), a discrimination-learning apparatus, and the presentation of cumulative records indicating number of textual responses acquired are all within the operant learning tradition. The reading materials he used were simply single letters, or consonant-vowel combinations, chosen to reduce response variation. There was little interest in, or even acknowledgement of, reading as a language process.

However, Staats recent work, while clearly a continuation of his early experiment, has a rather different formulation. Reading is still seen as a process of instrumental discrimination, and he feels that traditional learning principles and experimental techniques, using reinforcement contingencies, are appropriate for the acquisition of reading and for the study of the process involved.

However, he describes reading as a complex, cognitive skill many of whose components must be developed on the basis of already learned, more basic skills (including language repertoires); i.e., it is an instance of cumulative-hierarchial learning.

Gagne. Williams (1973), describing Gagne's view of the reading process, considers it another approach with a distinctively "learning" flavor. According to Gagne, there are eight distinct types of learning, ranging from signal learning to problem solving. Each is clearly distinguishable from the other, for it begins with a different state of the organism and ends with a different capability of performance. The eight learning types form a hierarchy and the prerequisite for almost any one type is that learning of the next lowest type already established.

Gagne has presented a learning hierarchy for the early stages of reading, the goal of which is decoding: specifically, mastery of the pronunciation rules for regularly spelled words. One important part of the behavior is the testing of "trial" pronunciations against familiar syllable sounds (tion, ity, etc.). The most basic ability required is that of reproducing single-letter sounds. Built on that is the identification of single letters by these sounds and built on that, pronouncing consonant and vowel combinations. Oral reproduction of syllables and syllable strings are skills subordinate to pronouncing printed words, and so they, too are included in the hierarchy.

Later stages of reading would include mastery of the rules for irregularities in the pronunciation of printed words, and following that, a variety of structures involving comprehension. In learning to read, acquisition of word sounds and the mastery of verbal concepts are basic, and if learning at the higher levels is to occur with facility, attention must be paid to these fundamental prerequisites. The models of the reading process described above are representative of the letter-sound model. The diagram on the following page illustrates this model. See Figure 3:2, Page 60.

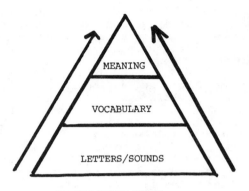

LETTER/SOUND MODEL

FIGURE 3:2

Diane De Ford's (1981) study found characteristics of beginning readers who learned to read with materials based on a letter-sound model or behavioral model as Williams classifies it. Materials based on the letter-sound model are typically referred to as phonic programs. These published materials begin instruction with learning letter names, letter sounds and the relationship of letters and sounds. The next step is blending letters and sounds in words and finally words are placed in phrases, sentences, and stories. The words to be practiced and learned are rigidly controlled, usually on the basis of letter-sound patterns.

De Ford found the following characteristics of beginning readers who learned to read by so-called phonic materials, predicated on a letter-sound model:

Letter-Sound Approach

1. The reader makes multiple attempts on words which usually have high graphic-sound similarity.
2. A high percentage of words are non-words.
3. The reader pronounces every word.
4. The reader omits and inserts words frequently.
5. The reader has a preoccupation with correct pronunciation.

Whole Language or Psycholinguistic Model

The philosophy of the author and the content and approach of this book are closely aligned with two psycholinguistic theories/models of the reading process. Therefore, the theories of Frank Smith (1971; 1975) and Kenneth Goodman (1967; 1969; 1970; 1973; 1975; 1976) will be described more extensively. The skills and letter-sound models of the reading process may be compared to the psycholinguistic models. It is submitted that Goodman's and Smith's psycholinguistic theories and models come the closest at this time to providing a realistic, sound theory upon which instructional practice may be based.

Goodman's Psycholinguistic Model of the Reading Process

Kenneth Goodman (1967) developed his psycholinguistic model of the reading process based on the study of oral reading. The research by Goodman (1969) has been basically descriptive, the goal being to describe what happens when a reader, at any stage of proficiency, reads orally. Goodman has based his models, which was originally called, "A Psycholinguistic Guessing Game," on a comparison of the reader's observed response (OR) and the expected response (ER). What has traditionally been called oral reading errors, substitutions, omissions, inserted words, and the like, Goodman calls miscues. Goodman (1967) states, "The insights into the reading process come primarily from errors, which I choose to call miscues in order to avoid value implications. The reader's expected response mark the process of their attainment, but the readers unexpected responses have been achieved through the same process, albeit less successfully applied. The ways that they (miscues) deviate from the expected reveal this process."

Kenneth Goodman's psycholinguistic model of the reading process has been in stages of development for over a dozen years, and as Goodman (1975) stated, the model is still not complete. Goodman produced an earlier model of the reading process, however only his revised model will be described, including implications for language learning, particularly reading.

Goodman (1967) sought to refute the common sense notion of the reading process which persist concerning the nature of reading. The common motion referred to is that, "reading is a precise process. It involves exact, detailed, sequential perception and identification of letters, words, spelling patterns and large language units." In phonic approaches (letter-sound model) to reading, the preoccupation is with precise letter identification. In word (skill model) approaches, the focus is on word identifications. Known words are sight words precisely named in any setting.

Goodman (1967), noted that, "reading is a selective process. It involves partial use of available minimal language cues selected from perceptual input on the basis of the reader's expectations. As this partial information is processed, tentative decisions are made to be confirmed, rejected, or refined as reading progresses. More simply stated, reading is a psycholinguistic guessing game. It involves an interaction between thought and language. Efficient reading does not result from precise perception and identification of all elements, but from skill in selecting the fewest, most productive cues necessary to produce guesses that are right the first time. The ability to anticipate that which has not been seen, of course, is vital in reading, just as the ability to anticipate what has not yet been heard is vital in listening."

Studies of oral language development cited earlier make it quite clear that the young child by ages five or six have closely approximated the grammatical model of the adult language in his or her linguistic environment. Although, as Chomsky (1969) demonstrated, syntactic development continues to grow between the ages of five and ten. Thus, the child learning to read possesses a well developed ability to utilize syntactic structures to encode and decode speech. This ability can be tapped and brought to use by the reader to increase efficiency and effectiveness during the reading process. The reader, of course, also has available graphophonic and semantic information which must be applied interrelatedly in the act of reading.

Goodman (1967) has equated the task of the reader to the task of the listener, although the reader in the oral reading must perform two tasks at the same time. Utilizing Chomsky's (1965) model of sentence production by speakers of the language and a model structure of the listener's sentence interpretation, encoding of speech reaches a more or less precise level and the signal which results is fully formed. But in decoding (listening), a sampling process aims at approximating the message and any matching or coded signal which results in a kind of by-product.

Goodman's (1973) psycholinguistic model of the

reading process which has undergone several revisions
and modifications was developed through miscue analysis
and a taxonomy of cues and miscues (1969). Goodman
(1973) has contended, "that miscue analysis, the comparison of observed response, with expected responses
of a reader reading orally a fully formed text for
comprehension," is a tool which in research contributed
to formed text for comprehension," is a tool which in
research contributed to development of a comprehensive
theory and model of reading. In the classroom or clinic
it can be used to reveal the strengths and weaknesses
of pupils and the extent to which they are efficient and
effective readers. But, it is only useful to the extent
that the user comes to view reading as the psycholinguistic process it is. Miscue analysis involves its
user in examining the observed behavior of oral readers
as an interaction between language and thought, as a
process of construction meaning from a graphic display.
The reader's use of graphic, phonological, semantic,
and syntactic information is considered."

Goodman (1973) has stated, "that one of the most
powerful uses of miscue analysis is in teacher education.
In the process of analyzing miscues of a reader, the
teacher or potential teacher must ask questions and consider issues he may never have thought about. Was the
meaning acceptable after the miscue? Did the reader
correct the miscue if it was not? If a word was substituted for another word, was it the same part of
speech? How close was it to the sound and shape of the
text word? Was the reader's dialect involved? Through
these questions, instead of the teacher counting errors,
the quality of the miscues and their effect on meaning
are the central concerns. Miscue analysis then is
rooted in a psycholinguistic view of reading (one that
sees thought and language interacting), but also it is
a way of redirecting the focus of teachers so that they
may see reading in this new perspective." In Chapter
IV, Evaluation of Reading, a detailed description of
miscue analysis which can be applied by teachers to
identify a reader's strength and needs will be given.

Goodman (1975) has provided a revised version of
the reading model based on newer insights concerning
the reading process provided by continuing analysis of
reader's miscues over a period of several years. In
the revised model, as in Goodman's earlier model of the
reading process, three kinds of information are available and used in language whether productive or receptive. These came from: (1) the symbol system which
uses sounds in oral language and graphic shapes in

written languages. For literature users of alphabetic language there is also a set of relationships between sounds and shapes; (2) the language structure which is the grammar, or set of syntactic relationships that make it possible to express highly complex messages using a very small set of symbols; (3) the semantic system which is the set of meanings as organized in concepts and conceptual structures. Meaning is the end product of receptive language, both listening and reading; but meaning is also the context in which reading takes on reality. The listener/reader bring meaning to any communication and conduct themselves as seekers of meaning. Figure 3:3 illustrates three kinds of information available to the listener/reader.

GRAPHOPHONIC,...

SOUNDS

SYNTACTIC...

PATTERN

SEMANTIC...

SIGNAL

MEANING

(SEMAPHOR)

LANGUAGE CUES

FIGURE 3:3

64

Goodman (1975), identified four cycles of his model of the reading process as illustrated and explained below: (See Figure 3:4)

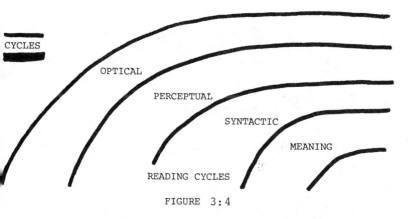

CYCLES

OPTICAL

PERCEPTUAL

SYNTACTIC

MEANING

READING CYCLES

FIGURE 3:4

Though reading is a process in which information is dealt with and meaning constructed continuously, it can be usefully represented as a series of cycles. Readers employ the cycles more or less sequentially as they move through a story or another text.   But the reader's focus, if they are to be productive, is on meaning, so each cycle melts into the next and the readers leap toward meaning.   The cycles are telescoped by the readers if they can get to meaning.

Goodman (1975), also has identified five processes as readers move through the cycles of reading. The brain is the organ of information processing.   It decides what tasks it must handle, what information is available, what strategies it must employ, which input channels to use, and where to seek information.   The brain seeks to maximize information it acquires and minimize effort and energy used to acquire it.   The five processes it employs in reading are:

1. Recognition - initiation. The brain must recognize a graphic display in the visual field as written language and initiate reading.   Normally this would occur once in each reading activity, though it is possible for reading to be interrupted by

other activities examining pictures, for
example and then being reinitiated.

2. <u>Prediction</u>. The brain is always anticipating
   and predicting as it seeks order and significance in sensory inputs.

3. <u>Confirmation</u>. If the brain predicts, it
   must also seek to verify its predictions.
   So it monitors to confirm or disconfirm with
   subsequent input what it expected.

4. <u>Correction</u>. The brain reprocesses when it
   finds inconsistencies or its predictions
   are disconfirmed.

5. <u>Termination</u>. The brain terminates the reading when the reading task is completed, but
   termination may occur for other reasons:
   the task is non-productive; little meaning
   is being constructed or the neaming is already known, or the story is uninteresting,
   or the reader finds it inappropriate for the
   particular purpose. At any rate, termination
   in reading is usually an open option at any
   point.

These processes have an intricate sequence. Prediction precedes confirmation which precedes correction.
Yet the same information may be read to confirm a prior
prediction and to make a new one. See Figure 3:5 below.

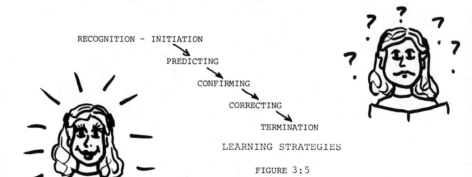

RECOGNITION - INITIATION

        PREDICTING

           CONFIRMING

              CORRECTING

                TERMINATION

LEARNING STRATEGIES

FIGURE 3:5

Goodman's (1975), revised psycholinguistic model of the reading process involves an interrelationship among cycles (optical, perceptual, syntactic, meaning); processes (recognition, initiation, predicting, confirming, correcting, terminating); language cues (graphophonic, syntactic, semantic); and inputs and outputs.

The process begins with the reader's recognition of the task as reading. The reader uses optical (cycles) scanning as the brain directs the eye in the direction of the graphic display using the graphic (print) as input from memory. The reader fixes--focuses eyes on print using light reflection from graphic displays. The visual field includes sharp and fuzzy input. The more information the reader has behind the eyes the less need there is to use all the graphic print. However, the beginning reader with a minimum of graphic knowledge needs more information behind the eyes and must develop other strategies. Conceptual development, experiential background, interests and situational context are significant factors which may enable the beginner reader to process print with a minimum of graphic knowledge. During the optical cycle the reader receives input from memory, including prior predictions of meaning, structure, graphic redundancy, expectation of locus of key graphic cues. During the optical cycle the reader's output includes the fixation cycle, prediction of relation of information to direction of display, the perceptual cycle and cues for image information. Figure 3.6 below illustrates the optical cycle of the reading process.

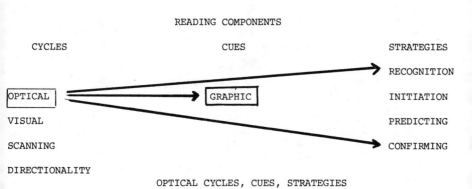

READING COMPONENTS

CYCLES   CUES   STRATEGIES

OPTICAL CYCLES, CUES, STRATEGIES

FIGURE 3:6

The optical cycles melts into the perceptual cycle in which the reader samples and selects cues from the graphic display using as input, fixation of cues available in sharp and blurred input, from memory sampling strategies and prior predictions and decodings to meaning output during part of the perceptual cycle includes selected cues in short term memory and feature analysis. The reader applies feature analysis during the perceptual cycle, choosing features necessary to choose from alternate letters, words, structures. Inputs include the sampled features and from memory assigns allo-system(s) (type style, cursive, etc.) and prior predictions. Output involves confirmation of prior predictions, corrections if necessary by returning to scan and fixate. If no system is available the reader tries the best approximation or terminates; if successful, the reader proceeds to image formation. As sampling-selecting graphic cues and choosing features related to prior predictions and confirming or correcting proceeds, the perceptual cycle continues as the reader forms an image of what is seen, and what is expected to be seen. What is seen is compared with expectations. During forming an image input includes feature analysis from memory, graphic, syntactic, and semantic constructs, prior predictions and cues from the parallel phonological system which is optional. The reader at this stage may go directly from the graphic display to the syntactic cycle (deep structure) to meaning without resorting to recoding or going from graphic shapes to sound to meaning. If no image is possible as output, the reader may return to feature analysis, or to sample more cues from the graphic display using the optical cycle to scan. The reader may confirm his or her prior predictions as output, or if correction needed, return to prior cycle of optical scanning, to locate the source of inconsistency. If an image is formed consistent with the reader's expectations, the reader stores the image in short term memory and goes to the syntactic cycles. Figure 3:7 on Page 69 illustrates the perceptual cycle of the process.

During the syntactic cycle the reader assigns an internal surface structure using input from image formation and from memory applies language rules for relating the surface display to the internal surface structure. The reader's knowledge of language patterns such as, question markers (who, what, when), verb markers (is, are, was), and noun markers (a, the, an), and tense, passive or active sentence construction enables the reader to assign an internal surface structure. There is input from prior predictions and

READING COMPONENTS

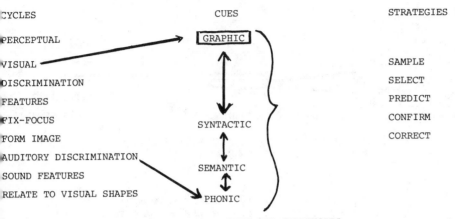

PERCEPTUAL CYCLE, CUES AND STRATEGIES

FIGURE 3:7

decodings. If no structure is possible, the reader may recycle to perceptual or optical cycles to scan back for more graphic cues. If inconsistent with prior predictions, the reader may try an alternate structure or correct by recycling and scanning back to the point of mismatch. If a structure is possible the reader goes to deep structure. The reader assigns a deep structure seeking clause and their interrelationship using input from the internal surface structure and from memory, transformational rules for relating the surface and deep structure, and input from prior predictions and decoding. At this stage in the process the reader takes compacted written language apart and put back together to see the relationships, using transformational rules to retain the order of the author's language patterns. If no structure is possible the reader may try an alternative. If still no structure, the reader recycles. If inconsistent with prior predictions, correct by recycling. If deep structure possible, the reader predicts graphic, semantic and syntactic features. Then the reader goes on to the meaning cycle. If oral reading, the reader assigns appropriate information contour. The reader may terminate at this point in no success. Figure 3:8 following illustrates the syntactic cycle in the process.

CYCLES	CUES	STRATEGIES

SYNTACTIC

SURFACE   GRAPHOPHONICS   SAMPLING
INTERNAL   SELECTING
DEEP STRUCTURE
ORAL LANGUAGE PATTERNS   SYNTACTIC   PREDICTING
WORD FUNCTIONS
CLAUSE RELATIONSHIPS   CORRECTING
QUESTION, NOUN, VERB MARKERS   SEMANTIC   COMPREHENDING

SYNTACTIC CYCLE, CUES, STRATEGIES
FIGURE 3:8

        The optical, perceptual, and syntactic cycles
melt into the meaning cycle as the reader constructs
meaning or decodes applying input from the deep structures from memory, stored experiences, conceptual constructs, lexicon and prior prediction. The reader in-
terprets and constructs meaning reducing uncertainty,
achieving a degree of agreement with the author. At
this point, the reader's output may be: if meaning not
acceptable, the reader may recycle to the point of inconsistency; if no meaning possible, the reader may try
an alternate deep structure or recycle to seek more information; if still no meaning, the reader may hold all
information in memory and return to scan; or terminate
if no meaning results; or, if acceptable meaning, the
reader goes on to assimilate or accommodate meaning.
The reader is not simply adding meaning, but if possible,
assimilating meaning, relating new meaning to known
ideas, or accommodating, modifying prior meaning. The
input involves decoding, from memory, prior predictions
and prior meaning and conceptual and attitudinal constructs. Output during the construction of meaning to
assimilate/accommodate includes; if no assimilation is
possible and no accommodation is possible, recycle to
correct or obtain more information; if still not possible, hold and return to scan for possible clarification as reading progresses; if accommodation is possible;
modify reading of story text to this point; modify predictions or meaning; modify concepts; modify word definitions; restructure attitudes. If the reading task
is incomplete, recycle and scan forward, predict meaning, structure and graphics. If the reading task is

complete then terminate. Figure 3:9 below illustrates
the meaning cycle in the reading process.

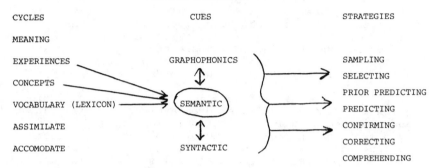

READING COMPONENTS

MEANING CYCLE, CUES AND STRATEGIES

FIGURE   3:9

The last reading model or theory described is
Frank Smith's (1971) version of the information-
processing point of view as Williams (1973) classified
this theory. Since there are more similarities than
there are differences, Smith's theory of the reading
process is categorized as a psycholinguistic model.
Also, since the Goodman psycholinguistic model was described in great detail, a brief description of Smith's
theories will be given.

Smith's Model of The Reading Process

Smith (1971) has described reading as a specialized, complex skill that involves several skills that
have to be understood. A common assertion is that reading requires special skills of visual discrimination,
the ability to discriminate between two letters, which
is an oversimplification and misses the main point. It
is only one aspect of reading. The child's problem in
learning to read, according to Smith, is to discover
critical differences, knowing what to look for and not
so much how to look. He suggests that the processes of
visual perception must be understood before the more
specific question of reading. Visual perception is

pertinent to understanding the skill of a mature reader and comprehension of prior knowledge and learning strategies a child brings to the task of learning to read.

Smith (1971) made a distinction between learning to read, and proficient or fluent reading. The beginning reader has to acquire special skills that will be of little use as the child develops reading fluency. Second, there is a major distinction between word identification and reading for comprehension. Smith has said, "it is possible to read for comprehension without actually identifying individual words."

Two processes of word identification are distinguished by Smith (1971) as immediate word identification and mediated word identification. Identifying a word by discriminating all or some of its component letters and putting together the sound of the word by some knowledge of spelling or phonic rules is mediated word identification. The ability to go directly from ink marks (code) to identification is immediate word identification.

The raw materials of reading are distinctive features. Features are elements of unusual aspects of words, the ink marks on the paper. This is the visual stimuli of reading, visual configuration, or visual array. Features may be common to more than one visual configuration, whether letter or word: i.e., "b", "d", "h", share one or more common features that "p", "n", "v", do not. Features are distinctive (to a reader) when discrimination permits a reduction in number of alternative letters or words a visual configuration might be. The more distinctive features discriminated, the more alternatives eliminated. (Smith 1971.)

Smith (1971) has made a distinction between fluent, skilled reading and beginning reading or when first learning to read. He has constructed a "working model" of a fluent reader. The fluent reader is a person who is able to make optimal use of all the redundancy available in the passage of a text. The reader's objective is to extract information from the written text to reduce uncertainty. The reader may engage in the reduction of word, letter or meaning uncertainty. The reader may use immediate or mediated identification to process letters, words and meaning. The fluent reader reduces uncertainty about letters, words, and meaning independently. One cannot read to reduce both letter and word uncertainty simultaneously. Any attempt to identify individual letters while "reading for words," or to identify words when the aim is comprehension, must inevitably result in delay and disruption of both identification processes.

Smith (1975) has described the importance of the role of prediction in reading. He has defined prediction as the prior elimination of unlikely alternatives. Prediction is the reduction of uncertainty. The fluent reader and even the beginning reader can develop prediction abilities because of the redundancy in language, redundancy in letters, words, or sequences of words, (syntactic) and semantic aspects. However, the fluent reader, having additional practice with written language is more highly equipped to utilize visual feature redundancies of letter and word identification than the beginning reader.

A Model of Beginning Reading

Smith (1971) has identified three aspects of the process of learning to read: the relevant skills and knowledge that a child has already acquired before he begins to learn to read; additional skills and knowledge that he requires in order to be able to read; and the available means and difficulties of acquiring the additional skills and knowledge.

The child brings a rich and fully functioning knowledge of the spoken aspect of his language, as was presented at some length in the previous section concerning oral language development. Smith (1971) has said, "the child has also developed a complexly differentiated and integrated cognitive structure, his internalized representation of the world. The child has developed processes of thought and perception, has established cognitive categories; established specifications for the distinguishing characteristics of objects and events and concepts, the child can integrate visual, acoustic and other sensory information with semantic attributes; and he continually develops and refines his store of knowledge by testing its implications and relations."

Smith (1971) has identified the additional knowledge a child requires to be able to learn to read. He has said, "the child needs to learn what are the distinctive features of written language and their relations to letters, words and meanings. The child must discover the features and establish feature lists for letters, words, and meanings himself. The child has to discover the visual, acoustic, semantic category

73

associations, the sources of redundancy in written language, and the child has to learn to read fast."

Smith (1971) has addressed the question of how a child actually does, and must, learn to read. He described the sources of information available and the difficulties involved in the learning-to-read process. "The child has to discover the distinctive features of written material, the significant differences by which letters, words and meanings can be differentiated. The child must be shown what the alternatives are. The beginning reader must build feature lists and categories to identify similarities and differences for letters, words and meanings. Through this process the child establishes rules and lists for functional equivalences. The child must build new categories which he or she must associate with a name."

The child has to learn how the rules of syntax are related to the written aspect of language, together with the relation of visual configurations and semantic interpretations. All this can come about only if the child is given examples, if he is shown what is the same and what is different. (Smith, 1971).

A diagram of the whole language (socio-psycho-linguistic) model of the reading process is below in Figure 3:10.

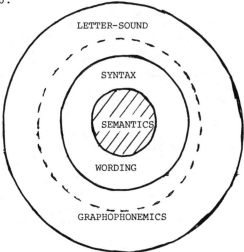

WHOLE LANGUAGE MODEL

FIGURE 3:10

The study by De Ford (1981) concerning the influence of instructional programs based upon these reading models, i.e., skills, letter - sound, and whole language (socio - psycholinguistics) and characteristics of beginning readers found the following characteristics in readers who learned to read in a whole language model:

Whole Language Approach

1. The less proficient and poorer reader produces syntactic acceptability.

2. The reader demonstrates less graphic and sound similarity in miscues produced.

3. The reader uses semantic cues more effectively producing acceptable meaning.

Ex. A kid

The boy got on the bus.

Drove away

The bus went fast.

Several different types of models and theories of the reading process have been described from the field of reading and related areas of psychology and psycholinguistics. The model, which in the author's opinion, provides a sound, theoretical base to guide a reading program in the elementary and higher levels are the psycholinguistic theories proposed by Kenneth Goodman and Frank Smith. Both models consider reading, writing, speaking, and listening as interrelated language processes and focus on implications from oral language development related to written language development. The following chapters in the book will illustrate the application of psycholinguistic theories based on the Goodman and Smith models of the reading process and sociolinguistic theories developed by M. A. K. Halliday concerning oral language development and the relationship of oral language to written language.

However, before moving to application of theories and models to instruction a discussion of written language processes will be given. The teacher should be aware of the linkage between oral and written language processes, particularly, how reading can be learned in some ways similar to the way that oral language was learned. Finally, key principles are presented concerning what teachers should know about written language.

Written Language Processes

Goodman (1980) has described English as an alphabetic system which uses a set of letters almost directly adapted from Latin which was in turn derived from Greek. The alphabetic system is a representation not of meaning directly, but of oral language. There is not a one-to-one correspondence since the units of written language (letters) represent the sound units of speech rather than meanings as in pictographic and other written language systems, i.e., characters in Chinese. Written language is arranged spatially and various arrangements are possible as used in other language systems, yet in English, print is arranged from left to right and top to bottom in successive lines with white spaces separating patterns of letters, just as oral patterns are marked by intonation contours such as pauses, pitch sequence and stress. The language patterns in written language require marking punctuation to set them off from other patterns, e.g., capital letters, indentation of paragraphs, etc. Intonation features are replaced to some degree in print by periods, commas, and other graphic symbols. In written language there is no one-to-one correspondence between visual and written language. The intonation pattern of a question like, "Do you understand?" is distributed over the whole sentence, while graphically represented by only a capital letter at the beginning and a question mark at the end.

Chomsky (1970) presented a view of English orthography which has emerged from recent work in phonological theory within the framework of transformational grammar. Traditionally, she stated, "the inconsistencies of English spelling are often a source of regret to the reading teacher and to those concerned with reading in general. Because English spelling is frequently not phonetic, because of the large number of words which are lacking in graphemephoneme correspondence, it is often concluded that the orthography is irregular and a relatively poor system for representing the spoken language. While it is true that English spelling in many instances is deficient as a phonetic transcription of the spoken language, it does not necessarily follow that it is therefore a poor system of representation."

Chomsky (1970) explained that the child, when he

76

learns to read, is not being introduced to a system of representation that is inconsistent with the language that he speaks. It is simply that the orthography bears an indirect rather than direct relation to his pronunciation. The direct correlation is to the lexical spelling, a level of linguistic processing that is beneath the surface, related to pronunciation by regular phonological rules that are part of the child's normal linguistic equipment. Letters correspond to segments in lexical spelling, which in turn are related to pronunciation through the medium of phonological rules. The correspondence is to something real in the child's linguistic system that he is equipped to handle.

The reader, to improve efficiency and effectiveness in using the orthography to get to meaning needs to process information at the lexical level, avoiding the phonological processing. With increasing experience, the reader should exploit the lexical nature of the orthography more and more effectively. Then, Chomsky, demonstrated that there should be no need to deal with words at the surface phonetic level, given an orthography that directly represents the underlying form of the word.

Gillooly (1973), defined writing to consist of the assignment (or mapping) of symbols to sound according to rules in order to represent spoken language. He goes on to analyze the symbols, sound base, and rules of correspondence of the English writing system. Gillooly's analysis will be briefly described.

Gillooly (1973) stated "one of the most persistent criticism of our writing system by those who would reform it is that it suffers from a symbol shortage." Linguists have identified forty or more phonemes in the English alphabetic system there are only 26 letters to account for the phonemes.

In the case of phonetic writing systems, individual graphemes (letters) are the functional units that are mapped on to sounds. In other systems, such as English, the graphemic units are more complex, involving not only single letters but also compounds (letter sequences) formed of more than one letter. Examples are the digraphs, "th", "ch", "ck", "oo", etc., that function in a different way from the simple, combined efforts of their constituent letters. As a consequence of these graphemic patterns, English orthography employs far more than 26 functional units. Researchers have identified at least 65 or more letter groupings.

Written English makes use of marker units which often are unsounded themselves and affect the sounds of other letters in their environment (as "e", in "mate", affects the sound of "a" and as the "t" in "thought" affects the sound of the diagraph "th." (Gillooly, 1973).

In alphabetic writing, which the English system is based on, the symbol stands for the most elemental unit of sound, the phonemes. Although our English writing system is phonemetically based, it is not a phonemic (or phonetic) writing system in the sense that each symbol stands in one-to-one correspondence with a single sound element.

Goodman (1972) has described how orthography is used in reading. He has stated three significant points: (1) Alphabetic systems do not operate on a letter-sound basis. If there are relationships between written and oral language they involve patterned relationships or sequences of sound related to sequences of letters. For the user of language, surface oral structure and surface written language are related through a common underlying structure; (2) Regularity ought not to be confused with complexity. An orthographic system can be regular and very complex. Rules of language, (phonological, semantic, syntactic) are learned by considerable exposure to written language; (3) The relationship of graphemes and allographs. The reader has to be able to relate several very different squiggles with the same abstract name or idea, e.g., "A" and "a" are the same but "A" and "H" are different. Perceptual categories must be operating to discriminate the differences and the similarities; the spelling system is standardized across dialects.

In addition to the symbol system and the complex sound base of English orthography, the alphabetic system employs rules of correspondence. According to Gillooly (1973), the rules of correspondence of a writing system determine how the symbols are mapped on to the sounds constituting the base of the writing system. Therefore, they establish the sound-symbol correspondence.

Smith (1972) has said, "the complex system of sound-spelling relationships discussed by Venezky may be the basis of idealized classroom phonics instruction but its relationship to the manner in which beginning readers actually identify words new in their experiences is largely imaginary. There are 166 rules of analysis

78

which would be a tremendous memory load. That a beginning reader would apply phonic generalizations fails to
account for morphological, syntactic and derivational
determinates of spelling which the readers learn to use
quite inductively."

Since English orthography is an alphabetic system
in which there is no one-to-one correspondence between
the symbols and sounds represented, it would seem that
the reader must learn to use larger lexical units, or
morphophonetic units. Chomsky (1971) has identified
that the English writing system represents regularities
which exist at a deeper level and it is not necessary
for the reader to deal exclusively with phonetics.

Relationship Between Oral and Written Language

Goodman and Burke (1976) have stated "that all
aspects of language (reading, writing, speaking, listening) have three language systems (graphophonic, syntactic, semantic) in common. When a speaker or a writer
is producing language, he is actively doing many things
to make sure his listener or reader will understand
what he has produced. For communication to take place,
readers and/or listeners must be actively trying to get
the message. They use their own language background
and experience to try to understand the message of the
speaker or writer. Language--both oral and written is
an active process."

Lundsteen (1977) has identified nine elements of
oral language and reading and explores the differences
and similarities between learning to talk and learning
to read. First, suddenness of onset. Oral language
acquisition appears to have no conscious beginning,
while reading (writing) instruction is introduced
abruptly. Goodman and Goodman (1977) noted, "For most
people, oral language competence develops earlier than
written language competence because it is needed sooner.
But children growing up in literate societies begin to
respond to print as a language almost as early as they
begin to talk. Traffic signs and commercial logos, the
most functional and situationally embedded written language in the environment, are learned easily and early.
Despite their differences and history of acquisition,
oral and written language processes become parallel for
those who become literate; language users can choose
the process that better suits their purposes. Readers
may go from print to meaning in a manner parallel to the
way they go from speech to meaning."

However, as described in Chapter II, oral language develops very early and without any conscious adult intervention or instruction. Traditionally, it has been thought that reading and writing must generally wait for school entrance. Possibly, children would learn to read and write in the same way they learn to talk if children perceived the need and functional use of reading/writing for communication purposes. Since oral language is dominant in a child's linguistic and experiential environment, the child learns oral language relatively easy and without much difficulty. Conversely, reading is not as purposeful a process as perceived by the child in an environment in which oral language is the early and dominant form of communication. However, there is evidence that some children do learn to read, particularily at the stage of oral language development when a syntactic structure is added to the phonological and semantic system. Soderbergh (1975) demonstrated how a child beginning at eighteen months of age begins to develop reading ability at the same time as syntactic ability was developing in oral language.

A second factor given by Lundsteen (1977) is the differences in the degree of anxiety when a child learns to talk and learns to read and write. Usually there is little anxiety when a child is learning to talk; however, anxiety when a child is learning to read may be great. The freedom from anxiety enables a child learning to talk to take risks, make predictions and leap toward meaning. Reading instruction sometimes inhibits a child from taking risks and may create a fear of making mistakes if oral reading is expected to be word perfect.

Third, Lundsteen (1970) has stated that frequently in learning to read some children are blamed but usually given understanding and help when they fail to learn to speak.

Fourth, the internal reward for learning to speak are obvious. The child experiences intrinsic reward through the ability to communicate. Internal benefits from reading may appear too distant and abstract to a child. (Lundsteen, 1977).

Fifth, Lundsteen (1977) has pointed out the factor of surface features of oral and written language which differ. Oral language has a surface structure using the sound system of the language while written language uses the graphic system. Written language is

80

more concise, abstract and requires special skills of visual discrimination.

Sixth, oral language is supported by social interaction generally in the context of a situation in which the child receives immediate feedback and associated at times with experiences. Reading instruction often leaves little room for dialoging as a natural accompaniment to the child's learning.

Seventh, in oral language learning, correcting, controlling, and forcing the child to imitate and respond apparently does not help, but similar techniques seem to be typical in reading instruction.

Eighth, Lundsteen (1977) has stated that most children have a fairly broad and deep understanding of what speaking and listening are needed for. But many children may not understand what reading is and what they are supposed to be doing.

Finally, oral language is learned without the control and breaking apart of language as is done with reading instruction.

Goodman and Goodman (1977) have maintained that the differences between oral and written language result from differences of function rather than from any intrinsic characteristics. While any meaning that can be expressed in speech can also be expressed in writing and vice versa, we tend to use oral language for fact-to-face communication and written language to communicate over time and space. Oral language is likely to be strongly supported by the context in which it is used; written language is more likely to be abstracted from the situations with which it deals. Written language must include more referents and create its own context minimally supplemented by illustrations. Written language can be polished and perfected before it is read; therefore it tends to be more formal, deliberate, and constrained than oral language.

Furthermore, Goodman and Goodman (1977) have contended that since the deep structure and rules for generating the surface structure are the same for both language modes, people learning to read may draw on their control of the rules and syntax of oral language to facilitate developing proficiency in writing language. This is not a matter of translating or recoding print to sound and then treating it as a listening task. Rather it is a matter of readers using their knowledge of language and their conceptualizations to get meaning from print, to develop sampling, predicting, confirming, and correcting strategies parallel to those they use in listening.

Finally, Goodman and Goodman (1977) confirmed what Lundsteen (1977) alluded to, that oral and written language differ more in how they are taught than in how they are learned. Although most oral language development is expected to take place outside of school, the expectation is that literacy development will take place in school programs under teacher's control. Attempts to teach oral language in school are not noted for being as successful as what children achieve outside of school. Similarly, literacy instruction is not totally successful. Moreover, capable readers and writers demonstrate the use of integration of strategies not included in the structured literacy curriculum.

Although there are similarities and differences in oral and written language development and communication, the four language processes are closely interrelated. The most significant relationship is the underlying basic property that oral language (speaking and listening) and written language (reading and writing) have similar language elements (phonological graphic, semantic, and syntactic).

What Teachers Should Know About Written Language

Goodman (1974) has noted, "all children have immense language resources when they enter school. By understanding and respecting and building on the language competence of kids we can make literacy an extension of the natural language learning of children. Teachers must know and understand kids, their language and the reading process in order to bring this about."

Goodman (1974) identified several key principles about reading and learning to read which teachers should understand if they are to help children be successful in reading. First, a rather obvious but often not understood principle is that reading is language, one of the four language processes. Frequently, reading has been thought of and treated as non-language. When instructional techniques and methods break apart the elements of language which function together and communication is not evident, reading ceases to be a language process. Second, readers are users of language. Readers construct meaning and bring meaning to the reading process in ways that speakers and listeners do. Third,

82

beginning readers are competent language users. Goodman (1974), stated, "literacy can become an extension
of the existing language competence of the learner if
we understand it and encourage children to rely on their
language strengths in learning to read." Fourth, language
exists only to communicate meaning. "Learning to read
requires relevant meaningful language in order for language users to make use of their existing language competence and of the meaning context in which language
process function. Any attempt to reduce the complexity
of language in reading by sorting out letters and word
parts or words increases the complexity of the learning
since it substitutes abstract language elements for
meaningful language," according to Goodman (1974).
Fifth, there is no defensible sequence of skills in
reading instruction. Goodman (1974) has stated, only
in its communicative uses are all elements of the reading process in proper perspective. Such sequencing was
not a necessary prerequisite to the original language
acquisition of the same learners. Children learn language because they encounter it whole and within the
context of meaningful use in meaningful situations."
Sixth, accuracy in reading is inconsequential. Goodman
(1974), declared "an effective reader is in substantial
agreement with the author and an efficient reader uses
the least amount of effort to comprehend an author's
meaning. Seventh, reading is a single process. Reading is decoding, the reader must go directly from print
to meaning. Any recoding or going from print to sound
and then to meaning slows down the reading process resulting in lower comprehension. Eighth, behavior and
competence is not the same. Goodman (1974) has stated,
the goal is comprehension, not to produce behavior in
the form of performance on tests . . . we are never
justified in saying that the performance we observe and
measure is the competence itself. . . . There is no
justification to superficial focus on behavior without
relating it to underlying competence." Ninth, tests
in reading are anchors against progress. Goodman (1974)
states, "Reading tests in current use lag far behind
current theoretical insights into reading and learning
to read."

    Finally, as Goodman (1974) has stated, "teachers
who believe in kids, who understand how language works,
and who can help kids capitalize on the language resources which they bring to school can solve the problem." There will not likely ever be a panecea in solving the problem of reading difficulty experienced by so
many children through technology, materials, organizations, and the like. Only the knowledgeable teacher

will be the answer.

Summary

Several models of the reading process have been described from different perspectives. Most theories and models of reading can be categorized under three headings: a skills model, a letter-sound model and a whole language model. Examples of each model were described to provide knowledge of different philosophies and beliefs about the reading process.

Goodman and Smith's psycholinguistic models were described extensively to provide information which is the basis for the application of assessment and instruction in the classroom.

Teacher knowledge of the orthography of written language helps to understand the reading process and what the reader has to deal with in the act of reading.

Finally, the relationship of oral and written language, the similarities and differences were described to enable teachers to help students to be successful in reading.

Questions to Investigate

1. What are significant relationships between the oral and written processes?

2. Do you think children can learn to read much like they learn to talk? Why or why not?

3. Explain how a knowledge of oral language development can help teachers assist children learning to read.

4. How is learning to talk and listen (oral language processes) similar and different to learning to read and write (written language processes)? What are the implications for learning experiences in school?

Reading References

Burke, Carolyn L. "Analysis of Oral Reading Miscues: Applied Psycholinguistics." Help for the Reading Teacher: New Directions in Reading. Urbana, Illinois: National Council of Teachers of English, 1975.

Burke, Carolyn L. and Goodman, Kenneth S. "When a Child Reads: A Psycholinguistic Analysis." _Elementary English_. Vol. 47, January 1970, pp. 121-129.

Chomsky, Carol. "Reading, Writing and Phonology." _Harvard Educational Review_. Vo. 40, 1970, pp. 287-309.

Chomsky, Noam and Halle, M. _The Sound Pattern of English_. New York: Harper and Row, 1968.

Clay, Marie. "Early Childhood and Cultural Diversity in New Zealand." _The Reading Teacher_. Vol. 29, January 1976, pp. 333-342.

De Ford, Diane E. "Literary: Reading, Writing, and Other Essentials." _Language Arts_. Vol. 58, Urbana, Illinois: National Council for Teachers of English, September 1981, pp. 652-658.

Gibson, Eleanor J. and Levin, Harry. _The Psychology of Reading_. Cambridge, Massachusetts: MIT Press, 1975.

Gillooly, William B. "The Influence of Writing System Characteristics on Learning to Read." _Reading Research Quarterly_. Vol. 7, No. 2, Winter 1973, pp. 167-198.

Goodman, Kenneth S. "Behind the Eye: What Happens in Reading." _Reading: Process and Program_. Urbana, Illinois: National Council for Teachers of English, 1970.

Goodman, Kenneth S. "Effective Teachers of Reading Know Language and Children." _Elementary English_, Vol. 51, September 1974, pp. 823-829.

Goodman, Kenneth S. "Miscues: A Window on the Reading Process." _Miscue Analysis: Approach to Reading Instruction_. Kenneth Goodman (ed). ERIC Clearinghouse on Reading and Communication Skills. National Council of Teachers of English. Urbana, Illinois, 1973.

Goodman, Kenneth S. "Orthography in a Theory of Reading Instruction." _Elementary English_. Vol. 49, December 1972, pp. 1254-1291.

Goodman, Kenneth S. "Reading: A Psycholinguistic Guessing Game." _Journal of the Reading Specialist_. May 1967.

Goodman, Kenneth S. "The Reading Process." In Language and Reading. Sandra S. Smiley and John C. Townes (Eds) Sixth Western Symposium on Learning Language and Reading. Western Washington State College, 1975.

Goodman, Kenneth S. and Goodman, Yetta. "Learning About Psycholinguistic Processes by Analyzing Oral Reading." Harvard Educational Review. Vol. 47, N. 3, August 1977, pp. 317-333.

Goodman, Kenneth S. and Goodman, Yetta. "Learning to Read is Natural." Paper presented at Conference on Theory and Practice of Beginning Reading Instruction, Pittsburgh, April 13, 1976.

Goodman, Yetta and Burke, Carolyn. "Reading: Language and Psycholinguistic Bases." In Reading: Foundations and Instructional Strategies. Editors: Pose Lamb and Richard Arnold. Wadsworth Publishing Co., Inc.: Belmont, California, 1976.

Gray, William S. "Reading and Physiology and Psychology of Reading." In C. W. Harris (ed) Encyclopedia of Educational Research, New York: MacMillan, 1960, pp. 1086-1088.

Hollander, Shiela K. "Reading: Process and Product." The Reading Teacher. Vol. 28, March 1975, pp. 550-554.

Holmes, Jack A. "The Sub-Strata Factor Theory of Reading." In H. Singer and R. B. Ruddell (eds) Theoretical Models and Processes of Reading, Newport: Delaware: IRA, 1975.

Lundsteen, Sara W. "On Developmental Relations Between Language Learning and Reading." The Elementary School Journal. Vol. 77, January 1977, pp. 192-204.

Pearson, P. David. "A Psycholinguistic Model of Reading." Language Arts. Vol. 53, March 1975, pp. 305-311.

Singer, Harry and Ruddell, Robert B. eds. Theoretical Models and Processes of Reading. International Reading Association, Newark, Delaware. Second Edition, 1976.

Smith, Frank. Comprehension and Learning: A Conceptual Framework For Teachers. New York: Holt, Rinehart and Winston, Inc., 1975.

Smith, Frank. "Phonology and Orthography: Reading and Writing." Elementary English. Vol. 49, November 1979, pp. 107-108.

Smith, Frank. Psycholinguistics and Reading. New York: Holt, Rinehart and Winston, 1976.

Smith, Frank. "The Role of Prediction in Reading." Elementary English. Vol. 52, March 1975, pp. 305-311.

Smith, Frank. Understanding Reading: A Psycholinguistic Analysis of Reading. New York: Holt, Rinehart and Winston, 1971.

Venezky, R. L. and Calfee, R. C. "The Reading Competency Model." In H. Singer and R. B. Ruddell (eds) Theoretical Models and Processes of Reading. Newark, Delaware: IRA, 1970, pp. 273-291.

Williams, Joanne P. "A Review of Several Theories and Models of Reading Acquisition." Paper presented at meeting of the American Educational Research Association. New York, Feb. 4-7, 1971.

CHAPTER IV

EVALUATION OF READING

Knowledge Competencies

1. What is the relationship of knowledge of the reading process, evaluation techniques and reading instruction?
2. What factors are important considerations when evaluating reading performance?
3. Why is miscue analysis a realistic way to assess reading performance and to plan instruction?
4. What are the advantages and disadvantages of informal reading inventories?
5. What methods can teachers use to observe reading and reading-related behavior to evaluate readers and to plan instruction?
6. What is a cloze test and how can the results be used to plan instruction?

The focus of this chapter will be on the development of teacher competency experiences. Chapter II, Oral Language Development, and Chapter III, The Reading Process, provides a sound theoretical base for relating teacher background knowledge of oral and written language learning processes to the evaluation of individual reading performance. The evaluation procedures described in this chapter are related to recent findings concerning how oral and written language is learned. The theories and models of language learning developed by Halliday (1973) and Smith (1978) and Goodman (1975) are related to the evaluation procedures described in this chapter. The diagram below illustrates the interrelationships between the theory of the reading process, evaluative procedures, reading instruction, and whole language reading approaches and organization.

The diagram on page 89, is a part of the total design of the teaching-learning model presented in Chapter I. The primary concern here is with the processing of written language or reading.

In this chapter a rationale for evaluating reading performance is described to establish a framework for specific types of evaluative procedures useful to teachers to identify strengths and needs in reading performance, and to assess progress in reading ability. Second, a description of the Reading Miscue Inventory

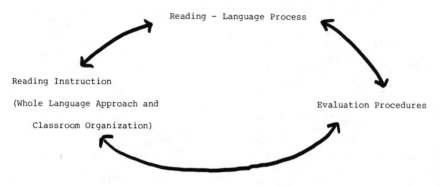

Psycholinguistic-Sociolinguistic

Reading - Language Process

Reading Instruction

(Whole Language Approach and

Classroom Organization)

Evaluation Procedures

Inter - relationships of Reading Process,

Evaluation, Procedures and Instructional Whole Language Approach

Figure 4:1

(RMI) developed by Goodman and Burke (1972), is given
to provide teachers with insight into the reading process and identify strengths and needs of readers. The
complete or modified RMI is described as an evaluation
instrument available to teachers to assess reading behavior. Third, the informal reading inventory (IRI),
Betts (1940) is presented as another evaluative technique. Fourth, the most valuable evaluative procedure
suggested for the classroom teacher is systematic,
planned observation of children and keeping records of
student's reading performance. Observation with record
keeping is also included in the teacher's use of the
RMI, modified versions of the RMI and IRI. Another
important aspect to evaluate is the child's interests,
attitudes, self-concept, values, or affective behaviors.
The use of teacher observation with record keeping, e.g.,
anecdotal records, interests and attitude inventories
and rating scales, are suggested and presented to obtain
background information about each child. In addition,
a teacher needs information about student's physical,
emotional, social and mental growth related to background experiences, concept development, interests,
attitudes and reading-language strengths and needs.

The cloze test (Taylor, 1953), (Bormuth, 1968) is

90

presented as another highly useful whole language technique to assess reading performance.

A Rationale For Evaluating Reading Performance

Evaluation of reading behavior at all stages and levels of reading development has involved testing and measurement. The basic purpose of evaluation has been and continues to be focused on identifying deficits or deficiencies in a reader's performance. Testing has been and is used as Goodman (1973) has stated, ". . . to provide a data base used increasingly as means (often a sole means) of evaluating pupil progress, teacher effectiveness, and program success." "Reading evaluation has consistently overemphasized identification of weaknesses to the exclusion of the strength that the reader, speaker, writer or listener possesses." Instructional approaches and practices have been related to the weaknesses identified by traditional individual and/or group "reading" tests. The so-called "reading" tests, survey, achievement and diagnostic individual and group tests, generally include subtests of the reading process.

The norm-referenced or criterion-referenced tests currently available are based upon a common-sense, semilogical view of what is assumed to be components of the reading process. The subtests include items such as: Identifying letter names, visual discrimination of visual forms, geometric shapes and individual letter and word forms, auditory discrimination of sounds which represent letters, sound-symbol correspondences, syllables of words, inflectional endings of words, prefixes, suffixes, vocabulary, word meaning, sentences, and paragraph comprehension, and the like. Various individual and group "reading tests" are constructed and include various combinations of what is thought to be the components of the reading process. The currently available tests fragment and isolate the language elements so that each language component is tested separately. Conventional reading tests include unnatural, fractionated language, e. g., letters, sounds, letter-sound relationships, words, parts of words (syllables, prefixes, suffixes, inflectional endings, etc.), individual sentences and short paragraphs. The tests contain language which frequently is not meaningful to the reader, the skills tested are decontextualized and lacks function, purpose or use to the reader.

Goodman (1973) has stated, only two basic uses of the reading tests are legitimate. They are as follows:

(1) To measure the effectiveness with which any
person uses reading to comprehend written
language. Within this, the two main concerns are (a) flexibility in comprehending
a wide range of materials and (b)degree of
proficiency as compared to other readers or
as compared to some absolute scale of proficiency in comprehending written language.

(2) To diagnose the strengths and weaknesses of
readers as an aid to planning instruction
which will help to make them more effective.

The evaluative procedures presented in the follow-
sections of this chapter are based upon a socio-psycholinguistic model of the reading process development by
Goodman (1975), Smith (1971) and Halliday (1973). (See
Chapters II and III). The basic objective of any form
of communication, speaking, listening, reading and
writing, is to convey or receive meaning. A basic premise is that evaluation of communication performance
must be based on meaning. Any evaluative and instructional approach which does not involve the reader in
comprehending meaning or constructing a message written
by a writer is not reading. The definition of the
reading process as stated by Goodman (1970)is that
"Reading is a complex process by which a reader reconstructs to some degree, a message encoded by a writer
in graphic language." The evaluative procedures recommended and described in this chapter and the instructional reading approaches suggested in Chapters V and
VI are predicated on the concept that reading is a
thought-getting, meaning-centered process.

Standardized, norm-referenced tests, criterion-
referenced tests and other informal tests which do not
provide readers with natural, whole language in meaningful print settings and in which language is not
functional have no real purpose. Such test procedures
are likely to provide inaccurate information to the
teacher regarding the reading performance and underlying competence of a reader.

Rousch (1976), identified three significant areas
of concern related to the testing of reading performance: (1) How we view performance tests of reading;
(2) Alternatives to present performance tests; and (3)
What has been discovered about some aspects of performance tests. He states that, "psycholinguistic research
demonstrates that children do not learn language in
small pieces; or in a way to put pieces together and

arrive at a coherent language form. Performance tests (norm-referenced standardized tests and criterion-referenced tests) assume that this is how language is acquired in a piecemeal fashion. Performance tests separate so-called skills that comprise subtests, e. g., visual perception, visual discrimination, etc. Such subtest items are not in a natural situation in the environment of the reader. The test items are presented out of the context of the meaning."

Rousch (1976), stated that performance tests of reading are: " (1) Incompatible with views of reading as a language process; (2) not based on a theory of reading specifically or on language development generally; and (3) ignore the language competence of the child and sees a child as one whose oral language needs to follow a pattern in order to read successfully."

Alternative means of evaluating reading performance suggested by Rousch (1976) include the need to consider the child's ability to process material meaningfully. He suggests miscue analysis, analyzing the oral reading miscues, which are deviations from the text, a reader makes, enabling a teacher to make decisions on the quality of the reader's deviation from the text.

The teacher's use of the miscue analysis, the informal reading inventory (IRI), cloze test and teacher observation in various oral reading instructional situations with appropriate record keeping techniques will be discussed in the following sections.

Finally, Rousch (1976), identified several reasons why performance reading tests are inadequate. First, the background knowledge of concepts developed in a story influences the quality of the miscue and the style of reading. Second, children are required to apply different thought processes on achievement reading tests and required answers on tests are vague. Third, the reader can answer test questions correctly without reading. Fourth, some children have the ability to answer correctly only by reading a key word. Fifth, there is the possibility of more than one correct answer.

In a position paper, Perrone (1976), raised several questions about test items found on a standardized test which need to be considered when used to evaluate pupil performance. Perrone asks, ". . . Are they (test items) clear? Are they fair? Do they address the particular educational concerns of teachers of young children? Do the tests provide <u>useful</u> information about individual children, about a class as a whole? Do they help children in their learning? Do they support children's intentions or learners? Do they provide essential information to children's parents?"

Perrone (1976), stated further, ". . . we have encountered few teachers able to provide an affirmative response to any of the foregoing questions. They do respond in the affirmative, however, to the following questions: Do teachers feel any pressure to teach to the tests? If the tests were not given, would there be fewer skill-sheets and workbooks, a broader range of materials, more attention to integrated learning? Would teachers prefer to use the time devoted to standardized testing for other educational activities? Do teachers feel they can assess children's learning in more appropriate ways than through the use of standardized achievement tests?"

Goodman (1973), identified design problems in constructing reading tests. Included among other problems cited previously, Goodman notes, "there is a distortion of actual reading tasks in group-administered reading tests. He provides the following examples:

(1) <u>Items too short</u>. Research on reading miscues has demonstrated that short items are harder to read than longer ones because reading involves building up expectations on the basis of redundancies. A sentence is proportionately harder to read than a paragraph, a paragraph harder than a page, and an isolated word the hardest of all. Since short items predominate in tests (words, phrases, sentences) reading test items will be harder than reading stories or other natural materials.

(2) <u>Words in isolation</u> are particularly hard to "read" because there are no grammatical cues from the sentence structure or meaning cues from the context to help identify the word meaning, yet many sub-tests deal with idolated words.

(3) <u>Comprehension questions that can be treated like nonsense</u>. Many questions are stated in such a way that readers may answer them by transforming the question to a statement and searching the text for a match without

94

necessarily understanding. They manipulate the sentence patterns as if they were nonsense like the jabberwack. Q - What did the momeraths do? A - The momeraths outgrabe.

The evaluative procedures described in this chapter are based upon a rationale of the reading process which views reading as a comprehension process. Reading is synonymous with meaning. The reading process is a composite of interrelated language cues, (graphic, sound, syntactic, and semantic) learning strategies, (predicting, confirming and correcting and integrating) experiences, thoughts, attitudes and social situation.

Evaluative procedures utilized by teachers should present the reading process to learners in a whole, natural and meaningful language so that the reader can apply all cues of language and learning strategies. There should be no fragmentation or isolation of language cues and strategies or skills. Components or elements of language, e.g., sounds, letters, parts of words, words isolated sentences and paragraphs are non-language items and do not in and of themselves communicate meaning. Fragmented reading tests deprive the learner of all the language information needed. The learner is unable to apply linguistic ability, and cannot bring experiential background and thoughts to the reading process, when bits or parts of language are presented in tests and learning situations. Moreover, the teacher is deprived of relevant information about the reader's strengths and needs, e.g., use of language cues, linguistic abilities, interests, attitudes, experiential background and concept development, when evaluative techniques and learning experiences are fragmented and reduce and/or eliminate the reader's use of language and strategies.

The preceding description has provided a rationale for evaluative procedures which should enable teachers to assess each child's reading performance in meaningful ways. In the following sections alternatives to currently used tests, particularly standardized reading achievement tests, diagnostic reading tests and criterion-referenced tests, will be given.

Alternative Evaluative Procedures

Goodman (1973), commented on the needs of future reading tests asserts that, "diagnostic reading tests

95

in the future will need to focus on reading as it really occurs in natural language. This suggests the type of task now found in informal reading inventories. But the diagnostic test of the future will be designed so that strengths as well as weaknesses of learners will be made clear. A shift will need to be made away from counting errors to analysis of performance, to get at the underlying competence."

Goodman (1973), also stated, "achievement tests will need to deal with comprehension in a range of reading situations. They will need to avoid irrelevance. And they will need to get at the reader's ability to use written language effectively. Group tests may well disappear. They sacrifice too much for the sake of economy of time." Finally, Goodman (1973), concluded by stating, ". . . the main improvement needed in the area of testing is in use. No test, however cleverly it is constructed can substitute for the insight professional teachers get from working closely with children."

The following alternatives to presently available standardized tests are proposed by Perrone (1976). One technique described is systematizing documentation through record keeping procedures. It is suggested that teachers within a school reach a consensus about what areas will be looked at in pupil learning by teachers. Documentation using record keeping techniques might include documenting the process of learning, e.g., information about children's originality, responsibility, initiative, etc.: documenting the content of learning, e.g., materials the children produce (such as writing, drawings); documenting the context of learning, e.g., basic human relationships. Another evaluative procedure might include interviews. For example, the pupil interview, focusing on how the child uses materials, pursues learning, relates to other children, etc. Other techniques recommended include, assessing a child's progress in reading, language development and math through systematic observations and frequent conferences which are recorded. Perrone (1976), raises the question, "Can a standardized achievement test really reveal as much as carefully kept records maintained over a period of time?" In education, informal reading inventories to monitor reading and teacher-prepared checklists and inventories are suggested as appropriate evaluation procedures.

Perrone (1976), concluded by describing the teacher's, children's and parent's role in assessment of learning. He suggests, ". . . for teachers to make a conscious effort to document in some of these ways,

they must step back and observe from time to time. To
make such observations meaningful, it is necessary to
have a wide range of learning activities available for
children to engage in during the observation. . . Being
free of standardized tests might encourage such classroom
environments." Moreover, Perrone recommends that . . .
"children participate in record-keeping, recording the
books they have read or the math concepts they understand."

Spiegel (1974), described the need for a holistic
approach to diagnostic remediation of reading and presented the theories of the reading process of Goodman
(1970), Moffett (1968) and Hunt (1970). The focus of
each theory is on reading as a meaningful, whole language process for communication of meaning. She states,
"The assumption that reading is a holistic process
(rather than an isolated skills process) would imply
many changes in remediation as well as diagnostic techniques. Among the implications for diagnosing reading
difficulties, Spiegel suggested are the following:
When using oral reading inventories, "the diagnostician
would examine each deviation from the text and count it
as an error only if it resulted in a change in the
meaning of the passage. Repetition and substitutions
that have been corrected would be viewed as encouraging
signs that the reader is making use of context and indeed is searching for meaning. Repetitions and corrections would not be counted as mistakes. The holistic
approach suggests that minute components are not the
important part of reading. What the reader understands
from what he has read is the major concern. . . The
second major change in the use of informal inventories
would be the adoption of a positive attitude on the
part of the diagnostician when analyzing oral reading.
The diagnostician should look for indications that the
reader is making intuitive use of semantic and syntactic
cues. Is he interacting with his language? Use of
formal reading diagnostic tests would be decreased, for
these tests do not treat reading holistically, but as
the sum of its parts."

The following sections will identify and describe
evaluative procedures which are consistent with reading
as a whole language process. The teacher should acquire
an understanding of various procedures enabling him or
her to assess a reader's performance in whole, natural
language context. The reader should be involved in
meaningful language for a purpose so that the reader's
language cues and learning strategies are focused on
meaningful interaction with an author.

Procedures for Analyzing Oral Reading Performance

Teacher observation of oral reading performance is not a new evaluation procedure. Informal listening to a child read by the teacher in the traditional reading group has been a time-honored and questionable practice. To the knowledgeable teacher oral reading by children in groups provides limited insight into a child's reading performance. Individual teacher-pupil conferences in which the child reads orally to the teacher and discusses what the story is about has been used by teachers as a part of the so-called "individualized reading program" for many years. This practice provides a teacher some input about the child's surface processing of written language and, to a degree, a sampling of the reader's understanding of the material read. In addition, informal reading inventories or graded oral reading tests have been used by teachers and "reading clinicians" to evaluate specific reading strengths and needs of a reader and to estimate the "reading levels" of the reader.

Since what happens during the silent reading process is unobservable, oral reading is one effective way for a teacher to attempt to evaluate reading performance in an effort to get to the reader's underlying competence. Traditionally, the teacher observation of oral reading performance, has involved the teacher or examiner counting the number of oral reading "errors" the reader made and using some pre-conceived criteria to determine the reading levels of the reader, e.g., "independent," "instructional," and "frustration" levels. Generally, several questions are asked of the reader to determine roughly the comprehension score of the reader of each graded passage read. The teacher or "diagnostician" may also examine the patterns of a word recognition "error" (miscue) to interpret a reader's sight vocabulary or certain graphophonic correspondences, syllabication, or various types of comprehension abilities, e.g., vocabulary, understanding the main idea, recalling details, or inferential or interpretive reading.

The basic limitations in conventional uses of oral reading to evaluate a reader's strengths and needs for the purpose of providing appropriate reading materials and instructional learning experiences are: (1) counting word "errors" and looking for patterns of specific word recognition difficulties is usually unproductive and unrelated to the psycholinguistic view of reading as a language process; (2) the oral reading

of paragraphs or brief passages limited in context is
unlike real settings; (3) a few questions following the
oral reading is hardly productive in determining a
reader's comprehension of the material read; (4) the
reader is at a disadvantage in applying his or her language abilities and learning strategies because of the
abbreviated text; and (5) the reader has little real
purpose to read the material.

Miscue Analysis: A Brief Background

Kenneth Goodman has provided new insight into the
reading process through a procedure known as miscue
analysis. Goodman (1973) stated, "Reading miscue research was undertaken for the express purpose of providing knowledge of the reading process and how it is
used and acquired. In turn, this knowledge can form
the basis for more effective reading instruction toward
the achievement of the goal of universal literacy.
Miscue analysis . . . is a tool which in research has
contributed to the development of a comprehensive
theory and model of reading. (See Chapter III: The
Reading Process.) In the classroom or clinic it can be
used to reveal the strengths and weaknesses of the pupils
and the extent to which they are efficient and effective
readers. Miscue analysis involves examining the observed behavior of oral readers as an interaction between
the language and thought during the process of constructing meaning from a graphic display. The reader's use
of graphic, phonological, syntactic and semantic information is considered."

Goodman and Burke (1972), stated the premise
that, "reading is not an exact process. All readers do
deviate from the text, and these deviations can be evaluated based on the degree to which the meaning of the
text is disrupted. Deviations in oral reading are
called miscues to suggest that they are not random
errors, but in fact, are cued by the thought and language of the reader in his encounter with the written
material. Goodman (1973) defined a miscue "as an actual
observed response in oral reading which does not match
the expected response. Nothing the reader does is
accidental. Both his expected response and his miscue
are produced as he attempts to process the print to get
to the meaning."

To provide background knowledge of miscue analysis and its development a brief history of the process
will be described. Goodman (1973) has stated "miscue
analysis as a research tool began in 1963. I started

with the goal of describing the reading process. The most basic task in doing this seemed to be to have subjects read, orally, a story they have never seen before, one which was somewhat difficult for them. . . . I was then led to development of an analytic taxonomy which considers the relationships between the expected response (ER) and the observed response (OR) from all possible angles. Each miscue is considered on all variables that are pertinent, and no attempt is made to establish a single cause--effect relationship . . . one had to look at the whole process and that the various kinds of information a reader used always interacted with each other." (See Findings of Research in Miscue Analysis, Edited by P. David Allen and Dorothy Watson (1976) for a complete version of Goodman's Taxonomy of Miscues.)

Goodman and Burke (1972) developed a less formal version of miscue analysis, the Reading Miscue Inventory, which includes significant variables from the taxonomy of miscues. In later sections of this chapter the use of the complete Reading Miscue Inventory designed by Goodman and Burke (1972), and other modified versions of using miscue analysis will be presented, including examples applying the RMI, and analyzing the miscues of individual readers from oral reading situations.

The development of the Goodman taxonomy of miscues has continued with revisions based on insights learned through continuous analysis of oral reading miscues of many readers. From the taxonomy, Goodman developed his theory and model of the reading process which also has undergone revision as new data about the reading process has accumulated. (See Chapter III: The Reading Process, for Goodman's revised model of the reading process.)

Miscue analysis focuses on the qualitative analysis rather than a quantitative assessment of oral reading miscues. The emphasis in miscue analysis is on an examiniation of how the reader is using linguistic cues, thought processes and experiences as she or he interacts with an author through the medium of print materials. The essential point for the teacher to consider is whether or not miscues interfere and disrupt the meaning of the message. The teacher must be concerned with how effectively and efficiently the reader is applying strategies and language cues in the comprehension of an author's meaning. Goodman (1972) comments, "research for the last ten years on reading miscues continuously

100

reaffirms the conclusion that when a reader's errors are simply counted and this quantitative information is used for placement, the reader may be encouraged to read materials that are either too simple or too difficult for him. The reader's miscues must be evaluated based on the degree to which the miscues disrupt the meaning of the written material. The qualitative analysis of miscues can enable a teacher to help a reader select appropriate written materials. It also provides specific information regarding a reader's strengths and weaknesses which can be used to plan a personalized reading program." Robinson (1972) is in agreement that a qualitative analysis of oral reading miscues is necessary to effectively evaluate the reading performance and to provide useful learning experiences in reading. He says, "rather than examining how or why errors or miscues are made during an oral reading performance, we have added up a number of types of errors to obtain quantitative scores to find reading levels. If we are truly concerned with assessing the learner's ability to cope with written language, the only important 'product' is process."

Page (1975) also questioned the conventional focus in reading diagnosis of oral reading on quantitative assessment or the error-counting procedure in placing readers in print materials for instructional purposes. He states, "oral reading errors traditionally have played a decisive role in setting reading levels for instruction." Page suggested "the analytic process in reading miscue research forces a re-thinking and the concept of error should be set aside. A more productive approach to diagnosis of reading performance is the analysis of the relationship between the reader's observed response and expected response." Page suggests, "a depth analysis of miscues beyond only the differences between the observed response and the expected response. The observed oral response is an outcome of the interaction between the reader and the writer. The oral reading response is only a glimpse of what is happening in the reader's thinking. Page (1975) illustrated the process as follows:

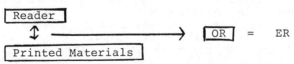

Interaction of Reader, Text, Observed
and Expected Response

Figure 4:2

101

In addition to the reader's interaction with the printed materials, the observer of the reader's interaction is also interacting with the printed materials in the reading situation. Page (1975) stated, "a consideration must be given to the observer's role in relation to the printed material. The expected response (ER) is not a foregone conclusion. The expected response is an outcome of the observer's interaction with the material read by the reader. There is considerable variability in dialect, background and though process of the observer which is different from the reader." In addition, Page stated, "there is variability in an observer's listening ability. Listening ability differs among and within individuals, i.e., fatigue, acoustics, dialect differences and the like." Page (1975) illustrated the complex relationships between the reader, printed materials, and observer related to observed and expected responses during oral reading as follows:

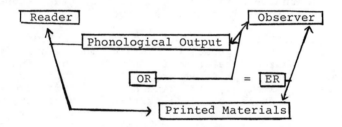

Relationships Between Reader, Text,
Observer and Miscues

Figure 4:3

Page (1975) drew several implications which are relevant to diagnostic techniques using miscue analysis to assess oral reading performance. Analysis of oral reading is a complex situation involving several variables, e.g., the reader, the observer's listening ability, the expected response, observed response and the printed materials. There should be recognition of the problem of interpreting expected responses (ER) and observed responses (OR) which are subject to variations. There is a need for insight into the complexity of the reading process. It is necessary to approach the analysis of oral reading errors with a good deal of thought about one's own perception, definitions and judgements.

102

Finally, we should be aware that oral reading observations are only surface indications of the reading process. We need to treat reading as a search for information by the reader rather than producing the sounds we expect. Comprehension is the only objective in reading.

The Reading Miscue Inventory (RMI)

The Reading Miscue Inventory developed by Goodman and Burke (1972) is an evaluative procedure which is an outgrowth of Goodman's Taxonomy of Oral Miscues (1975), discussed briefly in the preceding section.

Goodman and Burke (1972), stated "The procedures used in the Reading Miscue Inventory (RMI) give teachers the opportunity to examine and evaluate the interaction between the language of the reader and the language of the author. They help the teacher understand how a reader's thoughts and language are brought to the reading task, and how a reader's experiences aids his interpretation of the author's meaning."

It will not be necessary to provide a full explanation of the procedures to follow when using RMI to diagnose a reader's strengths and needs. Goodman and Burke (1972) have developed the Reading Miscue Inventory Kit which will help teachers learn how to use the RMI. The RMI Kit has four components: (1) the rationale for interpreting the oral reading behavior, (2) a self-instructional or in-service package with audio tapes and protocols for learning to record relevant oral reading behaviors, (3) student inventories and record forms and, (4) ways to help the student learn strategies. The RMI Manual, included in the RMI Kit, provides a complete description of the procedures for taping a student's reading, marking miscues, coding miscues, analyzing the retalling, preparing the reader profile, and a section for interpreting the reader profile to develop reading strategy lessons.

Here, only a brief overview of the procedures a teacher can use for administering the complete RMI will be given. The procedures for using miscue analysis are similar to a shortened or modified form of the RMI, which will be described later in the chapter, as well as systematic observations by the teacher in planned reading situations.

To administer a RMI the teacher should have available a large collection of print material, whole stories, both narrative and expository, at different readability levels. The reading material used for the RMI is a whole story with a beginning, middle and end, including a plot, theme, sequence of events and character. The story material should be slightly above the reader's so-called "instructional level" and should be somewhat challenging for the reader. As much as possible, the story should be within the background experience and conceptual development of the child. The concepts in the story should not be too far removed from the child's experience. The teacher will usually select the story for the child to read, knowing the background of the reader. However, the teacher could provide an opportunity for the reader to self-select the material from several stories which the teacher is sure will be of interest and related to the child's experiential background. In addition, the teacher will need a duplicate copy of each story read for a RMI. The duplicate copy, or story worksheet should be an exact reproduction, line-for-line of the original story. The teacher will use the worksheet to record the reader's observed responses or miscues. Each story used for a RMI should also include a retelling outline which identifies the story character, something about each character, the story events, plot, and theme.

Briefly, the six steps to follow to give an RMI includes the following:

1) Taping the oral reading and retelling of the selection.
2) Marking the miscues on the story worksheet.
3) Using the RMI questions and the coding sheet.
4) Preparing the RMI Reader Profile.
5) Interpreting the Reader Profile.
6) Planning the reading program for the reader.

Marking the Miscues

The types of miscues the teacher should record on the worksheet (the duplicate story) are the following:

1. Substitutions - Indicated by writing the substitution above the appropriate part of the test.

       a   door
   She ran into the store.

2. Omissions - Indicated by circling the word, words, or parts of words.

104

He worked (at home) every afternoon.

3. <u>Insertions</u> - Indicated by an insertion sign at the point where the insertion occurs. The insertion is then written above the line.

The boy hit $\overset{\text{at}}{\wedge}$ the ball.

4. <u>Reversals</u> - Indicated by the commonly used editor's transpositional symbol that shows which parts of letters, words, phrases, or clauses have been interchanged.

She <u>ran</u>⁄around the playground⎸<u>merrily</u>.

5. <u>Repetition</u> - A line is drawn from right to left to the point at which the reader began to repeat. At this point a letter is placed' within a circle indicating the reason for the reader's repetition.

A. Correcting a miscue - Ⓒ

Ⓒ helped
David⟍<u>helps</u> his father.

B. Abandoning a correct form - ⒶⒸ

ⒶⒸ in
She ran⟍<u>into</u> the store.

C. Unsuccessfully attempting to correct -

ⓊⒸ ⓊⒸ 1. head 2. hid
He had⟍<u>heard</u> alot.

D. Anticipating difficulty with a sub-sequent word - Ⓐ or Ⓡ

Ⓐ
Tony⟍<u>enjoyed</u> doing chemistry experiments.

The RMI Question and Coding Sheet

Goodman and Burke (1972) have provided an entire chapter in the RMI Manual explaining the RMI questions which are asked about each miscue. The Coding Sheet is used to record information related to each question about each miscue. Usually twenty-five miscues are adequate to analyze a reader's strategies and use of language cues related to the comprehension of the material read and to the identification of strengths and weaknesses upon which reading learning experiences can be planned.

Briefly, the nine RMI questions as given by Goodman and Burke (1972) and explained in depth in the RMI Manual are:

1. <u>Dialect</u>. Is a dialect variation involved in the miscue?

2. <u>Intonation</u>. Is a shift in intonation involved in the miscue?

3. <u>Graphic Similarity</u>. How much does the miscue look like what was expected?

4. <u>Sound Similarity</u>. How much does the miscue sound like what was expected?

5. <u>Grammatical Function</u>. Is the grammatical function of the miscue the same as the grammatical function of the word in the text?

6. <u>Correction</u>. Is the miscue corrected?

7. <u>Grammatical Acceptability</u>. Does the miscue occur in a structure which is grammatically acceptable?

8. <u>Semantic Acceptability</u>. Does the miscue occur in a structure which is semantically acceptable?

9. <u>Meaning Change</u>. Does the miscue result in a change of meaning?

Modified Procedures of Miscue Analysis

A modified version of the Reading Miscue Inventory is presented for the classroom teacher's use. Although a modified miscue analysis does not provide as much information about a reader's performance as the complete RMI, the techniques are appropriate procedures to be used by the classroom teacher. The modified procedure provides the teacher a qualitative analysis of a reader's behavior as the reader interacts with a writer in full language context.

The procedures for administering and marking

miscues are similar to that used for the complete RMI.
A whole story is selected or chosen by the teacher or
child to read. The teacher should have a duplicate copy
of the story, or worksheet which the child reads. The
teacher marks the various types of miscues on the story
worksheet, e.g., substitutions, omissions, insertions,
reversals, and corrections. The oral reading by the
child is usually audiotaped to preserve the reading so
the teacher can go back to review the child's reading.
The reader is not given any assistance during the oral
reading and is told before the oral reading that she/he
will be asked to retell everything she/he can remember
about the story. The teacher also asks follow-up, open-
ended questions after the unaided retelling. The teacher should prepare a retelling outline, including characterization, plot, theme, and events. As with the
complete Reading Miscue Inventory, the teacher transfers miscues from the story worksheet to a modified
coding sheet and analyses the expected response (ER) of
the text and the observed response (OR) of the reader.
The procedures at this point are modified in that not
all of the RMI questions are asked when comparing and
analyzing the reader's miscues. For some modified RMI
techniques a teacher may not use twenty-five miscues but
a lesser number. For a very quick evaluation the teacher may not include a retelling and simply analyze a
reader's strengths and needs from the miscues the reader
makes.

A Modified Reading Miscue Inventory (RMI)

        The adapted procedure of the complete Reading
Miscue Inventory appropriate for classroom use is a
technique which includes analysis of graphic/sound similarities of miscues produced by the reader and corrections. This version includes an analysis of syntactic
and semantic cues as well. The complete RMI categories
omitted are intonation, dialect and grammatical function
as well as the comprehension pattern and grammatical relationships. However, it does include a retelling score
used by the teacher with semantic acceptability to ascertain the degree of comprehension of the reader.

        Below is an example of how a teacher used a mod-
ified analysis to analyze the oral reading miscues and
retelling of a reader. The reader's name is Richard.
Richard is a child who has completed the third grade.
He reads approximately at a beginning third grade level.
The story Richard has read is Treasures Under The Sea
(Scott Foresman, 1976).

Study Worksheet and Marked Miscues

Third Reading Level (3^2)

Treasure Under The Sea

Wagon 1.

A few years ago a man named Kip Wagner found some old

coins on a beach in Florida.   He wondered where the

coins came from.   He wondered if the coins came from
the 2.
a ship that sank long ago.

Wagner began to study the coins.   Many coins had the
them 4.
date 1714 on them.   He learned that about that time ten
fall 5.
ships filled with gold, silver, and jewels sank near

Florida.   The ships were caught in a storm, and they
sunk 6.
sank.

Wagner and some friends began to read old books to find

out where the ships had sunk.
reed 7.
When they read the old books, they found that the ships
sank 8.
had sunk near the beach where Wagner found the old coins.
the 9.
They even found a map in an old book that showed where
10.   sank 11.
the ships (had) sunk.

(Then) Wagner and his friends decided to search for the
ship 13.   15.
ships,14. in the sea.
 ^ were 16. (C) driving 17.
The man wore (diving) suits, face masks, and flippers.
    (C) sank 18.
They had (tanks) filled with air so they could breathe

underwater.   It took a long time to find some of the
     a 20.   (C) became 21.   bird 22. 23.
ships and treasure (because) they were buried in (the) mud

at the bottom of the sea.

Wagner and his friends had to use equipment to uncover

108

the treasure that was buried in the mud and sand. They
could not ⟨look⟩ for the treasure for many months because
could not 24.
the sea was rough.   They had ⟨to be careful⟩ when they
roug 25.   ©became 26.

saw sharks in the water. Wagner and his friends did
                                              ship 27.
find gold and silver coins and jewels in the ships!
                                         treasures 28.
They found silver forks and dishes too. The treasure

they found at the bottom of the sea is worth millions of

dollars. They feel they will still find more treasure.

Coding Form

       The teacher then lists the first twenty-three
consecutive miscues made by the reader in the first
column and the word from the text. The teacher compared
each miscue with the text asking five basic linguistic
questions and recording a "Y" for "yes" or a "N" for
"no." The percentage of all "Y's" and "N's" were recorded at the bottom of each column. The procedures
for responding to each of the reader's miscues compared
to the text are similar to the procedures used with the
complete RMI. For example, for graphic similarity, if
two parts of the reader's miscue looks like the text
word, the miscue is marked "Y"; or a high degree of
similarity. If one or no parts of the word are visually
similar, the miscue is marked."N." The same procedure
is followed for coding sound similarity, correction,
syntactic (language) and semantic (meaning) acceptability.

       Given below is the completed coding form based
upon the miscues produced by Richard in his oral reading.

Evaluation of Oral Reading

Name Richard _____ Age 10 _____ Grade 3 _____ Date 7-21-77
Y=Yes   N=No

Reader	Text	Graphic Similarity	Sound Similarity	Correction	Language Syntactic Accept.	Meaning Semantic Accept.
1. Wagon	Wagner	Y	Y	N	Y	N
2. the	a	N	Y	N	Y	Y
3. Wagoner	Wagner	Y	Y	N	Y	Y
4. them	that	Y	Y	N	N	N

Reader	Text	Graphic Similarity	Sound Similarity	Correction	Language Syntactic Accept.	Meaning Semantic Accept.
5. fell	filled	Y	Y	N	N	N
6. sank	sunk	Y	Y	N	Y	Y
7. reed	read	Y	Y	N	Y	Y
8. sank	sunk	Y	Y	N	Y	Y
9. the	an	N	N	Y	Y	Y
10. -	had	-	-	N	Y	Y
11. sank	sunk	Y	Y	N	Y	Y
12. -	then	-	-	N	Y	Y
13. ship	ships	Y	Y	N	Y	N
14. ship. in	ship in	-	-	N	N	N
15. sea the	sea. The	-	-	N	N	N
16. were	wore	Y	Y	N	Y	N
17. driving	diving	Y	Y	Y	Y	N
18. sank	tank	Y	Y	Y	N	N
19. was	took	N	N	N	N	N
20. a	and	Y	N	N	N	N
21. became	because	Y	Y	Y	N	N
22. bird	buried	Y	Y	N	N	N
23. -	the	-	-	N	Y	Y
	% Yes	83	83	13	61	39
	% No	17	17	87	39	61

Retelling Outline and Retalling Score

The teacher used the following retelling format to informally record Richard's retelling of the story, including his unaided retelling and follow-up questions. She then assigned points for each aspect of the reader's comprehension of the characters, events, plot and theme. The breakdown of points awarded for each was: characters - 25 points; events - 35 points; plot - 20 points; and theme 20 points.

Retelling Outlining and Retelling Score

Unaided Retelling

Kip - 2
Wagner found coins on the beach, he read old books and got friends to read them too.

they found a map where the ships sank air tanks - 1
they got scuba diving gear (masks, flippers, suits) and went out to sea to look for it

to find it because it was buried-3
it took them months but they found silver and gold, forks, spoons, jewels they can find more, it is worth millions of dollars
they had to watch for sharks   and the sea was rough-3

Follow-Up Questions

Teacher: What is the plot of the story?
Richard: he looked for coins since he found them on the beach
Teacher: What was the problem in the story?
Richard: that he found the treasure

Characters -	23 points
Events -	28 points
Plot -	10 points
Theme -	5 points
Total	66 points

Analysis of Reading Performance and Instructional Strategies

Richard showed a fairly high degree of comprehension as indicated by his retelling score of 66. He is quite effective in using syntactic or language cues as shown that 61% of Richard's miscues were grammatically acceptable. He uses his knowledge of oral language and how it should sound when he makes miscues. This appears to be the reason he seldom corrects miscues because to him they obviously sound like he would say it. However, he does not monitor his reading effectively using acceptable semantic cues as indicated by the low percentage of miscues which are semantically acceptable, 39%. Richard shows a high dependence on graphophonic cues. Eighty-three percent of his miscues have a high degree of similarity to the text. It appears that Richard uses too much visual information at the expense of meaning even though his miscues frequently are syntactically appropriate.

Richard needs to reduce his overemphasis on graphophonics cues and focus his attention during reading on semantic cues with his strength in applying syntactic cues. Cloze procedure-type activities would be appropriate to help Richard move away from overemphasis of visual information and to help him develop prediction, confirming and correcting strategies and semantic and syntactic cues.

Miscue analysis is a very effective evaluative procedure to identify an individual reader's strengths and needs for the purpose of planning reading experiences which are appropriate. Oral reading situations provide teachers an opportunity to examine a reader's use of language cues and strategies always related to the reader's comprehension of the written language. Although miscue analysis is time-consuming, the information about each reader available to a teacher cannot be obtained using other standardized or informal type tests which fractionate and isolate the elements of written language. Frequent individual teacher-pupil conferences provide the setting for a teacher to have a child read a story selection in a natural reading situation. With continuous practice in using miscue analysis a classroom teacher will be able to reduce the time necessary to complete an oral reading assessment using a modified form of miscue analysis. The benefits to the children and teacher will be many and reading will become a more natural process of communicating meaning with others, similar to speaking and listening.

The next section will describe the use of informal reading inventories. The informal reading inventory (IRI) is similar in some respects to the miscue analysis, however, there are significant differences in the purpose and procedures which each can be used to provide information about an individual reader.

The Informal Reading Inventory

An Informal Reading Inventory, referred to as an IRI, has been used by classroom reading teachers and reading clinicians as an evaluation technique for many years. Traditionally an IRI has been used to identify so-called "independent," "instructional" and "frustration" reading levels. The results are then used to place children in appropriate reading materials. In addition, an IRI provides the teacher with information related to the reader's strengths and needs in word identification and comprehension abilities. The IRI is another technique to assess the oral reading performance of a reader in an oral reading situation. Also, an IRI can be used to assess silent reading comprehension, rate of comprehension, and listening comprehension. An IRI generally includes graded passages which begin at a low reading level such as a pre-primer level and progresses to increasingly higher readability passages through sixth, eighth or twelfth grade reading levels. A graded isolated word list is frequently used to identify the starting point for the reader to begin reading the graded passages. There are many limitations using a conventional IRI which will be discussed briefly in this section. However, an IRI has an advantage that other standardized and criterion referenced tests do not have and that is that the reader has the opportunity to inter-with whole language at least a paragraph or more in

112

length, and it is closely related to the natural act of reading.

In the following sections the purpose, proce- dures, design, administration and interpretation using an informal reading inventory will be described and illustrated.

The informal reading inventory, referred to as an IRI, is available as an evaluation technique to assess various aspects of a reader's performance. An IRI is considered to be an effective procedure to es- timate a child's reading "levels" for the purpose of selecting "instructional" and "independent" reading materials.

McCracken (1972) stated, "an informal reading inventory is a teacher's way of observing or reacting toward what she sees . . . sampling a child's reading performance is based on two premises: The teacher understands child growth and language growth well enough to recognize needs and achievements. The pupil comes first, and from his responses the teacher plans an in- structional program that enables the pupil to acquire greater language development."

What is an IRI?

An IRI, generally, is a set of graded passages which are read orally or silently by a reader beginning at a lower level of readability and progressing to high- er reading levels. Each passage from a preprimer level to a sixth, eighth or twelfth reading level is approx- imately 50 - 250 words in length. Each passage in- cludes a set of questions to be asked the reader follow- ing the oral or silent reading.

What is the Purpose of an IRI?

The IRI is used to obtain specific kinds of in- formation about a reader's performance. Among them are: (1) a means of appraising achievement levels in reading (independent, frustration, and instructional levels in comprehension and word recognition); (2) the determina- tion of specific reading strategy and use of language cues (skills), strengths and weaknesses; (3) evaluation of progress, (4) identify a reader's attitude, inter- ests and reactions to different materials.

Criteria for Evaluating Functional Reading Levels

There has been considerable controversy and lack of agreement concerning a set of criteria to be used to identify a reader's independent, instructional, and frustration reading levels. Betts (1957) identified the following criteria to be used with an IRI to determine a reader's functional reading level. At the independent reading level the reader should pronounce accurately 98% - 100% of the words and answers correctly and no less than 90% of the comprehension questions. At the instructional reading level the reader must pronounce accurately 94% - 97% of the words and answers correctly and no less than 75 - 90% of the comprehension questions. At the frustration level, the reader will pronounce accurately less than 90% of the words and answer 50% or less of the comprehension questions.

Several investigations concerning the percentages and criteria needed to determine independent, instructional and frustration levels have been conducted. Eckwall (1976) has found evidence supporting Betts' original criteria for frustration and independent levels. He concluded that the original criteria given by Betts is approximately correct if repetitions are counted as errors. Powell (1970), suggested that the word recognition criterion originally formulated by Betts is incorrect for designating the instructional reading level on an IRI. In another investigation reported by Powell and Dunkeld (1971), they focused on the discrepancies between various sets of criteria by which different authorities define the instructional levels and offer criteria, "which attempt to reflect the progression of the increase of language difficulty and the reader's response to this increase appear to be more suitable." Powell (1969) provided another set of criteria which is claimed, "more nearly resembles children's actual performance and allows for the interaction of increased language complexity and the age-grade of the child."

Hunt (1970) maintained that more than an assessment of the child's reading level is necessary and identifies other factors such as the effects of self-selection, interests and motivation upon reading levels.

Lowell (1970) also questioned the concept of independent instructional and frustration reading levels and suggests that more attention be given to reader interests and less attention to examiner judgement, finely differentiated levels of performance and oral reading.

114

Whether a reader has distinct functional reading levels and if it is possible to identify these levels are unanswered questions. It would appear that identifying functional reading levels using an IRI is a simplistic procedure when one considers the complexity of factors which are involved in the reading process. Variables such as motivation, desire to read, interest. conceptual development, experiential background, the testing situation, the interaction between the examiner and the reader, the content of the material, the physical and emotional feelings and attitudes of the reader, the length of the passages, the readability of the passages, and the like, influence the results obtained for the purpose of identifying functional reading levels.

Moreover, many IRI's and oral reading tests vary concerning the types of "errors" (miscues) which are counted in order to arrive at a determination of a functional level for word recognition. Some IRI's and oral reading tests count repetitions as "errors", others do not. Some count hesitations as miscues, others do not. In addition, insights into the reading process provided by psycholinguistics has questioned the value of simply counting "errors" to arrive at functional reading levels. It is proposed that a qualitative analysis of oral reading miscues is more productive and provides more accurate data concerning a reader's strategies and use of language cueing systems related to comprehension. If a reader makes miscues which do not significantly change the meaning intended by the author, such miscues would not be counted as "errors" in arriving at a determination of a functional reading level for word recognition. Traditionally, most IRI's and oral reading tests count as miscues any deviation from the text even though the miscue does not result in any change of meaning. Therefore, if miscues which do not affect the meaning are not included in the word count for identifying the functional level for word recognition, this will have an effect upon the results. The author questions whether quantitative word recognition information using an IRI is of any real value. A qualitative analysis of miscues will provide more valuable information to a teacher to evaluate the reader's use of graphophonic, syntactic and semantic cues and strategies such as predicting, confirming and correcting related to comprehension. It is proposed that the real essential information of significant importance to determine functional reading levels is the comprehension the reader demonstrates following the oral or silent reading of graded passages or stories. Despite the difficulties inherent in IRI's, this technique is a more effective evaluative procedure than norm-referenced standardized tests and criterion-referenced tests, because it enables a teacher to observe the reader in a somewhat natural reading situation in which the reader has the opportunity to utilize linguistic, experiential, and learning strategies in a modified whole language setting. There are still obstacles facing the reader when using an IRI which have been previously identified as disadvantages.

Marking Miscues

The types of miscues marked by an examiner using an IRI or other oral reading test are similar. The marking code and types of miscues or deviations from the text the reader makes are also similar to that of the RMI. The teacher must be familiar with some code and the different kinds of miscues to mark on a duplicate copy of the passages the child is reading orally.

The basic types of miscues to mark and the related code to identify each type of miscue is as follows:

Type of Miscue	Symbol to Identify Miscue
1. Omission	Then we could buy some summer clothes at (the) City Fair.
2. Insertion	all It is all⌃so deep that ocean liners can travel it for two thousand miles
3. Substitution	may be the gases made by the exploding charge push against the walls of the tube in all directions
4. Reversal	"Well, you can now, "this mother⌒said.
5. Word Pronounced by Teacher	P His little brother Howie said, "I want to go too."

116

(This is an omission which may be marked "P" if the examiner supplies a word when the reader hesitates at least five seconds.)

6. Correction   ©All

                            He wanted to make a rocket

                            that would really work.

7. Inadequate phrasing or   The men/told stories to ex-
    excessive hesitation

                            plain/ why the world/ is the

                            way it is.

If miscues are counted to arrive at "reading levels," numbers 6 and 7 above are not counted as miscues.

Administration of an IRI

The teacher will need a copy of the graded passages for the child to read and a duplicate copy to mark miscues and to check comprehension. An audio-tape recording should be made of the oral reading so the teacher can replay the child's oral reading to check to make sure all the miscues are accurately recorded and that comprehension is marked appropriately.

There are a variety of different ways to administer an IRI. The IRI may be administered only as oral reading followed by comprehension questions after each graded passage has been read. Or, the inventory may be read silently first, followed by a comprehension check and then reread orally to assess word recognition strategies using the same graded passages. Another procedure would be to have available two different IRI's, one for the child to read orally and check comprehension and one for silent reading followed by questions after each passage has been read silently to check for comprehension. In addition, a third IRI may be used to assess listening comprehension to use as a comparison between reading performance and listening performance to identify the possible difference between reading achievement level and capacity to understand through listening comprehension. However, the classroom teacher will seldom have time to administer an IRI very frequently, so the author suggests using only the oral reading technique if the conventional IRI is used. The administrative procedures which follow are based on only having the child read orally the graded passages.

It is important as in any testing, or for that

117

matter, instructional situation, for the examiner to establish rapport with the child. The teacher should talk briefly and try to relax the pupil. The teacher should explain what the purpose of the IRI is and what the child will be expected to do. The examiner needs to know the beginning level for the IRI. A classroom teacher who is familiar with each child's performance will have a very good idea at which grade level to begin. If an IRI is given at the beginning of the year to all children the teacher may refer to the previous year's record about the child related to the reading level at which the child completed the last year. If a new child has entered the classroom and the teacher has no knowledge of the child's reading background, the teacher may use a graded isolated word list to help estimate the starting point for orally reading the graded selections. However, this technique is strongly discouraged unless absolutely necessary since isolated word recognition is not reading and may produce inaccurate information about the child's actual reading performance. If an isolated graded word list is used to establish the beginning level the usual procedure is to start the child's oral reading one level below the level at which the child pronounced all the words correctly. Another "rule of thumb" technique to estimate the beginning level is to have the child start reading a graded passage at least two levels below his/her grade level, although this will not be an effective procedure for all children. The important point is that the child should experience success at an easy level so as to try to establish the "independent level" so that the testing can proceed to levels of increasing difficulty.

Once the beginning level has been determined the procedure at each successive graded level passage is the same. The child is asked to read the passage orally followed by the teacher asking prepared questions to check on comprehension. The types of questions usually include vocabulary, recall of the main idea, recall of details and inferences or interpretive-type questions. There may be 5-10 questions including for example, two or three vocabulary, two or three detail type questions, one main idea, and two or three inference questions. If percentage criteria are used to ascertain the functional reading level of the passage read, the teacher will have to quickly compute the word recognition and comprehension percentage to determine whether the child should continue reading the next graded passage or whether the inventory should be terminated. The teacher will need to have in mind the criteria percentage which will be applied. The teacher should have the child continue reading each graded passage and ask the comprehension questions following each passage until the teacher believes and/or the criteria indicate a "frustration" level has been reached and the inventory should be terminated. During the oral reading the teacher will usually mark the child's oral reading miscue and check the child's correct and incorrect responses to the comprehension questions. The author believes that the reading should continue until the reader's comprehension percentage falls within the range of the "frustration" level even though the word recognition percentage is already at a "frustration" level as determined using one set of criteria. However, other factors such as the reader's physical and emotional behavior may indicate a need to terminate the testing at any particular time during the testing session. The session should continue uninterrupted with the teacher behaving as a neutral but interested observer who is present to record and keep the process moving.

An Example of an IRI

The following IRI (Betts and Welch, 1964) was administered to a child enrolled in a remedial program. The child's name is Barry (fictitious) and he was in the sixth grade at the time of the test.

The teacher began the IRI by having Barry read the third reader level which established his "independent" level and continued until Barry reached the "frustration" level at the seventh grade level. The teacher only counted miscues which disrupted or changed the meaning intended by the author which accounts for the difference in the number of miscues the reader made during the oral reading and the number of word "errors" recorded after each graded selection. This, of course, will make a difference in the functional reading level assigned to a particular graded passage related to the word recognition criteria percentage used.

The teacher applied the following word recognition and comprehension percentage criteria to determine the child's functional reading levels for each graded passage.

Functional Reading Level	Word Recognition	Comprehension
Independent	100 - 97%	100 - 90%
Instructional	97 - 94%	89 - 75%
Frustration	90% or less	below 50%

Given below is the duplicate copy of the IRI, graded levels three through seven which were read orally by Barry and the oral miscue and comprehension check made by the teacher.

(118 Words)

Third Reader Level

A Rope Around The Sun

In each village on the cliffs there ~~was~~/ *were* a large meeting room. To enter this room ⓒ too, the/ Indians had to climb onto the roof and descend through an ~~opening~~ *the openings*.

Inside the round meeting room,/ a fire of/ ~~juniper~~ *jupiters* logs ~~burned~~ *burning* in the middle of the floor. ~~Beside~~ *Besides* the ⓒ ~~fire~~ sat/ the wise men of the tribe. They sang songs and told stories.

Around the walls/sat children of all ages. ⓒ They listened ~~eagerly~~ *early* to the wise men.

They ~~men~~/ told stories to explain/ why the world/ is the way it is. They explained the thunder and the moon and the stars. They explained the animals,/ too, and∧told why each/was different/ some wild, some gentle. *they*

No. of word errors 2 Percent Correct 98 Reading Level

 Independent

Comprehension Questions

½ 1. Name two things the wise men of the tribe did in the large meeting room? (sang songs and told stories)

+ 2. How did the Indians enter the meeting room? (climb onto the roof and descend through an opening)

+ 3. What was located in the middle of the meeting room? (Fire of log)

+ 4. Who sat around the walls of the meeting room? (children)

½ 5. What did the children do in the meeting room? (listen to the wise men sing songs and tell stories)

+ 6. What is the meaning of descent? (to go down)

+ 7. What did the stories told by the wise men explain about the world? (explained the thunder, the moon, the stars)

+ 8. What did the wise men explain about the animals? (why each animal was different, some wild, some gentle)

+ 9. What is the meaning of the word eagerly? (very attentive, with interest)

No. of Questions Missed _1_ Percent Correct _90_ Reading Level _Independent_

(157 Words)

Fourth Reading Level

Mighty River Of Brazil

The greatest river/ in the world lies in South America, running thousands of miles across Brazil into the
seas
sea. From the time of / its/ discovery to the present
©days
~~day~~, strange tales have been told of the / mighty/
©Am---
Amazon.

naming
These tales began with/ the meaning / of the river many years ago.
© ea--
One of the early Spanish explorers thought/that/
were
the/ long-haired/native men/ he saw/ there / women, and he was surprised to find the fierce fighters as well.

121

He had heard (in) his own country/ many tales of strange/

warlike/ women who were called Amazons. And so he

named/ the South/ American river the Amazon.

    No other river in the world carries (so much

water as the Amazon. It gathers the waters from half∧the

of South America and sends them in a great / yellow/
 flow   the   all
flood (out) to sea. It is∧so/deep/ that/ heavy/ ocean
                               s of
liners can travel it for (two) thousand∧miles.

No. of Word Errors 7   Percent Correct 96   Reading
Level Instruction

Comprehension Questions

+ 1. What is the name of the greatest river in the
    world? (Amazon River)

+ 2. In what country is the Amazon River located?
    (Brazil)

½ 3. From what country was the explorer who named the
    river the Amazon River? (Spain)

+ 4. Why did the Spanish explorer name the river the
    Amazon River? (he thought the long-haired native
    men were women. He had heard many tales of
    strange warlike women who were called Amazons)

½ 5. About how long is the Amazon River? (thousands
    of miles)

+ 6. Does any other river in the world carry as much
    water as the Amazon?

+ 7. Where does the water from the Amazon go? (out to
    sea, out to the ocean)

½ 8. What is the meaning of the word fierce? (aggres-
    sive, determined)

+ 9. How do you know the Amazon River is deep? (Ocean
    liners can travel it for thousands of miles)

+ 10. What is the meaning of explorer? (a person who
      discovers)

No. of Questions Missed 1½ Percent Correct 85 Reading
Level Instructional

(131 Words)

Fifth Reader Level

Outer Space

Take a tube, sealed at one end. Put into it/ a
ⓒchar---
charge of something that will explode. As the blast
                of
blows out∧ the open end at/the back, the/tube jumps
                       may be   pushed
forward. The gaseṡ made by the exploding charge push

against the wallṡof the tube/ in all directions. Since
                    farward   always to
they/ cannot get/out forward, the tube runs away and

leaveṡ them behind. That's a rocket.
                              ⓒ a---
The Chinese found/ this/ out/ about/ the year 1200,
                              The
when/ they invented / gunpowder. That first gunpowder

was very poor, as far as exploding powder went. It

burned slowly instead of/ going/ off all/ at once/ with

a bang. So when it was placed in/ tubes, the tubeṡ

moved forward, carrying some of the/ unburned powder

instead of/ blowing up.

And the Chinese had invented rockets.

No. of Word Errors 5 Percent Correct 96 Reading
Level Instruction

Comprehension Questions

½ 1. What does this story tell about? (how rockets
       were invented)

+ 2. Who invented gunpowder? (Chinese)

123

+ 3. When was gunpowder invented? (about the year
      1200)

- 4. What happened to a tube sealed at one end with a
      charge of something that will explode when the
      blast blows out the open end? (the tube jumps
      forward)

+ 5. What causes the tube to jump forward? (gases made
      by exploding charges against the walls of the tube)

½ 6. Why was the first gunpowder very poor? (it burned
      slowly instead of going off all at once with a
      bang)

+ 7. What is the meaning of explode? (a loud noise,
      to break apart, to blow up)

+ 8. Did all of the powder burn in the tube? (No)

No. of Questions Misses _2_ Percent Correct _75_ Reading
Level _Instruction_

(212 words)

Sixth Reader Level

An Early Scientist
cathered   © since
The huge/cathedral was silent except for the sound

of scattered/ footsteps on the stone floor. Here and
                                                                   s
there men and women were kneeling. The young student∧
                                                    he   d
Galileo, rose to leave. As he did so, his glance∧fell

upon the great/ hanging above him.

Someone had just come /to/ light the lamp. In
                                                    s
order to do so/ more easily, he drew it toward∧ him.
                 he
When he let it go, it swung back and forth, back and

forth. The young man/watched/ with/ growing interest.
              noticed   © al---
    Galileo noted that although the swinging became
                                      down
less and less as it died, the time each / swing/

124

neither increased/ or lessened. But how could he be
[C circled before "how could"] [it above "he"]
was
sure? There were / no / watches/ in those days,/

more than three hundred years ago. How could / he
strength [UC circled] 1. look 2. take
measure/ the length of/the time it took the swinging

object/ to make each swing exactly?
He heard the exactly the boys
His heart beat excitedly. The beat in / his body!

It was so/regular/ he could use it as a / timepiece.
observantly
He did and found he was/ absolutely right. The lamp

swing, like/ the/ pendulum of a big clock, took the same
it made
/time to make its first large movement as the last

small one. The swing was as regular as the beat of his
[C circled above "The"]

pulse.

No. of Word Errors <u>11</u> Percent Correct <u>95</u> Reading
Level <u>Instruction</u>

<u>Comprehension Questions</u>

- 1. What discovery did Galileo make from watching the
      lamp swing back and forth? (the lamp took the
      same time to make its first large swing as its
      last small one)

+ 2. Where was Galileo when he made his discovery?
      (in a cathedral)

+ 3. How did Galileo happen to look at the lamp?
      (someone came to light the lamp)

+ 4. How did Galileo measure the length of time it
      took a swinging object to make each swing?
      (he used his heart beat or pulse beat)

- 5. What is a cathedral? (a church)

+ 6. What is the meaning of a timepiece? (a watch)

+ 7. What did the swinging lamp resemble? (the pen-
      dulum of a big clock)

125

No. of Questions Missed 2 Percent Correct 71 Reading
Level Instructional

121 words)

Seventh Reader Level

Why Shells Produce Pearls

Century
Centuries ago, people were puzzled to know how
                              accent
pearls were formed, and the/ancients/ had many/
fantastic   of
fanciful stories and myths regarding them,/ but today we

know just how and why shells/ produce pearls, although

all/ are not formed / in exactly the same way. But in
                         with   Ⓒ for for --
every case pearls/ are formed when some foreign
Ⓒ ma-- ma--Ⓒ be=Ⓒ lo--   animals
matter becomes lodged in / the shell/ and the/ animal
cover
covers is with/ the same material/ as the / lining of
      shells   1. nar- 2. nairs
the shell, or the "nacre" as it is called. For this

reason, the pearls/are always/ of the same color/ and
        and   1. in- 2. inter-er
luster as the interior / of the shell, so that the more
        the
beautiful and lustrous the shell, the more beautiful
                    Ⓒ peer
and lustrous is the pearl.

No. of Word Errors 6 Percent Correct 95 Reading
Level Instructional

Comprehension Questions

- 1. Centuries ago how did people explain how pearls
      were formed? (fanciful stories and myths)

- 2. What produces pearls? (shells)

- 3. How are pearls formed? (foreign matter becomes
      lodged in the shell and the animal covers it with
      the lining of the shell)

+ 4. What is the "nacre"? (material which lines the
      shell)

- 5. Why are pearls always the same color as the in-
     terior of the shell? (the pearls are always the
     same color as the lining or the "nacre" of the
     shell)

- 6. What is the meaning of luster? (shine or gloss)

No. of Questions Missed 5 Percent Correct 17 Reading
Level Frustration

Analysis of Miscues

Name _____

	Reader	Text		Reader	Text
1.	were	was	23.	all	---
2.	the	an	24.	---	two
3.	openings	opening	25.	thousands	thousand
4.	jupiter	juniper	26.	of	---
5.	burning	burned	27.	of	---
6.	Besides	Beside	28.	gas	gases
7.	early	eagerly	29.	may	made
8.	they	---	30.	be	by
9.	seas	sea	31.	pushed	push
10.	presents	present	32.	wall	walls
11.	days	say	33.	far	for
12.	frightened	fighters	34.	always	away
13.	---	in	35.	to	---
14.	---	were	36.	leave	leaves
15.	Amazon	Amazons	37.	The	That
16.	water	waters	38.	take	takes
17.	the	---	39.	---	And
18.	it	them	40.	a	---
19.	into	in	41.	rocket	rockets
20.	flow	flood	42.	cathered	cathedral
21.	---	out	43.	since	silent
22.	the	---	44.	students	student

127

	Reader	Text		Reader	Text
45.	he	his	64.	the	a
46.	glanced	glance	65.	it	to
47.	towards	toward	66.	made	make
48.	he	it	67.	---	The
49.	noticed	noted	68.	---	as
50.	it	he	69.	Century	Centuries
51.	was	were	70.	accent	ancient
52.	strength	length	71.	fantastic	fanciful
53.	take	took	72.	of	and
54.	He	His	73.	with	when
55.	heard	heart	74.	animals	animal
56.	the	---	75.	cover	covers
57.	exactly	excitedly	76.	shells	shell
58.	the	his	77.	---	nacre
59.	boy's	body	78.	and	as
60.	---	could	79.	enter	interior
61.	used	use	80.	the	and
62.	observantly	absolutely	81.	peer	pearl
63.	swung	swing			

Interpretations of a Child's IRI

By applying one IRI, which by itself is totally inadequate to estimate the functional reading levels of a child and other reading performance, the teacher has arrived at an estimation of Barry's "independent," "instructional," and frustration" reading levels. The results of one IRI indicate that Barry can handle reading material at third grade and below independently. His "instructional" level ranged from fourth to sixth grade reading level and he reached a "frustration" level in comprehension at the seventh reading level. However, his word recognition remained at an "Instructional" level.

The teacher then listed the miscues Barry made at all graded reading levels to determine any significant patterns which may indicate strengths and weaknesses. It is possible to analyze his use of graphophonic, syntactic and semantic cues, and predicting, confirming and correcting strategies that were related to comprehension at each successively difficult passage. This process is similar to the procedure used for the modified version of the RMI previously illustrated. However, the classroom teacher may only have time to scan the miscues to quickly identify strengths and needs in the reader's use of language cues and strategies if IRI's are given to all children. For the purpose of demonstration, a complete interpretation and analysis of Barry's miscues is given.

The teacher wrote the following interpretation and analysis of Barry's oral reading behavior based on the IRI:

Barry's substitutions, omissions and inserted words usually are meaningful and do not affect the meaning which he demonstrates in his comprehension of the passage through the sixth reading level. He appears to be conscious of reading for meaning as indicated by some of the corrections he makes when a miscue doesn't make sense in the context of the story, or he is satisfied to substitute words that make sense to him and are to a degree grammatically acceptable. However, he frequently adds endings to words which do not have endings and makes them plural, e.g., "openings" for "opening;" "seas" for "sea;" "thousands" for "thousand;" "students" for "student;" or omits the plural "s" such as, "wall" for "walls;" "rocket" for "rockets." Several miscues changed the tense of the verb such as, "burning" for "burned;" "pushed" for "push;" "glanced" for "glance;" "was" for "were;" "take" for "took;" "swung" for "swing." These miscues which change the tense or plurality do not significantly interfere with his comprehension, but may cause confusion to some degree.

Barry also demonstrates difficulty in phrasing or reading orally with fluency as indicated by frequent pauses even on easier level materials. Regarding comprehension, Barry understood details except in cases where he was unfamiliar with the content, e.g., the teacher found that Barry knew little about shells and was not particularly interested in shells. This may account for the low comprehension score on the passage at the seventh reading level which was at "frustration" level. He showed strength in recognizing the main idea in easier selections but was unable to do so in more difficult passages. Vocabulary and use of semantic cues was strong except when the content became increasingly difficult. For example, "nacre" at the seventh level was not known as a concept, yet he was able to answer most inferential type questions indicating he could apply his experience and background to a particular reading selection.

Suggested Instructional Strategies

It would not be appropriate to generalize and recommend instructional strategies based on only one IRI. The teacher needs to synthesize other information available concerning the reader's behavior, such as RMI data, cloze test results, systematic planned observation with record keeping pertaining to the child in various reading situations, and so forth. However, for demonstration purposes, suggested instructional strategies for Barry will be proposed related to his performance observed on the IRI.

Instructional Strategies for Barry

1. Provide choices of self-selected reading material for independent reading at a third or fourth grade readability level related to his interests. Higher level readability materials such as trade books should be provided for self-selection if of high interest to him.

2. Stories, books and other materials for reading for instructional purposes should be at fourth to sixth grade reading level. However, reading materials for instructional practice may be at higher levels if Barry's interests, background experiences, and concepts are related to the material.

3. Design reading strategy lessons including variant endings of words such as "s", "ed", "ing, to determine possible difficulty.

4. To improve phrasing and intonation, provide high interest, familiar concept material at Barry's "independent" level.

5. To improve phrasing and intonation, provide assisted reading situations in which Barry reads along with an audio tape recording of the story material.

6. Have Barry tape record samples of his oral reading to listen to on a playback and have him

analyze his own reading and comprehension. Avoid
super-correct, accurate oral reading. The teacher
can assist Barry with an analysis of his reading
and help him identify his language use and
strategy strengths and weaknesses. Stress comprehension.

The preceding description of the informal reading inventory indicates it is an evaluation instrument
which may be useful to assess a reader's performance,
assuming a teacher is aware of the limitations involved
and is knowledgeable concerning its administration and
how to interpret a reader's behavior from the results
obtained. As with any evaluative technique the results
obtained will only be as valid and reliable as the
effectiveness of the teacher using the IRI. Yet, the
difficulties which are not currently resolved concerning criteria for determining functional reading levels
(if they ever will be), and the ambiguity about which
miscues are counted (if indeed they should ever be),
raises serious questions about the IRI. Nevertheless,
the IRI appears to be one way to evaluate reading performance.

In the next section, systematic observation with
accompanying record keeping techniques, will be presented. Systematic observation by the teacher, in situations in which children are involved in various planned
reading approaches, is advocated as the most important
evaluative procedure available.

Systematic Observation of Reading Performance With Record Keeping

It is appropriate at this point to refer
briefly to the "Teaching-Learning Model" given in Chapter I: Introduction, particularly within the context
of teacher observation of children's reading performance
and related record keeping techniques as one evaluative
procedure. The evaluative techniques presented in previous parts of this chapter are obviously forms of
teacher observation, particularly of oral reading, such
as the RMI, and IRI. However, in this section, the
focus is on a wider range of classroom learning situations in which a teacher may systematically observe in-
dividual/group reading behaviors to continuously evaluate various behaviors in the context of whole language
learning settings. The evaluative procedures described
earlier usually take place in structured "testing" situations. The teacher and child are well aware that the
situational context is different in a testing setting

than in daily classroom learning situations. The concern here with the teacher observation and record keeping is that assessment takes place in normal and natural reading-learning situations planned by the teacher and/or children, or which at times are spontaneous.

The teaching-learning process illustrated in the model involves complex interactions and variables which influence a teacher's observations of a reader's behavior. The Teaching-Learning model is involved when a teacher is observing, recording, interpreting, summarizing, and applying information obtained through the observation process. The teacher's knowledge of the communication processes, her ability to apply teaching strategies related to understanding of how children develop oral and written communication, and her affective behavior, i.e., attitudes, feelings, values, beliefs about her/himself and children, and the interpersonal relationships established between her/him and each child and the group, are significant factors related to observational procedures. Each child brings her/his background knowledge and views of the world, his or her language and cognitive abilities and skills, as well as unique affective behaviors which are constantly interacting with the teacher's competencies and personality, and with other children in the group. All these interacting factors need to be considered and teachers need to be aware of the complexity of the teaching-learning variables which influence teacher observation/record keeping when employed as an evaluation procedure.

The focus concerning systematic observation with record keeping is related to several significant components of the teaching learning model. However, it should be recognized that all components are functioning in the classroom to some degree at any given time. The components of specific concern as it affects teacher observations are: (1) Evaluative procedure: types of records and procedures (checklists, rating scales, inventories and anecdotal records); (2) Reading-language cues/strategies related to instruction (See Chapter V); and (3) Reading approaches, conditions and organization (See Chapters VI and VII).

Figure 4:4 on Page 133 illustrates the interrelationship of the teaching-learning components as related to systematic teacher observation and record keeping.

132

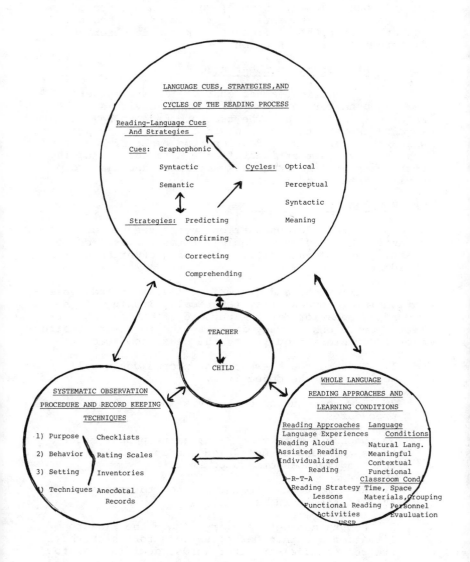

LANGUAGE CUES, STRATEGIES, AND
CYCLES OF THE READING PROCESS

Reading-Language Cues
And Strategies

Cues: Graphophonic
       Syntactic   Cycles: Optical
       Semantic   Perceptual
                                       Syntactic
Strategies: Predicting   Meaning
             Confirming
             Correcting
             Comprehending

TEACHER

CHILD

SYSTEMATIC OBSERVATION
PROCEDURE AND RECORD KEEPING
TECHNIQUES

1) Purpose   Checklists
2) Behavior   Rating Scales
3) Setting   Inventories
4) Techniques Anecdotal
              Records

WHOLE LANGUAGE
READING APPROACHES AND
LEARNING CONDITIONS

Reading Approaches Language
Language Experiences Conditions
Reading Aloud   Natural Lang.
Assisted Reading   Meaningful
Individualized   Contextual
  Reading   Functional
D-R-T-A   Classroom Cond.
Reading Strategy   Time, Space
  Lessons   Materials, Grouping
Functional Reading   Personnel
  Activities   Evauluation
USSR

RELATIONSHIP OF TEACHING-LEARNING COMPONENTS
IN THE OBSERVATION PROCESS
Figure 4:4

133

The following discussion will focus on two primary aspects. First, a description of methods of systematic observation. Second, the various types of record keeping instruments and procedures to record information about a reader's performance as observed in different reading situations.

Methods of Systematic Observation

Systematic teacher observation of learner's reading behavior is a complex task involving several interrelated factors. The teacher needs to have firmly in mind the strategies involved in the reading process which the learner must develop, the types of record keeping devices that identify the strategies, reading approaches or "instrumental" settings, and classroom environmental conditions.

The Purpose of Observation

Systematic observation by the teacher of reading behavior can provide valuable information applicable to planning appropriate reading-learning experiences for children.

Cartwright and Cartwright (1974) stated "Observation is a process of systematically looking at the recording behavior for the purpose of making instructional decisions." They identify the following instructional decisions required by the classroom teacher:

1. What to teach--what most people would call deciding on the objectives.

2. How to sequence objectives and teaching procedures.

3. Decide how to teach--what many people refer to as the need to decide on the appropriate teaching methods or procedures.

4. What materials to use and how to present them to the learners.

5. How to manage behaviors within the classroom situation and in other situations for which they are responsible--in other words, deciding how to discipline.

6. How to organize the time that is available during the school day.

7. How to group children for instruction.

8. How to set up the classroom environment.

9. How to evaluate the progress made by the learners toward objectives as well as the effectiveness of new instructional strategies.

10. Need to enlist the aid of resource person.

Therefore, the general purpose of observation is to monitor in individual/group situations reading behavior, so that each learner develops effectiveness and efficiency toward becoming a more proficient reader. The ten instructional decisions required of teachers identify specific purposes to provide a framework for the observational process.

Cartwright and Cartwright (1974) emphasized, "the first step in the process of observation is to determine the purpose. The observer should be thoroughly familiar with the purpose underlying the observation before observing and making the record." If the purpose is well defined, it will dictate the following guidelines for the procedure:

1. Who will make the observation

2. Who or what will be observed.

3. Where will the observation take place (there should be a variety of situations included).

4. When will the observation occur (there should be diversified time periods).

5. How will the observation be recorded.

Applying the guidelines given above to teacher observation of reading behavior, the classroom teacher, if she/he is the only adult present in the classroom, will obviously be responsible for all observation. Possibly, paraprofessionals or teacher aides are available at times to participate in observing learners in reading situations. The observer, whether teacher or paraprofessional or reading specialist, must know in advance of the observation, which child/children to observe and what behaviors will be observed. This provides the specific purpose for the observation.

For example, the classroom teacher is planning

135

to observe Susan and Billy who are in a first grade classroom. The classroom teacher, Ms. Brown, decides she needs more information about Susan and Billy's abilities to use semantic cues with predicting, confirming, and correcting strategies integrated with perceptual development of visual/auditory relationships (graphophonic cues), to comprehend story material. This identified who and what will be observed providing a specific purpose.

Before the observation of Susan and Billy for the specific reading behavior identified above, Ms. Brown should consider where the observation will take place. It will be assumed that Ms. Brown has observed Susan and Billy using semantic cues with predicting, confirming and correcting strategies related to specific graphophonic cues in previous reading situations. For this particular observation, Ms. Brown will develop a specific strategy lesson in which she has written a short story or found a story related to Susan and Billy's interests and background experiences. Ms. Brown has deleted significant meaning words in the story selection, providing the beginning letters of each deleted word to provide graphophonic cues. Billy and Susan are trying to predict, confirm and if necessary, correct, using semantic cues (the context) to replace the blank with words which make sense in the context. Ms. Brown will conduct the reading strategy lesson with Billy and Susan in a meaningful context. She will briefly introduce the story to them to provide a background information discussing with them what the story is about, then instructing them about what to do. (See examples of reading strategy lessons in Chapter V.) This will provide the setting for the observation.

The fourth point made by Cartwright and Cartwright (1974) related to setting purposes for observation is, deciding when the observation will occur. Continuing with the example of Ms. Brown, Billy and Susan, Ms. Brown has planned before the lesson that the observation during the strategy lesson will take place in the morning when the other children will be involved in individualized reading of self-selected books, assisted reading in which a few children will be reading-listening to stories at the listening center, and so forth. She plans on being free to work with Billy and Susan for fifteen minutes on the reading strategy lesson.

Finally, the teacher needs to plan in advance how the observation will be recorded. The record keeping devices available and procedures for recording behavior will be discussed and illustrated in a later section. In the example given above, Ms. Brown has decided to record information observed in the planned situation using a Checklist of Reading - Language Cues and Strategies (see example in later section, Types of Record Keeping Techniques).

Identifying the Reading Behaviors to Observe

Although redundant, it is important that the teacher identify in advance, as much as possible, the reading behavior to observe. As Boehm and Weinberg (1977) stated, "Generally, when teachers have used ob- servational techniques, they have been unstructured and highly dependent on remembering the observed be- haviors until an opportune time to record--usually the end of the day."

Planned and systematic observation involves knowing what behaviors to observe, how to arrange the environment (time, space, etc.) to observe and how to record the observed information for use. This is re- lated to the general and specific purposes of observa- tion as an evaluative process presented in the preced- ing section. The teacher's knowledge of the reading process based on insight into the socio-psycholinguistic model of the process identifies the reading behaviors to observe. The interrelated strategies and language cues of the reading process are given in the revised model of the reading process, Goodman (1976). (See Chapter III.)

In the next section, Types of Records and Re- cording Behaviors, examples of checklists and rating scales are illustrated which identify interrelated com- ponents of the reading process based on a psycholin- guistic reading model. (See Chapter V for a descrip- tion of the reading components, i.e., language cues and strategies.) In addition to teacher knowledge of reading-language cues and strategies for systematic ob- servation, the teacher needs to observe and record learner's interests and attitudes in a variety of sit- uations. Inventories, rating scales and anecdotal re- cord forms are illustrated later that identify specific behaviors for teachers to observe and to record learner's responses. During various reading situations, using different whole language reading approaches, the teacher should continuously monitor and observe the conceptual/ perceptual difficulty of the written material the learner is using. Several techniques were given earlier to estimate readability levels for the purpose of

providing appropriate reading materials to learners,
i.e., IRI, Cloze, and RMI. A more natural and valid
procedure is teacher observation, as children read in
a variety of situations with different materials for
different purposes over a period of time.

In summary, the teacher should identify in advance of observations, the reading behaviors which will
be observed and with which learners. The reading behaviors can be categorized under three general headings:
(1) reading language cues and strategies; (2) attitudes,
interests, and self-concept; (3) reading performance
level.

There are also other learner characteristics in
which the classroom teacher can apply systematic observational methods and recording devices. These characteristics or behaviors include physical, emotional and
intellectual attributes which are related to the reading process. Examples of the checklist and rating
scales to identify "non-reading" characteristics are
given in a following section, <u>Types of Records</u>.

The Setting for Observation and Procedures

The contextual setting in which observations
take place is a significant consideration related to
identifying the behaviors to observe and the recording
device to use to organize and summarize observed behaviors. Boehm and Weinberg (1977) identify four key
components of a setting as: physical features, objects,
people and activities. These factors will be discussed
later related to teacher observation of reading behaviors. However, before describing observational setting,
it is appropriate to focus briefly on the nature of observation and several related problems in the observation process.

In the observational setting, Boehm and Weinberg
(1977), stated, "the trained observer uses a systematic
strategy for collecting information from the setting.
What the observer focuses upon and the pattern of observations that result are not random but are guided by
the questions posed or the problem needing to be solved.
The categories for labeling components of the setting,
specific people in the observed situation, and behavioral activities that occur are precise and clearly defined.
In collecting and recording observations, the trained
observer uses a system that allows a sampling of the
situation, taking into account sources of bias. Through
a sufficient number of objective observations, he/she

is prepared to build valid inferences from a reliable rich data base of direct observations in natural settings."

The aim of systematic observations as Boehm and Weinberg (1977) emphasized is, objectivity. This is a difficult teacher behavior to achieve because of human nature and human bias. The observer's attitudes, feelings, mood, knowledge, perception and so forth are involved in the process. Nevertheless, the observation process can be more objective if there is a focus on behavior to identify, if observation is made over a period of time related to specific behaviors and in different settings. The observational process for evaluative purposes leading to instructional decisions, depends on making inferences from observable and recorded data, and drawing conclusions to make various decisions. Boehm and Weinberg (1977) note, "The strength of inferences depends on the prevalence of the frequency of the observed behavior that supports the inference. Sampling behavior over time eliminates the tendency to draw inferences on the basis of scanty observational data."

Cartwright and Cartwright (1974), identified several problems teacher's should be concerned with when using observation. The teacher should make observation a routine, a natural part in the classroom. There is a need for unobtrusive observation. The teacher will at times be a participant observer in certain learning situations. She/he will need to be actively involved in facilitating the activity and simultaneously observing a child or a group of children for a specific purpse. The teacher's presence will have some effect and influence on the behavior of the children. The aim is to observe children so that they will behave in natural typical ways. If reading instruction, approaches and situations are arranged by the teacher in which reading (and for that matter, spelling, listening and writing) and language is natural, meaningful, contextualized and functional, there will be a better chance that children will respond in natural ways. Artificial and contrived instructional situations are created by teachers when emphasis is on isolated skills using workbook pages, worksheets, games, flashcards, basal readers in round-robin oral reading and so forth. There is no real purpose that children can understand. In these contexts children and teachers are forced to act unnatural and teacher observations become unreliable and invalid resulting in observational data which may be inaccurate if used for instructional decisions.

139

Another problem in the observational process, which has been identified earlier, is that of too little data. Data collection through systematic observation and various record keeping devices should take place over a period of time to obtain an adequate sampling of different behaviors. The inferences and conclusions drawn from insufficient data due to infrequent observation will reduce objectivity, reliability, and validity. Caution needs to be exercised by the observer so that bias will not contaminate the observational data, conclusions and instructional decisions based upon possible biased observation. This is a difficult factor to control using observational methods, however, teacher awareness of this potential problem can help reduce observer bias.

Returning to a consideration of the setting in which observation takes place, the teacher-observer should be aware of the combined factors, including: physical setting, the persons involved and the activities. A description of suggested reading approaches, activities, organizational patterns and arranging reading-learning conditions will be given in detail in Chapters VI and VII. At this point the concern will be with the overall physical setting, various reading approaches/activities and the observational process.

The whole language classroom will have a different physical setting than the so-called "conventional" classroom. The classroom in which language learning is natural, meaningful, contextual, and functional will include activities, approaches and materials different from a classroom where language learning is fragmented and perceived as an end itself rather than a means to communicate meaning with others. The physical setting of a classroom suggested here will enable a teacher to utilize observation and record keeping productively to evaluate learner behavior. The physical setting should be flexible. Various arrangements of the physical setting will depend on the individuality of the teacher's preferences, types of materials and equipment available (desks, tables, chairs, books, magazines, newspapers, reference materials, etc. (see Chapter VII).

A significant amount of the teacher's observation of an individual child/small or large group of children should occur within the reading instruction and whole language reading planned by the teacher. This will provide a more natural setting for obtaining information in on-going activities for the purpose of immediate and future instructional decisions. The crucial

140

activity is the observation by the teacher of the child/
children in various learning experiences and the accurate perception and recording of behavior. Observing
and recording behavior will be a more complex task in
"normal" on-going group or individual learning situations
than, for example, in isolated, individual "testing"
settings. Generally, the teacher will need to cope with
more distractions if observation is taking place during
the time other children are involved in on-going learning experiences at the same time. The teacher will need
to develop the ability to concentrate on the specific
observation task while simultaneously being aware of
other activities going on in the classroom. This task
will take considerable practice and development of a
tolerance for distraction. The effectiveness of the
teacher's management experience in the classroom, organization of meaningful learning experiences, availability of appropriate reading-learning materials, wise
utilization of space and time related to activities, and
the learner's unique personality are important factors
related to the teacher's ability to employ observation
procedures during on-going activities.

To observe and record various reading behaviors
when children are engaged in different reading experiences, the teacher will need to develop ways to record
on-the-spot behaviors which may be forgotten if left
until the end of the day. The teacher should always
have a supply of blank index cards or a small note pad
available to jot down observed behaviors pertinent to
the purpose of observation. Then shorthand notes
written during the observational period can be transferred to the checklist, rating scale, inventory, or
anecdotal record in a more complete form at a later time.

Inventories and Questionnaires

Inventories and questionnaire-type recording
devices are useful to obtain information about children's interests, background experiences, concepts,
attitudes, feelings, values, concept of the reading
process and the like. Although the teacher should obtain data about these pupil characteristics in a variety
of settings over a period of time, it may be useful to
interview each child individually at certain times.
There are many inventories or questionnaires available
that include questions to ask children so that the
teacher can use the information in various ways to make
instructional decisions. The situation in which a
teacher interviews a child, observing and recording the
child's responses is a somewhat contrived setting

141

similar in some ways to a testing session. Therefore, spontaneity and naturalness of the child's responses may affect the validity and reliability of the information obtained using this approach. However, the information may be a useful supplement to data obtained through other observational methods and recording devices, i.e., on-going instructional experiences with checklists, rating scales, anecdotal records and the like.

Given below are examples of three types of inventories and questionnaires which may be used to obtain information about children's background experiences, interests, and concept of the reading process.

GETTING TO KNOW YOU - Part One

Name_____Date _____

Birthday_____Grade/Class_____

Please answer the following questions so that I can learn more about you. Don't worry about spelling.

1. What do you like to do on Saturdays?

2. What is your favorite T.V. program?

3. Tell me something about your pets if you have any.

4. What is the best vacation you have ever taken?

5. If you could be famous, what would you be famous for?

6. Tell me about the best gift you have ever received.

7. Tell me about the best gift you ever gave.

8. What would you like to do on your birthday this year?

9. If you start a collection what would it be?

10. If you could do anything this weekend, what would it be?

11. What would you like to be doing ten years from now?

12. What sport do you like best?

13. Tell me about your hobby, if you have one. If you don't have one, tell me about the one you would like to have.

14. What would you like to do very well?

15. What person or place would you like to know more about?

142

16. What new subject would you like to see taught in school?

17. What clubs or groups do you belong to?

18. What are two things you do in your spare time?

19. Name an historical event or period in history that interests you.

20. Tell me something about your family

GETTING TO KNOW YOU - PART TWO

Name _____Date_____

1. Do you like to read?

2. What is the best book you have ever read?

3. What kinds of books do you like to read? (biography, mystery, animal stories, war stories, fantasy, information books, science fiction, others).

4. Do you like to tell other people about what you've read?

5. Do you own any books? Tell about them.

6. How often do you read?

7. Do you read because you want to or because you have to?

8. Do you like to read?

9. Do you have trouble finding books you like?

10. Did your parents read to you when you were young?

11. Do you like to read alone or in a group?

12. Do pictures help you read the story?

13. Do you get the newspaper at your house?

14. If you get the newspaper, what section do you like best?

15. Who is your favorite author?

16. Do you have a library card?

17. How often do you go to the library?

18. Name a character that you have read about and tell why you like him/her.

19. If someone were going to select something for you to read, what should that person keep in mind so that he/she will pick out the perfect thing for you?

INTEREST SURVEY

1. Do you like to read?   YES   NO

2. What kind of stories do you like best?

3. What is the name of your favorite book?

4. Name any book that you have read more than once.

   Write how many times_____.

5. Write the name of any book you didn't like and tell why.

6. Do you ever read a book instead of watching television?

   YES   NO

7. Have you ever read a book because one of your friends said it was good?

   YES   NO

8. Give the names of some books that you have at home.

9. What are your hobbies and collections?

10. Do you read a book if you have seen the movie or T.V. program based on it?

    YES   NO

11. Name some of the last movies that you saw?

12. What do you want to be?

<u>READING INTERVIEW</u>

by Carolyn Burke

Name _____Age___Date_____

Occupation_____Educational Level_____

Sex_____ Interview Setting_____

1. When you are reading and you come to something you don't know, what do you do?

    Do you ever do anything else?

2. Do you think that (ask a teacher's name) is a good reader?

    Who is a good reader that you know?

3. What makes him/her a good reader?

4. Do you think that he/she ever comes to something he/she doesn't know when he's/she's reading?

5. Yes. When she/he does come to something she/he doesn't know what do you think she/he does about it?

    No. Suppose/pretend that she/he does come to something that she/he doesn't know, what do you think she/he does about it?

6. If you knew that someone was having a difficulty reading how would you help them?

7. What would your (a) teacher do to help that person?

8. How did you learn to read?

9. What did (they/you) do to help you learn?

10. What would you like to do better as a reader?

11. Do you think that you are a good reader?

YES_____ NO _____

ADDITIONAL NOTES:

Teacher observation will be more effective if the classroom is organized into various kinds of learning areas which, although spatially separate, function together in the total classroom environment. The teacher will have more opportunities to observe individuals and small groups in language situations (reading, writing, speaking and listening) if space in the room is designated for certain purposes, however, there may be overlapping of communication functions within the designated areas of space, i.e., reading, writing, speaking, listening areas, related to math, social studies, and science.

The teacher needs to consider the individuals involved within the classroom setting. Components such as space, time, materials, and grouping of learning must be analyzed and planned in order to effectively observe and record behavior. The teacher will need to be selective in identifying who will be observed, in what place, for how long (time in one situation and over a period of time) in what activity, and in what type of grouping situation (individual, small group, or whole class) related to what purpose.

Finally, the overall setting for observation includes the various reading approaches in which children will be involved. Evaluative information obtained by systematic observation will be more valuable if reading approaches planned by the teacher involve certain conditions conducive to language learning. These language conditions have been referred to frequently elsewhere in the text. They include for reading development, print materials and reading approaches in which language is natural and full, not isolated or fractionated into bits and pieces, i.e., letters, sounds, words, phrases, etc.; language that is meaningful, in a social structional context as much as possible, and functional. The reading approaches recommended that possess these language characteristics include: the language experience approach, reading aloud by the teacher (or others) to children assisted reading (reading along with a tape), individualized reading (self-selection) uninterrupted silent reading, directed-reading-thinking-activity (DRTA), reading strategy lessons and functional reading activities, and the like (see Chapter VI). The teacher will have ample opportunities to observe children reading in natural situations for the purpose of assessing specific strengths and needs in language cues and strategies, attitudes and interests, difficulty of materials and other characteristics.

In the next part various types of record keeping devices are presented that teachers can select for different observation purposes and procedures for recording behaviors.

Types of Records and Procedures for Recording Behaviors

To use the observational process effectively as an evaluative technique the classroom teacher needs to follow systematic procedures which have been previously identified. These procedures include: (1) identification of specific behaviors to observe; (2) selection of types of record keeping devices relating to the observable behaviors; (3) identification of the total physical setting, including persons, physical setting, and activities. The selection and use of record keeping devices and the teacher's role in recording behaviors are important in the observational process.

Checklist

The selection of a particular recording device will depend on the behaviors to be observed. Various types of recording devices are available, such as, checklists, rating scales, inventories, and anecdotal records. For example, a checklist (see Checklists of Reading-Language Cues and Strategies, A, B, C and D given on the following pages) would be appropriate for recording specific behaviors identified and selected in a planned reading approach such as observing an individual child's oral reading of a self-selected book as part of the sustained silent reading program. The checklist is based on Goodman's psycholinguistic model of the reading process including cycles, language cues and learning strategies described in Chapter III. The teacher may focus his/her observation on specific and interrelated behavior, for example, as listed on Checklist C, Syntactic Abilities. (See Checklist C on the following pages.)

CHECKLIST A

CHECKLIST OF READING-LANGUAGE

CUES AND STRATEGIES

Name_____Age____ Grade_____

	YES	SOME	NO
Visual Scanning (Directionality Abilities (perceptual images, syntactic, semantic cues/strateies) Applies Left-Right eye movement along line of print...............	___	___	___
1. Eye movement function in return sweep from line to line (return sweep).........................	___	___	___
2. Eyes scan from top to bottom of page.......................	___	___	___
3. Omits whole lines of print.....	___	___	___
4. Omits series of words in phrases........................	___	___	___
5. Omits words....................	___	___	___
6. Eyes fixate/focus on print.....	___	___	___
7. Applies above visual scanning with perceptual image, feature analysis, to predict/ confirm/ correct scanning..............	___	___	___

148

CHECKLIST A (Cont'd)

8. Applies above visual scanning
   with syntactic/semantic to
   predict/confirm/correct
   scanning...................... ___ ___ ___

9. Comprehension (Oral-written
   retelling).................... ___ ___ ___

Comments:

Interpretation:

Instructional Practice:

CHECKLIST B

CHECKLIST OF READING - LANGUAGE
CUES AND STRATEGIES

Name _____ Age____ Grade_____

Perceptual Abilities (visual
scanning, syntactic, semantic
cues/strategies)   YES   SOME   NO

1. Applies feature analysis/
   builds categories of
   letters in words with
   visual scanning............... ___ ___ ___

2. Discriminates visual like-
   ness/differences in graphic
   letter forms in words in
   language context:
   a. Consonnants (B,C,D,F,G..)... ___ ___ ___

   b. Vowels (A,E,I,O,U,W,Y...)
      (uppercase/lowercase letter. ___ ___ ___

3. Established visual sequence
   patterns of letters in words
   in context using prediction/
   confirming/correcting strategies ___ ___ ___

149

4. Applies syntactic cues
   with predicting confirming,
   correcting, strategies and
   visual scanning/visual fea-
   tures and visual patterns.....   ___   ___   ___

5. Applies semantic cues with
   predicting confirming,
   correcting strategies and
   visual features and visual
   sequence patterns............   ___   ___   ___

6. Discriminates feature list of
   letter/word sounds/visual
   categories of letters/words in
   context
   a. Consonnants (b,c,d,f,g,...)   ___   ___   ___

   b. Vowels (a,e,i,o,u,w,y,...)
      (upper and lower case
      letters)................   ___   ___   ___

7. Applies syntactic cues and
   prediction confirming,
   correcting strategies with
   letter/word sound/visual
   categories in context.........   ___   ___   ___

8. Applies semantic cues and
   prediction confirming,
   correcting strategies with
   letter/word sound/visual
   categories in the context......   ___   ___   ___

9. Forms/holds visual image and
   recalls visual image/pattern/
   sequence in context...........   ___   ___   ___

10. Comprehension (oral and
    written retelling)
    a. Characterization (recall
       Development)..............   ___   ___   ___

    b. Events (factual, inter-
       pretation, application)....   ___   ___   ___

    c. Plot (factual, interpretation,
       application).............   ___   ___   ___

CHECKLIST B (Cont'd)   YES   SOME   NO

   d. Theme (factual, inter-
      pretation, application).....   ___   ____   __

COMMENTS:

INTERPRETATION:

INSTRUCTIONAL PRACTICES:

CHECKLIST C

CHECKLIST OF READING-LANGUAGE

CUES AND STRATEGIES

Name _____ Age___ Grade_____

Syntactic Abilities (Visual
scanning, perceptual images,
semantic cues and predicting,
confirming, correcting strategies)

1. Demonstrates intuitive use of
   language patterns with scan-
   ning/perceptual units.........   ___   ____   __

2. Uses prediction strategies to
   anticipate language patterns...   ___   ____   __

3. Applies confirming strategies
   to monitor prediction of lan-
   guage patterns................   ___   ____   __

4. Uses correction strategies
   with knowledge of language
   patterns if not grammatically
   acceptable....................   ___   ____   __

5. Demonstrates intuitive use
   of grammatical function of
   words, i.e., nouns, verbs,
   adverbs, etc.)................   ___   ____   __

YES   SOME   NO

   a. Predicts using knowledge
      of word function in context   ___   ___   ___

   b. Confirms using knowledge
      of word function in context   ___   ___   ___

   c. Corrects using knowledge of
      word function in context   ___   ___   ___

6. Demonstrates intuitive use of
    knowledge of question markers
    (who, what, when, etc.) noun
    markers (a, the, an); verb
    markers (is, are, was, etc.)...   ___   ___   ___

   a. Applies predicting strategy.   ___   ___   ___

   b. Applies confirming strategy.   ___   ___   ___

   c. Applies correcting strategy   ___   ___   ___

7. Demonstrates use of transfor-
    mational rules to apply lin-
    guistic knowledge to print,
    i.e., perceives relationships
    of clauses.....................   ___   ___   ___

   a. Uses prediction strategies..   ___   ___   ___

   b. Uses confirming strategies..   ___   ___   ___

   c. Uses correcting strategies..   ___   ___   ___

8. Comprehension (Oral and written
    retelling).....................   ___   ___   ___

   a. Characterization (recall and
      development)...............   ___   ___   ___

   b. Events (factual, interpre-
      tation, application.......   ___   ___   ___

   c. Plot (factual, interpre-
      tation, application)......   ___   ___   ___

   d. Theme (factual, interpre-
      tation, application)......   ___   ___   ___

CHECKLIST C (Cont'd)

Comments:

Interpretations:

Instructional Practices:

CHECKLIST D

CHECKLIST OF READING-LANGUAGE CUES

AND STRATEGIES

Name_____Age____Grade____Date_____

Semantic Abilities (Visual scanning, perceptual image, syntactic cues with predicting, correcting, confirming strategies)	YES	SOME	NO
1. Possesses wide experiential background, i.e., varied experiences in home, environment outside home (trips, books, visits, etc.)..................	___	___	___
a. Applies prediction, confirming, strategies.........	___	___	___
2. Possesses store of concepts, i.e., has established categories of ideas, events, objects, feelings, etc...........	___	___	___
a. Applies predicting, confirming, correcting strategies..	___	___	___
3. Oral/Aural language reflects wide experiences/conceptual background (not only can verbalize but can also understand).......................	___	___	___

CHECKLIST D (Cont'd)   <u>YES</u>   <u>SOME</u>   <u>NO</u>

4. Understands multiple meanings
    of words in context of oral/
    aural and written languages....   ___   ___   ___

    a. Understands synonyms........   ___   ___   ___

    b. Understands antonyms........   ___   ___   ___

    c. Understands homonyms........   ___   ___   ___

5. Applies prediction strategies to
    anticipate appropriate meaning.   ___   ___   ___

6. Applies confirming strategies to
    accept or reject appropriate
    meaning......................   ___   ___   ___

7. Applies correction strategy when
    meaning inappropriate.........   ___   ___   ___

8. Comprehension (Oral and Written
    retelling)

    a. Characterization (Recall and
       Development)..............   ___   ___   ___

    b. Events (factual, interpre-
       tation, application).......   ___   ___   ___

    c. Plot (factual, interpreta-
       tion, application)........   ___   ___   ___

    d. Theme (factual, interpreta-
       tion, application).......   ___   ___   ___

<u>Comments</u>:

<u>Interpretations</u>:

<u>Instructional Practices</u>:

154

The teacher needs to be familiar with the specific and interrelated reading behaviors listed on the checklist before the planned observation in the instructional setting. Possibly, a more simplified recording device such as Worksheet A, Language Cues and Worksheet B, Learning Strategies, given below would be appropriate.

WORKSHEET A

WORKSHEET FOR LANGUAGE CUES

USED FOR OBSERVATION OF AN INDIVIDUAL OR GROUP

LANGUAGE CUES   RETELLING

NAME	GRAPHO-PHONIC	SYNTAC-TIC	SEMAN-TIC	CHARACTERIZATION	EVENTS	PLOT	THEME

COMMENTS:

WORKSHEET B

WORKSHEET FOR LEARNING STRATEGIES

USED FOR OBSERVATION OF INDIVIDUALS OR GROUPS

	LEARNING STRATEGIES				RETELLING			
NAME	PREDICT	CONFIRM	CORRECT	CHARACTERIZATION	EVENTS	PLOT	THEME	
								COMMENTS

COMMENTS:

Teacher observation with checklists to record information may be used to identify non-educational causes related to a reading language difficulty. Given below are checklists of symptoms of visual, hearing, speech, and emotional difficulties. Frequently, the classroom teacher may be the first person to identify possible physical and emotional/social symptoms that may contribute to and/or cause a language learning difficulty. A pattern of symptoms observed by the teacher over a period of time may result in the teacher notifying the parents of a possible difficulty and subsequent referral to specialist and further tests and treatment.

CHECKLIST OF VISUAL DIFFICULTIES

Name_____Date_____

Date of Last Professional Eye Examination_____

Checklist Completed By_____Referred_____

Symptoms	Check if Symptom Exists	
	Yes	No
1. Acuity low on test instruments	___	___
2. Specific difficulties detected with instruments.	___	___
3. Has had professional examination within one year.	___	___
4. Eyes or eyelids are red, bloodshot or swollen.	___	___
5. Eyes water after close work.	___	___
6. Squints or shields eyes when facing light.	___	___
7. Complains of frequent headaches.	___	___
8. Closes or covers one eye when reading.	___	___
9. Holds book at an odd angle when reading.	___	___
10. Turns head to one side when reading.	___	___
11. Complains that words look fuzzy or blurred.	___	___
12. Complains of seeing double images or lines.	___	___
13. Complains of painful, stinging, itching eyes.	___	___

157

CHECKLIST OF VISUAL DIFFICULTIES (Cont'd)

	Yes	No
14. Has difficult in reading from chalkboard or charts.	___	___
15. Reads significantly better when print is large.	___	___
16. Loses place more often when print is small.	___	___
17. Has trouble with the return sweep when reading orally.	___	___
18. Keeps moving book to different distances from eyes.	___	___
19. Frowns or seems to be in strain when reading.	___	___
20. Tires easily when doing close work.	___	___
21. Is irritable after close reading.	___	___
22. Selects books with large print and pictures.	___	___
23. rubs eyes frequently when reading.	___	___
24. Blinks or closes eyes often when reading.	___	___

CHECKLIST OF SYMPTOMS OF HEARING DIFFICULTIES

Name_____Date_____

Date of Last Professional Auditory Examination_____

Checklist Completed By_____Referred_____

Symptoms	Check if Symptom Exists	
	Yes	No
1. Inclines one ear towards speaker when listening.	___	___
2. Holds mouth open while listening.	___	___
3. Holds head at an angle when taking part in discussions.	___	___
4. Reads in an unnatural tone of voice.	___	___
5. Uses faulty pronunciation of common words.	___	___
6. Enunciation is indistinct.	___	___

158

CHECKLIST OF SYMPTOMS OF HEARING DIFFICULTIES (Cont'd)

	Yes	No
7. Invariably asks to have instructions and directions repeated.	___	___
8. Breathes through the mouth	___	___
9. Has discharging ears.	___	___
10. Frequently complains of earache or sinusitis.	___	___
11. Complains of buzzing noises in the ear.	___	___
12. Has frequent attacks of head colds.	___	___
13. Seems to be lazy, inattentive or indifferent.	___	___
14. Does not excel in games requiring observance of oral directions.	___	___
15. Cannot follow the "trend of thought" during oral discussion.	___	___

Interpretations:

Recommendations:

CHECKLIST OF SYMPTOMS OF SPEECH DISORDERS

Name_____Date_____

Date of Last Professional Examination_____Referred____

Symptoms	Check if Symptom Exists	
	Yes	No
1. Refuses to talk.	___	___
2. Exhibits unusual movements of the head when talking.	___	___
3. Shows persistent delay in uttering words or speech sounds	___	___
4. Is unable to imitate sounds.	___	___
5. Mispronounces particular patterns of words.	___	___
6. Has trouble getting lips in shape to form words.	___	___

159

CHECKLIST OF SYMPTOMS OF SPEECH DISORDERS (Cont'd)

	Yes	No
7. Cannot articulate some speech sounds.	___	___
8. Has unusual difficulty in learning specific phonetic units.	___	___
9. Stutters and stammers when trying to talk.	___	___
10. Talks in a high pitch voice.	___	___
11. Speaks with too much volume.	___	___
12. Speaks with too little volume.	___	___
13. Cannot sound certain letters in the alphabet.	___	___
14. Slurs sounds until they are not recognizable.	___	___
15. Speaks too rapidly for proper articulation.	___	___
16. Lacks inflection of the voice when speaking.	___	___
17. Voice lacks tonal quality.	___	___
18. Voice has undefinable unpleasantness.	___	___
19. Has poor rhythm--does not phrase properly.	___	___
20. Seems to get "out of breath" when speaking.	___	___

Interpretations:

Recommendations:

160

OBSERVATION CHECKLIST OF EMOTIONAL DIFFICULTIES

Student_____Date_____

    In comparison with the majority of pupils you have known, how often does this student exhibit the behavior traits listed below?

Traits	Less	About the Same	More	Excessive
1. Hostile agressiveness.	___	___	___	___
2. Disinterest in learning activities.	___	___	___	___
3. Difficulty in working with others.	___	___	___	___
4. A tendency to worry about trifles.	___	___	___	___
5. Afraid to face problems.	___	___	___	___
6. Always moving; never quiet.	___	___	___	___
7. Mind wanders.	___	___	___	___
8. Seems to live in another world.	___	___	___	___
9. Prefers to play and work alone.	___	___	___	___
10. Easily embarrassed.	___	___	___	___
11. Hesitates to respond in a group situation.	___	___	___	___
12. Is afraid to try new things.	___	___	___	___
13. Gives up easily.	___	___	___	___
14. Wants to monopolize teacher's time.	___	___	___	___
15. Interest flits from one thing to another.	___	___	___	___
16. Continually wants help from someone.	___	___	___	___
17. Brags about his accomplishments.	___	___	___	___
18. Ridicules the contributions of others.	___	___	___	___
19. Refuses to cooperate.	___	___	___	___
20. Seems jittery or nervous.	___	___	___	___

Interpretations:

Recommendations:

During the actual observation the teacher could record the reader's behavior related to the specific behaviors, i.e., use of syntactic cues with predicting, confirming and correcting strategies, on the worksheets and at a later time transfer the on-the-spot observations recorded on the worksheets to the complete checklist that is related to the worksheet (See Checklist C, Syntactic Abilities).

The teacher will need to develop his/her own personal code to record observed information for later retrieval and use on the worksheet and checklist. A checklist is a useful device to use if behaviors are known in advance and such behaviors are then quantified. There is no assessment of the quality of the behavior observed, therefore, checklists may provide a more "objective" view of the learner's behaviors assuming there is a pattern of behaviors observed over a period of time.

Rating Scales

Rating scales are appropriate recording devices to use when a qualitative assessment of specific behaviors is needed. The observer is involved in making value judgements when using rating scales to record observation of specific behaviors. The observer in the observation setting often will need to observe the child or small group of children in order to focus on the selected behaviors. For example, Rating Scale A, Types of Miscues in Oral Reading, illustrated below would be an appropriate device to use when the teacher takes a child aside and the child reads orally a self-selected or teacher-selected story. The teacher would focus his/her observation on the types of miscues the reader makes related to comprehension during the oral reading and complete the rating scale at some other time following the observation. The teacher could then analyze the quality of the different kinds of miscues which may develop or distort the reader's comprehension. Follow-up reading experiences could be planned on the basis of the interpretation of the data from this particular observational setting using a rating scale to record information. Obviously, this information needs to be synthesized with other evaluation data to plan appropriate reading-learning experiences for each child. The Rating Scale of Types of Miscues in Oral Reading can be found on Page 163.

RATING SCALE OF TYPES OF MISCUES IN ORAL READING

Name_____Age___Grade_____Date_____

1. Omission of Words/Punctuation

   1   2   3   4   5   6   7

Many omissions   Omission of words
change meaning   do not change meaning

2. Insertions of Words/Punctuation

   1   2   3   4   5   6   7

Inserts many words   Insertions do not
which change meaning   change meaning

3. Substitutions of Words/Punctuation

   1   2   3   4   5   6   7

Many substitutions   Substitutions do not
change meaning   change meaning

4. Repetition of Words, Phrases, Sentences

   1   2   3   4   5   6   7

Frequent repetition   Repetition to correct
and over correction   miscues are meaningful

5. Reversal of Letters, Words, Phrases

   1   2   3   4   5   6   7

Frequent reversals change   Infrequent reversals no
meaning   effect on meaning

6. Fluency

   1   2   3   4   5   6   7

Very halting, word-by-word Fluent, natural expres-
reading which affects   sive oral reading re-
meaning   flected by high compre-
                      hension

7. Comprehension (Oral and Written Retelling: Characterization, Events, Plot, Theme)

   1   2   3   4   5   6   7

RATING SCALE A (Cont'd)

Comments:

Interpretations:

Instructional Recommendations:

_____

      Rating scales may also be effective devices to record observations of children's attitudes, and feelings, particularly with respect toward reading. For example, the Attitude Survey below is one device to use for this purpose. The teacher administers the scale orally on the individual basis if possible, particularly for young children. Older children who are able to read the questions with understanding could complete this rating scale independently. When using rating scales or checklists, it is necessary to obtain information through other observational situations and with other record keeping techniques.

ATTITUDE SURVEY   STUDENT_____

Put a circle around the word that describes how you feel. You may circle more than one.

1. School makes me

    happy   excited   sad   interested   bored

2. My reading is

    excellent good all right not too good very poor

3. Reading books and stories is

    fun   exciting   interesting   boring bad

4. I think I am

    tall good looking plain happy smart short

      sad   dumb   good

Attitude Survey (Cont'd)

5. Teachers are

busy   helpful   hurried   funny

6. Other kids are

fun   friends   enemies   dull   good readers

poor sports   like me   different from me

Anecdotal Records

Anecdotal records are another record keeping device which is appropriate to use to record certain types of reading behaviors and other learning behaviors during various classroom situations.

Cartwright and Cartwright (1974) defined anecdotal records as, "brief accounts of some event that happened." An anecdotal record might be thought of as a "word pucture of an incident, behavior, or event that occurred." They recommended that, "anecdotal records are best used to record observations of unanticipated behaviors, incidents or events."

Since certain behaviors, incidents, or events are spontaneous, observing, and recording these activities using anecdotal records, tends to be highly unstructured. However, observation using anecdotal records can be valuable to record information which cannot be included using other types of records. Attitudes, interests, feelings, values and other affective behaviors as they occur in various situations may be recorded using anecdotal records. These observations are difficult to record using other devices, such as checklists, since it is difficult to anticipate affective behaviors in advance. Anecdotal records would be an inappropriate recording system for evaluating the reader's strengths and needs in use of language cues and strategies, i.e., predicting, confirming, correcting with graphophonic, syntactic, and semantic cues related to comprehension. Checklists and rating scales, generally would be better techniques for recording and interpreting these kinds of behaviors.

Cartwright and Cartwright (1974) suggested pre-planning the format of the anecdotal record. Examples of anecdotal format are given below:

ANECDOTAL RECORD

Name_____Date_____

Observer_____Time_____

Setting _____

Incident:

_____

INDIVIDUAL CONFERENCE RECORD

Name _____Date_____

Book_____Pages_____

Oral Reading

Comprehension

Observation and Plans

ANECDOTAL RECORD SUMMARY

Name_____

Observer(s) _____

        _____

        _____

This summary is based on _____ records taken
                           (no. of records)

from _____ to _____.
      (date)   (date)

Is there supporting information on file? Yes___ No___

If Yes, where is the information located?_____

What supporting information is available?_____

_____

Summary Statements:

Recommendations:

ANECDOTAL RECORD - DAILY

Name_____Date_____Time_____

Setting_____

Incident_____

Date_____Time_____

Setting_____

Incident_____

Date_____Time_____

Setting_____

Incident_____

Date_____Time_____

Setting_____

Incident_____

ANECDOTAL RECORD - WEEKLY

Name_____Date _____

Summary Statements:

Recommendations:

Cartwright and Cartwright (1974) noted, "The most important statement which can be given about the preparation of anecdotal records is that the individual preparing the record, the observer, should state exactly what happened in clear, concise language and should make the statement or report at the time the observation is occurring, if at all possible. Each anecdotal record should be limited to a description of one specific incident."

Observation with anecdotal records should be as factual as possible. This is also the case, of course, with other record systems as well. However, anecdotal records tend to be more subjective. The observer needs to be cautious of his/her bias, particularly when observing and recording incidents, behaviors and events in the affective realm. Sampling of behavior should be observed over a period of time in a variety of different situations. This practice as with other recording devices will provide more objective and reliable information. The observer must be cautious about his/her use of language when writing anecdotes observed. The observer should avoid making judgement statements, such as, "Jim was very good during the uninterrupted silent reading time today. He did not act badly as he usually does."

It is important also to keep the interpretation of records separate from the actual recording of incidents, behavior and events. Interpretations should be accomplished after a series of anecdotes are available over a period of time. A separate interpretation and summary form should be used. (See sample anecdotal records forms given previously.)

During the day the teacher should be aware of and anticipate the need to observe and record children's behavior when they are involved in various reading situations. He/she should have available index cards or a small notepad to briefly write down observed behavior. The observer may want to plan ahead of time in a planned instructional setting to focus her/his observation on one or two children concerning specific behaviors, i.e. observing the selection of reading materials to further identify interests in reading, or observation of one or two children over a period of time in a planned Directed-Reading-Thinking-Activities (DRTA). The focus of the observation in this particular situation may be to observe certain attitudes or interests of the two children such as, the interaction of each child toward peers (interested, friendly, critical, etc.), emotional factors (poised, relaxed, tense, anxious, self-confident, shy, etc.), and attitude toward reading and oral participation in the DRTA situation (enjoyment, uninterested, dependent, or independent). The teacher should unobtrusively as possible, jot down brief notes of his/her observation as the DRTA lesson progresses. These notes can be written in more detail at a later time and filed for reference and use.

Cartwright and Cartwright (1974) recommended that observation using anecdotal records be purposeful and systematic. They stated, "even though anecdotal records provide a way of keeping track of unanticipated behaviors, the observer should record incidents with a purpose . . . the selection of behaviors to record should be done in terms of some instructional decisions that need to be made about the pupil." Furthermore, Cartwright and Cartwright (1974) acknowledged that, "the task of keeping anecdotal records for all of the children for whom a teacher is responsible may be insurmountable. The trick in handling the volume of anecdotal records which will be needed is to work out some kind of pattern for collecting records about children. For example, a teacher may decide that he/she will always prepare at least one anecdotal record for some child, i.e., during group Directed-Reading-Thinking-Activity (DRTA), a language experience setting, an oral reading situation, or during a teacher-child conference as part of the individualized reading program and so forth.

Various anecdotal record formats were illustrated earlier. Cartwright and Cartwright (1974) suggested, "when the anecdotal record format is designed, the need to file the records should be kept in mind. For this reason, it may be desirable to prepare the form and mimeograph it on "4 by 6" or "5 by 8" index cards which can easily be filed alphabetically for children and then chronologically for each child. If index cards are used, the summary and recommendation form could be mimeographed on a different color index card for easy accessibility."

Another type of anecdotal record form might be designed to be mimeographed on standard 8½ by 11 paper, as suggested by Cartwright and Cartwright (1974). They explain, "these records could then be filed in manila filing folders, with each pupil having his/her own folder. The folders would probably be arranged in alphabetical order and the anecdotal records in each folder could be arranged in chronological order."

In conclusion, systematic observation by a teacher using checklists, rating scales, inventories and questionnaires and anecdotal records can be another effective way to evaluate individual reading behavior for the purpose of planning and providing each learner with appropriate reading experiences at various stages of reading development. Systematic observations with different types of record keeping devices is a highly complex task. To attain proficiency, the teacher must be knowledgeable concerning children's oral language development and the reading process, particularly related to recent insight from psycholinguistic and socio-linguistic theories and research investigations. The teacher-observer must be highly familiar with the reading-language cues and the comprehension process to effectively provide reading-learning experiences which enable learners to develop reading abilities over a period of time in developmental stages.

Successful use of observation with record keeping devices is also based on teacher understanding and application of appropriate observation methods. Methods include, setting a purpose, identifying specific behaviors to observe, consideration of the overall setting (physical setting, persons, and activities) and the selection of appropriate recording devices related to the purpose.

Finally, since most classroom observation of reading performance will take place during on-going reading activities, the teacher must plan and organize meaningful reading situations in which children are participating in real reading experiences in which the purpose of reading is to comprehend and to communicate with others through print. Hopefully, the information provided in this section will enable the teacher to be more effective "child-watchers" and therefore, obtain valuable information about each child to use for improved reading experiences.

The Cloze Test

The cloze test or cloze procedure is suggested as another evaluative technique which has been found to have potential for assessment of reading performance. The cloze test has value as an instrument because, like other assessment procedures described previously in this chapter, it provides the reader with whole language discourse. The reader using a cloze test has the opportunity to interact with the author in processing the written message applying all language cues (graphophonic, semantic, and syntactic) and strategies (predicting, confirming and correcting) in an integrated, unified approach. The focus is on comprehension of the message. However, the cloze test or procedure is significantly different from other whole language evaluative techniques presented earlier, i. e., RMI, IRI and systematic observation with record keeping, in one important way. The cloze procedure requires that certain language patterns are deleted.

In this section the following aspects of the cloze test will be described: (1) Background of the Cloze Procedure; (2) The Construction of a Cloze Test; (3) The Cloze Test as a Diagnostic Technique; (4) Administration and Scoring a Cloze Test; and (5) A Sample Cloze Test.

Background of the Cloze Procedure

Wilson Taylor developed the cloze procedure in 1953 as a new tool for measuring readability. Taylor (1953), defined the cloze procedure itself as "a method of intercepting a message from a 'transmitter' . . . mutilating its language patterns by deleting parts, and so administering it to 'receivers' . . . that their attempt to make patterns whole again potentially yield a considerable number of cloze units." He explains a cloze unit as "any single occurrence of a successful attempt to reproduce accurately a part deleted from a message . . . by deciding from the context that remains, what the missing part should be."

Taylor (1953) explained, "the cloze procedure is similar to the process of closure in Gestalt psychology. This theory states that a person wants to complete any pattern which is not complete. Although investigations have been done, its similarity to Gestalt experiments has not been confirmed."

The Construction of a Cloze Test

A cloze test can be constructed from reading selections of about 250 words or more (preferably more) on any grade level. Choose a representative passage from a basal reader, a study book or work book (that has whole reading selections), a trade book, or a content area textbook. If possible, try to have each graded selection a whole, complete story with a beginning, middle and end. A cloze test may include graded story selections beginning at a preprimer, primer, or first reading level and continue sequentially through the sixth, eighth or twelfth readability level. The cloze test appears similar to an IRI except that words are deleted for each graded passage, there are no comprehension questions following each selection and a key providing the deleted words for each passage is necessary.

After graded story selections have been chosen, type each passage, keeping the first and last sentence of the passage intact. Omit every nth word in the remainder of each graded passage. Every nth word may be every fifth or every tenth word. Deleted words are replaced by blanks the same length (about fifteen spaces).

Modified cloze test or exercises can be constructed by choosing a 250 or more word passage which is representative of a particular graded book, i.e., a basal reader or content area textbook and following the same procedure for designing a graded cloze test. The purpose may be to assess the reader's ability to comprehend the material at one particular readability level.

The Cloze Test as an Evaluation Technique

The cloze test can be used as an evaluative technique for assessing reading comprehension "levels." The teacher must have some knowledge of the reading materials appropriate for each child so that materials are challenging, yet not frustrating. To provide reading materials appropriate for each child, teachers frequently use oral tests, informal reading inventories, miscue inventories, and/or observation of readers in various oral and silent reading situations. Standardized "reading" tests are highly inappropriate for estimating "reading levels" as has been emphasized in the past, since they frequently overestimate children's "instructional levels" and are designed so that the test is quite unlike the actual reading process. The IRI previously described, provides an estimate of "reading levels," however, the concept of "reading levels" is ambiguous and unclear. Nevertheless, the IRI, through time consuming provides a general estimate of the "reading levels." The cloze test provides a quick and possibly appropriate measure for estimating reading comprehension "levels"

The cloze test can be used for determining a readers "independent," "instructional" and "frustration" reading levels for the purpose of: (1) placing children in graded materials, and (2) selecting reading materials for a group. However, it is well to recognize that results from cloze tests or any other evaluation procedure should be compared with other information to obtain a more complete profile of a child's reading performance. Possibly, as with other types of tests, including the cloze test, more valuable information is obtained by analyzing the quality of the child's responses to the individual items, i.e., in the case of a cloze test, the words the child replaces for the deleted words are more important than an estimate of "reading levels."

Administering and Scoring a Cloze Test

Administration

The teacher will need one copy of a graded set of reading selections, one selection which is given to the child to read silently. As with any testing situation, the teacher should try to relax the child as much as possible and conduct the test, if possible, in a place free from distraction.

The teacher giving the cloze test to the child may provide the following directions. "I have some stories (or a story) for you to read to yourself. In each story some of the words have been left out and replaced with a blank. The first stories are easier and then each other story will be more difficult. Now, you are to figure out or guess what each word is that has been left out and write in the word you think will fit in the blank in the story. Write only one word in each blank. Try to fill in every blank. Don't be afraid to guess. You may skip blanks you don't know and come back to them later. Try to spell each word the best that you can. I cannot tell you how to spell words. You have to try and think what the exact word is that has been left out. When you finish with one story let me know. Then we will go on to the next story. There is no time limit so take your time and do the best that you can. Do you have any questions?"

If a child has not done a cloze test before, you may provide a practice test using a sample story passage with deleted words and then begin with the test.

Determining where to begin having the child read is a problem similar to that when using the IRI, or any other oral reading test if used to estimate functional reading levels. It is important that the child begin reading a graded passage at an easy level, the so-called "independent level." Procedures for determining the starting level for the cloze test are similar to those for the IRI described previously.

The child should read silently, filling in the blanks, reading sequentially more difficult passages until a "frustration level" is reached, or it is obvious the child lacks the strategies to cope with the materials, i.e., using ineffective language cues and strategies. Then the test is terminated. The teacher will need to score each graded passage read using the accompanying key before continuing to the next higher selection. A computation will need to be done to score the test. The test could be given in more than one sitting to avoid fatigue.

Scoring the Cloze Test

To determine an estimate of a reader's "independent," "instructional," and "frustration" reading levels, the child must fill in the exact answer to receive credit. To evaluate a cloze test, the teacher counts the number of blanks in the cloze passage. Next, he/she calculates the number of blanks completed with exact responses.

There have been a variety of criteria suggested for converting cloze scores to readability or "reading levels." For example, Bormuth (1968) established the following criteria: Instructional level, 38 percent and Independent level, 50 percent. In a second study, Bormuth recommended 44% for the instructional level and 57% for the independent level.

In a study done by Ransom (1968) to establish reading level criteria for the cloze procedure, she constructed informal reading inventories and cloze tests from graded basal readers. The cloze criteria she discovered were: independent, 50 percent; instructiona, 30 percent; and frustration, 20 percent or less.

Alexander (1968), also compared cloze scores and informal reading inventory scores to identify criteria for the cloze test. He found the reading level criteria for the cloze to be: independent level, 62 percent; instructional, 47 percent; frustration, less than 47 percent.

It is obvious there is considerable variation among the percentage criteria recommended for determining functional reading level. This, it may be recalled, is highly similar to the different criteria suggested when using an IRI to estimate a reader's functional reading levels. However, the most accepted criteria used and suggested is as follows:

Percentage of Exactly Completed Words	Comprehension Level
45% or less	Frustration
45-50%	Instructional
60% or more	Independent

If a translation from percentage of exact replacement of words for a given passage to a functional reading level is desired, the following computation may be made:

1. Divide the number of words exactly replaced by the total number of blanks.

2. Multiply this figure by 1.67 to determine the average comprehension.

> Example: 22 exact replacements
> 50 blank spaces
> 22 divided by 50 = 44% correct replacement
> 44 multiplied by 1.67 = 73.48% comprehension

According to Bett's reading levels, the independent reading level requires 95 percent or better comprehension, while the instructional is 75 percent or better comprehension. The frustration level is at 50% or less comprehension. A percentage of 44 percent correct replacement on a cloze test would indicate the reader is slightly below the "instructional" reading level in comprehension according to the Bett's criteria. However, one may prefer to use another percentage criteria than Bett's for estimating functional reading levels. One example of a cloze test is given on Page 177.

Sample Cloze Test With Instruction to Students

Instructions

At the bottom of this page is a sample of a new kind of test. Each of these tests is made by copying a few paragraphs from a book. Every fifth word was left out of the paragraphs, and black spaces were put where the words were taken out.

Your job will be to guess what word was left out of each space and to write that word in the space.

It will help you in taking the test if you remember these things:

1. Write only one word in each blank.
2. Try to fill in every blank. Don't be afraid to guess.
3. You may skip hard blanks and come back to them when you are finished.
4. Wrong spellings will not count against you if we can tell what you meant.
5. Most of the blanks can be answered with ordinary words, but some will be numbers like ....3,427, or $12, or 1954 contractions like............can't or weren't abbreviations like..............Mrs. or U.S.A. parts of hyphenated words like....self- like in self-made

Sample Test

Below is a sample of one of these tests. Fill each blank with the word you think was taken out. You may check your paper when you finish it by looking at the answers which are written upside down at the bottom of the page. Write neatly.

The Beaver

Indians call beavers the "little men of the woods." But they____really very little. _____beavers grow to be _____ or four feet long____weigh from 30 to _____ pounds. These "little men____the woods" are busy____ of the time. That___why we sometimes say, "___busy as a beaver."

____know how to build ____that can hold water.

177

____use their two front____to do some of ____ work.
Cutting down a ____ with their four sharp-____teeth
is easy. A ____can cut down a ____four inches thick in
____15 minutes.

Summary

The selection and use of evaluation procedures
to monitor and report reading development needs to be
related to a socio-psycholinguistic theory of the reading process. The tests must be like the actual reading-
learning process. Evaluation procedures are used in
contextual settings with all language cues and strategies available to the reader. Assessment instruments
that fragment the reading process are not reading tests
and the results produced are misleading. Using results
from isolated skills tests lead to inappropriate instructional practices.

Evaluation procedures that are like the actual
learning-reading process and that are whole language
are recommended. The whole-language evaluation procedures include: the reading miscue inventory, informal
reading inventory, teacher observation in real reading
settings with record keeping techniques and the cloze
test.

The most valid and reliable evaluation procedure potentially is teacher observation accompanied by
record-keeping devices. Observation and monitoring of
reading development must take place in reading situations in which the learner has access to all language
cues and strategies, in connected texts. Then the
teacher can monitor the learner's strengths and weaknesses related to comprehension and plan appropriate
strategy lessons and other reading experiences.

The next chapter, Reading Instruction, describes the language cues, strategies, and cycles of the reading process and examples of teacher-planned strategy lessons. The reading process and instructional program is viewed from a skill-centered process and a whole language process. The strategy lessons described are related to evaluation of student's reading performance and other characteristics using miscue analysis.

Teaching Competencies

1. Administer at least one RMI to a child at an age/grade level of your choice. Prepare the materials you will need for the RMI. Tape the child's oral reading, mark the miscues, conduct retelling, complete the Coding Sheet and Reader's Profile. Interpret/analyze the child's performance. Recommend instructional strategies.

2. Administer at least one informal reading inventory (IRI) to a child at an age/grade level of your choice. Prepare the materials you will need for the IRI. Tape the child's oral reading. Mark oral reading miscues, conduct retelling/questioning, list miscues for analysis, identify functional reading levels. Interpret and analyze reader's performance. Recommend instructional strategies on basis of result.

3. Plan to systematically observe a child/group of children in a natural reading situation. Plan which children to observe, the purpose of the observation (specific reading behaviors such as language cue systems, strategies, comprehension, interests, attitudes, etc.), identify the setting for the observation, select the type of record keeping technique to utilize. Conduct the observation. Record observations for at least four observations using a checklist rating scale, inventory, and anecdotal records. Information obtained using observations with each type of record keeping device should include: language cues and strategies, reading levels, interests, and attitudes.

4. Administer a Cloze Test to at least one child at any age or grade level of your choice. Prepare the materials you will need. Conduct the Cloze Test. Identify the reader's functional reading levels as determined by the Cloze Test. Interpret other information about the reader's performance.

5. Administer any other types of tests such as survey/ achievement tests, diagnostic tests or other oral reading tests (norm-referenced), criterion refer- enced, intelligence, or psychoeducational tests, to a child of your choice. Score and interpret the child's performance. Suggest a possible instruc- tional decision based on test results.

6. Complete an indepth case study of one child of your choice, particularly a child who is experiencing difficulties in reading. Administer various diag- nostic/evaluative techniques suggested in this chapter, i.e., RMI, IRI, observation with record keeping, cloze test, other appropriate tests. Iden- tify the child's reading levels, strategies/ needs in language cues/ strategies, interest, attitude, reading potential, learning style, etc. Synthesize all data. Design a reading program for the child related to information obtained.

Affective Behaviors

1. Provides an evaluation setting and uses evaluation procedures which enable the student(s) to demon- strate his/her strengths in learning to develop feelings of self-worth.

2. Utilize evaluative procedures and results which promotes the individual's self-esteem enabling each individual to accept self and relate positively toward others. Provides an atmosphere of learning which is cooperative rather than competitive.

3. Develops each child's self-confidence using evalua- tive techniques which provide security through a focus on individual mastery and control of learning at individual rates and stages of human development.

4. Evaluation is success-oriented so that each individ- ual develops a sense of purpose moving toward self- actualization and self-realization, recognizing his/ her talents as well as weaknesses.

5. Provides a classroom environment and atmosphere in which evaluative procedures take place in natural learning situations as much as possible so that each individual can demonstrate his/her strengths and minimize weakness.

Questions to Investigate

1. Explain and justify various evaluative techniques related to psycholinguistic principles of the reading process developed by Kenneth Goodman and Frank Smith (see Chapter III for explanation of Goodman and Smith's model of the reading process).

2. Identify several factors the teacher should carefully consider which are significant to the evaluative process if the teacher is to obtain useful information about the child's reading performance and progress to utilize for instructional decisions.

3. Discuss the statement made by Kennth Goodman, "Reading diagnosis and evaluation has consistently overemphasized identification of weaknesses to the exclusion of the strengths that the reader, speaker, writer or listener possesses." Can deficits in learning/reading be minimized and can children improve in a program that focuses on strengths? How might this be accomplished?

4. Discuss the results of an RMI that you gave to a reader. What strengths and weaknesses did you identify? What would you suggest for future learning-reading experiences?

5. How do you think currently available survey/achievement tests, diagnostic tests (norm-referenced), and criterion-referenced tests can be improved to make them more like the actual reading process? Should such tests be eliminated? What alternative diagnostic/evaluative instruments could be used in their place to assess reading performance and report reading progress?

6. Discuss the results of any one modified or adapted form of an RMI such as those described in this chapter or any form you design. Identify the reader's strengths and needs. What are the instructional implications related to the date obtained?

7. Discuss the results of systematic observation of a child or several children over a period of time related to the specific purposes using various record keeping devices to record observed behaviors. Identify the strengths and weaknesses and implications for making instructional decisions.

Reading References

Alexander, Henry W. "An Investigation of the Cloze
    Procedure as a Measuring Device Designed to Identify
    the Independent Instruction and Frustration Reading
    Levels of Pupils in the Intermediate Grades." Un-
    published doctoral dissertation, University of
    Illinois, 1968. Dissertation Abstracts Internatio-
    al 29 (1969), 4314A-4315A, University Microfilms
    No. 69-10 625.

Betts, Emmett. Foundations of Reading Instruction.
    New York: American Book Co., 1957.

Betts, Emmett A. and Welch, Carolyn. Informal Reading
    Inventory. New York: American Book Co., 1964.

Boehm, Ann E. and Weinberg, Richard A. The Classroom
    Observer: A Guide for Developing Observation
    Skills. New York: Teachers College Press,
    Teachers College, Columbia University, 1977.

Bormuth, John R. "The Cloze Readability Procedure."
    Elementary Education, Vol. 45, April 1968. Pg.
    429-436.

Cartwright, Carol A. and Cartwright, G. Phillip. Dev-
    eloping Observational Skills. New York: McGraw
    Hill Book Co., 1974.

Dunkeld, Colin G. The Validity of the Informal Reading
    Inventory for the Designation of Instructional Read-
    ing Levels: A Study of the Relationships Between
    Children's Gains in Reading Achievement and the
    Difficulty of Instructional Materials. (Doctoral
    Dissertation, University of Illinois) Ann Arbor,
    Michigan: University Microfilms, 1970. No. 71-
    14733.

Goodman, Kenneth S. "Analysis of Oral Reading Miscues:
    Applied Psycholinguistics." Reading Research
    Quarterly, Vol. 5, Fall, 1969, pp. 9-30.

Goodman, Kenneth S. "Do you Have to be Smart to Read?
    Do you Have to Read to be Smart?" Reading Teacher,
    Vol. 28, April 1975, pp. 625-632.

Goodman, Kenneth S. "The Reading Process." Presenta-
    tion at Miscue Seminar. University of Arizona,
    Tucson, Arizona, December 1976.

Goodman, Kenneth S. "Testing in Reading: A General Critique." In Robert Ruddell, (Ed.) Accountability and Reading Instruction: Critical Issues. Urbana, Illinois: National Council of Teachers of English, 1973.

Goodman, Yetta. "Kit Watching: An Alternative to Testing." National Elementary Principal, Vol. 57 June 1978, pp. 41-45.

Goodman, Yetta M. "Miscue Analysis for Inservice Reading Teachers." Miscue Analysis: Application to Reading Instruction. Urbana, Illinois: National Council of Teachers of English, 1973.

Goodman, Yetta M. and Burke, Carolyn L. Reading Miscue Inventory: Procedures for Diagnosis and Evaluation. New York: MacMillan Co., 1972.

Halliday, M.A.K. Explorations in the Functions of Language. New York: Elsevier, 1973.

Lowell, Robert E. "Problems in Identifying Reading Levels with Informal Reading Inventories." In Reading Difficulties: Diagnosis, Correction and Remediation. Edited by William K. Durr, pp. 120-126. Newark, Delaware: International Reading Association, 1970.

McCraken, Robert A. "Informal Reading Inventories: Diagnosis Within the Teacher." The Reading Teacher. Vol. 26, December 1972, pp. 273-277.

Moffett, James. A Student Centered Language Arts Curriculum, Grades K-6: A Handbook for Teachers. New York: Houghton Mifflin Co., 1968.

Page, William D. (ed.) Help for the Reading Teacher. Urbana, Illinois, ERIC, National Conference on Research in English, 1975.

Page, William D. and Barr, Rebecca C. "Use of Informal Reading Inventories." In Help for the Reading Teacher: New Direction in Research. Urbana, Illinois: National Conference on Research in English, ERIC/CRCE, 1975.

Perrone, Vito. "A Position Paper on Standardized Testing." Childhood Education. October 1976, pp. 10-16.

Powell, William R. "Reappraising the Criteria for Interpreting Informal Inventories." In Reading Diagnosis and Evaluation. IRA Proceedings, Vol. 13,
Part 4, edited by Dorothy L. De Boer, pp. 100-109,
Newark, Delaware: International Reading Association, 1970

Ransom, Peggy E. "Determining Reading Levesl of Elementary School Children by Cloze Testing," in J. Allen
Figurel (Ed.), Forging Ahead in Reading, Proceedings
of the International Reading Association, 12, Part
I. Newark, Delaware: International Reading Association, 1968

Rousch. "Testing." In Findings of Research in Miscue
Analysis: Classroom Implications. Allen, P. David
and Watson, Dorothy J. (Eds). Clearinghouse on
Reading and Communication Skills, National Institute
of Education; Urbana, Illinois: National Council
of Teachers of English, 1976.

Smith, Frank. Understanding Reading. New York: Holt,
Rinehart and Winston, 1978.

Spiegel, Dixie Lee. "Holistic Approach to Diagnosis
and Remediation." The Reading Teacher. Vol. 27,
January 1974, pp. 370-374.

Taylor, Wilson L. "Cloze Procedure: A New Tool for
Measuring Readability." Journalism Quarterly,
Vol. 30, Fall 1953, pp. 415-433.

Tortelli, James P. "Simplified Psycholinguistic Diagnosis." The Reading Teacher, Vol. 29, April 1976.

CHAPTER V

READING INSTRUCTION: LANGUAGE CUES,

STRATEGIES AND COMPREHENSION

Knowledge Competencies

1. What factors are involved in viewing reading instruction from a socio-psycholinguistic perspective?
2. What are the differences in reading instruction comparing a skills reading model and a whole language model?
3. What are reading strategy lessons in whole language instruction?
4. How are graphophonic cues learned in a skills program compared to a whole language instructional program?
5. How can reading instruction help a reader to use syntactic and semantic cues?
6. How can reading instruction help a reader to use predicting, confirming, correcting and integrating (comprehending) strategies?
7. How can language cues, strategies and cycles in the reading process be integrated through reading instruction?
8. What are the differences between traditional and newer views of the comprehension process?

In this chapter a description is given of the components of the reading process related to reading instruction. The emphasis is on reading as a socio-psycholinguistic process involving an interaction between the author and the reader. Chapter III, The Reading Process, described several models of the reading process. The theories and models of Kenneth Goodman and Frank Smith in Chapter III have identified the components of the reading process. The components include: the cycles the reader goes through during reading, language cues, and strategies.

The reading components include what has been conventionally called "reading skills." Psycholinguistic insight into the reading process rejects the notion that reading is a separate assortment of skills organized in some arbitrary hierarchial sequence. Rather, the reading process is an integration of various language cues and strategies which function together. The underlying premise is that reading can be learned as other language processes are learned, naturally and integrated. Reading is a language process using written symbols to represent meaning as speaking and listening utilize spoken symbols to convey and receive meaning. The difference between learning to speak, listen, read and write is the purpose for which each language process is used. Reading should be viewed as an alternative language process to communicate meaning. Figure 5:1 identifies the different characteristics when viewing reading as skills-oriented and from a psycholinguistic view:

Skills Model	Psycholinguistic Model
1. Reading is made up of separate skills	1. Reading is an integrated process
2. Reading has a hierarchal skills sequence	2. Reading has no one sequence of skills
3. Reading is treated as non-language	3. Reading is language-centered
4. Applying reading skills leads to meaning	4. Reading is meaning-centered
5. Reading is a separate process from speaking, listening and writing.	5. Reading is an alternate language process
6. Reading is a passive process	6. Reading is an active process
7. Reading is a precise practice	7. Reading is an inexact process
8. Form precedes function in reading.	8. Function precedes form in reading

CHARACTERISTICS OF THE PSYCHOLINGUISTIC
AND SKILLS READING PROCESS

FIGURE 5:1

A distinction is made between "reading instruction" and "reading experience." Reading instruction is viewed as an intervention on the part of the teacher in the learning process. Reading instruction is the result of planning and the use of teacher-prepared or published materials related to identified needs of the learner. Reading instruction is generally based on needs determined by evaluation procedures such as miscue analysis or observation of the learner's reading performance in a reading situation. Reading experiences, on the other hand, are natural reading settings in which the reader develops and uses reading strategies on his/her own. The teacher's role is to arrange and provide the conditions and materials to facilitate reading development through a variety of planned reading experiences. Reading is learned by "real" reading. (See Figure 5:2 below.)

Reading Instruction	Reading
1. Teacher intervention is based on a specific evaluation of reading.	1. The teacher arranges, guides and provides the conditions for reading.
2. Reading is frequently separated from other language processes.	2. The teacher integrates reading with speaking, listening, writing and content learning.
3. The teacher prescribes instructional activities and materials, i.e., workbooks, skill sheets, basal reader stories.	3. The teacher provides varied materials in a whole language setting. i.e., books, magazines, etc.
4. The focus is on teacher-purpose related to identified skills.	4. The focus is on the learner's purpose, interests, etc.
5. Learning to read is a skill-by-skill process.	5. Reading is learned by reading and writing by writing.
6. The teacher diagnoses skills.	6. The teacher observes in "real" reading situations which may lead to instruction.

CHARACTERISTICS OF READING INSTRUCTION AND READING

FIGURE 5:2

As Frank Smith has indicated, children learn to read by reading. There is a risk of interfering with a child's natural learning process when reading instruction is planned by the teacher. Even though a sophisticated evaluation procedure such as miscue analysis is used, there is a risk that the teacher has not accurately identified a reader's strengths and weaknesses. Planned reading instruction for an individual child or group of children identified to have similar needs may miss the mark. Frequently, instruction becomes contrived and unnatural when the teacher intervenes by providing instructional activities. However, reading in schools today is not at the point where children are able to learn to read only by "real" kinds of reading. Possibly, understanding the reading process is still not sophisticated enough to eliminate all forms of reading instruction.

Nevertheless, most reading in the classroom should be planned to provide reading experiences for children to learn to read by reading. Presently, reading instruction should be a part of the total reading program utilizing whole language types of reading strategy lessons based on evaluated needs. There should be no fractionating of language cues and strategies of the reading process. This will only make the process more difficult to learn and use.

The next chapter, Whole Language Reading Approaches, describes methods emphasizing "real" reading experiences.

A Socio-Psycholinguistic Perspective of the Reading Process

Reading instruction must be presented to children at various learning stages in a natural setting in the classroom. The readers at any developmental stage should have all linguistic cues and strategies available to process written language. Reading is a psycholinguistic process because it involves thinking and language. Reading is a language process in which the reader constructs the meaning of a written message. The message of any written communication is available to the reader in context. Fragmenting or breaking apart written language destroys or distorts meaning and makes the reading task more difficult for the reader. The beginning reader and older "poor" readers need the full language context as much or more than does the proficient reader.

Reading is an active interaction between an author and a reader. Both the author and the reader possess thoughts, language, and experiences. The reader uses prior experiences and knowledge of language to construct the author's experiences and language patterns and to decode from print to meaning. The efficient reader uses the least visual information (print) to get to meaning. The more non-visual information the reader brings to the print the less visual information is required to construct meaning. The reader's task is to sample from the visual cues, select the most significant cues, test the significant features of the visual information with semantic and syntactic cues, predict and confirm whether what has been processed makes sense and sounds appropriate. If meaning is disrupted and/or not grammatically acceptable, the reader has the option of correcting by reprocessing using graphic and/or phonemic, syntactic and semantic cues, or to continue reading, attempting to build meaning. The reader's focus must always be on constructing meaning and when meaning is destroyed, the reader must have other strategies to overcome or eliminate nonsense. If the reading process is too difficult, the reader should have the option of terminating the task. (See Figure 5:3. on Page 190.)

Processing written language is similar in many respects to processing oral language. Written and oral language are communicative processes. Reading and writing, like speaking and listening, are learned naturally and easily when four factors or conditions are available to the learner.

Reading is a Unified Process

Written language should be kept intact for the learner at any stage of reading development. There should be no artificial fragmentation of written language. The components of written language include the following:

1. Linguistic Cueing System

    a. graphophonemic cues

    b. syntactic cues

    c. semantic cues

(See Figure 5:4 on Page 191.)

189

AN INTERACTION BETWEEN AUTHOR AND READER

FIGURE 5:3

Graphophonemic

SH CAT

OI E -ING

Syntactic

Noun Verbs

We went to the park.

Semantic

Vocabulary

Experiences

Meanings

LINGUISTIC CUEING SYSTEM

FIGURE 5:4

191

2. Learning Strategies
   a. sampling
   b. selecting
   c.. testing
   d. predicting
   e. confirming
   f. correcting
   g. comprehending

(See Figure 5:5)

PREDICTING

The man caught a
big _____ in the lake.

CONFIRMING

The man caught a
big ___fish___ in the lake
      ~~dish~~

CORRECTING

The man caught a
big ℮ fish in the lake.
    ⌐ dish

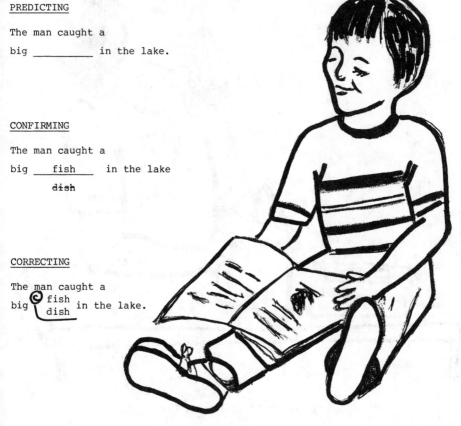

LEARNING STRATEGIES
FIGURE 5:5

According to psycholinguistic insight of the reading process, language learning proceeds from whole to part. The reader must have available all linguistic cues and should be able to apply learning strategies in an integrated approach. It is easier for a reader to process larger language units than smaller language units. A story is easier to read than a paragraph; a paragraph is easier to read than a word; and a word is easier than letters.

There is no meaning in the print itself. The reader brings his/her experiences, thoughts, and language to the language encoded in print by the author. There is no meaning or communication possible if graphophonemic cues are presented to the child in isolated exercises. Learning to read is more difficult if reading instruction emphasizes isolated words for recognition and pronunciation without meaningful context. The reader is limited in applying sampling, selecting, predicting confirming, correcting and comprehending strategies if only limited linguistic cues are available. There is no purpose for communication when letters, letter-sound correspondences, parts of words, isolated words and sentences are given to children apart from meaningful context.

According to Kenneth Goodman (see Chapter III), the reading process also includes cycles which involve the readers in applying linguistic cues and strategies during the act of reading. The cycles are sequenced from one to another as a reader processes print to get to the deep structure and meaning. The cycles include:

1. Optical
2. Perceptual
3. Syntactic
4. Meaning

If reading instruction is frequently limited to drill on isolated linguistic units, such as graphophonemic cues, then the reader is unable to complete all the cycles in the reading process. For example, the reader is limited to the perceptual cycle, or is restricted to the optical cycle, i.e., recognizing words from left to right. The reader has no opportunity to move into the whole optical cycle, including processing written language from left to right, return sweep right from left to the next line, and from the top of the page to the bottom in a whole connected text.

The reader will not be able to complete the

cycles in the reading process, the syntactic and meaning cycles. The reader is prevented from applying his/her linguistic knowledge of the structure of language (syntax) and his/her prior experiences and vocabulary (semantic). The most effective language strength and support the reader brings to the reading process are removed when the reader cannot progress to syntactic and meaning cycles.

The reading process must be kept intact and available to the reader. The reader must have available all linguistic cues and strategies to apply as the reader moves through the various cycles during the process of reading. (See Figure 5:6)

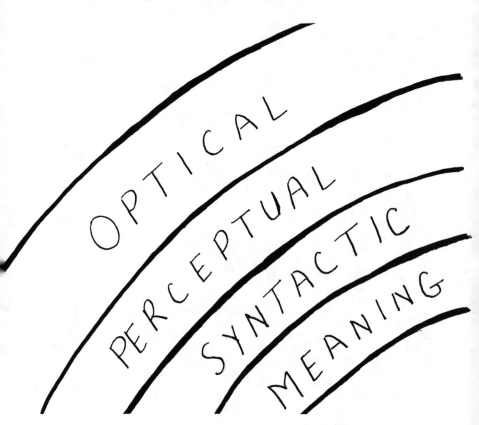

CYCLES IN PSYCHOLINGUISTIC READING PROCESSES

FIGURE 5:6

Reading Involves Natural Language Patterns

Reading will be easier if the written language children are to read is natural. Contrived language patterns make reading more difficult. Children have already learned to communicate verbally and to understand oral language in natural language structures. Children bring linguistic strengths to the reading process.

Reading ability will develop over time if written language learning is presented at the beginning and continuously in a natural form. It should be recognized, however, that written language patterns are usually more formal, complete, and precise than oral language structures. The writer needs to encode more information than the speaker to communicate a message to a reader. In written communication there is generally no face-to-face situational context. Written language must provide more of the context than does oral language. Therefore, children need to develop an "ear" for written language patterns.

At the beginning stage of learning to read in skill-centered programs written material for children is usually controlled. The control of the written language includes: vocabulary, control of words based on graphophonemic rules, high frequency words, and sentence length. In effect, this imposed graphophonemic, word and syntactic control results in unnatural, frequently difficult language patterns for the beginning reader to process. The language patterns are not highly predictable. There is little need to impose control on the reading material for children by arbitrarily controlling the frequency of letter patterns, length of words and syntactic structures. Young children and developing readers at a later stage are able to process written language patterns if reading materials are related to prior experiences, concepts, and interests. It is more important that written materials are fully formed, have predictable natural language patterns of high interest to readers, and that the conceptual load is related to the child's experiences.

Reading Involves Meaningful Context

A third condition is that reading should be learned in a meaningful context. The linguistic cues (graphophonemic, syntactic, and semantic) and learning strategies (sampling, confirming, correcting, and comprehending) develop when written language is whole

195

and meaningful to the reader. Reading experiences must include print materials related to the reader's linguistic strengths, experiences, concept development, interests, and purposes.

The reader possesses his/her own meaning potential to process print. Even the beginning reader at the acquisition stage of learning to read, as well as the developing reader at a later stage, needs exposure to the written language that is highly interesting and relevant to his/her own experiences, interests, and purposes. The reader will need to use fewer visual cues and more non-visual information can be applied when written material is related to experiences and involve whole text.

The brain is capable of processing meaningful information more easily than nonsense. The reader is able to make connections linking what is known (prior experience) to the print representing concepts and experiences encoded by a writer. The more the brain has to process unrelated bits and pieces of abstract visual or non-visual information, the greater the difficulty the brain has storing information in short and long memory, and retrieving information. If reading instruction emphasizes abstract letters, letter-sound correspondences, parts of words, isolated words and isolated sentences, the brain becomes overloaded and short-circuiting results. Kenneth Goodman (1976) explained the nature of short-circuits which may occur during the reading process in the following way:

> Any reading which does not end with meaning is a short circuit. Readers may short-circuit in a variety of ways and for a variety of reasons. In general, readers short-circuit: (1) when they can't get meaning or lose structure; (2) when they've been taught or otherwise acquired non-productive reading strategies; (3) when they aren't permitted to terminate non-productive reading.

Theoretically, a short-circuit can occur at any point in the process.

Goodman provided examples of short-circuits. These include: (1) letter naming which is spelled out unfamiliar words; (2 recoding which includes matching print to sound with no meaning resulting. Recoding may take place on several levels. Letter sound recoding is

the most superficial. Sounds are matched on a one-to-
one basis to print. This sounding out requires the
reader to blend sounds to synthesize words. Pattern-
matching recoding involves the reader fitting spelling
patterns to sound patterns. Readers focus on features
which contrast patterns, such as, rat-rate, hat-hate,
mat-mate; (3) internal surface structure recoding involves using the rules needed to relate print to underlying surface structures. Instead of going beyond to
deep structure, however, the reader generates an oral
surface representation. This recoding can produce words
with approximate intonation patterns; (4) syntactic
nonsense is readers may treat print as syntactic
nonsense, generating an appropriate deep structure without going beyond meaning. Even proficient readers
resort to this short-circuit when conceptual load is
too great or when they lack relevant background. With
this short-circuit the oral reading may be relatively
accurate and yet involve little comprehension; (5) partial structures is when readers may resort to one or
more of these short circuits with alternating periods
of productive reading. Furthermore, because the brain
is always actively seeking meaning, some comprehension
will often "leak" through even the most non-productive
short-circuit. It will most likely result in fragments
of meaning, a kind of kaleidoscope view, rather than
integrated understanding.

Therefore, learners need reading materials and
experiences which avoid the short-circuits to meaning
described by Goodman. To avoid short-circuiting, reading instruction and experiences must be meaning-centered.
Readers must be able to identify and relate their background experiences and knowledge of language to the
processing of print. Graphic and phonemic cues will be
learned within whole text if written language is presented in meaningful context. Non-visual information
can be applied by readers as a test for constructing
meaning. Non-visual information, including semantic
and syntactic cues, stored in the brain can be applied
to process the printed message.

Reading is Functional

Reading is a language process must be purposeful and serve useful functions. This is as significant
for the child beginning to read as for the proficient
reader. The child developed oral language ability to
use language to communicate meaning to others and to
receive information because language was functional.
Michael Halliday (1975) has identified several "models"

of oral languages functions which are useful in understanding the purposes for processing written language.
During the process of learning oral language, the child
is also learning the uses of language. Reading ability
develops as written language forms are learned when
reading has a purpose.

Traditionally, form has preceded function in
reading instruction. The learner is presented the
graphic and phonemic symbols of written language and is
gradually expected to learn to read, beginning with
small linguistic units of print, to increasingly larger
units of print. Generally, there is no meaningful context or natural whole language patterns available for
the learner to bring his/her linguistic knowledge to
apply to the abstract visual-sound patterns. There is
form but no real purpose or function to communicate or
construct meaning related to experiences, interests,
and linguistic ability. The form, or surface representation, supercedes the purpose for reading. Reading instruction currently consists of learning the form of
written language in a piecemeal, fragmented way, separate from any real purpose to communicate actively with
the author in a meaningful setting. Most reading instruction presents the fragmentary elements of written
language form first in isolated drill and practice and
then requires the learner to transfer the elements into
connected written discourse with larger linguistic units
such as sentences, paragraphs, and stories. The learner
recognizes no internal need to process the written message when there is no function.

The learner must be involved in recognizing the
function and purpose of reading at the earliest stages
of learning to read. There should be no distinction between function and form of written language. Halliday's
"models" of oral language learning can be applied to
functions of learning written language. (See Chapter II
and Chapter VI.) Written language is used to satisfy
personal needs (instrumental); to regulate and control
behavior (regulatory); to interact with others (interactional); to develop individuality (personal); to discover and find out about the environment (heuristic); to
create and invent (imaginative); and to inform others
(informative). Also, Frank Smith has identified additional functions of language which provide purpose for
writing and reading: to enjoy jokes, puns, riddles
(divertive); to record historical events (perpetuating);
and to record legal contracts and records (contractual).

The teacher needs to be aware of the uses and

purposes of written language related to the interests and experiences of the learners. Printed information in various contexts and purposes should be presented to learners in integrated, natural language patterns, meaningfully related to background experiences and interests. There is no need to emphasize the surface form of language separate from the function or communicative message of the print. The learner will, developmentally, abstract the orthographic rules of written language if the printed information is viewed as having a useful purpose. Methods and approaches relating reading experiences to function will be discussed fully in Chapter VI, <u>Whole Language Reading Approaches</u>.

Components of the Reading Process

The significant focus of the reading process is comprehension. There is no other reason for reading than to construct meaning from print. The reader has the task of using printed symbols arranged in a linear way to get to the underlying meaning intended by the writer. Therefore, reading is synonymous with comprehension. The phrase "reading comprehension" is redundant. The processing of written language is referred to as reading. However, there is no reading unless there is comprehension by the reader.

A Reading Skills Model

Observing the reading process from a skills-oriented model, the components or skills are identified as separate categories which are to be learned in a highly sequential program. Current reading instructional programs are based on a set of prescribed sequence of isolated skills. The components or skills in a highly sequential "skills-model" builds from one skill to the next. The major classification of components are generally referred to as word recognition, word identification, or word attack skills, comprehension skills, and study skills. The "skills" model of reading is represented by several theoretical models (See Chapter III). Much of the research in reading, reading tests, published instructional material, teaching techniques by classroom teachers, reading and language textbooks, and courses in training reading teachers also emphasize a "skills Model." The "skills syndrome" of the reading process has been accepted and perpetuated by all segments of the educational establishment. Obviously, most lay persons and legislators at local, state, and national levels, subscribe to the skills approach to reading. Federal education agencies, including the

United States Office of Education, of which the National
Institute of Education is a funding agent for educational proposals in reading and other educational areas,
identify funding programs as, "Basic Skills." Thus,
the tendency is to perpetuate the myth that reading is
a collection of separate skills learned in a hierarchal
form leading to comprehension. (See Figure 5:7 below)

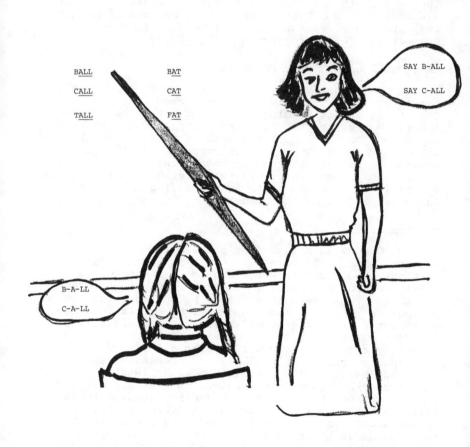

SKILLS-CENTERED READING INSTRUCTION

FIGURE 5:7

Conventional reading research, reading tests, reading materials, and reading methods identify the components of the reading process as separate and distinct. Word recognition skills are generally separated from comprehension skills and study skills are separated from word recognition and comprehension skills. In addition, word recognition skills are further subdivided and classified into sub-skills such as: sight vocabulary, phonic analysis, structural analysis, context clues, and dictionary skills. Furthermore, comprehension skills are sub-categorized into sub-skills which include: main idea, details, sequence of events, predicting outcome, drawing conclusions, and so forth. The comprehension process is fragmented and identified by levels as well as separate skills. Various comprehension taxonomies or classification systems identify separate comprehension skills. For example: literal (meaning, recall), interpretative (inference), critical (analysis, evaluation), and creative (application, synthesis); or some other similar categorization of thinking levels are used to supposedly identify the various skills and levels of comprehension. The identification and fragmentation of word recognition and comprehension skills and the subdivision of these sub-skills, seems to be for the simplification of conducting research, publishing reading texts and reading instructional materials, and for the convenience of teaching techniques in the classroom. There is no evidence that reading as a language and communication process is learned or used in this manner (see Figure 5:8 on Page 202).

A Whole Language Model

Socio-psycholinguistic research provides an alternative theory to the "skills-model" of the reading process. There is a need to test the assumption that language is learned more efficiently and effectively when the components or "skills" are integrated, related, and fully accessible to the learner. There is no need to make distinctions and classifications of separate "skills" for children to learn to read. There is no need for teachers to have long lists of separate word recognition skills and sub-skills of word recognition, or to have lists of separate comprehension skills and levels to assist learners to learn to read. It is doubtful that teachers need to possess knowledge of phonic and structural analysis rules to help children learn to read. Certainly children do not need to know lists of phonic and structural analysis rules to read.

SKILLS-CENTERED READING INSTRUCTION

FIGURE 5:8

Teachers do need knowledge of linguistics as it is applied to language learning. There is a need for teacher knowledge of linguistic terminology to understand the socio-psycholinguistic nature of the reading process. Teachers need to understand the developmental nature of the reading process and language development.

Psycholinguistic insight into the reading process is at the point where it can be stated, that the fundamental knowledge teachers must possess to influence children's ability to read, includes: knowledge of child development; knowledge of the language; learning and reading processes; insights into the children's interests and experiences; and knowledge of various print and non-print materials, including children's literature.

However, since classroom reading instruction is fundamentally skills-oriented, in this chapter traditional reading skills are described along with newer socio-psycholinguistic concepts of the reading process. In this section the components of the reading process from a socio-psycholinguistic perspective will be presented and when necessary, these components will be identified with traditional word recognition and comprehension skills.

The reading components involved in the reading process are identified in Kenneth Goodman's psycholinguistic model, described in Chapter III, The Reading Process. The major components of the reading process are: Linguistic cues, reading strategies and cycles, and the interrelationship of these components. Each major component includes sub-components such as the following: Linguistic cues (graphophonemic, syntactic, and semantic); reading strategies (predicting, confirming, correcting, and comprehending); and cycles (optical, perceptual, syntactic, and semantic). All sub-components under the major components are integrated within the total act of reading. Comprehension and so-called word recognition are integrated together. There is no arbitrary separation between the components of comprehension and word recognition.

Reading Strategy Lessons

In a later section, instructional examples are given illustrating various reading strategy lessons related to components of the reading process. Most of the strategy lessons have been prepared by classroom and remedial reading teachers who have been enrolled in the author's graduate reading courses and workshops. Some of the lessons have been used with children in the teachers' classrooms. The strategy lessons are examples describing how reading instruction may be planned. Strategy lessons need to be adapted or modified by teachers to be applicable to learners in any reading situation. The strategy lessons provide practical ideas to serve as examples for teachers to design their own lessons and/or to select commercially published materials to use with lessons. In addition, strategy lessons should be used only with learners who need a specific type of lesson, highlighting a specific language cue/learning strategy.

There is no way teachers should use the same strategy lessons designed for all children unless there is a common need. The examples of strategy lessons in this chapter can be adapted by teachers, but ultimately, lessons need to be planned for the children in their classrooms. Finally, the strategy lessons, unless indicated, are not related to specific age, grade, or "reading levels." However, some examples of strategy lessons are clearly for readers at primary levels and others are for intermediate or higher levels. Frequently, strategy lessons designed for younger readers can be modified for older readers with similar needs using material related to student's interests and experience.

Strategy lessons are useful for reading instruction if the oral reading miscues of children have been carefully examined. Strategy lessons should not be given indiscriminately to all children. Lessons should be designed only for readers who need specific types of instruction to strengthen linguistic cues, i.e., graphophonemic; strategies, i.e., predicting or correcting as linguistic cues and strategies are applied during the reading process.

Yetta Goodman and Carolyn Burke (1980) have identified criteria for selecting and writing materials for strategy lessons. Goodman and Burke state: "Context is a significant aspect of any learning situation. In writing materials for reading strategy lessons at least seven criteria must be considered to insure that the context of the material will be supportive as possible of the reading strategies the student is developing. These criteria must indicate concern for the reader, for language, and for the content of the written material."

Goodman and Burke identify the criteria for strategy lessons as:

<u>Concern for the Reader</u> - (1) Strategy
lessons are most effective when they
are used only with students who need
them. (2) Strategy lessons are most
effective when they are used at the
critical moment.

<u>Concern for the Language</u> - (3) The
language of strategy lesson material
is similar to the language of the
learner. (4) The language of the
strategy lessons shows concern for
literary quality. (5) The language
of the reading strategy lesson material minimizes ambiguity and uses
appropriate redundant information.

<u>Concern for Content</u> - (6) The content
of the reading strategy lesson material is interesting to the reader.
(7) The content of the strategy lesson
material is significant to the reader.

Goodman and Burke provided a description of
reading strategy instruction. They explain . . . "the
purpose of reading strategy instruction is to make students aware of the language and thought cues available
to them as readers and to support their developing use
of reading strategies."

According to Yetta Goodman, "the teacher's role
in reading is significant. The teacher must discover
which reading strategies the reader is using effectively
and which strategies the reader needs help to develop.
The teacher should also be able to find or write, if
need be, materials with linguistic strengths that enable
the reader to develop effective strategies. These written materials which provide the reader with supportive
reading are called reading strategy lessons. Reading
strategy lessons help make learning to read a less abstract task and make it possible for readers to use
their language competence to the fullest as they discover how to become independent readers."

Goodman continued, "a strategy lesson is a carefully constructed instructional plan developed for an
individual or group of readers. Evidence that a reader
needs the support emphasized in the lesson could come
from a miscue analysis of a student's reading (see Chapter IV, <u>Evaluation of Reading</u>). Strategy lessons help
readers focus on aspects of written language they are

not processing effectively . . . learning by using specifically focused material which is as much like "real" reading material as possible gives readers all language cues intact so they can interrelate the specific strategy into a total language setting."

Goodman and Burke suggested a lesson plan format for teachers to use to organize reading instruction. The strategy lesson format used in various examples given in following sections in the chapter utilizes this format:

Reading Strategy Lesson Format

1. Purpose: The purpose includes the specific reason or objective for the lessons. The purpose identifies specific linguistic cues and/or strategies which have been identified by miscue analysis, observation of reading, as needed by the reader.

2. Initiating: This part of the overall strategy lesson is the introduction of the lesson to the student(s). The initiating phase should capture the interest of the student(s). The context of the reading material should be as closely related to the student(s)' experiences and interests as possible. It may be useful to introduce and clarify new concepts.

3. Interacting: In this stage of the strategy lesson the student(s) and teacher discuss the content related to the lesson. The teacher and student(s) interact to present their ideas about the reading material.

4. Applying: The application phase of the lessons include having the student(s) apply the language cues and strategies which have been identified as the purpose of the lesson.

5. Expanding: Learning activities are planned to provide further related experiences for students to refine and develop effectiveness and efficiency in language learning. Explanding learning experiences may include: independent reading, writing, listening experiences, art, dramatic activities, and possibly to other areas of the curriculum.

6. Evaluation: Teacher evaluation of lesson

objectives. Through observation of above activities and/or through oral reading/ writing samples.

As indicated previously, the reading process based on a socio-psycholinguistic model includes integrated components such as: language cues and learning strategies, which are applied by the learner during the act of reading. The purpose of reading at all levels and stages of development is comprehension or the construction of meaning from the print.

In the following sections, the major components of reading are identified, explained, and illustrations of reading strategy lessons are given related to the components. As stated earlier, the components are divided into sub-components, although it would be clearly understood that during the process of reading the reader is integrating all components and sub-components to construct meaning from written language. The description of the language cues, learning strategies and cycles are related to Kenneth Goodman's model of the reading process described in Chapter III, The Reading Process.

Linguistic Cueing System

The language systems learners have access to include the graphophonemic, syntactic and semantic systems.

Graphophonemic Cues

The graphophonemic system includes the graphemes or letters and phonemes or sound system of a language. In English language there is a relationship between the graphemes (letters) and phonemes (sounds) which are represented in written language by visual symbols. Although there is not always a one-to-one relationship between letters and sounds in English, the spelling system or orthography is fairly regular and systematic.

The reader at the acquisition stage (pre-school to primary grades) has a well-developed phonological system of his/her language. In a print-oriented society, the young child has some knowledge of the relationship between print (letters) and sounds. However, this knowledge of letter-sound correspondence has been learned indirectly and informally. There is growing evidence that 3-4-5 year old children know some of the relationship between a letter and sounds. This is evident from the work of Charles Read (1975) who has identified the invented spelling of young children. In their early writing, children appear to abstract the significant letter-sound relationships in words when they spell. There is a developmental nature to the spelling of children. For example, young children will spell "ladder" as "ldr," selecting significant letters to represent sounds of written language. The early spelling of "girl" may be "grl." This indicates the child's growing awareness and development of grapheme-phoneme relationship.

In addition, there is evidence that young children at pre-school ages know that printed language communicates or represents meaning. Young children know the meaning of significant printed langauge on signs, food products, labels, TV commercials in their environment.

Young children are able to go directly from printed language in context to meaning without resorting to recoding or sounding out individual letters and sounds represented by letters. Still later, young children are able to learn likeness and differences in letter/sound patterns in words. Obviously, children at a literacy acquisition stage have not learned all letter-sound correspondences and other graphophonemic relationships still need to be learned. However, it is not necessary to directly teach or isolate grapheme-phoneme relationships in any highly organized and sequenced hierarchy of skills. If beginning and developing readers are immersed in whole, meaningful, contextual, and functional written language, they will be able to abstract and apply graphophonemic cues when necessary.

The relationship of letters and sounds or graphophonemic cues are but one language system. These cues need to be integrated with syntactic and semantic cues readers already have developed to a great extent. At the same time, readers at any level of development possess learning strategies which have been operating since birth. The learner has the capability of predicting, confirming, correcting and integrating information to make sense during the process of reading. Children have had considerable practice in making sense of their world. Learning to read is essentially no different from other learning the child has accomplished. During reading the learner uses the visual representation of language to construct meaning. This involves the optical and perceptual cycles of the reading process. The learner processes the visual information, resorting to recoding or phonological cues related to visual cues if necessary, and uses syntactic and semantic cues to predict and confirm, if necessary correct, as the eyes scan the print, and fixating and focusing on significant visual information.

The reader should be continuously monitoring what is read to make sense. Comprehending strategies help the reader integrate what the reader already knows with the information being processed during the reading task.

Current descriptions of the reading process from theoretical "skills" models and reading tests and commercially published instructional materials based on a skills model, isolate graphophonemic cues into separate parts. The graphophonemic cues are usually classified as word recognition, or word identification, or word attack skills. The word attack skills are then further fragmented into sub-skills, such as: sight vocabulary (high frequency words), phonic skills, structural skills, context cues, and dictionary skills. Scope and sequence charts accompanying basal reader materials identify each type of word recognition skills, and when it is introduced, practiced, and reviewed at different "reading levels." Elaborately sequenced word recognition skills are found in instructional reading materials.

The graphophonemic system in a psycholinguistic model of reading on the right includes the following word recognition skills in a "skills" model on the left in Figure 5:9 on Page 210.

Sight Vocabulary

A sight vocabulary generally refers to words that a reader automatically pronounces and recognizes at sight. In addition, sight words are the high frequency words called function or structure words that hold sentences together. These words usually include prepositions (in, under, over, around, on); conjunctions (and, or, but, therefore); pronouns (I, he, she, me, they, them); adverbs (when, then, there, through, though); auxillary verbs (are, were, was, has, had); adjectives (big, large, small, little); and others. There are several lists of basic or high frequency words such as the Dolch 220 Word List, Kuceria-Francis, and others.

Generally, a sight vocabulary in traditional reading programs is developed with flash cards, isolated

209

Word Recognition in a
Skills Model

Word Recognition in a
Psycholinguistic Model

1. Sight Vocabulary

   A. High frequency

   B. Automatic

2. Phonic Analysis

   A. Consonants

      1. Single

      2. Blends

      3. Digraphs

   B. Vowels

      1. Long

      2. Short

      3. Digraphs

      4. Diphthongs

      5. R-controlled

3. Structural Analysis

   A. Syllabication-Accent

   B. Plural

   C. Possessive

   D. Contractions

   E. Compound

   F. Prefix-Suffix

4. Context Clues

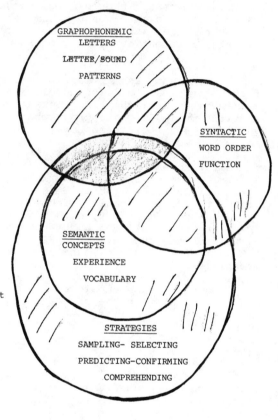

GRAPHOPHONEMIC
LETTERS
LETTER/SOUND
PATTERNS

SYNTACTIC
WORD ORDER
FUNCTION

SEMANTIC
CONCEPTS
EXPERIENCE
VOCABULARY

STRATEGIES
SAMPLING- SELECTING
PREDICTING-CONFIRMING
COMPREHENDING

OPTICAL   PERCEPTUAL   SYNTACTIC   MEANING

CYCLES

Word Recognition in a **Skills and Psycholinguistic**
Model of Reading
FIGURE 5:9

210

word games, language experience stories, worksheets, workbooks, and independent reading. Since Basal reading material are used in most classrooms for reading instruction a large portion of the time, the high frequency sight words and other words are introduced in graded readers in a controlled, systematic way. In so-called "phonic" models or phonic-oriented reading materials, a sight vocabulary is generally learned by synthesis. A sight vocabulary is developed by presenting the reader with individual letter/sound relationships. Then blending isolated letters and sounds into words in repetitive practice using worksheets, workbooks, word flashcards, tapes with letter/sound combinations, and the like.

Phonic Skills

Most basal reading material and so-called "phonic" programs identify and sequence specific phonic rules and skills. The phonic skills are ordered in various ways from program to program. There is no research base for the establishment of any one sequence of phonic skills. Therefore, there are differences in the sequences in which separate phonic skills are introduced and reinforced in workbook lessons and within stories which control words on the basis of letter-sound correspondences.

The phonic skills and rules include all consonants, vowels, combinations of consonants and vowels, and the letter(s)-sound correspondences. Basal reader and other phonic programs provide a list of phonic analysis or word attack skills. Also, other reading method textbooks publish checklists of phonic skills. Given below are the most frequently listed phonic skills, however, it is not an exhaustive listing:

1) <u>Initial and ending consonants</u> (b, c, d, f, g, h, j, k, l, m, n, p, r, s, t, v, w)

2) <u>Consonant Blends</u> (br, cr, dr, gr, pr, tr, scr, spr, str, thr, bl, cl, fl, gl, pl, sl, spl, sc, sk, sm, sn, sp, st, sw)

3) <u>Consonant Digraphs</u> (sh, wh, th, ch, ng)

4) <u>Silent Consonants</u> (as in ladder, know, night, wren, often, neck, comb)

5) <u>Vowels</u> (short and long a, e, i, o. u, and sometimes y, w)

211

6) <u>Vowel digraphs</u> (ee, oa, ai, ea)

7) <u>Vowel dipthongs</u> (ou, ow, oi, oy)

8) <u>Vowel followed by r</u> (ar, er, ir, or, ur)

9) <u>Vowel followed by l</u> (al, el, il, ol, ul)

10) <u>The oo sound</u> (as in: boot, foot, blood)

According to Frank Smith (1971) there are 166 phonic rules and 45 exceptions to the rules.

Structural Analysis Skills

Again, basal reading and other published material identify various structural analysis skills as a sub-skill of the general area of word recognition skills. The structural analysis skills generally include: 1) syllabication, 2) prefixes and suffixes, 3) plural forms, 4) contractions, 5) possessive forms, 6) inflected forms, 7) accenting, and 8) compound words. Examples of each sub-skill are presented below:

<u>Syllabication</u>. There are several rules or generalizations for dividing words into syllables. The most common rules are:

A) There are as many syllables as there are vowel sounds. Syllables are determined by the vowel sounds heard, not by the number of vowels seen.

B) Syllables divide between double consonants or between two consonants (hap/pen, bas/ket).

C) A single consonant between vowels usually goes with the second vowel (fa/mous, ho/tel).

D) As a general rule do not divide consonant digraphs (teach/er, weather/er).

E) Word endings such as ble, cle, dle, gle, kle, ple, tle, zle, constitute final syllables (mar/ble, han/dle).

F) In general, prefixes and suffixes form separate syllables, such as re, un, dis, less, able (re/form, un/able, comfort/able).

212

Prefixes and Suffixes. The following are generalizations or rules about prefixes and suffixes:

A) Common endings which begin with a vowel are
   usually sounded as syllables (er, est, ing).

B) One vowel words ending in a single consonant
   usually double the consonant before adding an
   ending when it begins with a vowel (run-running,
   stop-stopped).

C) Prefixes added to words result in new words
   often with quite different meanings (clear-un-
   clear, place-displace).

D) Suffixes are word endings added to root words
   and give different words (hope-hopeless).

Plural Forms. The following are generalization for
plural forms.

A) When words end in: s, ss, ch, sh, x plurals are
   formed by adding "es" (bus-buses, dress-dresses,
   lunch-lunches, fox-foxes, dish-dishes).

B) When a word ends in "y", its plural is formed by
   changing "y" to "i" and adding "es" (fly-flies,
   baby=babies).

Contractions. Contractions result from major structural
changes in words (cannot, can't, would not-wouldn't,
I am-I'm).

Possessive Forms. All word forms which involve adding
"'s" (Bill's coat, Mother's hat) and "s'" (James' toy).

Inflected forms. Adding inflected forms such as ly, ing,
ed, er, est.

There are certain generalizations which include:

A) Adding suffixes following "y" or final "e".
   Change the "y" to "i" before adding a suffix
   beginning with a vowel (busy-busier, busiest)
   An exception is if the suffix begins with "i",
   leave the "y" (cry-crying, dry-drying).

B) Drop the final "e" before adding a suffix beginning with a vowel (large-larger, largest).

Accenting. The following are generalizations for accenting syllables in words:

A) In compound words the primary accent usually falls on the first word (sail'boat, fish'er·man).

B) In two syllable words containing a double consonant the accent usually falls on the first syllable (cop'per, mil'lion).

C) When "ck" ends a syllable, that syllable is usually accented (chick'en, rock'et).

D) Syllables comprised of a consonant plus "le" are usually not accented (ta'ble, un'cle).

E) In two syllable root words the accent usually falls on the first syllable except when the second syllable contains two vowels (be·lieve, sur·prise').

F) Prefixes and suffixes as a rule are not accented (lone'ly, un·hap'pi·ly).

G) Two syllable words ending with "y" are usually accented on the first syllable (cit'y, ear'ly, ba'by).

H) Adding suffixes to some longer words may cause a shift in the primary accent (u·ni'verse-u·ni·ver'sal, mi'cro·scope-mi·cro·scope').

I) In many longer words the primary accent falls on the syllable before the accent.

Compound Words. All root or base words combined to form different words (railroad, sailboat, everyone).

Context Cues

The skills model of the reading process identifies context cues as one of the skills a reader can apply with phonic, structural, and sight vocabulary to "unlock" words. Context cues have traditionally been categorized and identified as the following:

1) Experience Clues. The word to be recognized is related to the reader's experiences and makes sense. For example, "The postman brought a letter from Aunt Mary."

214

2) Comparison or Contrast Cues. The author constructs the message so the reader can compare
or contrast the meaning. For example, "Rabbits
have short tails and cats have long tails." Or,
"I'm so hungry. I never get enough to eat."

3) The Synonym Clue. A word is a repetition of the
same idea or word, "Nancy laughed as she ran.
She looked like a happy girl."

4) The Summary Clue. One word or idea describes a
whole set of conditions, "They marched in line
just like a parade."

5) Mood or Situation Clue. A word may be suggested
to the reader because of the setting or mood,
"The day did not look good, but the children
wanted to go on a picnic. Soon Nancy called
Jack, "Now we can't have a picnic, look at the
rain!"

6) Definition Clue. An author sometimes provides
a definition for a word or idea, "A home on a
boat is called a houseboat."

7) Familiar Expression Clues. Certain language
patterns that have become common and familiar,
"She was as proud as a peacock."

Reading strategy lessons are given in a later
section to illustrate the development of various graphophonic cues with syntactic and semantic cues and strategies.

Syntactic Cues

The syntactic system refers to the relationship
that words, phrases, clauses, sentences and paragraphs
have to each other. It includes the relationship involving word order, tense, number, and gender. Grammar is a more common term often used in place of syntax.
All children can use the rules of their own grammar system rather proficiently by the time they come to school.
(Goodman, Burke, and Sherman, 1980)

The pre-school child intuitively develops and
uses the rules of his/her grammar. Words are ordered
and sequenced to convey meaning. Children intuitively
know where nouns, verbs, and other words function in
their utterances. They have built a grammatical

215

language structure which provides a tremendous linguistic strength to apply in learning to read. During oral language development the young child has integrated the syntactic system into the developing phonological and semantic system. Although young children cannot identify a noun or a verb, they know where words function in utterances. A five year old is able to predict what language structures fit in the appropriate slot to make sense. For example, if given the following sentences orally, and asked to fit in the appropriate word, the five year old can do this easily: "We are going to eat _____ at McDonald's." The child is able to predict and confirm an appropriate noun to fit the pattern.

In a whole language reading program instruction integrates the graphophonemic cues available to the reader with the syntactic cues and semantic cues. The natural learning strategies within the child can be applied and used in the construction of meaning. Reading strategy lessons are planned to provide the reader access to all linguistic cueing systems. The readers must be able to bring his/her intuitive knowledge of syntactic rules to reading.

Conventional reading instruction attempts to help children develop use of syntactic cues generally through isolated phrases, sentences, paragraphs, and contrived sentences within unnatural stories, particlarly at the acquisition literacy stage or "readiness" stage of learning to read. The practice of presenting isolated sentences in workbooks, skill ditto sheets, and sentences or phrase games, is evident in most published instructional materials. The isolated sentences, frequently in lists, are unrelated to any real experiences or interests of the child. The general practice is for the child to fill in missing words in the context of a sentence or paragraph structure.

Reading strategy lessons are illustrated in a following section focusing on the development of various syntactic cues with the support of graphophonemic and semantic cues, and strategies of predicting, confirming, and correcting.

Semantic Cues

The semantic system includes the non-visual information and meaning an individual has contructed through experiences. It involves, according to Smith (1971), the theory of the world each individual has in his/her head. The semantic cues available to a language user includes the network of cognitive structures of events, ideas, and feelings. Each individual develops an interpretation of the world and constructs concepts which enable an individual to make sense and organize the environment. Halliday (1975) referred to the semantic system as a meaning potential. The individual is developing a meaning potential, a system of meaning relationships. Language is used to symbolically represent concepts and the reality of events, objects, ideas and attitudes.

The reader, who may be a beginning, developing, or proficient reader, has available experiential background, concepts, and vocabulary (lexical items) to bring to the reading process. These experiences, concepts, and vocabulary (lexical) are not isolated items stored in the brain, but rather, a network of related cognitive structures. The reader has the capability of applying known concepts, experiences, and language (prior experience) to the print to construct meaning from the message. The reader must be able to relate his/her semantic knowledge to the message encoded by the author. This is necessary with all readers, but especially at the acquisition stage of reading. The closer the reader's conceptual knowledge and experience is to the author's message the easier will be the reading task. Less visual information or graphophonemic cues are necessary if the reader can apply his/her meaning potential (semantic cues) and linguistic strengths (syntactic cues) to the reading process.

Conventional reading instructional practices isolate vocabulary items or words. It is common practice to define words for their lexical meaning. Children are given lists of words to look up meanings in the dictionary or glossary. Another frequent activity in commercially published workbooks, ditto skill sheets, and vocabulary games are isolated sentences and paragraphs, usually unrelated to the reader's experiential background. Students fill in the blanks with words to fit the context. The student has little or no access to apply linguistic cueing systems to the construction of meaning. These instructional practices provide the learner no real meaningful incentive or purpose to learn. The student cannot bring his/her full semantic potential to the development of sense or meaning. In addition, the reader is limited in applying various learning strategies, such as, predicting, confirming, and correcting when isolated vocabulary items are emphasized. The reader should have the opportunity to relate the message encoded to his/her cognitive structures.

217

Examples of reading strategy lessons to develop
reader's use of semantic cues integrated with graphophonemic cues and syntactic cues are given in a following section in this chapter.

Reading Strategies

Reading-learning strategies are another major
component together with linguistic cues involved in the
reading process. Goodman (1975) states, "reading strategies are the myriad ways readers process information
when dealing with written language. They are the methods
readers use to construct the message as they perceive
the author produced it. Reading strategies are natural
to the reading process and occur continuously as the
reader strives to construct the author's meaning."

Goodman identified the universal strategies
which readers constantly apply. "These strategies include: 1) selecting graphophonic, syntactic, and semantic cues; 2) predicting graphophonic, syntactic, and
semantic information; 3) confirming those predictions
by asking themselves whether the results of the predicting strategies produced acceptable language; 4) applying correction strategies when the confirmation strategies supply evidence that the predictions were not
successful; and 5) deciding which bits of information
should be held in short-term memory for further examination and which bits finally should be integrated into
the reader's meaning system." (see Figure 5:10 on Page
219.)

As the reader is processing the linguistic information system (graphophonic, syntactic, and semantic
cues) the reader is also constantly applying strategies
(selecting, predicting, confirming, correcting (if necessary) and comprehending during the cycles (optical,
perceptual, syntactic, and meaning) of the reading process. The cycles of the reading process will be described and components identified as developed by Kenneth
Goodman (1976) in his revised model of the act of reading in a following section in this chapter (also, see
Chapter III).

For readers to make sense from print and for the
natural learning strategies to operate, there must be
whole, meaningful, natural language to process. The
reader's application of strategies in reading is similar to what the child has done in other learning tasks.
In learning to talk, the child selected significant
sound, grammar, and meaning features, predicted how

STRATEGIES

PREDICTING

CONFIRMING

CORRECTING

COMPREHENDING

READING STRATEGIES

FIGURE 5:10

these structures fit into the communicative setting, confirmed whether it made sense, and corrected if what was spoken did not receive a positive response. Thus, the child gradually developed spoken language to communicate with others in the environment. The young child learning to talk applied problem-solving strategies in whole language, meaningful situations in which language was available. Learning to process written language to construct meaning involves the same strategies. However, it is necessary that the reader have available the full context, and for the beginning reader, the text should be closely related to the child's experiential background, concepts, language patterns, and interests.

Goodman (1976) indicated, "the strategies of prediction, confirmation, and correction have an intrinsic sequence. Prediction precedes confirmation which precedes correction. Yet, the same information may be used to confirm a prior prediction and make a new one."

219

Each reading strategy is identified and described below. Then, illustrations of reading strategy lessons focusing on one or more of the strategies and linguistic cueing systems are given in a later section.

Selecting Strategy

During all cycles of the reading process the reader, according to Goodman's psycholinguistic model (1976) and Smith's theories (1971), is selecting significant graphic cues from the visual array, and phonemic cues if necessary are selected related to graphic cues. The reader also applies syntactic cues (linguistic knowledge about grammatical acceptability and function) and semantic cues (experiences, concepts, and vocabulary). The brain directs the eye to the significant visual features in the print and organizes the print relating the written marks on the page to non-visual information stored and retrieved in the brain. The process is selective because the brain can only process so much information at one time to get information into short-term memory and evantually to intermediate-term or long-term memory. The more the written language to be processed relates to the reader's store of non-visual information, e.g., linguistic system, prior knowledge, the more the brain can effectively select and process the least amount of visual information and use more non-visual information.

Predicting Strategies

As the brain is actively searching and selecting visual, sound, syntactic, and semantic cues in the processing of print, predictions are made based upon expectations. Predictions make use of the graphic system of language. The reader, even the beginner, has developed expectancies about letters, letter patterns, and whole configurations of words. The reader at the acquisition stage, as explained previously, has some knowledge of letter features, letter pattern and word features from print in the environment. However, this knowledge is not completely organized into a system. Further development of visual regularities in the written orthography will take place as the child is exposed to meaningful, whole, natural language patterns in learning situations related to the child's interests, experiences, and language structures.

As the brain is processing the visual properties of written language, the learner has available sound or phonemic cues to relate to the print. Evidence is accumulating that four and five year old children can encode in written forms letters and spelling patterns which approximate the adult spelling patterns in words. Therefore, the learner has knowledge of phonemes applicable to make predictions about print, if necessary, to recode from written letters, sound-spelling patterns, or words equivalent to oral patterns.

The most significant linguistic cues, syntactic and semantic, are available to the reader to predict during the reading process. The young reader has a well-developed syntactic system, knowledge and use of how language is ordered, to convey meaning. The young child possesses a meaning potential that has developed into a network of cognitive structures about the world.

Frank Smith (1975) described the role of prediction in reading. He states, "it is not necessary that prediction be taught, for prediction is as much a part of spoken language comprehension as it is of reading. Children with sufficient verbal ability to understand written language that is read to them, have both the competence and the experience to direct their ability in prediction to reading." He gives four reasons for prediction: 1) Individual words have too many meanings; 2) The spellings of words do not indicate how they should be pronounced; 3) There is a limit to how much of the "visual information" of print the brain can process during reading; 4) The capacity of short-term (or "working memory") is limited.

According to Smith (1975) prediction is, "the prior elimination of unlikely alternatives. Prediction . . . does not mean wild guessing, nor does it mean staking everything on a single outcome. Rather, prediction means the elimination from contention of those possibilities that are highly unlikely, and the examination first of those possibilities that are most likely."

Thus, readers use selection and prediction strategies applied to available linguistic cues in written language (visual information) and knowledge about language and the world (non-visual information). During the reading process readers have access to confirming strategies which help to verify or disconfirm predictions; enabling readers to correct by possibly reprocessing to select other linguistic cues to construct meaning. Next, confirming strategies are discussed.

221

Confirming Strategies

Confirming strategies are a natural part of the learning process and are used by the learner during the reading process. The learner is actively involved in selecting and predicting from graphophonemic, syntactic, and semantic cues available when written language is presented in whole language context. As the learner predicts, he/she tests the predictions to determine appropriateness of graphic and possibly phonemic information, syntactic and semantic data. Confirming strategies enable the reader to monitor the meaningfulness of the message. If what has been read is ambiguous or anomolous, the reader has the option of disconfirming prior predictions and applying several techniques. Confirmation is closely related to the selection and prediction strategies during the reading process. Goodman (1976) stated, "If the brain predicts it must also seek to verify its predictions. So it monitors to confirm or disconfirm with subsequent input what it expected."

Goodman, Burke, and Sherman (1980) described what readers do during the confirming strategy. "As readers we ask ourselves two questions to test our predictions or hypotheses: 1) Does this sound like language to me? 2) Does this make sense to me? If the answer to both questions is "yes" and if we decide the material is worthwhile, we continue to read. However, if the answer is "no", the following optional strategies are available:

1. Stop and rethink the problem.
2. Regress, reread, and pick up additional cues until the material makes sense.
3. Keep reading in order to build up additional context; this may generate enough understanding to decide what went wrong.
4. Stop reading because the material is too difficult."

Correcting Strategies

As readers are engaged in the reading process during the optical, perceptual, syntactic, and meaning cycles, selecting, predicting, and confirming (disconfirming) from graphophonemic, syntactic, and semantic cues, there are correction strategies available. Learners naturally apply correction strategies when their hypotheses are rejected. When there is no sense at any point during the act of reading, readers have the option of correcting or continuing to read, holding the ambiguity in memory for possible later clarification.

Goodman (1976) referred to correction as, "the brain reprocesses (information) when it finds inconsistencies or its predictions are disconfirmed."

Recht (1976) stated, "research shows that self-correction is a positive indicator that the reader is comprehending. The correction should not be regarded as an error, but rather as evidence of the reader's successful interaction with the text." From a study she conducted concerning self-correction strategies, the following conclusions were stated: 1) the self-correction process provides information about a reader's interaction with the text and about the reading process as a whole; 2) students should be encouraged to correct their miscues during oral reading. Self-correction is a learning process. The teacher should not prompt or immediately correct a reader when he/she miscues. The reader needs opportunities to develop the correction process. It was found the highest percentage of corrected miscues is found among the most proficient reader.

Goodman (1970) has found, "children learn to correct their own errors. In a previous study of fourth graders, Goodman concluded that "virtually every regression which the children in this study made was for the purpose of correcting previous reading. They were less likely to correct miscues when the resulting passage sounded like language and was meaningful to them, . . . the children were more likely to correct when language prior to and including the miscue was meaningful and sounded like language to them but then conflicted with the remainder of the passage. . . . When children attempted corrections of their own miscues, they were successful at least 75 percent of the time."

At all stages of reading development, including the acquisition stage (readiness), readers need whole language text. The language text must be related to the reader's experiential background and language patterns as much as possible. The reader will have the opportunity to exercise and develop self-correction strategies when meaningful expectations about the message are predictable. Reading should be an active process in which the reader has access to all linguistic cues and learning strategies. The whole context of language enables a reader to monitor his/her selection, prediction, confirmation, and correction of linguistic cues. The reader can apply his/her syntactic and

223

semantic knowledge to confirm or disconfirm whether
what is read is grammatically and semantically acceptable, and reprocess, correct, or continue reading, when
there is ambiguity. The reader is limited in applying
correction strategies when letters, words, phrases, sentences, or isolated paragraphs are emphasized in reading
instruction.

Comprehending Strategies

Comprehending is considered distinct from comprehension, although a part of the comprehension process. Comprehending is what the reader does during the
reading task. The reader's goal is to construct meaning as the reading process continues, attempting to
assimilate (relate new information to prior knowledge),
and accommodate (modify new ideas to old ideas) information. From Goodman's (1976) revised model of the
reading process, during the meaning cycle the reader's
focus is on making sense from the deep structure using
prior predictions from graphic cues (if necessary,
phonemic cues) and syntactic cues. The reader applies
stored experiences and conceptual knowledge to test the
semantic acceptability of the message. If there is semantic unacceptability, the reader has the options to
recycle, try an alternative deep structure, hold all
information in memory and re-scan for more cues, or
terminate if no meaning results. Therefore, comprehending may be defined as miscues that are semantically
acceptable, plus, miscues that are semantically unacceptable and corrected as the reader processes print.

Comprehension, on the other hand, can be described as the end result or what is understood or recalled when the reader completes a reading task. However, comprehending is naturally a part of the comprehension process. Comprehension is the reader's construction of the meaning of the author's message as information is processed and interpreted by the reader.

Comprehending strategies involve the reader's
prior knowledge and experiences which are applied to
constructing the author's message. The reader's theory
of the world or semantic potential is related to the
development of meaning. When reading material is purposeful to the reader, and the information to be constructed is related to the reader's knowledge and experience, comprehending strategies are enhanced and
comprehension is likely to occur. The reader has the
opportunity to use other strategies and linguistic cues
flexibility and selectivity during the process of

224

developing and integrating meaning. Comprehending strategies are developed from the beginning stages of reading as reader's make use of non-visual information without resorting to an over emphasis on graphophonemic cues. Comprehending strategies are learned naturally and effectively when reading makes sense.

In a later section various examples of strategy lessons will be given to illustrate the development of learning strategies with linguistic cueing systems.

Cycles of the Reading Process

In Chapter III, The Reading Process, Goodman's (1976) revised model of the reading process from a psycholinguistic view was described. The components involved in the reading process include the linguistic cueing systems (graphophonemic, syntactic, and semantic), the learning strategies (selecting, predicting, confirming, correcting, and comprehending) integrated within the cycles of the process.

The reading process appears to be the same for all levels and stages of reading development. The reader at the literacy acquisition stage has access to the same process as the highly proficient reader. The beginning reader and the proficient reader have access to the same linguistic systems and strategies and proceed through the same cycles. The significant difference between the young reader and the older proficient reader is the control of the linguistic systems, strategies and background experiences. The reader at the acquisition stage needs to develop the concepts of the reading process, such as, abilities required during the optical cycle of the process. However, some young children have already discovered the directionality of print from previous experience, i.e. parents, or others who have read aloud to the children.

The cycles identified by Goodman (1976) in the reading process include: 1) optical; 2) perception; 3) syntactic; 4) meaning. Each cycle is continuous and melts into the next cycle during the process of reading. The reader must have total access to full, whole written language to apply and integrate linguistic cues and learning strategies. Limiting or restricting "reading" instruction to isolated graphophonemic, syntactic, or semantic cues prevents the reader from developing reading ability.

Examples of reading strategies are given related to a description of each cycle and linguistic cues and strategies available to the reader. However, it should be understood that reading must be learned as an integrated language process rather than isolating or fragmenting parts of the total process for testing or instruction.

Optical Cycle

Even before the optical cycle has begun, the reader must recognize the task as reading a familiar language and initiate the process, according to Goodman. The reader activates strategies in memory. The graphic display provides the input to begin the optical cycle. The young learner exposed to print through various book-type experiences, such as frequently being read aloud to, may already recognize the task as reading. Children who have parent models they see reading various materials may develop the concept that reading has something to do with print. If picture books are available to the child in his/her environment, there is exposure to concepts of books and print.

The reader needs to learn and apply visual scanning of print. Through various listening experiences, such as, being read to, the child develops the directionality of reading. The basic concepts of directionality that the young child must learn is that print is processed from left to right across the line of print on the page, a return sweep from right to left to the next line, proceeding from top of the page to the bottom.

During the time the eyes are scanning the graphic display, the reader must fix and focus at a point in the print. This behavior requires coordinating the eyes and knowing where and how to look. The young child has already learned to focus visually on objects in his/her environment as the brain controls eye movements to fixate on significant features and organize the incoming message through the eyes along the optical nerve, to the brain for processing. The graphic display needs to be organized as the brain organizes and categorizes other visual information in the visual field. However, the reader needs to understand that print is arranged in an arbitrary manner and is processed in certain directions.

The teacher can facilitate the learning of print directionality during various whole language learning experiences. It is important that the child is immersed in print related to meaningful experiences. Reading aloud books and stories to small groups of children is a natural way for children to learn how print is read. The teacher should run his/her finger under the line of print as it is read. Language experience stories dictated by children and written by a teacher or aide can facilitate and develop understanding of the visual scanning process, training the eyes to move in the required direction. Again, the teacher or aide would use his/her hand to demonstrate the necessary eye movement from left to right, return sweep from right to left to the next line, reading from the top of the page to the bottom. Functional reading activities, such as, printed messages in learning centers, can be useful to illustrate the directionality of print. Coordinating beginning writing with reading can develop the concept of how print is arranged to convey a written message. The teacher can encourage and provide opportunities for children to write even at a very early stage, pretending to write even though spelling rules and other written conventions have not been learned. At a later stage variations of assisted reading techniques can be utilized to develop visual scanning of print. A teacher or aide can read individually with a child using the echoic or impress method. Basically, the teacher/aide and child read a story together. The teacher/aide would direct the child's eyes by running his/her finger under the line of print being read. Later, young learners or even older learners having difficulty reading can read along with a story and a tape to listen to the story as the eyes follow the print.

However, reading is not only a visual task. As previously emphasized repeatedly, the reader has access to other linguistic cues and strategies and non-visual information to bring to the reading task. The reader has access to meaning (semantic) structure (syntactic) and prior predictions, as well as, confirming, correcting, and comprehending strategies to utilize with graphic redundancy. Moreover, the print must represent experiences of high interest and related to the background experiences and conceptual development of the reader. The reading material must be purposeful and functional for the reader.

As the reader recognizes and initiates the task of reading beginning with the optical cycle, the process moves into the perception cycle.

Perception Cycle

According to Goodman (1976) the perceptual cycle involves the reader in sampling and selecting cues from the available graphic display: applying feature analysis, or choosing features from alternate letters, words, and structures; and forming an image of what is seen and expected to be seen.

The graphic display provides the input for the reader to sample, select, and choose significant visual cues. The brain directs the eyes to focus and fix on graphic array. The reader applies sampling strategies and prior predictions from memory. The reader analyzes the visual features sampled relating and assigning graphic shapes and distinctive feature to known categories. The beginning reader must gradually build letter categories to differentiate shapes of individual letters and word structures or sequences and patterns of letters in words.

As a child is exposed to the graphic display in meaningful, whole language print situations, he/she will abstract the significant visual features and patterns of graphic features in various allosystems (type style, cursive, etc.). It is not necessary to isolate individual letters for practice to develop visual discrimination of visual features. Word patterns comprised of individual distinctive letter forms are more concrete when presented to the child in connected print in a meaningful context in which the child can relate experiences and language patterns to the graphic display.

The reader forms an image from feature analysis applying from memory graphic, syntactic, and semantic constructs and prior predictions. If necessary, the reader applies phonological cues related to visual cues to predict, confirm, and possibly correct if there is confusion or distortion in meaning. The phonological system, which for young children is already well-developed, provides a back-up system for the reader if visual cues, syntactic cues, and semantic cues with appropriate or flexible strategies prove inadequate in the construction of meaning. Even the learner at the literacy acquisition stage may bypass the phonological system and learn to process print directly to meaning. However, the beginning reader may have to resort to recoding (matching visual cues with auditory cues) more frequently than the proficient reader. It should be understood that whenever a reader, beginning or proficient, has to apply "sounding out" techniques the comprehension process is disrupted.

During the perception cycle the reader has the option to correct, if necessary, by returning to visual scanning and fixing the eyes on the graphic display, to try and approximate or terminate; or if no image is formed, return to feature analysis; or return to scan for more information. If sampling, selecting, feature analysis, and image formation is confirmed, the reader continues to the syntactic cycle, according to Goodman (1976).

The perceptual abilities of readers can be developed in ways similar to visual scanning since the two cycles in the reading process are closely related. Readers develop sampling, selecting, feature analysis, and image formation through meaningful exposure to connected written discourse. Whole language experiences such as, reading aloud so children can visualize the print display, assisted reading, i.e., echoic, impress, read-along, language experience stories, functional-type reading activities, i.e., meaningful print messages in learning centers, on bulletin boards, are several methods to help children develop visual perception.

Again, many opportunities for writing with spelling instruction also develop visual and auditory perception. As children learn letter formation and related phonological correspondence of letters and letter patterns, this print awareness transfers to reading. However, writing like reading should be highly meaningful, purposeful settings where children write as an alternate system of communication to communicate to someone. Meaningful writing activities, even at the earliest stages, include: written records of science experiments, creative stories, letters, invitations, thank you notes, diaries, personal journals, and the like.

Syntactic Cycle

As the reader is visually scanning the graphic display, fixing and focusing the eyes at a point in the print; sampling and selecting significant visual features; forming a perceptual image using prior predictions, confirming (or disconfirming), correcting, if necessary, by re-scanning, recycling, the visual information is stored in memory. The reader moves into the syntactic cycle, as Goodman (1976) describes the process, by assigning an internal surface structure applying linguistic rules to relate the surface display to the

internal surface structure based on prior predictions
and meaning. Then the reader assigns a deep structure
to his/her linguistic knowledge, i.e., applying transformational rules for relating surface and deep structure. The beginning reader has developed knowledge of
oral language patterns, grammatical function of word
structures, and sequencing of grammatical structures.

If no structure is possible, the reader has various options during the syntactic cycle. The reader
can recycle to perception or optical cycles; try alternate structures or correct by recycling and scanning
back to point of confusion. If an internal surface
structure sounds appropriate within the reader's linguistic patterns, it is possible to go to the deep
structure. Again, the reader has various alternatives
if no structure is possible. The reader can recycle,
correct, if inconsistent with predictions by recycling,
or if deep structure is confirmed, the reader goes to
meaning. If confusion exists, the reader can terminate
at this point.

Reading experiences to develop learner's abilities during the syntactic cycle of the reading process
include approaches which also are conducive to development during the optical and perceptual cycles. The
learner is an effective language user and the syntactic/
semantic strengths are available to apply to any reading task that is within the learner's linguistic and
experiential background. It's important, however, to
keep in mind that there is no exact one-to-one correspondence between oral and written language. That is,
written language tends to be more precise and fully
formed than oral language. More information is necessary generally in written language than in face-to-face
oral language settings. The author needs to provide the
reader with more information, to build a meaning context
for the reader. The speaker, on the other hand, is not
as restricted because the situational context provides
more clues for the listener. Therefore, readers, particularly young readers, need to develop "book language."

Teachers can help children at the literacy
acquisition stage of learning to read to develop familiarity with written language structures by frequently
reading aloud, using assisted reading and language experience stories. The most effective method to help
young readers relate their oral language patterns to
written language patterns is through language experience stories. Language experience stories enable the
learner to link his/her linguistic knowledge and

experience to written language. The child is also applying other linguistic cues (graphophonemic and semantic) and strategies during the optical and perceptual cycles described above.

Reading aloud to children develops models of "book language." Particularly effective for young children are highly predictable language books, stories, nursery rhymes and the like. Stories with repetitive written patterns enhance relating print to meaning. Children easily and naturally identify with repetitive language patterns and soon learn to memorize and even "read" the book or story themselves. Syntactic structures and meaning become highly predictable in repetitive story material.

Assisted reading, previously described, provides the learner with the shapes of word structures, the patterning of words in sentences in high interest materials. Various forms of assisted reading, i.e., echoic, impress, tape/book, provide the reader opportunities to apply syntactic cues during the reading process. Highly predictable print is suggested for assisting reading as with reading aloud to children.

The reading process is not complete until the reader has constructed meaning from the author's message. The last cycle, the meaning cycle, has been described by Goodman (1976).

Meaning Cycle

From the deep structures, prior knowledge, experiences, and concepts, the reader moves to decoding meaning applying prior predictions. If meaning is not acceptable, the reader can recycle to a point of inconsistency; or, try an alternate deep structure, or recycle to seek more information; if still no meaning, the reader may hold all information in memory and return to scan; or terminate if no meaning results. The reader may also, continue reading and attempt to construct meaning from additional meaning provided by the author. If meaning is acceptable, the reader goes on to assimilate and accommodate meaning. If assimilation is possible, (i.e., relating new information to previously learned information) meaning is constructed by the reader. If assimilation is not possible, the reader may accommodate prior meaning (i.e., modify new meaning to previously learned meaning). The reader uses prior predictions and meaning from memory. If meaning is not assimilated or accommodated, the reader has options to

231

recycle to obtain more information; or, hold and return to the optical cycle to scan for possible clarification as reading progresses. Accommodation is possible when the reader modifies meaning, modifies predictions of meaning; modifies concepts; modifies word definitions; as restructure attitudes. If the task is complete the reader terminates the process. If the task is incomplete the reader may recycle and scan forward, predicting meaning, structure, graphics (Goodman, 1976).

Reading experiences related to the meaning cycle, as well as previously described cycles, e.g., optical, perception and syntactic, include reading aloud, assisted reading, language experience, individualized, self-selected reading, sustained silent reading and directed-reading-thinking-activities (D.R.T.A.) Through reading aloud the learner relates written language to his/her understanding of the world; receives input from images related to past experiences or builds new experiences; develops vocabulary and concepts. Assisted reading provides a semantic context; relates experiences and conceptual knowledge to material read/listened to; applies conceptual knowledge of the world to print. Language experiences provide meaningful concepts to relate to prior knowledge and experiences. Self-selected and sustained silent reading provides the context to practice real reading in purposeful settings. Directed-reading-thinking-activities (D.R.T.A.) focuses the learner's attention on constructing the author's meaning as well as developing self-interpretation through predicting, reasoning and logical thinking.

Attitudinal Construct

Values and attitudes of the learner are other significant components of any learning process and certainly of reading-language learning. Learning to read is not thought to have the compelling attraction that learning oral language possesses. However, young children are curious about their environment, including the print that surrounds them. Printed symbols and logos are a natural part of the young child's world. Recent studies of young children's awareness and knowledge of print indicates they have a concept that written symbols represent meaning. Therefore, young children possess a natural orientation to print and an interest and disposition to figure out the print in their environment. The need to learn print, as far as books is concerned, is not similar to the need to use oral language. Nevertheless, young children exposed to all types of print, non-book or book, have varying degrees of curiosity about print.

<u>READING COMPONENTS</u>

<u>INTEREST/ATTITUDES</u>

DESIRE TO READ

ATTENTION TO TASK

CONCEPT OF READING

PURPOSE OF READING

ATTITUDINAL CONSTRUCT OF THE READING PROCESS

FIGURE 5:11

At the literacy acquisition stage of learning
to read (preschool-primary) attitudes and values about
print can be encouraged and developed by home and
school in a variety of natural ways. Reading aloud by
parents and teachers help children develop a love and
appreciation of books. They learn that stories are for
enjoyment and relaxation. They develop attitudes that
books bring pleasure at the same time that children are
familiarized with written symbols. Reading aloud enables
children to relate talking and listening to reading and
writing. Frequent reading aloud to children develops
the concept that print conveys meaning that someone
else has written.

Reading aloud to children builds attention by
listening for increased longer periods of time. Children develop attention to task when listening experiences are meaningful and interesting to them. Independent reading which will occur later requires con-
centrated effort and attention for a sustained period
of time. However, at no time should children be forced
to listen to stories read to them that are uninteresting.
They should always have the opportunity to reject and/or
terminate the activity when it becomes boring and uninteresting.

Assisted reading also is effective at certain
times for children to develop a desire to read to themselves, develop attention, awareness of the function of
reading, and concepts about print. Assisted types of

reading is a natural extention of reading out loud. Stories or books with accompanying tape or records are easily available to parents or teachers. In addition to developing positive attitudes and values such as appreciation, enjoyment, and relaxation, assisted reading can naturally develop understanding about the mechanics and concepts about print in books. Assisted reading utilized with language experience stories, can indirectly, help children learn the spaces, capital letters, punctuation, and directionality. Processing print in meaningful stories through assisted reading, language experience stories, and reading aloud expose children to discover the concepts of printed language. Parents and teachers can naturally direct children's attention to characteristics of written language in whole, connected stories.

Developing Comprehension Abilities

Comprehension is the beginning and end result of communication with language. The whole purpose of any form of communication, verbal or non-verbal, is to convey or construct meaning. There is no other purpose or function of communication. The infant is fully equipped to process information through his/her sensory apparatus. The brain has the capability to organize and construct meaning coming in through the senses. Oral and written language are communication modes to organize, interpret, store, and retrieve representational information about self, others, and the environment. Language, oral or print, has no meaning itself. Language is used to represent symbolically the world. Language is used to represent and construct a theory of the world as Smith (1978) indicates.

Comprehension can be thought of as the reduction of uncertainty, according to Smith. Learning is possible when there is comprehension. There is no learning when there is no comprehension. Young children naturally learn and, therefore, comprehension is evident. Learning and comprehension are accomplished by children in meaningful situations. To learn and comprehend children must be able to relate prior information to new experiences. They must be able to link learned concepts to new concepts. Language helps to facilitate the child's increasing conceptual knowledge. The prior knowledge of the world must be assimilated and accommodated with new knowledge. Teachers need to help children reduce uncertainty, or develop comprehension, in a variety of meaningful ways.

234

Traditional Views To Develop Comprehension

There has been little disagreement that the purpose of reading is for comprehension. The basic controversy about reading has concerned how the reader constructs meaning from written language. Traditionally, it has been maintained that if a reader can recognize and pronounce words in isolation, in a phrase, sentence, paragraph, and longer connected text that comprehension will occur in the brain. This simplistic view has resulted in research tests, teaching techniques, and instructional materials that separate and identify skills in the reading process, such as, word recognition, phrase recognition, vocabulary study, sentence and paragraph comprehension. Each of the identified skills is presented in various practice type activities and are supposed to add up to the reader's comprehension of connected written discourse.

Wheat and Edmond (1975) stated, "Over the years reading comprehension has been explored and explained from various perspectives. In fact, more than sixty years ago, Huey raised questions concerning comprehension which are not yet answered. Furthermore, the process of reading comprehension has not yet been defined or conceptualized with any degree of general consensus, despite the fact that almost without exception reading authorities and practitioners feel comprehension is the most important outcome of the reading process."

There have been several comprehension taxonomies developed to identify and categorize levels and types of thinking abilities which may be related to the reading process. Bloom (1956) has identified categories of cognitive thinking abilities. Sanders (1966) has taken Bloom's taxonomy and revised it to include several of Bloom's categories. Sanders has classified thinking abilities and teacher's questions into several categories. The categories are:

1. Memory - recognizing or recalling information as given in the passage. Sanders distinguishes four kinds of ideas on the memory level of thinking.

2. Translations - expressing ideas in different form of language.

3. Interpretation - trying to see relationships among facts, generalizations, values, etc. Saunders recognizes several types of interpretations.

4. Application - solving a problem that requires the use of generalizations, facts, values, and other appropriate types of thinking.

5. Analysis - recognizing and applying rules of logic to solution of a problem; analyzing an example of reasoning.

6. Synthesis - using original creative thinking to solve a problem.

7. Evaluation - making judgements based on clearly defined standards.

Gallagher and Aschner (1969) developed a classification scheme which includes a four-category system designed to suggest the various kinds of questions that elicit responses from the different cognitive thought levels. The categories identified are: 1) cognitive - memory, 2) convergence, 3) divergence, and 4) evaluative thinking.

Much emphasis has been placed on identifying the separate components and levels of cognitive thinking abilities. Reading comprehension tests instructional materials, and teacher questioning techniques have been developed related to the identification and categorization of isolated cognitive abilities. Several investigations of teacher's questioning have conducted to determine the types and levels of questions teachers ask children in reading situations (Guszak, 1967, 1969). Most studies conclude that teachers ask mostly memory, factual, or literal recall questions. Thus, traditionally, comprehension has been tested, developed, or thought to be improved by segmenting cognitive processes into separate sub-skills. Furthermore, it has been postulated that comprehension is arranged in some hierarchal order, from low level cognitive abilities, implying that the development of one level of thinking is a prerequisite to development of higher order thinking. It is as if the brain has several separate sections which operate on different levels independently of other sections. One compartment for memory of facts, terms, generalizations; one for translation, interpretation, application, synthesis, analysis, and evaluation or some other categorization system.

The categorization and classification of cognitive abilities are for the convenience of conducting research, designing tests, instructional materials, and teacher questioning techniques. Comprehension is more complex than simply separating identified thinking abilities into categories and levels. This may be a first step in organizing our knowledge of various cognitive aspects of the comprehension process during the reading process, however, such a fragmented view of the process may distort and inhibit developing comprehension of readers. We fall into the similar illusion concerning comprehension as we do with word recognition by testing and teaching separate skills. Language for communication functions must be kept whole, meaningful, and intact. Any attempt to fragment by testing and asking isolated questions purported to be at different levels and types related to isolated units, i.e., words, phrases, sentences, and paragraphs, distorts the comprehension process. Comprehension, as word recognition, is more than a sum of the parts. Learning and comprehension is made more difficult for readers when teachers apply various questioning techniques to conform to separate categorization systems. Finally, it is highly unlikely that teachers can "teach" comprehension in reading or listening. The reader and listener must develop his/her comprehension in a variety of situations for the unique purpose perceived by the learner related to his/her cognitive structure and interpretation of experience.

Figure 5:12 below compares a skills-oriented with a whole language view of comprehension.

Skills-Oriented	Whole Language
1. The print signifies meaning.	1. There is no meaning in print.
2. The reader absorbs author's meaning	2. The reader constructs meaning.
3. Comprehension is a sequence of skills.	3. Reading is interpreing and inferring.
4. A teacher can "teach"/ "test" comprehension skills.	4. There is no hierarchal structure in comprehension.
5. If a reader recognizes words it equals meaning.	5. A reader doesn't need to pronounce words to get to meaning.
6. Comprehension taxonomies identify levels/types of thinking.	6. The reader's knowledge of story structure influences comprehension.

CHARACTERISTICS OF COMPREHENSION IN A SKILLS-ORIENTED AND WHOLE LANGUAGE READING PROGRAM

FIGURE 5:12

237

Newer Views To Developing Comprehension

If comprehension is not a collection of separate
skills arranged hierarchally according to levels, then
what is it? The answer to this question is not complete.
Yet, there are several interesting descriptions of
theories and models of the comprehension process. A
review of most studies of the comprehension process
addresses specific skills that contribute to comprehension instead of treating comprehension as a global process (Baker and Stein, 1978). Several recent investigations concerning the comprehension process focus on
identifying how the listener and reader process whole
text. One of the more promising techniques applied has
been discourse analysis or "story grammar."

Baker and Stein identified two models to investigate the comprehension process. One model developed
by several researchers represents the semantic content
of a passage (i.e., Crothers (1972), Frederieksen (1972),
Kintsch (1974), Meyers (1975)). The Kintsch theory of
language comprehension will be presented later. A
second model is the "story grammar" (Mandler and Johnson
(1977), Rumelhart (1975), Stein and Glenn (1978),
Thorndyke (1977). According to Baker and Stein, the
"story grammar" is applicable only to a limited class
of prose materials: the "story."

Another productive area of investigation into
the comprehension process is schema/theoretical models
of language processing. Adams and Collins (1977) explained the structural organization of schema/theoreti-
cal models in the following way: "A schema is a description of a particular class of concepts and is composed of a hierarchy of schemata embedded within schema.
. . . Each schema at each level in the hierarchy consists of descriptions of the important interrelationships, where these directions are themselves schema defined at the appropriate level of specifity." Schema
theory related to the comprehension process will be
described more fully in a following section.

Kintsch's Theory of Semantic Content

Royer and Cunningham (1978) described Walter
Kintsch's theory of language processing. Kintsch proposed that the meaning of text can be represented in the
form of a text base, which is a structural list of propositions. Propositions consist of a predicate with one
or more arguments, and an argument is a concept, of a
proposition itself. Concepts are realized at the

language level by a word (or words if there are synonyms) or at times by a phrase. In essence, propositions are idea units representing a simple idea.

Kintsch (1974) stated, "It is suggested that propositions represent ideas, and that language or imagery expresses propositions, and hence, ideas. Thinking occurs at the propositional level; language is the expression of thought."

Royer and Cunningham (1978) provided an example of Kintsch's representational system. The sentence "A great black and yellow V-2 rocket forty-six feet long stood in the New Mexico desert," would be represented as: 1) (BLACK, ROCKET), 2) (GREAT, ROCKET), 3) (YELLOW ROCKET), 4) (V-2, ROCKET), 5) (LONG, ROCKET), 6) (FORTY-SIX FEET), 7) (STAND, ROCKET), 8) IN, 7, DESERT), 9) (NEW MEXICO, DESERT). This example illustrates several of the conventions used in the representation system. The names of concepts, as distinguished from words, are written in capital letters, and the predicates in the prepositions are written first. In addition, the propositions are numbered such that when one proposition serves as an argument for another (as in six and eight above), the number of the proposition is written rather than writing out the proposition in its entirety.

Royer and Cunningham (1978) also described "another aspect of Kintsch's representational system which is text cohesion. Text cohesion is a concept which captures the difference between a list of numbered propositions derived from random phrases. Kintsch suggested that the difference lies in the degree of argument repetition. As an example, note that eight of the nine propositions in the sample sentence show the argument ROCKET. Thus, an index of the degree of cohesion present in the text is the extent to which arguments are repeated across propositions."

Royer and Cunningham (1978) continued, "Kirtsch has presented evidence to the effect that coherence in text is directly related to the ease of understanding of the text. Thus, a text which is highly coherent (having much argument repetition) will be easier to understand than one which is less coherent."

"In essence, what Kintsch is saying is that new information in text will be understood more easily if it has recently been preceded by related information.

Text will be understood more easily if the incoming arguments can be related to knowledge already in memory," according to Royer and Cunningham, (1978).

Furthermore, "Kintsch's theory contains a number of instances of the critical role of prior knowledge in constructing a memory representation for a linguistic event. First, Kintsch proposes a pattern matching phase in which an incoming linguistic message (consisting of perceptual elements) is matched to a semantic memory trace which consists of phonemic, graphemic, syntactic, semantic, and experiential features associated with a given word. The perceptual and semantic elements than combine to form an encoding for the event. Thus, prior knowledge, in the form of semantic memory elements, is involved very early in the comprehension process."

Finally, Royer and Cunningham (1978) discussing Kintsch's theory, stated, "prior knowledge also influences memory representation in Kintsch's theory through the role of short-term memory. Propositions which are already in short-term memory are presumed to influence both the pattern matching phase and the encoding phase of the representational process. If needed, propositions can also be called from long-term memory to aid in text interpretation. This would occur, for example, when the propositions presently in short-term memory were not relevant to the interpretation of incoming propositions."

Story Grammar and Story Schema

Story grammar and story schema are newer techniques applied in research toward understanding the comprehension process. Most of the investigations using schema theory and story grammar has been pure research rather than applied. However, there are some implications for reading development using schema theory and story grammar.

Rummelhart (1977) has developed a comprehension model. According to Rummelhart, "the notion central to a comprehension model. . . is the schema. A schema is an abstract representation of a generic concept for an object, event, or situation. Internally, a schema consists of a network of interrelationships among the major constituents of the situation represented by the schema. Moreover, a schema is said to account for any situation that can be an instance of the general concept it represents."

Mandler and Johnson (1977) use the term "story schema." They explained, "story schema to refer to an idealized internal representation of the parts of a typical story and the relationships among those parts." Furthermore, Mandler and Johnson state, "we use the term 'story schema' to refer to a set of expectations about the internal structure of stories which serves to facilitate both encoding (speaking and writing) and retrieval (listening and reading)."

Baker and Stein (1978) described a story schema which is similar to schema developed by others (i.e., Mandler and Johnson (1979), Rummelhart (1975), Thorndyke (1977)). They stated: "A simple story can first be broken down into two parts: a setting category, plus an episode structure. The setting begins the story with the introduction of a protagonist (character) and normally includes information about the social, physical, or temporal context of the story (setting). The episode is the primary higher order unit of analysis and consists of five categories of information. These categories serve particular functions in the story and occur in fixed temporal sequence. The initiating event category contains an event or action that changes the story environment. The major function of this change is to evoke the formation of a goal. The goal is included in the internal response category. Internal responses also include affective states and cognitions, and they serve to motivate a character's subsequent overt behavior. Overt actions that are directed towards goal attainment are classified as attempts. The result of an attempt is the consequence, which marks the attainment or nonattainment of a goal. The final category is the reaction, which can include either a character's response to the consequence of broader consequences of the goal attainment."

One example of the above story structure applied to a simple story provided by Baker and Stein (1978) is as follows:

Setting: 1. Once there was a big grey fish named Albert

                2. who lived in a big icy pond near the edge of the forest.

Initiating

Event: 3. One day, Albert was swimming around the pond

	4	when he spotted a big juicy worm on top of the water.
Internal Response:	5.	Albert knew how delicious worms tasted
	6.	and he wanted to eat that one for his dinner.
Attempt:	7.	So he swam very close to the worm
	8.	and bit into him.
Consequence:	9.	Suddenly, Albert was pulled through the water into a boat.
	10.	He had been caught by a fisherman.
Reaction:	11.	Albert felt sad
	12.	and wished he had been more careful.

Baker and Stein stated, " . . . there are rules governing the kinds of information that should appear in a story and the order in which this information appears." They further explained, "one of the major conclusions that has emerged is that knowledge of the structure of stories is critical to an understanding of stories."

Mandler and Johnson (1977) explained the construction of story schema from two sources in the following way, "one source comes from listening to many stories and consists of knowledge about the sequencing of events in stories, including how they typically begin and end. The other source comes from experience and includes knowledge about causal relations and various kinds of action sequences. However, the units which eventually form a story schema either condense or ignore many aspects of logical and experiential knowledge about the world. Only those perceptions, feelings, actions, and events which have to do with the ongoing plot or story line are represented in the schema, even though these may subsume other logical and psychological conditions."

Various researchers (i.e., Mandler and Johnson (1977), Baker and Stein (1978), and McConaughy (1980)) have identified differences in the construction of stories by young children, older children, and adults. Several studies (Piaget (1926), Fraisse (1963), Brown (1975), Stein and Glenn (1978)) of children's recall of stories have found differences in retelling of sequence of events and temporal order related to differences in the structure of the stories. Mandler and Johnson (1977) stressed, "The uncertain evidence in this area of study (i.e., different story structures) suggest again that the structure of the materials being used must be carefully examined before we can reach a sound conclusion about children's reproduction of temporal and causal sequences."

Mandler and Johnson examined the qualitative aspects of four short stories analyzed according to their grammar. Children in the first and fourth grades and college adults, listened to and recalled the stories. Adults recalled more information than the fourth graders, who in turn recalled more than the first. Age differences were observed in the amount recalled from specific categories, but the patterning of recall was similar. Settings were best recalled by first graders, closely followed by initiating events and then consequences. Recall was progressively worse for attempts, reactions, and internal responses. Fourth graders had the same ordering of category recall except that attempts were as well recalled as consequences. Adults recalled attempts, settings, initiating events, and consequences equally well, but reactions and internal responses were still significantly worse. It was concluded that young children and adults are both aware of structural components in stories.

Baker and Stein (1978) stated, "it appears that knowledge about the structure of stories develops during the preschool years. Most children's exposure to stories begins before they can even talk, so it is not surprising that a story schema is acquired so early. The schema goes through refinement during the elementary school years, with an increasing focus on internal goals and response."

McConaughy (1980) also found developmental progression in story schema used by children and adults. She explains, "The schema vary in both the components of story information they include and in the ways in which this information is organized." Her study involved college students and fifth grade children reading one of several stories and then writing a summary of the story, telling only what they consider to be the most important parts for meaning of the whole story. Conclusions were described indicating children's summaries, called single description schema, provide the basic information for remembering the temporal sequence of

243

actions and events explicitly stated in the story. It
includes only the beginning and ending components of the
story (the setting, initiating events, and resolution)
and may also fill in some details about intervening
actions and events (attempts and outcomes). The adult
summaries represent use of what is called the social
inference schema. The social inference schema not only
includes the basic components for the sequence of action
and events but also adds story components which explain
the character's actions. Thus, the social inferences
schema includes the goal of the character and his internal response."

Since story grammar or story schema is still
relatively a new approach to understanding the comprehension process, there are as yet few suggestions for
comprehension development in classroom settings. However, there are implications available from story schema
which may be useful for teachers. Several implications
and methods based on newer views of the comprehension
process are described in Chapter VI.

Planning Reading Strategy Lessons

There are situations when the teacher may help
readers at various times by providing reading instruction. Teacher intervention into a learner's reading
development is based on monitoring the reader's reading
performance. In Chapter IV, Evaluation of Reading,
several evaluative techniques were described which may
provide the teacher insight into the reader's strengths
and needs. The most powerful evaluative procedure suggested was miscue analysis. The teacher may plan appropriate reading strategy lessons related to information
about a reader's use of linguistic cues and strategies
in a whole story context. The teacher should obtain
other information about the student, including: experiences, interests, and concepts the reader has about
the reading process.

Reading strategy lessons, as previously described, are instructional settings in which specific reading strategies and language cues are highlighted in
full language context related to an analysis of a reader's miscues. The teacher should plan lessons only for
student(s) who will benefit from the instruction, and,
if possible, at the critical moment. Reading strategy
lessons should use natural language patterns, avoiding
ambiguous patterns. The language should be highly predictable. The reader should be able to develop a
specific linguistic cue or cues and strategy which is

244

emphasized with the support of other cues and strategies. The content of strategy lesson material must be interesting and closely related related to the learner's interests and background experiences.

Reading strategy lessons should be a part of the total reading program at any developmental level of reading. The instruction should be integrated within a whole language reading program. Reading strategy lessons can be expanded into various reading, listening, writing, and speaking learning experiences. The lessons can also grow out of whole language approaches as a teacher monitors the oral reading language performance of learners in reading situations, i.e., conferences with an individual child reading orally; ReQuest (oral reading by a pupil as the teacher and pupil take turns reading, retelling, and questioning in a story context); Directed-Reading-Thinking-Activity (DRTA); and so forth.

The following reading strategy lessons are divided into four classifications for the convenience of description. First, strategy lessons that highlight predicting and confirming graphophonemic cues; second, predicting and confirming syntactic cues; third, predicting and confirming semantic cues; and fourth, other reading strategies. The examples of strategy lessons are not organized according to specific age/ grade levels. However, some strategy lessons are clearly designed for readers at the acquisition stage, while others are appropriate for later stages of reading development. Most examples of strategy lessons presented may be adapted to different reader's needs and levels of performance.

Developing Graphophonemic Cues

The examples of strategy lessons for developing predicting and confirming graphophonemic cues within a whole language context are limited to only specific letter-sound correspondences. However, other graphophonemic relationships can be substituted if miscue analysis has determined a reader's need. Lessons 1-13 are examples of strategy lessons that focus on specific letter-sound relationships:

Developing Graphophonemic Cues

Determining Lesson 1

Focus: Graphophonemic cues - with syntactic and semantic cues.

Purpose: To assist the students in developing the use of graphophonemic cues in clarifying the initial "ch" digraph. Also to develop the use of sampling, predicting, and correcting strategies in reading for comprehension.

Introduction: My classes all are from 2 to 6 in size. A group of five students began by listening to a taped story called "Charlie, The Tramp" by Russell Hoban, after some introductory questions by me about the kind of animal the students thought the story was about, what was meant by "tramp", etc. . . As they listened, they followed along with the tape by following in the book. (We are able to get book bags of many stories which contain 5 or 6 books with the tape).

Interaction: After listening, we had more discussion about beavers, their activities, etc. and about Charlie's behavior. The class retold the story which I wrote on the board as they gave it to me. We paid particular attention to the sequence of events since many of my students need attention in that area.

From their dictated story on the board, they then located words beginning with "ch" and listed them on chart paper. (Charlie, chew, chop, children, etc.) The class then adds to the list any other words which they can think of beginning with the same sound. Each time a student contributes a word they try to use it orally in a sentence.

Expansion: Since my daily class period is only approximately thirty minutes in length, this is all I did for one class meeting. However, the following day the students

246

used the sentences from chart paper including "ch" words. The word in sentences begins with "ch" in each case
and they read trying to determine what
sounds correct or makes sense. I have
taken the words from the list they gave
me the previous day and it is available
for them to use in selecting words.

Further expansion may be done by
having each student make up his or her
own sentences including a word beginning
with "ch" and then exchanging with a
classmate. They may also see if they
could make up a silly sentence using as
many words starting with "ch" as possible (Example: Cheating Charlie chews
chewing gum and chomps chiggers.)

Evaluation: Observance in the use the children make
of the expansion exercises will easily
determine if the student is understanding what he is doing. Furthermore,
spacing the interaction exercises over
a period of a couple days helps me to
determine whether or not the student is
developing the graphophonemic cues. We
go over written exercises immediately
after completion to make necessary corrections and comments.

Determining Lesson 2

Focus: To develop use of graphophonemic cues
with predicting and confirming strate-
gies. The "ch" letter-sound relationship.

Introduction: The children have experienced much difficulty in mastering the digraph "ch"
sound. After a discussion using familiar objects, such as: chair, chart,
chain, place a story on the overhead
projector. Allow the children to read
the story so that the story makes sense.

Interacting: After the children have read the story
from the overhead, hand them the story
with deleted "ch" words and allow them
to fill in the blanks with words they

247

like best. Then have the children read
their story to their classmates.

Expanding: Have the children draw a picture of the
                story and label the "ch" words.

Evaluation: As children read their stories to their
                classmates, the teacher will know if
                he letter-sound of "ch" has been mas-
                tered. The teacher will also know if
                the children understand what they have
                read.

Charlie and Chester

Charlie is a little mouse who loves to eat
cheese. One day his mother said, "Charlie, if you eat
too much cheese, you will not be able to hop out of
your chair when Chester the cat starts to chase you."

Charlie said, "I'll take that chance because I
love to eat cheese."

Now Chester the cat was very charming. He pro-
mised Charlie a piece of cheddar cheese if he would come
sit by the chimney with him. But Charlie was no chump.
He knew that Chester was licking his chin. So he ran
to his mother and cried, "Chester wants to eat me so
I'm glad I took your advice."

Determining Lesson 3

Focus: Graphophonemic cues

Purpose: To develop graphophonemic cues while
                learning the "th" sound. Also, pre-
                dicting repetitious phrases - syntactic.

Introduction: The students listen to the story, Thim-
                ble, Thimble, Is My Name read aloud by
                the teacher.

Interaction: The children can join together to say
                the repetitious phrase. Activity for
                seatwork can be filling in the "th"
                words.

Expanding: Bring a sewing basket and articles that
                begin with "th" to be put into the bas-
                ket. The children can act out the story.

248

Evaluation: As the children work on their activities, observe those having trouble with the "th" sound. Check to see if they understand that more cues are given if they finish the sentence or go to the following sentence.

Thimble, Thimble, Is My Name

Mrs. Thimble lived in a sewing box all by herself. She got lonesome and invited others to live with her. Mr. Thread came rolling along and moved in. Then came thirteen pins. They moved in also. Next, came thin button and thick button. Pin cushion and tape measure tried to get in, but could not. Not in this basket. A queer looking thing was invited in to live. The basket seemed full, but when Mrs. Thimble went out to take down the sign, she met thumb and invited him in saying, "There is always room for one more."

Determining Lesson 4

Focus: Graphophonemic Cues

Purpose: To learn about the consonant blend "br" using graphophonemic cues.

Introduction: Introduce the story. Focus on "br" words in story.

Interacting: Read story silently. Reread story orally.

Expanding: Write story with "br" words.

Evaluation: Observe oral rereading for recognition of "br" words. Note which ones are having difficulty then, and when the lesson is reviewed orally. Give these children individual help.

The Two Brave Brothers

When it is warm, my brother and I get our lunch at home. When there is snow in winter, we put our lunch in a brown paper bag. We often bring it to school on a sled.

After school we made a snowman with a broom in his hand and a bright scarf around his neck. Some boys

249

threw bricks at our snowman, trying to knock him down.
We tried to be brave and fight them off, but they took
brances off a tree and ran after us. When we got home
we were out of breath. Mother called us the two brave
brothers.

Determining Lesson 5

In this activity the reader will be encouraged
to use graphophonemic cues when encountering new words.
It is hoped he will be able to employ the author's
rhyme scheme as well as semantic cues to come to the
realization that a double medial consonant often indicates a preceeding short vowel.

This generalization (rule) will not be given to
the reader before the exercise. Through the following
activities, it is hoped the reader will be able to come
to this conclusion on his/her own.

This activity would be for a child able to recognize and reproduce short vowel sounds, but having obvious limitations for working out words with these
sounds.

The students would listen to the poem read a-
loud. Following this, he/she would again listen to the
poem, this time with a copy in front of him/her so that
he could follow. On his/her copy the double medial consonants would be marked in green. The student would be
asked to guess the reason for the markings (to indicate
double medial consonants).

The poem would then be reread (perhaps the
following day). This time the students would listen
while referring to a copy on which the double medial
consonants had been marked in green and the preceeding
vowels marked short.

The student would then be asked if he/she could
make any generalizations. If he/she could, the student
would then be invited to imitate the author's style.
The first step might be to take some of the marked words
and change only the short vowel. If the student can do
this, it is quite likely he/she is secure with the generalization he/she has discovered.

250

Determining Lesson 6

Focus: Graphophonemic Cues

Purpose: To develop use of graphophonemic cues while learning consonant "t" sound, and "tr" blend.

Introduction: Lead a discussion about twins. Tell the children that in the story they will read, there are several words that begin with "t" and "tr". Have children read story silently.

Interacting: Reread stories orally to the class.

Expanding: Play: I am going to Boston and I am taking a _____. Child must repeat all words before and add a new "t" word. Write a story using words beginning with "t".

Evaluation: As children reread orally, observe who needs more help with "t" letter-sound relationships and check to see if they understand that more cues are given if they finish reading sentence, or even go to the following sentence.

Gina and Tina are twins.

They like to play with their toys.

One of their favorite toys is a doll called Tammy.

Tammy is a talking doll and the girls take good care of her.

Tammy can walk and talk.

Gina and Tina often take her to town when they go to shop.

Gina and Tina have a trunk for Tammy's clothes.

The girls have a tricycle also.

They take Tammy for a ride on the tricycle.

Gina and Tina enjoy Tammy so much that it is a thrill to watch them play with her.

Determining Lesson 7

Focus: Graphophonemic Cues

Purpose: To familiarize the child with graphic stimulus and instill a love of reading and books. Show that reading can be fun.

Introduction: Since there is only one copy of the book, I will use an opaque projector. The lesson will involve graphic-phonic stimulus, rhyming words, and predicting repetitious phrases that the children will anticipate and enjoy.

Interacting: The story used is <u>Never Tease A Weasel</u> by Jean Conder Soule. We will follow along and read the story from the screen.

Expanding: The children may want to read the book by themselves. We may discuss teasing and what can happen to those who get teased or those who tease too much.

Evaluation: Listen to retelling of the story to measure comprehension and sequence of events.

Determining Lesson 8

1. In order to prepare for this strategy lesson, the poem "What Is Pink?" by Christina Rosetti, would be read aloud to the children on different occasions.

2. The poem would be expanded on by discussing other possibilities for each question—perhaps in rhyme.

3. Finally, the children would be given a copy of the poem.

4. We could then read the poem together until all were secure in the words and meaning.

5. At this point, we would begin to explore some of the graphophonic cues. Each child would need a box of crayons and a number of copies of the poem.

6. Our first exploration would be of the color words. Read the poem and as we reach a color word, we will color-code it.

7. At a later date, we would explore the structure of a question by:

    a) picking out the word "what",
    b) picking out the question marks,
    c) writing questions of our own using the "What is _____?" format. Our questions could take the form of riddles to be answered by classmates.

8. At still a later date, we could explore rhyming words, taking note of the following points:

    a) rhyming words have different beginning sounds but the same vowel and ending sounds:

pink	red	yellow	green
brink	bed	mellow	between

    b) sometimes the rhyming words sound almost the same but do not look the same:

    white - light   blue - through

    c) poetry need not always rhyme:

    violet - twilight

9. Expansions of these points would include:

    a) expanded color word list - using poster board and a large box of Crayola crayons: write the color word/words and paste the crayon beside it.

    b) expanded work on word patterns and phonetic generalizations (examples, light, bright, fight, etc.)

    c) as colors are added to color-word chart above add a new stanza to the original poem.

Notes: This poem is found in "Sounds of Numbers" by Bill Martin, Jr. and Peggy Bragan. The illustrations are delightful and a teaching tool in themselves.

As mentioned earlier, the children would need new copies of the poem to be supplied at different points. Also, the preliminary work would be aimed at preserving the character of the poem. These preliminary explorations (pictures, etc.) would be collected into individual booklets and the follow-up work added to this booklet.

Observing children as they read orally will often reveal difficulty with structure or function words, such as: through, though, thought; for, from, off, of; was, saw; when, then; what, that; and so forth. These are called habitual associations. Frequently, habitually associated words in reading are caused by instruction which isolates words on flash cards, word lists, and ditto worksheets for practice. Words having highly similar graphic features should be presented in a highly unambiguous meaningful context. These words have a very low semantic profile and are easily confused when given to readers in isolation. The reader is unable to apply syntactic and semantic cues and is limited in using prediction, confirming, and correcting strategies with graphophonemic cues. Using miscue analysis and observing repeated miscues will inform the teacher about a reader who may benefit from strategy lessons designed to reduce or eliminate this difficulty.

The typical way of dealing with a reader experiencing difficulty with highly similar graphic shapes is to write a short story in which one form is embedded in the story. One form is used repetitively and predictably throughout the selection. Then a second story uses the other form in another way. Finally, both items are used within the context of the story in a highly predictable and unambiguous manner.

Strategy lessons for habitually associated words should be given only to a reader who has demonstrated repeated difficulties with the similar graphic items. This is the approach to use with all types of strategy lessons. Sometimes strategy lessons may be planned to determine if there is a consistent difficulty with some specific graphophonemic cue. Determining lessons would be planned for readers who have had miscue analyzed in one or two story contexts only. If the determining lessons demonstrates more difficulty, than other strategy lessons should be planned to develop the reader's use of the specific graphophonemic problem. However, the teacher must be aware that it may not be the graphophonemic difficulty, but rather, related to syntactic/

semantic cues and strategies. The following lessons
illustrate reading strategy lessons designed for readers
experiencing difficulty with highly similar graphic
structures.

Determining Lesson 9

Focus:	Habitual Association
Purpose:	To develop graphic discrimination be-tween <u>through</u> and <u>thought</u> by focusing on the use of through in a story.
Introduction:	Tell the child there are three stories about a little boy named Joe. Read each story silently.
Interacting:	When the child is finished, he could read the story orally. Discuss each story.
Expanding:	Ask the child to write a story or several sentences using the word <u>through</u> and <u>thought</u>.
Evaluation:	Have the child read the short stories containing the words <u>through</u> and <u>thought</u> to see if he has learned the graphic discrimination.

A Walk In The Woods

Joe walked through the door, down the sidewalk,
and through the gate. He was going for a walk through
the woods. As he walked through the bushes and the
trees, he saw a little deer. When the deer saw Joe,
it ran off through the woods. As Joe walked on through
the woods, he saw many more little animals running
through the grass. Finally, it was time for Joe to go
home. When he got home, he walked through the door
saying to his Mother, "I just had a nice walk through
the woods."

A Picnic

Joe thought it looked like a good day for a
picnic. He thought it would be fun to ask his friend,
Tom, to go on the picnic.

"But what if it rains?" Joe thought to himself.

He thought he would invite Tom anyway. Then Joe thought about what he would need for the picnic. He thought it would be good to bring peanut butter sandwiches and Kool-Aid.

Soon it began to rain. Joe thought to himself, "Well, maybe we can go on a picnic tomorrow."

Joe and Tom

Joe and Tom didn't know what to do. They had played inside all day because it had rained. Soon the rain stopped and the sun peeked through the clouds.

Tom said, "Let's go out and play baseball." Joe thought that was a good idea.

"Okay, Tom, we can run through the puddles, too!"

Joe and Tom got their bat and ball and ran through the door. On the way to the baseball field they ran through water puddles. They played ball for a while. Soon it started to rain again. They thought that it hadn't been such a good idea to play baseball.

When Tom and Joe got home they were soaking wet.

"Who thought it was a good idea to play baseball," said Joe.

Determining Lesson 10

Habitual Association Was-Saw

Jane got a new pair of glasses from the eye doctor. The doctor put the glasses on Jane's face and told her to look in the morror. Jane saw herself in the glasses for the first time. She did not like what she saw. "Oh no," said Jane. "I hate these glasses."

The doctor told Jane to go outside and look around. Jane saw an airplane high in the sky. She saw a cat coming down the sidewalk a block away. She saw many things that she never saw before. "Maybe these glasses aren't so bad after all," she thought.

Wendy was taking her dog, George, for a walk down the street. It was late at night and everything was very lonely and dark. Suddenly, Wendy heard footsteps behind her. She was afraid to turn around. Was it a ghost? Was it a wild animal? What was it? Wendy walked faster and faster. When she turned the corner toward home, the streetlight was bright and suddenly she could see that her friend, Ton, was walking his dog, also, and had been following Wendy.

What Andy saw was enought to make anyone happy. It was Andy's birthday and his parents bought him a new ten-speed bicycle. It was the neatest bike Andy had ever saw. He saw that it had a brown leather saddle and it was a full 26-inch bike. Andy couldn't wait to take his bike down the street to show his friends. He saw that his friend, Tony, was standing on the corner so he jumped on his bike and away he rode!

The following examples of strategy lessons focus on specific structural relationships in word functions, referred to as compound words, monophonemic structures, inflected endings, and contractions.

Determining Lesson 11

Focus: Compound Words

Purpose: To develop the child's ability to
                    recognize compound words and use them
                    in the context of a sentence.

Introduction: Use posterboard, felt markers, and
                    scissors to make a set of game cards
                    as shown:

I must buy another _____ for class tomorrow
----
note   book

```
+---------------------------------------------------------------+
| They didn't drown because each one was                        |
| wearing a _____.                                  |
|---------------------------------------------------------------|
|    life                        jacket                         |
|                                                               |
+---------------------------------------------------------------+
```

Tell the child he needs to separate the small cards from the large ones and put the large cards in a stack and the small cards face up on his desk.

Interaction: Have the child read the sentence on the top large card. A word is missing-- it is a compound word. Tell him to look through the small cards and make a compound word that will make sense in the sentence.

Expanding: Have the child write sentences using compound words--draw in the compound. Example: I like to stand in the _____.

Evaluation: Game pieces will fit together if compound word is properly formed. Encourage child to read to you his sentences using pictures for the compound words.

Determining Lesson 12

Focus: Morphophonemic Structures

Purpose: To develop the use of graphophonemic cues while learning the ending "ght".

Introduction: Lead a discussion that there are many words that end with the letters -ght. The letters -gh are silent. The t is sounded.

Interacting: Give copies of the sentences below to the children. Have them complete the sentences with words ending in ght.

258

1. Where were you when the _____ went out?

2. I think I _____ do my homework now.

3. You _____ a really neat shirt.

4. Dad _____ a ten-pound bass.

5. Make a turn to the _____ .

6. John _____ me how to play chess.

7. Our country has _____ for its great freedom.

8. This baseball cap is too _____ .

9. Gee, Mom, I _____ you said I could go!

10. Dad said we _____ go to the sports car races.

Expanding: Write riddles about the -ght words. Share them with the class.

Evaluation: Have the children read some of their sentences to see if they have used acceptable words.

Determining Lesson 13

Morphophonemic Structures

The following lessons were planned for one student who confused forms of the words start/stare. Because the stories were simple and one story related to the Social Studies activity of making leis, the children read the stories silently, then orally as a group, discussed forms of the words start/stare that made sense, then completed the word selection and Cloze type exercises individually. Any corrections were discussed individually where needed and often were self-corrected as the student read the story orally.

Start/Started

As Sam started to walk home from school, it began to rain. Sam started to run fast so that he wouldn't get very wet. He came to the corner and didn't see any cars coming. As he started to run across the street, he heard a horn start to blow at him. He

jumped back on the sidewalk. Before he <u>started</u> across
the street again, he looked carefully to see if there
were any more cars. When he was sure it was safe, he
<u>started</u> walking across the street.

Start/Started/Starting

As the children were <u>starting</u> to make the leis
for their luau, Tony asked Steve to trade some green
tissue paper for some of Steve's red paper. Steve was
glad to trade with Tony.

Steve was just ready to start his red and green
lei when Mike asked if he would trade some red tissue
for yellow tissue. Steve gladly traded some of his
red tissue for the yellow tissue.

Before Steve could start his red, green, yellow
lei, Joe asked him to trade red tissue for blue tissue.

At last as Steve <u>started</u> his lei, he saw that
it was going to be pretty. He now would be wearing a
red, green, yellow, and blue lei for the luau. He was
glad that he hadn't <u>started</u> his lei before he had
traded with his friends.

Start/Started/Starting

Choose the word that makes sense in each sentence.

1. Dad (start, started, starting) the car.

2. Matt and Bill had (start, started, starting)
   swimming across the lake.

3. When we got to the ball park, the game had
   already (start, started, starting).

4. When mother was ready to (start, started,
   starting) doing dishes, she asked me to help.

5. Dad asked me if I knew how to (start, started,
   starting) the lawnmower.

6. They are (start, started, starting) the game
   right now.

7. Wait until we all sit down at the table before you (start, started, starting) to eat.

8. The baby is (start, started, starting) to
   cry.

Use start, started, starting to make the sentences make sense.

The children went to the cafeteria to eat their lunch. Just as Sally _____ to eat her lunch, she lost a tooth. She could feel that a new tooth was _____ to come in. When Sally was ready to _____ eating again, she was careful not to chew on the new tooth.

The third grade boys were going to play a base-ball game in the park. Sam said he would be there by the time the game was ready to _____ . He was to be the catcher in the _____ line-up. When he got to the park, the game had already _____ . Sam saw that Bill was taking his place as catcher. He _____ to cry but the coach said he could play later in the game.

Stare-Stared-Staring

Bob was going to the pet shop to pick out a new puppy. As he got there, he stopped at the window. There was a little brown puppy staring right straight at him. Bob stared back at the puppy. The little puppy began wagging his tail.

He stared up at Bob, as if to say, "Please, take me home!? The longer Bob stared at the little brown puppy, the more he knew that he could take that puppy home and love him forever.

John stared at the broken window. He couldn't believe his eyes. He didn't think he had hit the ball so hard. Just than he saw someone on the other side of the broken glass staring back at him. It was his father staring straight at him and he didn't look very happy. John stared at his father and his father stared back at John. Finally his father said, "Come in the house, son."

261

Stare/Stared/Staring

1. The little boy (stare, stared, staring) at the little puppy in the window.

2. The children stood at the window (stare, stared, staring) at the pretty snow that was falling.

3. Mother told us not to (stare, stared, staring) at the boy in the wheelchair.

4. Dick (stare, stared, staring) at the checkers to try to plan a way to beat his dad in the game they were playing.

5. Everyone (stare, stared, staring) as the best player on the team struck out.

6. The little girl (stare, stared, staring) at her new doll.

7. Sally (stare, stared, staring) at the torn place in her new dress.

8. The new student cried because the children had been (stare, stared, staring) at him all day.

Forms of stare - start

"Don't stare at me," said Mother. "You heard what I said. Start doing those dishes now, or you are going to bed."

Tommy didn't mean to make his mother cross, but it wasn't easy going to a new school. All the boys and girls seemed to be staring at him all day. He didn't like to be stared at. It made him feel funny.

At last, Tommy stopped staring at his mother and started to cry. Mother put her arms around Tommy and he started to tell her how hard it was starting to go to a new school and having everyone stare at you all day.

In each sentences, there is a word used incorrectly. Cross out the incorrect word, and write the correct form above it.

1. Clyde and Mark starting walking to school.

2. Dad will started the lawnmower for you.

3. The boys were started the baseball game.

4. Does school starting the same time this year?

5. He has start to walk home.

6. Our school was started to save box tops to buy playground equipment.

7. The little boy stare at the puppy in the window.

8. Mother told me not to stared at the boy in the wheelchair.

9. Dick staring at the checkers to try to plan a way to beat his dad in the game they were playing.

10. The little girl sat stare at her new doll.

11. Sally staring at the torn place on her new dress.

12. Everyone stare as the best player on the team struck out.

Developing Syntactic Cues

Readers from the beginning need to have opportunities to apply the grammatical structures of language or syntactic cues they already know to the reading process. Many readers who begin reading instruction with an emphasis on sequential isolated letter, letter-sound relationship, and word-centered approaches tend not to apply their knowledge of how language goes together. Other readers are not easily influenced by repeated isolated graphophonemic instruction and naturally use their understanding of how language is ordered. They apply what they know from oral language to written language. The written language presented to children at the literacy acquisition stage of reading should be connected discourse. This will enable each learner to relate his/her oral language abilities to written structure.

The development of applying syntactic cues to the reading process should not be separate from graphophonemic and semantic cues. Frequently, instructional materials present the learner with isolated language structures, such as phrases, sentences, and short paragraphs. These instructional practices tend to short-circuit the learner's efforts to apply syntactic and semantic cues and predicting, confirming, and correcting

263

strategies. The learner is unable to use the redundancy
and constraints in language to predict language structures and construct meaning. The effective reader is
able to construct meaning by predicting and confirming
syntactic structures that sound like language. The
reader's focus on constructing meaning is possible as
the reader applies transformational rules by monitoring
grammatical structures that are produced. However, producing a surface syntactic structure does not always
result in meaning. Some readers are adept in producing
appropriate surface syntactic structures, but have not
developed a deep structure and decoded the message.

There is a close linkage between syntactic and
semantic cues in the reading process. It is thought
that meaning is possible when the reader goes through
the syntactic system. This view proposes that meaning
results as the reader processes the grammatical structures. In other words, there can be no construction of
meaning unless the reader has produced a representation
of the author's language structure. However, the reader
must focus on building meaning if syntactic cues are to
be useful. The sense of the language enables the reader
to predict appropriate graphophonemic and grammatical
cues.

The Goodman model of the reading process takes
the point of view that meaning is possible as the reader
processes syntactic cues to get to the meaning. Frank
Smith, on the other hand, proposes that the use of syntactic cues is predicated on meaning. The reader's sense
of the printed information enables a reader to use
knowledge of linguistic structures. Miscue analysis related to Goodman's model of the reading process is
based on the former view. Meaning is constructed
through the reader's use of syntactic structures. The
reader should monitor his/her reading to determine if
what is being read, "sound like language." At the same
time, the reader is to be aware of meaning--"Does it
make sense?"

Reading strategy lessons are planned related to
miscue analysis using the Reading Miscue Inventory
(see Chapter IV). A reader's profile may show a weakness in grammatical relationships, including either
difficulty in substituting structures of similar function or constructing appropriate grammatical structures,
or both. Strategy lessons may be designed for a reader
who frequently substitutes different word functions,
such as, confusing nouns for verbs, nouns for pronouns,
prepositions for conjunctions, etc. However, most

readers have a relatively high ability, based on intuitive knowledge of how words function in language, substituting structures that have the same function, even though the substitution may be a non-word, i.e., "destrived" for "decided." A reader may experience frequent difficulty with specific clause markers, i.e., noun markers such as: "a", "an", and "the"; verb markers, i.e., "are going. . . ", "is going", "was going", "were going", "has gone", "have gone" (indicating tense; and question markers, such as: "why", "why", "how", "when", "which." Habitually associated words that have a high graphic similarity cause some readers difficulty. Frequently these highly similar graphic word structures may have the same grammatical function but different meanings in text. Structures such as prepositions are easily confused: "in", "on", "into", "onto"; "for, "from", "of", "off"; "through", "though", "thought." Adverbial clauses and adjectives frequently result in substitutions that may cause minor or more significant changes in meaning. There are generally more options available to the reader concerning adverbs and adjectives. The author's choice of adverbs and adjectives may differ from the reader's language experience and predictions. The ineffective reader, relying heavily on graphophonemic cues, not monitoring for meaning and who doesn't bring his/her syntactic cues to the process, may substitute non-word structures that have high graphophonemic similarity. The more effective reader will often substitute synonyms or word structures that are highly graphically dissimilar, yet retain the same grammatical function as the author's structure. For example, the ineffective reader may read: "She ran happily down the dusty, winding road," as "She ran hugly down the dity, wending road." The effective reader may read: "She ran merrily down the curved, dirt road."

Determining Lesson 1

Focus: Syntactic Cues: Nouns

Purpose: To develop predicting strategies with nouns.

Introduction: This is a story about Scott. I have left some words out of the story. See if you can be a detective and discover the words that belong in the blanks.

Interacting: Present copies or use the overhead and work together (see story).

265

Expanding:	Do you think Scott had a good idea? What would you do? Write possible solutions on the board to be read.
Evaluation:	Observe who needs further help in this type of activity.

Scott came out of the house and locked the _____ behind him. This was the first time his mother let him have the house key.

Scott's mother had gone to the airport to pick up his _____ who was coming for a visit. She would be away for more than two hours.

Scott was afraid he might lose the _____. He knew that he would have to keep it in a safe _____.

"If I put it in my shirt _____, it might fall out when I play with the _____," though Scott. "And I have a _____ in my pants picket, so that won't do."

"I can put the _____ on a string around my _____," thought Scott. "Then I can't lose it."

Answers:	door, grandfather (or relative or frient), key place, pocket, boys, hold, key, neck.

Determining Lesson 2

Focus:	Syntactic Cues: Verbs
Purpose:	To provide practice in predicting and to review verbs as action words.
Introduction:	Here is a story about a girl just your age. See if you can fill in the missing words in the story. The missing words are action words which tell what someone is doing.
Interacting:	Pass out the stories and read the first sentence together. Supply the missing words.

Expanding: Think about what would have happened if Jan had not heard her mother call. We will talk about your new ending when we have finished reading our stories.

Evaluation: Check to see if anyone is having trouble. Tell children any words you think they will not know.

Jan _____ straight home from schoo. and _____ her clothes. Then she _____her mother if she could _____ out to play. "Yes," said her mother, "but you must_____ home in one hour. I will need you to _____ the table for supper. You do not have a watch so I will _____ you when I want you._

Jan ____ her friend Amy. They _____ a ball back and forth on the sidewalk. Then they _____ their bikes.

Jan _____ close to her house and _____ for her mother to call. Mother _____ at 4:00 and Jan _____ home to _____ the table.

Answers: Went, changed, asked, go, come, set, call, played, threw, rode, stayed, listened, called, went, set.

Determining Lesson 3

Focus: Syntactic cues: Verbs

Purpose: To develop use of syntactic cues with predicting verbs to comprehend a story.

Introduction: The child or children have just finished listening to the story record, Bread and Jam for Frances. They are given an activity sheet with missing words. Those who can do it alone will go ahead, while I work with the others.

Interacting: The children will read the sentences and predict the missing verbs in the story.

267

Everyone was at the table. Father was
_____ his egg. Mother was _____
her egg. Gloria was _____ egg, too.
Frances was _____ bread and jam.
and so on.

Comprehension Questions:

1. Why didn't Frances eat her eggs?
2. What did Frances eat for lunch and dinner?
3. What happened when Frances got to eat all the bread and jam she wanted to?
4. Do you think that Frances will eat her food from now on?

Expanding: The children may want to go to the book and read it for themselves or look at the pictures. They may also make a list of foods that they like to eat, foods that are good for them, and discuss why.

Evaluation: Observe individual children to check use of predicting and syntactic cues.

Determining Lesson 4

Focus: Syntactic cues: Pronouns

Purpose: To strengthen the child's use of pronouns.

Introduction: Take a story from the basal reader that contains some pronouns. Point out some of the pronouns and have the child tell you who the pronoun is referring to. Make sure this is a story the child has already read so he is somewhat familiar with it.

Interaction: Have the child read the story independently and insert the correct pronouns. When this is finished, let him read the story orally so he can hear his correct or incorrect responses. If a response is incorrect, help him find the person or thing being talked about.

Expanding: Draw a line from each pronoun to the person or thing it refers to.

Evaluation: Have the child write a story about his family and underline all the pronouns he uses.

Determining Lesson 5

Focus: Syntactic cues: Adjectives

Purpose: To develop syntactic cues with emphasis on the function and placement of adjectives in the sentence structure.

Introduction: The children have been listening to the book, A Ghost Story by Bill Martin, Jr., read aloud by the teacher or on tape. Lead a discussion in which the children are given the opportunity to describe various objects around the room.

Interacting: Hand them a worksheet with only the word "dark" left out. They may read along with you or read by themselves and discover how the story sounds without the describing word. Discuss which way they like the story best. Discuss how this story would change if other adjectives were used in place of "dark." For example: In a bright, bright woods; In a green, green woods. Discuss why the words "dark, dark" always come in front of the words being described.

Expanding: Whenever a story such as this one is presented to the child in the Literacy Acquisition Stage you might be prepared to deal with any fears the child might have. The children might enjoy drawing a picture of something "spooky" in an attempt to bring their fears out in the open and deal with them.

Evaluation: Observe whether the children can discover other describing words in favorite stories.

Determining Lesson 6

Focus: Syntactic cues - word endings "er" and
                 "est"

Approaches: Reading Aloud and Language Experience.

Purpose: To aid students in developing ability
                 to use syntactic cues, to clarify the
                 use of endings on root words (er, est).
                 Also to develop the use of sampling,
                 predicting, and correcting in order to
                 obtain comprehension in reading.

Introduction: After asking class to think of the
                 biggest thing they had ever seen or
                 could think of and using their suggest-
                 ions for comparison questions (Do you
                 think a whale is bigger or smaller than
                 a bus? Was King Kong bigger or smaller
                 than a skyscraper? What is the biggest
                 animal, person, vehicle you have ever
                 seen?) the class listened while I read
                 aloud "The Biggest Bear" by Lynd Ward.

Interaction: Questions were asked using words with
                 "er" ending.

                 Is Todd bigger than Eric?

                 Who is taller - Rosa or Alice?

                 Which runs faster - rabbits or boys? etc.

                 Students answered using words with "est"
                 endings.

                 Todd is the biggest.

                 Alice is the tallest.

                 Boys run the fastest. etc.

                 The following story was then read by
                 each student and words were chosen to
                 fill in the blank spaces.

                 Determining Lesson 7

Focus: Syntactic cues - word endings "ed", "ry".
                 "er", "ing"

In these exercises, the student will use base words and forms of words depending on which sounds correct and makes sense.

Exercise I

It was time for lunch and Danny was hungry for a big peanut butter and jelly sandwich. As he went to the cupboard, Danny saw there was no bread.

He decided to run to the bakery for some freshly _____ bread. Danny walked into the _____ and found Mr. Hill, the _____. Mr. Hill was busy _____ bread. Danny bought two loaves of the bread Mr. Hill had just _____.

It was time for lunch and Danny was hungry for a big peanut butter and jelly sandwich. As he went to the cupboard, Danny saw there was no bread.

He decided to run to the bakery for some freshly baked bread. Danny walked into the bakery and found Mr. Hill, the baker. Mr. Hill was busy baking bread. Danny bought two loaves of the bread Mr. Hill had just baked.

Determining Lesson 8

Focus: Syntactic cues: constrasting relation-
                ships

Purpose: Using syntactical cues and redundancy
                to predict contrasting relationship in
                meaning.

Introduction: This lesson is designed for students in
                a 10th grade remedial reading class who
                had difficulty recognizing contrasting
                relationships of ideas in a story pre-
                viously read.

Interacting: The teacher wrote this sentence on the
                chalkboard and asked the students to
                read it.

Sentence: Mary loves the new house,
but Diane _____.
Teacher: This unfinished sentence tells
us how two girls feel about their new
house. Mary is happy about it, but how
do you think Diane feels?
Student's response: Sad and unhappy.
Teacher: Why?
Students: She doesn't like the new
house.
Teacher: How do you know this?
Student: The word "but" is the clue!
(Other responses were given)
Teacher: It tells us, even before we
finish the sentence, that Diane's feelings will be different from or opposite
of Mary's:

The teacher completed the sentence
with the student's response. The student's completed sentence read like
this: Mary loves the new house, but
Diane hates it.
Teacher: Because "but" is a word showing that a different idea is coming, it
is called a contrast word or signal.
The teacher wrote these contrasting
words on the chalkboard and told the
students to watch out for them in print
to help them find different or opposite
ideas in print.

Contrasting words: however, but, even
though, never the less, yet, although
whereas, on the other hand.

The teacher then asked the students to read another sentence written on the chalkboard and guess ahead with
the next sentence.

I tried to carry the milk bottles home
carefully, nevertheless, . . .

272

(a) I didn't drop a single bottle.

(b) I stumbled and they are shattered.

(c) I left them at the store.

The students responded that sentence (b) made sense.
The contrasting signal, nevertheless, indicated that a
different idea followed.

Expanding activities: Activity I

The students are to choose the one sentence that makes
the most sense for each set of sentences. They are to
circle the contrast signal in the correct sentence
and underline the two main sentences twice.

1) a. Duncan didn't like school; on the other hand, his
       brother had a good job.

   b. Duncan didn't like school; on the other hand, he
       was on the honor roll.

   c. Duncan didn't like school; on the other hand, he
       was on the hockey team.

2) a. Although there was nothing funny, Bill began to
       laugh.

   b. Although there was nothing funny, Bill was very
       serious.

   c. Although there was nothing funny, Bill thought it
       was a real tragedy.

Determining Lesson 9

Focus: Syntactic cues: grammatical relation-
                ships

Purpose: To develop syntactic cues using
                predicting strategies. To improve
                awareness of grammatical relation-
                ships.

Introduction:	A week or two earlier the students each wrote a story about their experiences during a field trip to Washington, D.C.
Interacting:	During the first exercise, the students are given copies of their own stories with specific words deleted. They must complete them and compare them to their original paper. The student and teacher should discuss any differences that occur. During the second exercise on a different day, each student is given a copy of another student's story with words deleted. These, too, must be completed at their desks. Again, any variations from the originals should be discussed, e.g., did the alternative words make sense or alter the author's intended meaning, etc.
Expanding:	Have students write "newspaper articles" describing the trip or have students make a scrapbook of the trip.
Evaluating:	Circulating throughout the room and make sure no students are experiencing difficulties.

Sample Story

My Trip to Washington, D.C.

Last week I went to Washington, D.C. with the rest of my class. It was a lot _____ fun. We did _____ different, exciting things. I'm not sure which one _____ liked best. I would like to write about some of the things we _____.

During our first _____ there, we visited _____ Smithsonian Museum. After than, we _____ lunch. Then we took a tour of the _____ House. We did not _____ the president, though. Then we went back _____ motel. The _____ day we visited the Capitol Building. There _____ many people there. Then we went _____ the Washington Monument. We also _____ the lincoln and Jefferson

Memorials. That night we ate _____ in a fancy restaurant.
_____ third day in Washington was our _____ day before
we went home. We toured more _____ of the Smithsonian
Museum. _____ also visited the FBI building, the Library of Congress, and the Botanical _____. We all
_____well that night _____ we were so tired!

The _____ morning we drove back _____. I
really enjoyed my _____ to Washington. I hope some
day I can go back again.

Sample Answersheet

My Trip to Washington, D.C.

Last <u>week</u> I <u>went</u> to Washington, D. C. with the
rest of my class. It was a lot <u>of</u> fun. We did <u>so</u> many
different exciting things. I'm not sure which one <u>I</u>
liked best. I would like to write about some of the
things we <u>did</u>.

During our first <u>day</u> there, we visited the
Smithsonian Museum. After that we <u>ate</u> lunch. Then we
took a tour of the <u>White</u> House. We did not <u>see</u> the
president, though. Then we went <u>to</u> our motel. The
<u>next</u> day we visited the Capitol Building. There <u>were</u>
many people there. Then we went <u>to</u> the Washington
Monument. We also <u>visited</u> the LIncoln and Jefferson
Memorials. That night we ate <u>dinner</u> in a fancy restaurant. <u>Our</u> third day in Washington was our <u>last</u> day before we went home. We toured more <u>of</u> the Smithsonian.
<u>We</u> also visited the FBI building. That afternoon we
went to the Supreme <u>Court</u> Building, the Library of Congress, and the Botanical <u>Gardens</u>. We all <u>slept</u> well
that night because we were so tired!

The <u>next</u> morning we drove back home. I really
enjoyed my <u>trip</u> to Washington. I hope some day I can go
back again.

275

Developing Semantic Cues

To develop effectiveness as a reader, it is necessary that the reader apply available semantic cues with graphophonemic and syntactic cues, predicting and confirming meaning. The reader has access to his/her own background experience, concept development and vocabulary. Predicting, confirming and correcting strategies with semantic cues enable the reader to monitor reading for meaning.

Miscue analysis may provide the teacher information to identify reader's strengths and needs in predicting, confirming and correcting strategies with semantic cues. Many poor readers who have had extensive isolated skills instruction tend not to apply their prior knowledge, conceptual development and vocabulary to what is being read. A reader's greatest resource is his/her knowledge of language structure (grammar) and semantic potential. Unfortunately, an extreme focus on graphophonemic information at the beginning and continuous stages of reading development, diverts the reader's attention from applying semantic cues. Frequently poor readers demonstrate a high use of graphophonemic cues and, as a result, a low comprehending ability (e.g., miscues that are semantically unacceptable and not corrected). Usually this pattern also correlates with a low overall comprehension of the material.

The strengths and weaknesses of a reader's use of the semantic cueing system must be examined in relationship to the reader's syntactic and graphophonemic cueing system as well as correction strategies. In addition, the teacher must observe the reader's overall comprehension of a given selection in relation to the semantic quality of the miscues.

There are several types of strategy lessons a teacher may plan related to a particular reader's weaknesses in applying semantic cues and predicting, confirming and correcting strategies. However, most readers who have an observed need to develop more effective use of semantic cues, generally show an overanalysis on graphophonemic cues. The miscues generally show a high graphophonemic similarity, but result in meaning loss.

Some readers also indicate a weakness in applying syntactic cues. This type of reader produces many unacceptable grammatical structures and as a result there are many unacceptable semantic structures.

Reading strategy lessons for developing semantic cues are given below. A brief description follows illustrating the reader who may benefit from each type of lesson. Sometimes strategy lessons should be used as determining lessons. The determining lesson is designed to identify whether a reader, in fact, has a real difficulty predicting/confirming semantic cues. The assessment of a reader's difficulty with applying the semantic cueing system may be indicated from several analyses of the reader's miscues. There needs to be an on-going monitoring of a reader's performance to assess how effectively a given reader is integrating all cueing systems and strategies in the construction of meaning.

The Cloze Procedure: Selected Deletions

Any reader who shows the following miscue pattern may benefit from a cloze procedure with selected deleted structures:

> graphophonemic - high
> syntactic - high to low
> semantic - low
> correcting - low
> comprehension - low

A reader with the above pattern needs to rely less on the graphic display and more on his/her natural predicting strategy with prior knowledge and experience. The deleted words may be every fifth word, or if the reader is also expressing difficulty with grammatical structures, certain function words or parts of speech may be deleted.

The reading material used for cloze with selected deletions should be related as much as possible to the reader's experiences and interests. This will enable the reader to be successful and develop the awareness that one doesn't need all the print. For young readers the passages should be relatively brief, while older readers will be able to handle longer material.

Using cloze with selected deletions is not a natural way to read. We don't find blanks when we read. It should be understood that cloze is only one instructional technique and should not be overused. Cloze tends to be a contrived instructional activity not like real reading situations. Therefore, it is suggested that cloze activities be used only with readers who have an extreme reliance on graphophonemic cues resulting in very low comprehension. The deleted cloze technique eliminates the reader's over-dependence on graphic information.

The strategy lesson may be done orally or have the reader read the selection silently and predict the structure to fill in the blank. The reader should be told to read through the entire selection predicting the structure that will make sense.

When constructing the passage the beginning should be kept intact. If the selection is a paragraph there should be no deletions in the first and second sentence. If using several paragraphs don't delete words in the first paragraph, this allows the reader to construct meaning before encountering deletions. Any synonym or word which means the same as the deleted structure should be accepted. The synonyms, or words similar in meaning supplied by the student or different meanings should be discussed by the teacher with students. If the words are written by the student misspelling is accepted as appropriate.

The following are examples of lessons using cloze with selected deletions:

Determining Lesson 1

Focus: Predicting - Semantic Cues
                          - Syntactic Cues

Objective: Pupil will understand how context cues are
                used in reading.

Motivation: This story has some missing words. As you
                read, I want you to supply the missing
                words.

Development: Accept reasonable responses. If necessary,
                remind the child to read the rest of the
                sentence and try to think of a word that
                makes sense in the sentence. If the child
                cannot supply a word, suggest two or three
                words from which a choice is made.

Expanding: Have child draw a picture related to the
                story.

Evaluation: Observe the child to see if he or she
              uses semantic cues to predict.

        One day Tom was going down the street. All
of a sudden he saw a billfold! He picked it up and
looked for an identification card. He found one.

        _____ Tom saw a twenty _____ bill. What
should he _____? No one had seen _____ pick up
the billfold. Tom _____ take the money and _____
away the billfold.

        Tom _____ to take the money _____ of the
billfold.

        Then _____ thought, "What if this _____ really
needs the twenty _____?" "Besides, the money is _____
mine."

        Tom found a _____ booth and called the _____.
A man answered.

        When Tom _____ the man he had _____ the bill-
fold, the man _____ greatful.

        Tom took _____ billfold to the man's _____.
The man thanked him _____ his honesty.

        Tom _____ like the richest boy _____ town.

                Determining Lesson 2

Focus: Predicting Meaning Using Cloze Procedure

Purpose: To help the pupil use context, semantic
                syntactic and predicting cues.

Introduction: The teacher selects a paragraph eliminat-
                ing every fifth word, and replaces it
                with a blank line.

Procedure: The pupil predicts possible words as he
                or she reads the selection. Discuss the
                predicted words with the pupil.

Evaluation: Listen to the pupil's predictions to find
                out if they are semantically acceptable.
                Continue with other stories until the

                        279

pupil is better able to get meaning from
the printed material.

Example: This would be a quiet evening, Joan
thought. It ____ my first time alone at
_____.

Then she heard a _____ in the basement. She _____ herself that she would
be _____ and find out what _____ noise
was.

She walked to the basement door _____
turned on the light. _____ crept down
the steps.

All _____ a sudden, something
rushed _____ her. Joan screamed.

Then _____ saw that it was _____
cat, Buster. He had _____ over a bucket.

"What _____ relief!" said Joan.

The Picnic

One day Anna and Janet decided to have a picnic
in the park. They fixed cheese sandwiches and got something to drink. The girls put a blanket on the ground
and poured the cold drink into cups. Just then they
heard a buzzing noise. It sounded like a bee.

"If we sit very _____, it may go away," said
Anna.

Sure enough, it soon ____ away. The girls
went on _____. A little later a butterfly landed on
Anna's _____.

"Don't move," said Janet, "It'll go away."

Sure enough the butterfly flew up to a branch
on a _____. The girls continued to enjoy their picnic.
Suddenly the girls heard a loud _____.

280

"What's that?" asked Anna.

"Oh dear," said Janet. "Here comes my _____
brother.

William came _____ over to the girls. He was
yelling at the top of his _____.

"Oh boy!" he _____. "I want to have a picnic
too."

"I guess this is the end of our quiet picnic,"
said Janet. "This is one noisy visitor who won't go
_____."

Determining Lesson 3

Focus: Predicting Semantic Cues

Purpose: To associate oral and written language.
                To use context cues.

Introduction: Tell pupils that they are going to help
                tell a story by saying a word each time
                you pause. Read the story, pausing when
                you come to a blank. When a child sug-
                gests a word, write it on the chalkboard
                for pupils to read.

Expanding: The children will draw a picture to il-
                lustrate their favorite part of the story.
                Some children may enjoy trying to read
                the story by themselves.

Evaluation: Observe children's ability to make use of
                prediction.

Cloze Method - Key Word Deletion

Some readers become very uptight about continuing to read when they come to an unfamiliar structure
or word. If readers have the impression, which too many
readers have, that each word must be pronounced exactly,
then they usually resort to a sounding out process.
Readers who do this frequently produce miscues with high
graphophonemic similarity and usually have low semantic
profiles, resulting in lower comprehension over a whole
story or selection. A teacher may identify readers who

have developed a habit of sounding out words by listening regularly to samples of the readers' oral reading.

In group oral reading situations and during
silent sustained reading, the teacher should encourage
readers to sample the graphic cues, select the most
appropriate graphic cues, e.g., usually the first letter
or combination of letters, possibly the ending letter(s),
and predict an appropriate meaningful structure. The
reader needs to be encouraged to continue reading past
the unfamiliar structure. If the structure is significant to meaning, the author will usually repeat the
structure throughout a selection. It must be demonstrated to the reader that the unfamiliar structure will
possibly become more evident as the reader builds meaning by continuing to read. However, readers must have
the opportunity to terminate their reading when there
are too many unknown concepts and structures.

The teacher can design specific reading strategy lessons for groups of readers who do not continue
reading when they encounter unfamiliar structures. Unknown structures may be caused for several reasons. The
reader's background knowledge and conceptual development
may not be closely related to the author's message.
The author's writing style and grammatical structures
may be unfamiliar to the reader. However, if miscue
analysis confirms that the reader has strength using
graphophonemic cues, syntactic structures are not
usually difficult, and the information is within the
reader's experiential background, it may be assumed that
the reader's difficulty is in applying predicting and
confirming strategies and semantic cues. The cause of
difficulty could be the unfamiliar grammatical structures and concept difficulty.

The following examples of strategy lessons illustrate a modified cloze technique deleting a key word
throughout the passage. The reader should be encouraged
to continue reading past the blank, to pick up more
meaning cues from additional text provided by the author.
The exercises can be done individually or in groups.
Strategy lessons can be done orally or instructions given
and completed independently by each child, depending on
the teacher's preference. Generally, predicting and
confirming strategy with semantic cues is beneficial
for readers if done orally. Each reader can be called
upon to state his/her prediction as the blank occurs
each time in reading through the passage. The predictions of each reader can be written down using the overhead projector or chalkboard and discussed whether the

structure is appropriate to the meaning. The group continues to predict and confirm/disconfirm as each predicted structure is written down and reading continues
through the story. Predictions that don't make sense
are eliminated and further predicted structures written
until either confirmed or disconfirmed and corrected.

The following strategy lessons are examples of
using semantic cues:

Determining Lesson 1

Focus: Predicting and confirming semantic cues

Purpose: To develop use of semantic cues with predicting and confirming strategies. To
teach students to continue reading to gain
additional confirmation of meaning from
context.

Introduction: The passages with key word deleted or nonsense word substituted are projected overhead on a transparency. Tell the students
they will be reading one sentence at a
time. Each time the mystery word is used,
they are to list their predictions as to
what it might be. As they continue reading, they should delete from and add to
their list of predictions until at the
end of the selection, they should be able
to confirm an accurate prediction.

Interaction: Discuss the cues the students used to
confirm their predictions.

Expanding: For those students interested, make
copies of the book available.

Evaluating: Check work in class. Collect students' papers to make sure all have completed the assignment.

Mother said, "You better take your _____ to
school. You will probably need it when you come home.
The _____ is in the hall closet." John ran to get the
big, black _____. He carried it on his arm as he

went to school and put it in his locker when he came
into the schoolroom.

When school was out John ran to the window.
It was raining cats and dogs. Mother was right, he
did need the _____. It would be fun walking home
in the rain under the big, black _____.

Determining Lesson 2

Focus: Predicting/Confirming Semantic Cues

Purpose: To develop semantic cues through use of
              prediction.

Introduction: We will read a story together. The story
              tells about something most boys and girls
              like.

Interacting: Use overhead projector. Reveal one sen-
              tence at a time. Write guesses on board
              each time. Cross out ones that won't fit
              and go on. The word is cookies.

Expanding: Let children draw, color, and cut out
              their favorite kind of cookie. Have a
              cookie jar display. Put names of cookies
              on or near them.

              Have children bring favorite cookie recipe
              to school and see if they can read it.

Evaluation: Observe children as they try to "guess"
              answer. Give more help in this area to
              children who show need for it.

I like to eat _____. They are so good.
They are sweet. _____ come in all shapes and sizes.
My mother likes to bake _____. But sometimes we buy
them in the store. At Christmas time we make sugar
_____ and decorate them. I like chocolate chip
_____ the best. Some people call me a _____
monster!!!

284

Nonsense Word for a Real Word

Another strategy lesson to develop predicting strategies with semantic cues is to substitute a nonsense word for a real word in a text. The nonsense word is repeated throughout the text. The reader is encouraged to make predictions about what the real word could be and to continue reading if meaning is not evident. This is not unlike an actual reading situation in which a reader meets unfamiliar structures and may treat a word in text as a non-word. Readers need to be directed to keep their focus on building meaning, expecting that the author will provide more information in the ensuing text. The reader must develop the use of non-visual information to each reading task. Even though a particular structure in text is unfamiliar readers should know that continuing to read ahead will provide more information to construct meaning.

The following are examples of strategy lessons using nonsense words for a real work:

Determining Lesson 1

Discuss the following points:

1. You will meet words you don't know--we all do.
2. You will not usually sound these words out.
3. You may feel safe in skipping the word, and reasonably confident that you can figure out the meaning as you go along.
4. If it is an important word you will meet it many times in the selection. This is assurance of a good many contextual clues for your aid.
5. If you are reading silently there is no <u>need</u> to sound out the word--you are reading for meaning, not pronunciation.

In the following selection there is a strange word. You <u>cannot</u> sound it out. However, you can work out the meaning. As you read be aware of the first point at which you work out the meaning; also be ready to cite added evidence to support the meaning you have worked out.

The XBT

People like to travel. Across the land they go in cars, trains, buses, or by any means they can.

Over the water they go in ships. Up in the air people
fly. Soon they visit the far-off planets. But there is
one trip men will not take. They will never visit the
XBT.

The XBT is a giant ball of burning gas. It is
much too hot for people to visit. In some parts the XBT
is twenty times as hot as the kitchen stove. The hottest
parts of the XBT are found in its center. The center of
the XBT is 6,000 times as hot as the kitchen stove. A
rocket ship would melt long before it reached the XBT.

We could not get along without the XBT. Our
plants could not grow without the XBT's light. Without
plants there would be no animals because animals eat
plants. Without plants and animals there would be nothing for people to eat. Without the warm rays of the
XBT there could be no life on Earth.

On Earth we get only a small part of the XBT's
heat light. But the XBT gives us what we need.

FOLLOW-UP
A brief discussion would follow centering on
the points the children were asked to be aware of:

1) first point at which the meaning was
   worked out.
2) added evidence to support the hypothesis.

I think this would also be a good time to remind the children about the particular problems names
pose to a reader in the acquisition stage. They should
be able, from the information gained in this lesson, to
make a valid generalization.

Determining Lesson 2

Focus: Semantic Cues

Purposes: To develop use of semantic cues and to
                  teach students that if they continue

286

reading they will be able to confirm their
predictions.

Introduction: Present each student with a paper containing sentences one through four. Have
them read the sentences, predicting what
"Oops" could mean.

Interaction: Discuss various answers, then write sentences five and six on the board. Now
the students can confirm or reject their
previous predictions.

Expanding: Students might be encouraged to try to
write some "mystery word" paragraphs to
share with each other.

Evaluation: Observe each student's predictions and
give more help to anyone who seems to
need it.

OOPS

We are getting ready for the Oops.

The Oops is a big place.

We pay money to go to the Oops.

At the Oops we see many people.

At the Oops we see many animals.

Most of the animals are in cages at the Oops.

Determining Lesson 3

Producing Real Words Instead of Non-Words

Purpose: To help the reader concentrate on meaning
while reading.

Construction: Teacher selects or writes an interesting
passage containing a significant noun or
verb which is repeated a number of times.

Procedure: The reader must predict an appropriate
word to replace the non-word.

Example A:

The skidoo was standing by the lake. He had been here all morning. The skidoo had a long pole with a line on it. The skidoo had a net and a pail. He also had some worms in a can. The skidoo put a worm on the line. The skidoo threw the line in the water. He waited very quietly. The skidoo saw his line dip into the water. He pulled up quickly and caught a fish.

Example B:

The children were going to the creeble. They had two dollars to spend. Mother drove them to the creeble. First, they had to buy a ticket; then, they bought a box of popcorn. They sat in nice, soft seats. First the cartoon came on and then the main picture started. Going to the creeble is lots of fun.

Developing Concepts by Continuing to Read

All readers need to develop the strategy of continuing to read on beyond an unknown or unfamiliar structure or concept. Teachers need to develop early the idea that correct pronunciation of words is not the important thing in reading. The reading process and comprehension is slowed down when readers use excessive sounding out procedures. More importantly the reader should get close to pronunciation of a structure or even omit an unfamiliar word if necessary in order to keep the process going. Again, however, if the conceptual load or graphic structure are too advanced for a reader there is always the strategy available of terminating the process. If the reading is necessary but too difficult, then more emphasis needs to be placed on concept development through non-reading activities, e.g., films, field trips, pictures, demonstrations, and so forth, before reading.

The reading strategy lessons illustrated below are similar to previous types but different in that real words representing a key concept is the focus of the lesson. These lessons can be useful to demonstrate to readers that continued reading often will enable readers to construct meaning. The reader must be aware that reading is an active process and that he/she brings experience, concepts and vocabulary to the process in interaction with the information provided by the print.

Listening to retelling of stories read by children and analyzing miscues for semantic acceptability and unacceptability, whether corrected or not corrected, can provide the teacher information concerning readers who need examples of strategy lessons given below. The teacher can write or find commercial material which focuses on a key concept. Sometimes the problem is not with the processing of print but with lack of prior knowledge to bring to the main concepts represented by the print.

If this is the case, then the teacher should plan and provide concept building activities to clarify and develop concepts before reading takes place. This will be true usually with content material but also with some narrative selections.

The example of strategy lessons below illustrate development of concepts through reading building meaning from text and using prior knowledge:

Determining Lesson 1

Developing concepts using short stories. Write short stories to develop concepts of words children had trouble with on the RMI Coding Sheet. Read the stories with an individual child or in small groups and discuss.

Concept: Customer

Mr. Brown opened his grocery early each morning. Many people came to buy groceries soon after he opened the door.

Mr. Jones was the first customer. He needed to buy mild for his children's breakfast.

Mrs. Smith was the second customer. She needed to buy bread for her children's lunches.

Mrs. Green was the third customer. She bought hot dogs for a picnic in the park.

The fourth customer was Sam Davis. He bought apples to put in his lunch.

The fifth customer was the police officer. She stopped to buy a morning paper.

Mr. Brown was happy to have his grocery. He thanked each customer for coming to his store.

289

Concept: Remind

Betty was a forgetful little girl. Mother had
to remind her each morning to comb her hair before she
went to school. Daddy had to remind her that it was
time to go to school. Her teacher always had to remind
Betty to write her name on her papers.

One day Betty's mother, daddy and teacher decided they would help Betty learn a lesson. Mother did
not remind Betty to comb her hair. Daddy did not remind
her that it was time to leave for school. Her teacher
did not remind her to write her name on her papers.

Betty will never forget that day. She had to
walk to school because her daddy left without her. She
got to school ten minutes late. The boys and girls
stared at Betty because her hair was in such a mess.
She got a zero in math because there wasn't a paper
with her name on it.

After that, Betty was not so forgetful. Mother
did not have to remind Betty to comb her hair. Daddy
did not have to remind Betty that it was time to go.
Her teacher never had to remind Betty to write her name
on her papers.

Betty learned her lesson.

Developing concepts using related concepts in Short Stories.

Concept: Strong - strength

Mike was very strong. He ate good food and
slept 8 to 10 hours each night. He lifted weights and
got plenty of exercise each day. This helped to make
him strong.

One day Mike's baseball team was playing a game.
It was the ninth inning, the score was tied, and there

were two outs. It was Mike's turn to bat. He stepped
up to the plate. The first two balls were pitched too
high. Mike could see that the next pitch was coming
right across the plate. He hit the ball with all of his
strength. It was a home-run. Mike's team had won the
game.

Mike knew that eating good food and getting
plenty of rest and exercise had given him the strength
to hit the ball hard.

Use any of the concept stories at a later time as a
Cloze type exercise to be completed individually.

Concept: Use strong or strength in the blanks.
Mike was very _____. He ate good food and
slept 8 to 10 hours each night. He lifted weights and
got plenty of exercise each day. This helped to make
him _____.

One day Mike's baseball team was playing a
game. It was the ninth inning, the score was tied, and
there were two outs. It was Mike's turn to bat. He
stepped up to see the plate. The first two balls pitched
were too high. Mike could see that the next pitch was
coming right across the plate. He hit the ball with all
of his _____. It was a home run. Mike's team had won
the game.

Mike knew that eating good food and getting
plenty of rest and exercise had given him the _____ to
hit the ball hard.

Determining Lesson 2

Gaining Meaning from Words that are Significant and Unfamiliar

Purpose: To develop competency in using context cues.

291

Construction: Teacher should select a story with an unfamiliar but significant word which is repeated several times. The word should be so well explained within the material that the reader will be able to construct a meaning for it.

Procedure: The student should read the story first; then, through discussion with the teacher or in a small group, he should indicate how the meaning of the word developed from the accumulated context.

Example A:

Jean had to <u>mend</u> the jacket. She had torn it accidentally. She wanted to wear the jacket to school, but she needed to mend the hole before it got larger. Jean got the needle and thread. She began to mend the hole in the jacket.

Example B:

The vegetables are in the <u>colander</u>. After the vegetables were picked, they were washed in cold water. The water drains off the vegetables and goes through the little holes in the colander.

Example C:

<u>Lasagne</u> is very good. It has cheese and meat in it. You can get lasagne in a restaurant, or you can cook lasagne at home.

Determining Lesson 3

Purpose: To help children use context, semantics, and syntax to predict an unknown word.

Introduction: I want you to read each story and then tell me what you think the underlined words mean.

Interacting: Present a copy of the stories below to
               each child participating in the activity.
               Encourage them to read all of each story
               before guessing.

Expanding: Draw a picture of each item described and
               label it with the new word.

Evaluation: Observe child's responses to see if they
               make sense.

People call me a <u>Siamese</u>. I have a long tail
and whiskers. I purr when someone pets me. What am I?

People call me a <u>marlin</u>. I live in the ocean.
I swim alone. I can leap into the air above the water.
What am I?

People call me a <u>Newfoundland</u>. I am big and
have a black coat. I bark and wag my tail. What am I?

Determining Lesson 4

Student reads:
    George is little.
Teacher asks:
    What might George be?
Student reads:
    George is black and white.
Teacher asks:
    What are all the possibilities?
Student reads:
    George is playing with a ball. Now George is
    barking. George is a <u>canine</u>.
Teacher asks:
    What is George?

Determining Lesson 5

<u>Using Immediate Context to Build Concepts for Words.</u>

Purpose: To develop competency in using context
                cues.

Construction: Teacher selects or writes three or four
                clues, riddle style, about a specific ob-
                ject.

Procedure: The reader must predict an appropriate
                response.

<u>Example A</u>:

I live on a farm.

I am sitting on my nest.

Eggs are in my nest.

What am I?

    (Hen)

<u>Example B</u>:

I make cars go.

I make lawn mowers go.

I look like water.

You can get me at the service station.

What am I?

    (Gas)

<u>Example C</u>:

I am in your house.

I have a pillow on me.

You get in me at night.

I am your _____.   (bed)

Determining Lesson 6

    1) A riddle form where children list as many
possibilities that fit the clue as they can supply.
They continue to eliminate, correct, and add on possibilities as more clues are given.

294

1. Jeanie is my friend.
   She is small.
   She loves to fly.
   She loves magic tricks.
   Her favorite color is black.
   Her favorite holiday is Halloween.
   (Jeanie is a witch).

2. I am tall.
   I never move.
   I don't eat.
   I hold lots of people.
   I have lots of windows
   I am found in big cities.
   (I am a skyscraper).

3. I am small.
   I am red.
   I am something to eat.
   I do not grow on a tree
   I am put on a bacon, lettuce, and mayonnaise sandwich.
   (I am a tomato).

Determining Lesson 7

Focus: Predicting Strategy

Purpose: To develop comprehension through predict-
              ion.

Introduction: We will read some riddles together and
              guess the answers. Be thinking as we read
              the clues, do not guess until you are
              called on.

Interacting: Show a sentence at a time on the over-
              head projector. Call on children to read
              them. Stop after a few clues and let
              children guess.

Expanding:	Let children who know a riddle ask others. Or have children draw a picture of Ellen after she has grown up.
Evaluation:	Keep this an activity just for fun--not to be graded. Some children will have difficulty guessing the answer.

What Am I?

I am square.
I can be round or a rectangle.
I have four legs
Sometimes I have a cover on me.
You can eat off of me.
I am a _____.

*****

Tell What I Am

Boys and girls like me.
I fly in the sky.
I have a tail.
I am red but I can be any color at all.
I am a _____.

*****

Who is Ellen?

Ellen is a baby but she is not little.
She has big feet but cannot run.
She can walk very fast.
She drinks water and takes baths.
She is gray and has a trunk.
Who is Ellen? Ellen is an _____.

Key: 1) table; 2) kite;   3) elephant

Determining Lesson 8

Focus:	Syntactic and Semantic Cues
Purpose:	To use and extend vocabularies through the descriptions of sensations revealed by senses. To write, read, and evaluate both group and individual reports. To make use of syntactic and semantic cues.
Introduction:	Give each child an orange slice and ask

296

what it looks like, how it feels, how
it smells, tastes and sounds when they
eat it.

Interacting: Write the reactions on the board:

An Orange Slice

It looks like the sun going down.

It feels squishy, sticky and spongy. (etc.)

Read the group story and then have children write their
own story. Later they may read compositions to class.

Expanding: Have candy of another taste, size, shape
and texture of a Tootsie Roll. Follow
procedures listed above. This would be a
good time for developing long e words -
sweet, feel, teeth, etc. (graphophonemic
cues.)

Determining Lesson 9

Focus: Predicting - Semantic Cues

Purpose: To help students understand that words
often must have more exact meaning before
we can understand exactly what the author
means.

Introduction: Write the first sentence on the board. It
is a warm day. Discuss that warm can mean
many things. Does it mean warm enough to
go swimming? Underline warm to show it is
a word we need to know more about. Tell
children we will read some sentences like
this and underline the words which we need
to know more about.

Interacting: Pass out mimeographed papers to children
which they will underline as we did on the
board.

Expanding: Draw a picture to show that you think the
author could have meant when he said it
was a warm day.

297

Evaluation: Pass among children to see if any are
having trouble. When finished, have
children read their sentences aloud and
correct their own papers, before handing
them in.

It was a <u>warm</u> day. <u>warm</u>

Mr. Green is an <u>old</u> man. <u>old</u>

Bill said he had eaten only a <u>little</u> candy. <u>little</u>

This book is too <u>easy</u>. <u>easy</u>

It's a <u>long</u> way to the next town. <u>long</u>

It's <u>hard</u> to play the piano. <u>hard</u>

Al's bike is <u>better</u> than mine. <u>better</u>

We will come home <u>early</u>. <u>early</u>

<u>Soon</u> we will have another holiday. <u>soon</u>

Harry brought home a <u>large</u> fish. <u>large</u>

The policeman said we were driving too <u>fast</u>.   <u>fast</u>

We don't watch television very <u>often</u>. <u>often</u>

Determining Lesson 10

Purpose: To develop use of semantic cues by predicting rhyme.

Introduction: Child listens to tape of <u>I Know an Old</u>
<u>Lady Who Swallowed A Fly</u>. All of the
things the old lady swallows are left out
of the tape. Through the use of context
cues and rhyme the child will predict the
missing words which happen to be animals
or insects, which they will have been told
before listening to the tape.

Interacting: This may be one child or a few predicting
the answers or missing words. After they
have listened to the tape they will have
an activity to do at their seats.

1. I know an old lady who swallowed a ___.

2. I don't know why she swallowed a ____.

3. I guess she'll die.

and so on. . .

298

Expanding: The children may want to do a rebus pic-
                    ture activity to show the things the old
                    lady swallowed.

                    e. g. I know an old   who swallowed a

                    They may want to have a puppet show show-
                    ing the old lady and animals she swallowed.

                    They may want the old lady to swallow
                    different things (pie, chair) and change
                    the rhyme in the verse.

                    They may want to learn the song to the
                    verse.

Diagnosis
& Evaluation: Observe individuals and check on use of
                    semantic cues.

                    Determining Lesson 11

Purpose: To use semantic cues to predict sequence
                    and rhyme.

Introduction: The teacher reads the old rhyme, This
                    Old Man aloud to the children. After
                    reading ask the questions: When did you
                    realize that we were actually counting
                    to 10 in this rhyme? When did you figure
                    out which words in the story would rhyme?
                    Did you notice that when you catch on to
                    the author's plan the story is easier to
                    read?

Interacting: Hand the children a worksheet with more
                    words missing with each verse. Ask them
                    to supply the correct words.

Expanding: After completing the worksheet the chil-
                    dren might enjoy singing the familiar
                    song. They could add new verses as they
                    count higher.

Evaluation: As the children complete their worksheet
                    the teacher must observe them closely to
                    see that everyone understands the sequence
                    of the rhyme.

                              299

Naming Strategies

Readers who are highly influenced by isolated skills instruction and give evidence of excessive sounding out of unfamiliar structures, usually think they have to pronounce names of characters and places accurately. This habit naturally slows down the reading process and is likely to lower comprehension. They think that all words are of equal importance and value and must be recognized and pronounced. They need to know that wasting time trying to exactly pronounce an unfamiliar name is counter-productive to constructing meaning.

The reader who habitually tries several pronunciations of unfamiliar character names and places throughout a story should be told to do one of several things. The reader can be told to say "blank" when she/he comes to a difficult name and go on; or read the name as the first letter of the name, e. g., "Mr. A" for Mr. Antonopolos, and continue reading. The important thing for the reader is to have the concept of character or place and not to accurately pronounce the name.

However, simply encouraging or telling readers to do this does not always change the habit of trying to sound out unfamiliar names. The teacher can write naming strategy lessons which may be helpful in dealing with unfamiliar names of characters and places in print.

The following are illustrations of naming strategy lessons.

Determining Lesson 1

Teaching children to skip over proper names when they do not affect meaning of story (using Mr. B. and Mrs. S. instead of the name they can't pronounce.)

Mr. Banowski went to the store to get the groceries for his wife. As he walked into the store he got many "Hello's" from the grocer and the other shoppers. Everyone liked Mr. Banowski because he always wore a smile. He went down aisle after aisle picking up the items on the list. Mr. Banowski also picked up some cookies as a treat for the children on his block who often came to visit. He felt lucky that the children

didn't mind talking to an "old" man. He walked home
whistling and thinking how nice it was to live in a
small town like Smile Town. Yes, thought Mr. Banowski,
I'm really a lucky man.

The Family Reunion

Mrs. Siskowicz had just come to visit her
family in the United States. The trip from Yugoslavia
had been long, but that was all forgotten in all the
hugs and kisses. Everyone was talking at once as they
all got into the car. So many things had happened in
the five years since they had last been together.
Mrs. Siskowicz couldn't remember ever being so happy.
Her grandchildren had grown into beautiful young men
and women, and one was even expecting her own child!

All that day she received gifts and "Welcome-
to-the-United States parties." After supper Mrs. Siskowicz began to finally feel tired. She kissed her
family goodnight and went to bed. Mrs. Siskowicz
knew all her dreams would be sweet and filled with
pleasant thoughts of her stay in America.

Determining Irrelevant Information

It is important that readers monitor the reading process as they are reading using semantic cues and
predicting what will make sense. When what is being
read is not making sense or confirmed, there is a need
to correct by reprocessing, to sample more graphic
cues, resorting to phonological cues (sounding out) and
applying syntactic cues, or continuing to read to construct meaning if they are not corrected, particularly
if uncorrected structures represent important concepts
and ideas. Such miscues distort the author's message
and produce different meaning than that intended by the
author. One of the basic causes of readers producing an
inappropriate deep structure is a preoccupation with
graphophonemic cues.

301

To focus reader's attention on monitoring the
reading process for meaning and to make sense strategy
lessons may be written. This strategy lesson materials
include obvious irrelevant information which is inappropriate in the context. The material is analogous to
what a reader does when miscues seriously distort the
essential meaning--producing nonsense structures--unre-
lated to the context of the author's message.

The following are examples of strategy lessons
to assist readers who read nonsense, the miscues disrupt
the meaning and who do not correct. The exercises could
be done orally or silently. The students are asked to
identify the irrelevant information which changes the
meaning of the message or distorts the meaning.

Lesson 1

Direction: Students read paragraph to determine irrelevant information.

At last the day of the big game came! We had
worked hard all winter, waiting for this day. We watched
the game nervously. The train came into the station.
The other team hit a run! Our team sighed. Our team
hit a run! The blue birds flew over the ship. The
whole team cheered! Then the game was almost over and
the teams were still tied. We thought of our long winter of work. Our best player went up to bat. The
squirrel ran into the tree. She hit a home run! And
we won the game.

Lesson 2

Ann and Tom couldn't believe what they were
seeing. The clowns were fantastic. The roaring lions
made everyone shiver. The house in the middle of the
block was painted green. The tightrope walkers did such
dangerous acts that the crowd just stared. The children
had never seen a circus like this one!

302

Benjy waited for a present to come in the mail. For two weeks Benjy waited. Walter drove to an artist's studio in the country. The mailman finally brought the present after two more days.

Betsy loved to go to the theater. The person who guessed the right answer would win a diamond ring. She would go there whenever she had any free time. She always went to the theater on Saturday. He was an admirer of her drawings.

Lesson 3
Irrelevant Information
The student must find the sentence that is irrelevant.

Grizzly bears live on land away from people. They are strong and weight about 800 pounds. Their thick fur coats are mostly brown. They have long claws that they use to dig up food from the ground. My father digs up the ground to plant a garden.

Discriminating Between Significant and Insignificant Information

Many readers develop the habit of trying to pronounce every word when they read. They had been influenced early in reading instruction that exact recognition and pronunciation of every word is important. They become passive readers who focus on graphophonemic cues and often experience difficulty understanding what they are reading. An analysis of miscues would demonstrate high use of graphophonemic cues, a weakness in comprehending strategies, eg.g., miscues that are semantically acceptable and miscues semantically unacceptable but corrected, and generally a low retelling score, or comprehension. This reader profile may also indicate other types of strategy lessons such as those presented previously are needed. However, the word-by-word reader needs to know that not all the print is significant. They need to know that although the author encoded the full message there is a redundancy in written material, particularly, narrative material. The developing reader needs to be selective and active in sampling, selecting and predicting significant information. Comprehension of narrative material is enhanced when the reader is selective and flexible in processing significant print which carries the essential meaning.

The following lessons are examples to help readers determine significant from insignificant information:

Determining Lesson 1

Purpose: To develop students' use of semantic cues with comprehending strategies.

Introduction: Tell students they are to read a short story and pick out any descriptive information that is redundant (unnecessary, or repeating what has already been said). They are to circle such words or phrases on their worksheets.

Interacting: Students may work in small groups to compare their answers and discuss their choices. Teachers should guide and advise each group discussion.

Expanding: Have students try to write such stories themselves for others to read. For those interested, have copies of the book available to read.

Evaluating: After group discussions, collect the papers to take note of any students who are having difficulty.

Developing Correcting Strategies

One of the most important strategies a reader must develop to become an effective reader is self-correction. The effective reader self-corrects when what has been read doesn't sound appropriate or make sense within the context. Some teachers interfere with a child's development of correction strategies by intervening when a child is reading orally. Another harmful intervention practice is allowing other children in an oral group reading setting to say the word when a student is reading and comes to an unfamiliar word. Much learning takes place when readers self-correct. However, readers need the opportunities to correct themselves when reading.

Oral reading miscues need to be examined in relation to syntactic and semantic acceptability within the sentence and story context. Readers who show a reading profile indicating a loss of meaning according to their comprehending pattern, a weakness in grammatical relationships and a low retelling score (comprehension) usually are not correcting miscues. Frequently, non-correctors are using graphophonemic cues to a great extent. They are not concerned about meaning because they are too involved in processing the print, or recoding, matching the print to sound. Any meaning that gets through is usually because the reader has a prior knowledge to bring to the story, or there may be a general but sketchy understanding.

Strategy lessons may be planned to focus the reader's attention on the need to self-correct when meaning is disrupted and distorted. The following are examples of strategy lessons to develop self-correcting strategies:

Determining Lesson 1

Focus: Correction strategies

Purpose: To correct those elements which are disruptive to meaning.

Construction: Write some lessons which contain a misprint or anomalous information. For example, place male pronouns where female pronouns should be; or write a story and add a few lines which contain obvious misinformation.

Procedure: The reader first reads the selection, and then corrects those elements which are disruptive to the meaning.

Example A: John was playing with his dog. John threw a ball. The dog went to get it. The dog brought the ball back to her and dropped it at her feet.

Example B: It was very hot day. The children wanted to go swimming. They went to talk to

Mother. She said, "Do not forget your
mittens. Your hands will get very cold
without them."

Lesson 2

The student must read the paragraph and find the words
that don't make sense and correct them by putting in the
correct word.

Timmy went to visit his grandmother and grand-
father who lived on a farm. They had many animals on
their farm. There were horses, cows, chickens, tigers
and rabbits.

While Timmy was visiting, he helped Grandmother
do the chores. They went into the barn to milk the
chickens. After that they had to gather the eggs all the
rabbits layed. When all the work was done, Timmy put
the saddle on the tiger and rode down the lane.

It was time to go back home. Timmy shook feet
with his grandmother and climbed in the rocket with his
father and mother and rode down the road toward the city.

Lesson 3

Directions: Student locate and circle words that do not
make sense and correct them by inserting a
new word.

Tom walked slowly into the school room and dropped his books on his desk. The books were covered with
mud. Tom had fallen by the star on the way to school
and he was cold and wet and he wanted to go bread. Tom
had also been late, and the mouse said he would have to
make off the lost time. Tom painted at the floor and
laughed. The story makes you feel that Tom had a wonderful day.

The purple pond lay still in the afternoon moon-
light. Only the shadows of trees moved softly over the

306

water. Orange fish were running close to the bank of
the pond, and a large blonde frog nodded on a rock nearby. This makes you feel that it was a busy day.

Lesson 4

Students should realize that oral reading is language.
They need to understand that correcting oral miscues
verbally is an accepted practice.

By reading passages that contain obvious miscues, students will be forced into a situation where they must
correct the miscues for passage to have meaning.

The American alligator was once found in the
mountains, swamps, and rivers of the South. This am-
phibian was known to die to an old age. However, people
began to pet alligators so much that that kind of animal
almost disappeared.

People found that alligator hair made poor
leather shoes, belts, and pocketbooks. Everyone seemed
to want something made of strong alligator leather. So
the butterflies were killed in great numbers.

It was only when people saw that the alligator
was in safety of disappearing that laws were passed to
stop the killing. Even so, the number of wild alligators is small today. Farms or ranches have now been set
up to keep the alligator dangerous.

Punctuation and Meaning Strategies

Written language uses graphic cues such as
punctuation marks to guide the reader to meaning. Punctuation is an arbitrary convention that readers need to
learn. The writer uses punctuation to aid the reader to
process the print to meaning. It is similar to what the
speaker does for the listener by pausing at appropriate
places, e.g., at the end of an idea or rising voice to
indicate a question or falling intonation for a declara-
tive utterance. However, the reader cannot consciously
process punctuation cues or visual symbols such as periods, question marks and commas and still focus on

307

meaning. Punctuation is better developed through written instruction on the mechanics of language needed by the writer. Frequently, the reader will pause or use appropriate inflection during oral reading if the reader's focus is on meaning.

When listening to a pupil read orally it is apparent that some readers omit or insert punctuation and it goes uncorrected. Omission and insertion of pauses reflected in the reader's intonation pattern may be caused by the author's unfamiliar writing style. The syntactic structures of the author are unlike the reader's grammatical structure. Nevertheless, readers during oral surface reading may pause or not pause frequently and still have a good understanding of the author's message. There is apparently a phenomenon of silent correcting or the reader's prior knowledge of the topic is so great that inappropriate intonation does not affect meaning.

There are determining strategy lessons for readers who demonstrate low comprehension possibly because of inability to recognize punctuation marks, especially at the end of sentences. These lessons may help readers become more aware of pausing at the end of a sentence rather than continuing to the next sentence without pausing.

Lesson 1

Reading Punctuation

Read the following sentences.

I am going to the show with Jack. Jack is one of my friends. Friends are good to have. Have you made new friends today? Today is a good day for playing baseball. Baseball is a favorite game of my friends. Friends can always find something to do when they get together.

Lesson 2

For punctuation problems, use a story where last word of one sentence is the same as the first word in the next sentence.

308

Jack is one of my friends. Friends help you
when you need it. It is nice to have a friend to share
secrets. Secrets can even bring friends closer together.
Together with a friend you can play school. School is
a good place to make new friends. Friends can walk
home with you. You and everyone in the world need
friends.

My mother loves to make gifts from flowers.
Flowers are so pretty that everyone loves to receive
one of Mom's gifts. Gifts can be made from real,
dried, or silk flowers. Flowers Mom has include roses,
daisies, mums, and carnations. Carnations are my favorite flowers. Flowers can make great gifts for you. You
probably have a favorite, too.

Comprehending and Sequence Strategies

Overall comprehension is improved when a reader
understands the structure or scheme of a written selection. Frequently understanding the sequence of events
within a story or informational material is important.
Having children do retelling following oral reading of
short stories and miscue analysis can provide the teacher information about a reader's strengths and weaknesses in sequencing events and understanding story structure.

The following lessons are examples of strategies for readers who have difficulty retelling events
and organizing the beginning, middle and end of stories:

Lesson 1

Focus: Sequencing events

Purpose: To put ideas in sequence using semantic
                cues.

Introduction: Ask the children for suggestions as to
                what they do each day at school in order;
                i.e., collect lunch money, take attendance,
                reading, recess, math, lunch, etc.

Interacting:	After the children have completed the worksheet independently, go over the exercise orally, allowing children to correct their mistakes using a pen or crayon. Discuss reasons why certain things happen before others. Allow for difference of opinion if correct.
Expanding:	Draw a series of pictures depicting the story in sequence.
Evaluation:	Take note of those children who have difficulty with sequence while working independently, during oral discussion, and while drawing the pictures of the story in order.

Semantic Cues

Number these sentences in the order in which they happened in the story.

____ People may have noticed that seeds grew into plants if left in the earth.

____ Big machines are used to plant and cut wheat.

____ People mixed flour and water to make bread.

____ People just lived on meat, nuts and berries with no kind of bread at all.

____ People tried crushing wheat into flour.

____ Trucks take bread to the stores.

Lesson 2

Focus:	Sequencing events
Purpose:	To develop the need for reading, to follow directions and develop sequence.
Introduction:	I will read the children a story about a treasure hunt. We will discuss what things could be treasures.
Interacting:	We will determine a treasure, then we will hide it and write clues to direct someone to the treasure. Each child can devise his own treasure hunt for another child to

follow, and each child will get a chance to hunt for a treasure.

Expanding: Discuss the fact that treasures can be many things and that different people consider different things to be treasures. Have the children make a list of some of the things they would consider to be treasures. The children can then compare their lists.

Evaluation: Observe the children as they prepare their hunt and as they look for another's hidden treasure.

A Sample of a Treasure Hunt

Hide a candy bar on the coat rack under a hat.

Write clues such as:

Start:
1. Look to the right and walk three big steps to the colors board. (Clue found on color red.)

2. Here you are! Now go four steps north to the library table. Look in the books. (Clue is on a book mark.)

3. You found me! You are getting closer to the treasure. Now go three steps west to the listening center. Look around! (Clue on the back of the record player.)

4. Ha! Ha! Ha! Go four steps farther west to the sink. Wash your hands. (Clue on paper towel.)

5. Go south to the teacher's desk. Look at the date. (Clue is on the calendar.)

6. It is almost time to go! Look at the coat rack. Don't forget your hat! (Candy bar is under the hat.)

Lesson 3

Focus: Following directions.

Purpose: To develop a child's awareness of sequence in reading and to plant a flower for a science experiment.

311

Introduction: Bring a flower to show the children--
suggest they may start a flower to take
home later in the year. Have a large
chart showing the steps to plant a flower.
(Provide small paper cups, flower seeds,
soil, a spoon, water and a tray.) Give
each child the following worksheet:

_____On top of the seeds place 1 more
spoonful of soil in the cup.

_____Put a little water in the cup.

_____Take a paper cup and write your
name on it.

_____Pat it gently.

_____Put 10 seeds in the cup.

_____Put your cup on the tray.

_____Put 2 spoonfuls of soil in the cup.

Interaction: Tell each child to read the chart titled
"How to Plant a Flower." Then have them
look at the worksheet and write the number by the sentences to show the right
order. Have them check their paper with
the chart and then follow the steps to
plant their flower.

Expanding: Draw a picture and write a story about
how you think your flower will look.

Evaluation: Check the worksheet with the chart before
planting the flower. Hopefully if the
correct order was folloed the flower will
grow!

Lesson 4

Focus: Prediting story ending.

Purpose: To develop comprehension while encouraging
creative writing.

Introduction: Read the ending of a story to the students.
Ask them what might have happened in the
beginning of the story. Discuss the fact
that there isn't any right answers--the
author of the book had an idea and they
can have different ideas. Everyone's
story could be different.

Interacting:	Write down three or four story endings on the board or on a worksheet (samples below). Tell children to choose an ending and write a story that goes with the ending.

What a day it had been! Sue could not remember when she had seen such wonderful sights. The entire family enjoyed themselves, but not the long drive home seemed a good place to sleep and dream of the exciting amusement park.

How happy the villages were when Jack came down from the mountain. He was carried and cheered throughout the village and was soon nicknamed "Jack the Giant-Killer." No longer would the villagers have to live in fear of the mean giant.

Expanding:	Illustrate the story and make it into a book. Share with the class.
Evaluation:	Read the student's stories to see if the beginnings and endings of the stories follow a particular topic.

Lesson 5

Focus:	Finding the main topic.
Purpose:	To increase a child's comprehension while satisfying his obvious enjoyment of poetry.
Introduction:	Read a poem to the child. Give him a set of title cards and poem cards. These may be cut from old basal readers and pasted on posterboard. Separate the title from the poem.
Interaction:	Have the child spread the titles out on his desk so that he can see all of them. Now have him read a poem and then look at the title cards. Have him decide which title would fit the poem he read.
Expanding:	Encourage a group of children to write short poems with titles. Then separate the titles from the poems. Exchange with other classmates and see if they can

313

"match" them. The children can illustrate their poem too.

Evaluation: The title and poem cards can be numbered on the back for easy checking. Read over the poems and titles to see if the child understands the relationship.

Lesson 6

Focus: Identify fact and fantasy.

Purpose: To read carefully to discover if the story is real or make believe. Read to have fun.

Introduction: We will talk about what is meant by real and make believe and how to tell the difference.

Interaction: We will read stories to decide if they are a real or a make believe story to the other children. The rest of the children will be asked to decide which it is. Some of the children may want to write a story for the rest of the class to read and talk about. The place and importance of both real and make believe stories will be brought out.

Evaluation: Observe the children to see if they are enjoying the activities and stories.

Summary

Reading is a socio-psycholinguistic process involving an interaction and transaction between an author and a reader in a social contextual situation. A distinction is made in this chapter between reading instruction and reading. Reading instruction is defined as an intervention on the part of a teacher. There are times when teachers need to intervene in the reading development of learners. For example, observation by a teacher during oral reading using miscue analysis may indicate strengths and weaknesses which need planned instruction to assist the reader. Moreover, reading programs today emphasize teacher intervention and instruction. The conditions do not warrant most students learning to read by real reading.

A comparison was made between skills instruction and reading instruction based on a whole language,
socio-psycholinguistic model of reading. If direct
reading instruction is necessary for students, such instruction should involve reading components, integrated
into whole language context. Currently, reading instruction fragments and separates skills. A whole language
perspective views reading instruction in four important
ways: reading is a unified process; reading involves
natural language patterns; reading involves meaningful
context; and, reading is functional. All reading instruction should be planned on the basis of the above
criteria.

Reading strategy lessons were proposed as a
way for teachers to provide reading instruction for
students who need support. Strategy lessons highlight
specific language cues and strategies which need
strengthening for certain learners. Goodman and Burke
(1980) have identified criteria teachers can apply when
planning and using strategy lessons with readers. A
reading strategy lesson format teachers can use was
presented. Most strategy lessons are designed from
teacher observation and analysis of miscues as students
read in whole language text.

The components of the reading process from a
socio-psycholinguistic view were identified as: language
cues, reading strategies, and cycles of the reading process. The components are related to Goodman's (1976)
model of the reading process. A comparison was made of
the linguistic cues from a skills reading model and a
whole language or socio-psycholinguistic model. Traditional word recognition skills were related to graphophonemic cues in a whole language model. The strategies
and cycles related to language cues were described in
the context of reading instruction and reading experiences.

The conventional view of comprehension as a
collection of isolated skills, types and levels of comprehension represented by taxonomies was compared with
newer views of comprehension as a global process. Propositional anaylsis, schema theory and story grammar were
recommended as promising methods to understand the comprehension process.

Finally, examples of reading strategy lessons
were described according to the following types of
lessons:

(1) developing graphophonemic cues; (2) developing syntactic cues; (3) developing semantic cues; (4) developing correcting strategies; (5) developing meaning strategies; and (6) developing comprehending strategies.

Teaching Competencies

1. Plan a series of reading strategy lessons using a whole language approach to focus on specific graphophonemic cues/strategies with syntactic and semantic cues/strategies to read for comprehension with students at any reading stage. Select meaterials appropriate to children's interests, experiential/conceptual background. Write your lesson plan. The plan should include: (1) Purpose (2) Initiating Activities; (3) Interacting Activities; (4) Expanding Activities; (5) Evaluation Activities: and (6) Materials Activities. Observe children during the lesson and apply observation and record keeping to monitor child(ren) performance. (See Chapter VI for Whole Language Reading Approaches that can be integrated with strategy lessons.)

2. Plan a series of reading strategy lessons using a whole language approach. Focus on syntactic cues/strategies (predicting, confirming, correcting) with graphophonemic and semantic cues/ strategies to read for comprehension with students at any reading stage. Select materials appropriate to interests, experiences, and conceptual development. Write your plan. See the suggested strategy lesson format above No. 1. Observe to evaluate.

3. Plan a series of strategy lessons using a whole language approach. Focus on developing semantic cues/strategies (predicting, confirming, correcting) with graphophonemic/syntactic cues/strategies to read for comprehension with students at any reading stage. Select materials which are appropriate. Use the strategy lesson format suggested in this chapter. Observe using record keeping techniques described in Chapter IV.

4. Plan reading strategy lessons for students at any stage, i.e., preschool - grade 3, grade 4 - 6, grade 7 - 12, adult level, using content or information-type material, i.e., science, social studies, math,

health, etc. Focus on integrating graphophonemic, syntactic, semantic cues with strategies (predicting, confirming, correcting) to develop comprehension. Possibly focus on a particular language cue and strategy which is relevant to strengths and needs of an individual or group. Select and provide appropriate materials. Possibly integrate strategy lesson with whole language approaches described in Chapter VI. Observe with record keeping procedures to monitor reading performance in content or informational materials.

5. Plan reading strategy lessons to develop study strategies with students at any developmental level. Develop use of graphophonemic, syntactic, semantic cues/strategies as appropriate to the task. Focus on locating information. Selecting and organizing information to develop comprehension. Provide appropriate materials. Observe to evaluate study strategies in whole language content. Keep records of performance.

Affective Behaviors

1. The teacher accepts individual differences and needs in reading development of students.

2. The teacher respects the strengths and weaknesses of students' reading abilities.

3. The teacher motivates and encourages each student's reading development.

4. The teacher provides each student with successful reading instruction.

5. The teacher is supportive during reading instruction.

6. The teacher provides a learning environment that is non-threatening and encourages risk-taking.

7. The teacher treats each student's efforts in learning to read with dignity.

Questions to Investigate

1. How do readers (at the reading acquisition stage) develop distinctive features of letters, words and meanings?

2. What are graphophonemic cues? How can children apply their phonological development in oral language to reading?

3. What is meant by syntactic cues? How can children apply knowledge of syntactic development to reading?

4. What are semantic cues? How can children apply semantic knowledge to reading?

5. How are language cues (graphophonemic, syntactic and semantic) used interrelatedly with strategies (predicting, confirming, and correcting)? How can reading instruction develop language cues and strategies to help readers?

6. Discuss the significance of visual processing to reading. Auditory processing to reading.

7. Discuss the significance of interests to reading.

8. Discuss the significance of physical characteristics (vision, hearing, coordination, health) to reading. Emotional characteristics: Social characteristics.

9. How important are background experiences to reading? Oral language to reading?

10. Discuss whether comprehension is a combination of indivisible, global ability or specific, identifiable skills.

11. Identify what you believe are the differences in reading development at the various stages of reading.

12. Is the reading process different for informational and story-type written materials? How is it different or similar?

References:

Adams, Marilyn J. and Collins, Allan. A Schema - Theoretic View of Reading, Technical Report No. 32, University of Illinois at Champaign - Urbana, April 1977.

Bloom, Benjamin S. Taxonomy of Educationsl Objectives: The Classification of Educational Goals: Handbook I: Cognitive Domain. New Yori: David McKay Company, 1956.

Carlson, K. L. "A Different Look at Reading in the Content Areas" In W. D. Page (Ed) Help for the Reading Teacher: New Direction in Research. Urbana, Illinois: National Conference on Research in English. ERIC/CRCS, National Institute of Education, 1975.

Crothers, Edward J. "Memory Structure and the Recalling Discourse: In Language Comprehension and the Acquisition of Knowledge," edited by Roy O. Freeble and John B. Carroll. New York, NY: Wiley, 1972.

Fredericksen, C. H. "Effects of Task Induced Cognitive Operations On Comprehension and Memory Processes." In J. B. Carroll and R. D. Freedle (Eds.) Language Comprehension and the Acquisition of Knowledge. Washington, D.C.: Winston, 1972.

Gallagher, James J. and Aschner, Mary Jane. "A Preliminary Report on Analysis of Classroom Interaction." The Nature of Teaching. Edited by Lois N. Nelson. Waltham, Massachusetts: Blainsdell Publishing Company, 1969.

Goodman, Kenneth S. "The Reading Process." In Proceding of Western Learning Symposium. Billingham, Washington, 1974.

Goodman, Yetta M. "Reading Strategy Lessons: Expanding Reading Effectiveness." In Help for the Reading Teacher: New Directions in Research. 1975.

Goodman, Yetta M. "Using Children's Reading Miscues for New Teaching Strategies." The Reading Teacher. Vol February 1970.

Goodman, Yetta M. "Using Children's Reading Strategies for New Teaching Strategies." The Reading Teacher. Vol. 23, 1970, pp. 455-459.

319

Goodman, Yetta; Burke, Carolyn; with Sherman, Barry. Strategies in Reading: Focus on Comprehension. New York: Holt, Rinehart and Winston, 1980.

Goodman, Yetta M. and Greene, Jennifer. "Grammar and Reading in the Classroom." In Linguistic Theory: What Can It Say About Reading.

Guszak, Frank. "Teachers' Questions and Levels of Reading Comprehension." The Evaluation of Children's Reading Achievement Perspectives, Newark, Delaware: IRA, pp. 97-109, 1969.

Halliday, M.A.K. Learning How to Mean: Exploration in the Development of Language. New York: Elseview, 1975.

Kintsch, Walter. The Representation of Meaning in Memory. Potomac, Md: Erlbaum, 1974.

Kintsch, Walter. The Representation of Meaning in Memory. Hillsdale, New Jersey: Lawrence Erlbaum Associate, 1974.

Mandler, J. M. and Johnson, N. S. Remembrance of Things Passed: Story Structure and Recall. Cognitive Psychology, 1977, Vol. 9, pp. 111-151.

Read, Charles. Children's Categorization of Speech Sounds in English. ERIC Clearinghouse on Language and Linguistics, ERIC Clearinghouse on Reading and Communication Skills. NIE, Urbana, IL: NCTE, 1975.

Recht, D. "The Self-Correction Process in Oral Reading." The Reading Teacher, April 1976.

Royer, J. M. and Cunningham, D. J. On the Theory and Measurement of Reading Comprehension. Technical Report. Center for the Study of Reading. University of Illinois, June 1978.

Rumnelhart, David E. Toward an Interaction Model of Reading. Center for Human Information Processing. Technical Report No. 56, University of California, San Diego, March 1976.

Rumnelhart, David E. "Notes on a Schema for Stories." In D. G. Bobrow and A. M. Collins (Eds) Representation and Understanding: Studies in Cognitive Science. New York: Academic Press, 1975.

Sanders, Norris. Classroom Questions - What Kinds? New
York: Harper and Row, 1966.

Smith, Frank. "Learning to Read by Reading." Language
Arts. Vol. 53, March 1976, pp. 297-299.

Smith, Frank. Understanding Reading. New York: Holt,
Rinehart and Winston, 1971.

Smith, Frank. "The Role of Predictions in Reading."
Elementary English. Vol. 52, March 1975, pp. 305-
311.

Smith, Frank. Understanding Reading. New York, Holt,
Rinehart and Winston, 1978.

Stein, Nancy L. How Children Understand Stories: A
Development Analysis. Center for the Study of Reading. Technical Report No. 69, University of Illinois
at Champaign - Urbana, March 1978.

Thorndyke, P. "Cognitive Structures in Comprehension
and Memory of Narrative Discourse." Cognitive Psychology, Vol. 9, 1977, pp. 77-110.

Wheat, Thomas E. and Edmond, Rose M. "The Concept of
Comprehension: An Analysis." The Journal of Reading. Vol. 68, April 1975, pp. 523-527.

CHAPTER VI

WHOLE LANGUAGE READING APPROACHES

Knowledge Competencies

1. What are the characteristics of many current reading programs?
2. What are the characteristics of whole language reading programs?
3. What is the rationale for teacher reading aloud, assisted reading and the language experience approach being classified as whole language reading approaches?
4. In what ways does sustained silent reading help readers develop skills, comprehension and interest in reading?
5. How does the Directed-Reading-Thinking-Activity (DRTA), schema story approach and ReQuest develop comprehension? How is each approach similar and different?
6. What is functional reading and functional reading activities?
7. What are the differences between skills learning center activities and whole language learning center activities?

Psycholinguistic research concerning language learning has provided principles and generalizations upon which to base a reading program. The theories and models of language learning presented in Chapter II, Oral Language Development and Chapter III, The Reading Process, have contributed to an understanding of language learning processes. There is now available considerable evidence about language learning that children can learn to read and write the way they learned to talk and listen. The theories, hypotheses and models of the reading process developed by Kenneth Goodman, Frank Smith and Michael Halliday's theories of functional oral language learning, need to be applied in school reading programs at all levels.

A variety of whole language reading approaches have been developed during the past two decades, from 1960 - 1980. Some of the methods have an even longer history in the total school reading program, e.g., teachers reading aloud to students, individualized reading programs (self-selected materials) and the language experience approach. Newer techniques have been proposed, such as: assisted reading, sustained silent reading, directed-reading-thinking-activity (DRTA), Request, schema stories, written conversation, reading strategy lessons, functional-type reading, and "whole" language learning center activities. All the approaches identified above are whole language methodologies enabling the learner to communicate with language in a natural and meaningful way.

This chapter will provide a brief overview of the following: (1) the status of current reading programs; (2) whole language approaches to develop a comprehension-centered reading program at various developmental stages of reading.

The teacher, at any grade level, within the classroom or in special classes outside the classroom, has a formidable and complex task. There is no one blueprint available that can be implemented by a teacher. Each teacher must make educational decisions related to the unique situation and the individual learner and group of learners. Suggestions and examples are offered in this chapter toward the goal of implementing socio-psycho-linguistically-sound theories into educational practice. How a teacher translates socio-psycholinguistic principles into practice will depend upon each different situation.

Current Reading Instruction

Most reading instruction at all levels is preoccupied with teaching and testing isolated skills. Particularly at the acquisition stage of reading, there is an extreme emphasis on teaching separate graphophonemic relationships and a word-centered focus. There is usually a separation and fragmentation between practice on isolated skills and actually reading. The fragmentation of so-called "skills" of reading, e.g., word attack, comprehension and study skills, is characteristic of reading instruction at higher levels. Most reading instruction is dictated by commercially published basal reader materials referred to as either "whole word," "phonic," "linguistic," or other skills-centered supplementary materials. The commercially published reading materials are prescriptive in nature since they identify and sequence word recognition and comprehension skills to be tested and taught. Each "program" has its own sequence and hierarchy of skills, none of which are based on any empirical research. The underlying theory upon which "skills" programs are built, if there is one,

324

is that pronunciation or word recognition equals comprehension. The common assumption at the beginning level is that if a reader knows alphabet letters, can relate letters to sounds and blend letters/sounds into words, that comprehension will occur (see Figure 6:1). The focus in most commercially published reading programs, whether the so-called meaning-emphasis or "whole word approach," phonic-emphasis, "linguistics" materials, or some other skill-oriented materials, is not on comprehension, certainly at the beginning level of reading. The emphasis is on separate skills/though eventually the "skills," e.g., letter-sound relationships and words are embedded into sentences and stories. Frequently, these stories have difficult syntactic structures and are stilted, artificial and contrived.

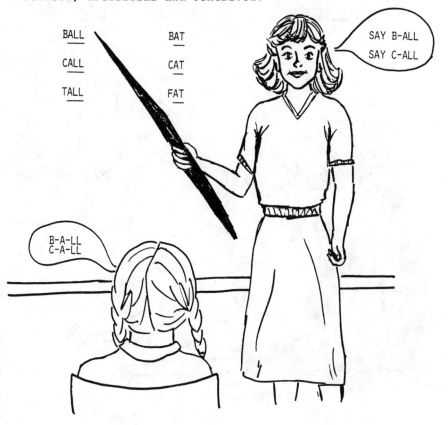

SKILLS-CENTERED READING INSTRUCTION

FIGURE 6:1

Current practices and materials in reading instruction teaches children that reading is an exact process. Frequently, all reading miscues are treated as
equal. Error-free reading is considered good reading.
Teachers or other pupils during group oral reading often
interfere with a reader's performance in unproductive
ways, e.g., unnecessary prompting to "sound it out";
insisting on super-correct oral reading; discouraging
guessing or predicting; not allowing reader's to regress
or self-correct and the consideration that all regress-
ions or repetitions are bad (see Figure 6:2).

SKILLS-CENTERED READING INSTRUCTION

FIGURE 6:2

The reading period and reading groups, high, middle and low, have become an institution in American schools. Reading instruction is scheduled at a certain time each day, and if one were to walk into almost any classroom in an elementary school there would be two or three reading groups. The dominant materials for reading instruction during the reading period and for each group are commercially published materials, e.g. basal readers, workbooks and "purple passion sheets," or commonly referred to as "ditto sheets." Look into almost any classroom during the reading period and you will usually see the teacher with a group reading orally a story from the reader. The teacher would be asking questions while other groups are at their desks working on skill workbooks and worksheets. Occasionally some children may be reading a book. There may be a reading corner or "center"; but it is seldom used. There may even be a writing or listening center; however, these too are infrequently used. The preoccupation with group oral reading, teacher questioning and completing workbooks and worksheets on "skills" takes up too much time for children to do real kinds of reading and writing.

All too often reading has no real function or purpose for children. If reading instruction consists of separate, fragmented practice on skills apart from meaning, prescribed reading materials, a separate reading period, and little time to read a variety of materials for different purposes, then is it any wonder that some children make no sense out of reading and see little value in learning to read.

However, there have always been teachers who have intuitively known that all reading must be comprehension-focused and used for meaningful purposes. They have known that so-called "skills" are learned and developed within a comprehension-focused reading program. Some teachers have developed individualized reading programs (self-selection of materials), used the language experience approach and have scheduled sustained silent reading in their classrooms. Frequently, these whole language methods have replaced or supplemented conventional published basal reading materials. Some teachers have moved away from the traditional two or three achievement reading groups and oral group reading to a variety of different organizational plans. The philosophy and principles of the "open classroom" concept are still evident in some classrooms.

There are hopeful signs that teachers are becoming more dissatisfied with highly organized skills-

327

sequenced, management systems to teach reading. Goodman and Watson (1978) stated: "In growing numbers, teachers are questioning the basis on which their reading programs are developed. These educators fear they are asking students to spend time and energy on activities that, at best, have little to do with becoming good readers, and, at worst, are interfering with the reading process. Many of these teachers have faithfully attended to skill building, only to discover that while their students may improve on drill and skill exercises, they continue to struggle with written language, including social studies, math and science materials; and rarely, if ever, become eager readers who enjoy a wide variety of literature."

Goodman and Watson (1978) continued: "As teachers become disenchanted with highly specific skill-oriented programs, they begin to rethink their own ideas about reading and learning. This has led them to discard some of their previous practices and to search for activities and procedures suitable to a reading program that is student-centered in nature, keeps language and thought in tact, and has comprehension as its focus."

Unfortunately, many teachers, though willing to discard skills-oriented programs, and whose creativity is stifled because of highly rigid skills-management systems, are locked out from implementing a whole language reading program. Even though there has been a profound breakthrough in understanding the sociopsycholinguistic nature of the reading process and there are available a variety of meaning-centered reading approaches and materials to use in reading programs, teachers are finding it difficult to eliminate and/or reduce skills programs in the classroom. In some school systems, skills programs are mandated by higher authorities, e.g. boards of education, superintendents, curriculum coordinators, principals, etc. Teachers are required to schedule a large part of the time having students drill on isolated skills. There is little time left for real reading/writing experiences. The classroom teacher does not always have much flexibility in selection and use of materials for reading. The situation should be more encouraging in remedial reading, learning disabilities classes and developmentally disabled classes. Teachers in special classes usually have more independence in the selection for reading experiences. However, often special teachers, LD teachers and teachers with slow learner children, do not have a background knowledge of reading as a socio-psycholinguistic process. Remedial reading, learning disabilities

328

and developmentally disabled programs are generally highly skills-centered. As a result, special teachers are usually compounding the reading problems of children referred for special help in reading.

There are, of course, no easy solutions to the problem of replacing or at least supplementing a skills-oriented program with a whole language reading program. The problem has to be approached at many different levels. Basically, it is a problem of lack of knowledge of the reading process and/or a "we-have-always-done-it-this-way" attitude on the part of teachers, administrators and the public. Too many teachers have not kept up with the development of socio-psycholinguistic theories about language learning. It is appalling the number of classroom teachers and reading specialists who are not members of the National Council of Teachers of English or the International Reading Association. Many teachers do not read the professional journals published by these organizations. However, it is not only teachers who are agents of change. Teachers need the support and cooperation of school administrators, boards of education, and the public. Superintendents, principals and instructional coordinators must become knowledgeable about what reading is and how it is learned based on psycholinguistic theories.

Moreover, tradition and convention are slow to change. Attitudes and ideas about reading instruction are etched in stone and handed down from one generation to the next. The public or parents have preconceived ideas and attitudes about how reading should be taught. They are influenced by the mass media about the teaching of reading. Schools generally reflect the prevailing attitudes and ideas of the society. Administrators and teachers, too, have preconceived ideas and opinions about how reading is learned. Generally, these ideas and attitudes are based on common-sense thinking, rather than socio-psycholinguistic insight into the reading process. Conventional ideas about reading tend to be perpetuated by many forces. Even within the so-called reading establishment there are wide differences in research findings and opinions about the reading process and how reading is learned. Therefore, it is understandable why the public, parents, boards of education, administrators, and teachers resist new ideas and insights about the reading process.

In the final analysis, teachers and parents will need to take the lead in educating the public and administrators about socio-psycholinguistic theories related to the reading process and the development of whole language reading programs. Teacher-educators will need to be more influential at pre-service and in-service levels to develop teachers who are knowledgeable about the reading process, know how children learn and how to implement a reading program focused on comprehension. School administrators will need to support teachers who are testing and implementing whole language practices based on a socio-psycholinguistic knowledge of the reading process.

New evaluation procedures must be developed to assess the reading progress of children in real and varied reading situations and for different purposes. Traditional tests do not really monitor the reading process. They merely sample parts of the total reading process and distort the reading process. Traditional tests contribute to skills-oriented reading programs and published reading instructional materials, e.g. workbooks, skill sheets, drill skills, and are mirror images of "reading tests." The reconstruction of reading programs from "skills-centered" to whole language programs are likely as more teachers realize that many children fail at reading and dislike reading despite achievement test scores indicating a higher percentage of children reading at or above grade level.

In the next section a variety of whole language approaches are described from which a teacher can select methods and materials appropriate for learning to read. Some techniques are more suitable for learners at certain stages of reading development than others. Some approaches are more appropriate for some learners than for other learners. Only the teacher, who knows her/his students as individuals and as a group, can make the decisions and judgements from available materials and resources which best fit an individual learner or group of learners at a particular time.

For each whole language approach a brief background will be given, including examples of how teachers may plan various approaches. The lesson plans are lessons that have been applied by classroom and remedial reading teachers the author has had in reading courses and workshops.

Chapter VII describes how to organize and manage a whole language classroom.

Whole Language Reading Approaches:

A whole language program at any level of reading development stresses comprehension. The focus of all language processing is on constructing meaning. Language is learned and used for communication purposes. As much as possible language learning is related to each student's experiences, interest, and learning development. In addition, children's questions and curiosity are nurtured and horizons are expanded. Language experiences in a whole language classroom are related to each child's life and purposes now--not for some future goal. Written language (reading and writing) and oral language (speaking and listening) development are learned naturally in various whole language situational contexts. There is no contrived separation between learning oral language and written language. Written language processing is an alternative form of communication for certain functions and purposes. Reading and writing are learned as a natural extension of speaking and listening.

In a whole language program language is used as a way to communicate ideas to and with others. Language learning does not take place as an end itself. The only justifiable end result of language is communication about self, others, and the world. In a whole language reading program there is no need to transfer isolated skills drilled apart from language use. All the components of the language system are available to the learner all the time. The learner is immersed in functional, whole and meaningful communication. There should be an integration and coordination of language learning to construct ideas about the environment and to learn more about self and others using language to communicate one's thoughts, feelings and experiences. Also, language is used to receive ideas and experiences from others. There is also a joy and self-fulfillment that comes from the use of language, both productive and receptive language.

The whole language classroom is life-centered, student-centered and language-based. Life is not compartmentalized into neat subject areas, such as social studies, science, health, physical education, art, and mathematics. Language learning is not separated into periods of time, e.g. reading, writing, and spelling periods. The separate distinction of subject areas and language in the traditional classroom needs to be reconsidered. Such distinctions present obstacles to learning since the transfer of skills and subjects

331

"learned" in isolation is highly questionable. The whole language classroom is a reflection and image of reality. Students learn when they perceive a purpose for learning. Content to be learned should be related to students' life problems and concerns. The old cliche, "start where the child is," is still a truism today. Content and language learning must begin and build upon the students' experiences and interests. Children naturally have an inclination to expand and explore ideas when they have successfully assimilated and accommodated prior information with new ideas. Learning and using language processes becomes easy and natural when learning experiences are based on prior language ability and knowledge. The wholeness of content and language enables each learner to progress at his/her own ability and within his/her background experiences.

Each approach presents language in natural whole language, it is meaningful, in a context and is functional. The whole language approaches described are the following:

* 1) Reading Aloud to Children
* 2) Assisted Reading
* 3) Language Experience
  4) Self-Selected Reading and Sustained Silent Reading (with student-selected miscues)
  5) Directed-Reading-Thinking-Activity
  6) Schema Stories
  7) ReQuest
  8) Functional-Type Reading Activities
  9) Written Conversation
 10) Whole Language Activities for Learning Centers

* Specialized materials such as "predictable language books" and wordless picture books are particularly related to reading aloud to children, assisted reading and language experience approaches. (See Appendices D and G.)

Reading Aloud to Students

It has become clearly evident from research and experience that reading to children helps them learn to read. All things considered equal, the child who has been read to frequently during preschool years and school years has a better chance of becoming a successful reader than a child who has not had the opportunity. Obviously, there are other factors contributing to reading effectiveness. However, being read to is clearly a very important variable in reading development.

READING ALOUD

FIGURE 6:3

How Reading Aloud Helps Reading Development

The preschool child up to the age of five or six has already internalized the linguistic system of his/her environment. The young child at school entrance can produce and receive language utterances. The linguistic competence of the child is considerable by the time he/she comes to school. Oral language learning and to some extent written language has been a natural learning process.

Parents, significant others in the child's environment, nursery school teachers and teachers at various levels in school, provide an exposure to print and an awareness of books when they read aloud to a child. The Book Program in a Research Oriented Preschool at the University of Waikato, New Zealand (1976) described how reading aloud contributed to reading development. Holloway (1974) stated, "Reading aloud to children develops a complex set of literacy skills. Reading to children develops an attitude where books are valued and used. The child develops a high expectation of print and comes to believe that books bring a special range of pleasures obtained in no other way. Reading to children, especially on a one-to-one basis or in a small group, provides a close personal, intimate relationship and interaction. It is very similar to the situations in which a child learns to talk. Frequent reading aloud to a child helps him/her to construct language models for written language or book language. As the child is read to he/she becomes familiar with written symbols as something different from other visual experiences. The child may try to produce written symbols in print-like scribbles at an early age. Reading aloud helps the child begin to understand conventions or directionality in print. The young child learns that stories in books unfold from the print by moving the eyes from the top of the page to the bottom from line to line and across each line of print from left-to-right and a return sweep of the eyes from right-to-left down to each succeeding line of print. Reading to a child helps him/her to learn to listen for increasing periods of time to continuous language interrelated in terms of plot, theme and characters. Finally, reading orally to a child develops ability to attend to language without reference to the sensory world around him or her at the moment and to respond to language in complex ways creating sensory or emotional images from past experiences. Reading aloud opens a new dimension of fantasy and imagination to his/her experiences allowing creation of images which appear nowhere in the sensory world, e.g. angels, giants, witches, monsters, etc. Being read to enables the child to escape from the here and now into the past and the future."

Eastland (1968) explained the purposes for read-aloud stories in the following statement: "Reading aloud develops in the child a deep enjoyment of the printed word. The "read-aloud" story is the necessary intermediate step leading the child from dependence on the story-teller to independence in reading. It is a readiness phase. Reading to children develops understanding and compassion for the world around him. The materials presented orally to the class graphically demonstrate to the children what is best in literature and

334

and has a far-reaching influence on the children's
future reading tastes and attitudes and new interests
are born. The teacher's way of reading in meaningful
phrases becomes part of the child's "inner ear." Eventually the child's independent reading reflects this
habit of phrasing and he/she seem to "hear" the speeches
in his/her book as clearly as if the story characters
were actually talking to him/her. The child's independent reading is no longer a laborious translation of
symbol into word meaning. It is a true thought communication between author and reader."

        To summarize, reading aloud to children in the
home, at school or anywhere, develops motivation to read
independently and that books are enjoyable and fun activity worth the effort of learning how to read. Reading
aloud helps the development of language: listening and
speaking vocabularies are expanded, syntactic structures
are developed and different language is heard, e.g.
regional differences, slang, etc. Conceptual development is enhanced through reading aloud. Objects, things
and experiences are classified, sorted and categorized
into cognitive structures. Prior knowledge and experiences are assimilated and accommodated with new experiences and knowledge through exposure to a variety of
books and stories. Cramer (1975), stated, "Reading to
children enriches their language. Unconscious and conscious memorization of words, phrases and syntax often
results."

        In the next section there will be a consider-
ation of the teacher's selection of books and stories
and other print appropriate for reading aloud to children.

Selection of Read-Aloud Materials

        Obviously, it is important for the teacher
to have a wide knowledge of children's books. Teachers
have the formidable task of keeping up with all the
books available on the market today. Taking a course
in children's literature would be particularly appropriate, especially if several years have elapsed since
enrollment in a course. However, there are other techniques to consider. Since a personal examination of
each title is time-consuming, a teacher must rely on the
judgement of others in becoming familiar with books and
selecting appropriate books. To aid in book selection
the teacher must rely on lists of books which are published. The following book lists should be consulted:

                        335

1. The Booklist and Subscription Books Bulletin: Current Books. Published by the American Library Association.
2. Children's Catalog. Published by H. W. Wilson Co. with regular supplements. A complete annotated listing.
3. Horn Book. Published by Horn Book, Inc., New York. Published six times a year.
4. School Library Journal. Published by R. R. Bowker Co., New Yori. Various professional journals report on books published and review books.

Various professional journals report on books published and review books.

1. Childhood Education Magazine. Published by Childhood Education International. There is a review of books in each issue.
2. Language Arts. Published by the National Council of Teachers of English. Urbana, Illinois has a monthly "Books for Children" section. Also articles on authors and illustrators of children's books appear.
3. The Reading Teacher. Published by the International Reading association, Delaware, N.J. Each October a section called "Children's Choices" features books recommended by children.
4. The New York Times. Has a column each week, "For Younger Readers" and in the Fall each year devotes one issue to a book review section of children's books.

The teacher should also consult various publishing companies for catalogues of children's books. A few to be considered are:

1. Scholastic Publishing Company
2. Garrard Publishing Company
3. Bowmar Publishing Company

Interests and Age Factors

There are important factors about children that teachers should consider when selecting stories and books to read aloud to children. The two primary factors are interest and age of children.

Interests are usually a reflection of age, sex, background experiences and psychological maturity. The teacher should be aware of play interests, movies, television and hobbies. Of course, books and stories to be read to children should also go beyond immediate interests and experiences and expand the child's interests into new areas. However, generally children at preschool and primary levels need to have stories read to them that are closely related to their interests and prior experiences.

Studies of children's reading interests show definite trends related to age. Preschool children from ages two to four are usually interested in picture books, nursery rhymes, Mother Goose rhymes, animal stories, Dr. Seuss books, fairy tales. Kindergarten and primary children like animal stories, stories about children, fairy tales, folk tales, riddles. Middle grades or fourth through sixth, generally are interested in informational books children of other lands and cultures, heroes, explorers, history, animal stories, tall tales, fantasy, humor. Upper grade students, grades seven and eight, usually like books similar to intermediate age children and, also, mystery and adventure books. Older students are becoming interested in problems in the adult world.

Eastland (1968) suggested the following criteria for assessing the suitable "read aloud" stories for primary age children: "The story should be appropriate for the developmental level of the group (or individual) to understand, enjoy and empathize with the characters. The story should have a simple plot which can be satisfactorily treated in a single story period without exceeding attention span. The story should be action-centered and involve only enough description to set the child's own imagination to work. It should have a plot and characters which are well developed and ring true within the framework of the story. In the main, the text of a good "read aloud" tale should capably tell the story without the support of accompanying illustrations. Whole stories to be read aloud should always deal with material of interest to children. The stories selected should not be those written in the primary vocabulary. Read aloud only those stories which you enjoy."

Donald Bissett (1978) compiled a bibliography of literature appropriate for reading aloud to children. This bibliography is categorized under general headings and can be seen in Appendix A.

337

Bonnie Chambers at Bowling Green State University compiled a bibliography including books suitable for reading aloud to children at various age levels. See Appendix B.

Carolyn Bradley, a second grade teacher in Springfield City Schools in Ohio has identified books enjoyed by primary age children. Appendix C contains a list of books appropriate for second, third, and fourth greaders. The * denotes a longer book taking about twenty minutes a day for about two weeks.

Lynn K. Rhodes (1981) compiled a bibliography of predictable books for use with children to read aloud to them. The bibliography in Appendix D identifies predictable trade books, predictable stories found in instructional materials, and written down songs.

Jane L. Decker, a Title I Reading Specialist at Grant Elementary School, Columbia Public Schools in Columbia, Missouri, compiled a bibliography of books appropriate for reading aloud to children and for other related whole language activities, e. g., reading and writing. See Appendix E.

The books listed in the Appendixes that are appropriate for the teacher to read aloud to children are also suitable for children to self-select to read independently. Books read aloud to children should be displayed in the classroom available for interested children to read themselves.

Sometimes books should simply be read aloud by the teacher, aide or older student for pure enjoyment. There need be no follow-up questioning, project to write an experience type story, or to apply what has been listened to, such as, making chicken soup after reading aloud Maurice Sendak's Chicken Soup With Rice. However, at times, after listening to a book there are various ways to naturally integrate and coordinate other language processes, reading, writing, dramatizing, art and music. This is particularly the case during thematic units to bring all things together in a unified relationship. It would seem quite meaningful to follow up reading aloud Judith Viorst's Alexander and the Terrible, Horrible, No Good, Very Bad Day, with having the children dictate for the teacher to write down or for the children to write their own version of their terrible, horrible, no good, very bad day. Nevertheless, there is neither the time nor the necessity to plan expanding learning experiences after most "read aloud" stories.

338

The teacher will need to selectively decide the interest the children show toward the book, whether the book
lends itself to natural follow-up activities, and which
children may benefit from future language experiences.

In a later section several examples of lessons
emphasizing reading aloud to children are given. These
lessons suggest several ways to extend and expand listening to books read aloud by teachers or others.

Establishing a Read Aloud Climate

Ronald Cramer (1975) offered suggestions for
teachers to develop a climate of receptivity on the part
of the children to teacher read aloud times in the classroom. The read aloud period should be a time for enjoyment and relaxation. There should be informality and
naturalness. Cramer suggests all distracting materials
and objects be kept out of reach of children. The read
aloud session should be an integral part of the daily
classroom schedule. It may be scheduled at a specific
time each day for reading aloud to the whole class. The
teacher will need to establish a few simple guidelines
for children including no talking or walking around when
a story is being read aloud. Finally, the teacher or
other person should not read too long at any one time.

Planning Read Aloud Sessions

One teacher at any grade level with 25-30 children will experience difficulty in reading aloud to individuals and small groups. If there are no paraprofessionals, student teachers or older students available to help, most reading to children will necessarily
have to be on a whole group basis. Reading to the large
group is appropriate if the book is fairly long and requires reading over several days and/or the book is of
general interest to all children.

However, most reading aloud to children, especially to learners at the acquisition literacy stage
(preschool - primary) should be individually and in
small groups. Listening to stories read should be a
close personal interaction between the person reading
and the child/children listening. Young children who,
unfortunately, have not experienced being read to frequently or not at all, particularly need the close one-
to-one relationship. They need to see the print and illustrations as the story is read to them. They need to

be able to interact with the person reading, to ask questions and to make comments. The teacher must know which children have or have not experienced being read to in their home. Additional personnel available in the classroom, such as teacher aides and/or older students from other rooms can read aloud individually or in small groups to children to assist the teacher. If you are the only person with a large group of children, then read-along-with books, stories, and tapes will need to supplement live reading aloud. However, the child loses the personal contact when using assisted reading.

Whether reading aloud to children in a large, small group or to an individual child, there are certain procedures to follow to make listening to stories an enjoyable and beneficial experience for children.

Eastland (1968) recommended the following procedures for presenting "read aloud" stories. First, it is important to plan in advance what you will read. Read it aloud to yourself before presenting it to the class. Boyd and Jones (1977) suggest essential steps in planning to read aloud: 1) orally and silently read the piece to grasp the overall meaning; 2) locate key ideas and groups of words for ease of breathing and emphasis; 3) discover the author's organization and literary unity of the story; 4) get aquainted with the personality of the author; 5) answer the question: "Why did the author write this?" --to inform, describe, convince, persuade, interest, amuse, entertain, stimulate, impress, etc.; 6) decide upon the predominate mood, e.g., serious, humerous, tragic, joyful, etc. and read in this vein; 7) note the flow of language, its melody and rhythm; 8) understand the symbolism.

Eastland (1968) further recommended the teacher draw the children into an intimate group so children benefit from physical and visual contact, especially with preschool, kindergarten, and primary children. Next, set the stage with a few well-chosen words to introduce the story or with a simple question. It is important to keep the introduction brief. Handle the book carefully and with respect. Be sure to pause until you have each child's attention before beginning to read. The teacher or other persons reading aloud to children should use appropriate inflection and avoid extreme facial or vocal animation. Boyd and Jones (1977), stated that good oral reading is interpretative reading. Good reading aloud requires the skill of an actor, the ability to establish a feeling of empathy, and to make the listener laugh, smile, feel sad or joyful.

During read aloud time the teacher should pause at appropriate places to allow the child's mind to catch up or race ahead in anticipation, according to Eastland (1968). She suggests avoid asking what will happen next because it is difficult to draw children's attention back into the story. Other considerations during reading aloud is the importance of eye contact with the audience as much as possible. When reading to one child or a very small group (2-4) with very young children, the person reading should help the child/children follow the print by running his/her finger under the lines of print.

Linda Lamme (1976) described an attempt to develop more objective ways for teachers to determine the quality of their oral reading to groups of children. She videotaped teachers as they normally read aloud to their classes. The videotapes were analyzed using a preliminary form of a Reading Aloud to Children Scale (RACS).

The results in this study indicated the following teacher reading aloud behaviors:

1) Child involvement in the story reading was the most influential item on the scale. Teachers had children orally "read" the refrains or predict what would happen next, or fill in words from time to time.

2) The second most influential reading behavior was the amount of eye contact between reader and the audience.

3) The third characteristic of good oral reading was putting expression into the reading.

4) A related item was the quality of the reader's voice; tended to put variety in their voices and not read at too high or low a pitch, or too soft or loud a volume.

5) Teachers who pointed to words and pictures in the book were better overall readers.

6) Familiarity with the story was scored as the next characteristic.

7) Selection of the book, particularly the quality (size and color), was important.

341

8) Grouping children so that all could see.

9) Highlighting the words and language of the story was significant.

Lessons Illustrating Reading Aloud to Students

Reading aloud to children by teachers should not be haphazard or an incidental activity to fill in time. The teacher should view reading aloud to children as an integral part of the overall comprehension-centered reading program in the classroom. Lesson planning including the factors described above should be considered when reading aloud.

Several examples of teacher-planned lessons focused on reading aloud to children are given below:

Lesson 1

Purpose: To build up language models; to help children relate to the world around them by responding to book language by using images and emotions from their past experiences, and to bring a special range of pleasure that can be obtained in no other way.

Plan: To read aloud, The Longest Journey in the World, by William Morris.

For: Group of six children, 2nd grade.

Where: Quiet, relaxing place that is free from distractions.

Initiating: "Have any of you gone on a long journey?" After listening and capitalizing on some of their experiences, I would say, "We are going to read about a little caterpillar who thought he went on a very long journey."

Interaction: Lively discussion of humorous concepts such as the comparison of the football to a mountain and a stuffed animal to a dragon. Let the children take turns in reading the book to themselves or to others.

Extending:	The children would draw pictures and write or dictate a comparable story.
Evaluation:	Observe how the children caught on to new concepts; did what they read make sense to them.

Lesson 2

Purpose:	To provide a model to help develop in students an appreciation of the pleasure books can give, to encourage good listening habits for themselves as well as being respectful of others; need to be able to listen.
Organization:	I use this book with 3rd and 4th grade students, particularly if I have a class of boys. They related readily to the characters and situations. The book is called "How to Eat Fried Worms;" and since its reading takes more than one of my 30 minute sessions, I make sure I read consecutively over two or three days. My classes like to sit on a rug we have provided for the story area. In fact, the children frequently like to stretch out on the floor around me as I read, but with this story, they stay close enough to see the illustrations clearly. At the end of the day's reading, I either read the title of the next chapter or ask questions to try to get them to predict what will happen next. If I must stop in the midst of a chapter, I try to choose the place carefully so as to maintain interest in the next reading.
Evaluation:	Students have gone to their regular classroom to retell the story to classmates; so there are many times when teachers come to borrow the book to read to their own classes. That tells me a lot about the success of the approach.

Reading Aloud Activity

Gulliver's Travels, by Jonathan Swift
Retold in simple language by Marie Stuart

Read Gulliver's Travels to a third grade reading class. Group children around so that as many as possible can see the book as it is being read to them. If all cannot see, take turns on following days letting children sit close so they can follow along. Be sure to show illustrations to everyone, two times with this book.

Read only a short time the first day then increase the time if children show a lot of interest. (Fourth graders loved this book, especially the illustrations.) Be sure to explain the unusual terms used.

After the book is finished, tell the children that they will find the book in the reading shelf if they would like to see it again. (Fourth graders look at it over and over. It has really captured their imagination.)

Assisted Reading

Assisted reading is a whole language, comprehension-centered approach, particularly appropriate for children at the acquisition stage of reading development, for older students who have not had success in reading, and so-called "reluctant" readers at various age levels.

The rationale of assisted reading as a viable method for developing reading ability is given below. In addition, various methods of assisted reading, suggested print materials and organizing space for assisted reading are described for classroom application. Finally, samples of teacher-planned lessons emphasizing assisted reading are presented.

Rationale of Assisted Reading

Assisted reading is not a discrete methodology, but usually accompanies reading aloud by a proficient reader to a younger developing reader. Assisted reading is simply and naturally providing support and help

necessary for the child to develop familiarity with
print in order to process the print to construct meaning. Various techniques of assisted reading may be included with other comprehension-centered approaches
described later in this chapter; e.g., Language experience approach, DRTA, ReQuest, functional-type reading
activities, and the like. The assisted reading procedure may take different forms as presented in the
following section, but all forms are fundamentally
based on helping children process print into meaning.
Generally, assisted reading enables children to relate
oral language to written language, or to bridge the gap
between what has been learned (speaking) and what is to
be learned (reading).

Assisted reading is a natural extension and
supplemental method to reading aloud to children. As
Hoskinsson (1975) described assisted reading, it involves learning to read by immersion in written language.
Hoskinsson (1974) stated, "Assisted reading is based on
the assumption that children may process written language in a manner similar to the way they process spoken
language." When parents, teachers or others read aloud
to a child there is the opportunity for the child to
follow the print and to relate his/her linguistic knowledge and experience to written language. Listening to
stories in complete text enables the learner to bring
prior knowledge, experience and oral language to print
to construct meaning.

Hoskinsson (1974) offered the notion that,
"Since children are not denied the full context of
spoken language while learning to speak, they should
not be denied the full context of written language while
learning to read."

Assisted reading provides the learner the
sound of language with the orthographic forms of written language. The learner has the opportunity to
transfer linguistic competence to print. Learning to
read is facilitated as the child applies conceptual
knowledge and linguistic strengths to the reading process. Assisted reading provides the learner with all
linguistic cueing systems, e.g., graphic, syntactic and
semantic. The learner has the possibility of applying
learning strategies, e.g., sampling, testing, predicting,
confirming, and correcting in a safe, secure environment. The child can use as much of the print as necessary with the support of the phonological or sound system of language. All the sound patterns and orthographic patterns are presented in a meaningful context.

The learner is literally "bathed" in the sound and written forms of the language.

Assisted reading is not a total or complete "method" for the development of reading effectiveness. It is one of several comprehension-centered reading approaches available to the teacher, particularly at the acquisition stage of reading. The beginning reader has the difficult and complex task of learning the graphic configurations and orthographic regularities in the print to get to meaning represented by the print. Assisted reading is one among other approaches that allows the reader to go directly from print to meaning without excessive recoding or going from sound to print and then to meaning. Along with other whole language approaches, assisted reading will enable tht reader at the acquisition stage to gradually abstract the significant visual features and graphic patterns to process the meaning. Assisted reading is effective in developing the graphophonics cueing system, syntactic system, and semantic system. Considerable assisted reading experience provides meaningful text for the child to discover and abstract significant letter-sound pattern features and relationships. There is no need to present letters, sounds, and letter-sound features and words in isolated practice and drill apart from whole context. Obviously, the print material must be of high interest and related to experiential background for the child to benefit from assisted reading. Assisted reading, as other comprehension-centered approaches described in this chapter, may be supplemented with a variety of word analysis and "traditional" practice activities usually found in skills-oriented reading programs. However, children should be allowed to choose "skills" activities only as another free-choice activity.

Methods of Assisted Reading

Assisted reading is not a new or novel approach to helping children read. For years parents have naturally read to their child while the child sits close by looking at the print and pictures and listening to the story. Teachers also have used forms of assisted reading by setting up a listening station, e.g., a tape recorder, a book or story and a tape of the story to listen to while following the story. Yet it has only been recently that several types of assisted reading or "read along" has been legitimatized as a powerful and effective technique to develop reading ability.

ASSISTED READING

FIGURE 6:4

Assisted reading appears to be most effective
with preschool age children and certain primary age
children who have not made sufficient progress in reading. Also, older severely handicapped readers may benefit from some forms of assisted reading in conjunction
with other whole language approaches described in this
chapter.

The teacher needs to be highly selective in
determining the type of assisted reading that will be
beneficial to a given child. There is as yet no empirical evidence to guide the teacher in making this decision. However, the teacher can try various methods
of assisted reading with a particular child and carefully observe which techniques appear most effective.
Again, assisted reading is not an exclusive technique,
but is effective for some children together with other
comprehension-centered approaches. Frequently, assisted
reading techniques may be effectively integrated with
other whole language approaches, such as, ReQuest, in
which the teacher and child(ren) read orally/silently,
each asking the other questions about the story, and

occasionally, reading aloud together when appropriate to do so.

The basic techniques or types of assisted reading are: (1) Echoic reading; (2) Neurological Impress Method; (3) Read Along (book/story and audio tape recording or record). Variations of the above may include: teacher/aide with a child, and reading couples or pairs (child with child). (See Figure 6:5.)

READING COUPLES: ASSISTED READING

FIGURE 6:5

The ideal and most effective use of assisted reading is on a one-to-one basis with the teacher, aide or another child who can read reading with a child who cannot read as effectively. This setting provides a close, personal relationship similar to situations in which the child learns oral language. The one-to-one relationship also encourages direct, immediate feedback and interaction about print and meaning. This one-to-one situation is not necessary for most children much of the time, except for very early beginning readers and primary age and older learners who are essentially highly ineffective readers. The assisted reading method is very time-consuming and only necessary as a direct approach for highly selective learners.

Echoic Reading

There are a least four types of echoic reading which may be selected by the teacher and tried with very young learners and older ineffective readers. The essential technique with each type is that the reader reads first and the learner listens while following the print and repeats a segment of the text read by the teacher/aide/parent or child. The first procedure is (1) word-by-word approach, next, (2) a sentence or phrase approach, and, (3) the teacher reads omitting key words which the student predicts to fill in the deleted word to make sense; and (4) the child reads and the teacher supplies word structures the child cannot recognize. The learner's individual preference and learning style should be considered in using various approaches. Some children may be frustrated using the sentence/ phrase, predicting or reading approach, while the word-by-word method may be effective. The aim should be to develop the child's ability to "read" assisted by another person beyond the word level to larger chunks of language such as phrases or sentences. (See Figure 6:6, on page 350.)

The word-by-word and phrase/sentence methods are essentially the same. For the preschool "non-reader" the teacher or aide (parent) may read to the child three or four times with the same story or different stories to develop a love for stories and increase attention span. Picture books with little print may be used initially. It is helpful for the reader to focus the learner's attention to the print by moving his/her finger under the line of print as it is read aloud. The pictures should be discussed and the reader should respond to questions and comments made by the learner.

ECHOIC READING

FIGURE 6:6

The book should be "read" together until it is completed in one sitting. The word-by-word approach involves the reader reading one word at a time and the
child immediately "read" the word pronounced by the
reader. The phrase/sentence method increases the language unit. The teacher reads a sentence at a time and
the child repeats the sentence immediately. When doing
echoic reading with a child the teacher should provide

positive verbal support such as, "good," "right," and so forth. Schnecberg (1977) suggested that discussion and concept development are implemented before and during the reading.

Neurological Impress Method

Hollingsworth (1970) devised the impress method involving unison reading in which the child and teacher read aloud simultaneously. The teacher is seated slightly behind the child and the teacher and child hold the book. As the child and teacher read in unison, the teacher's voice is directed into the ear of the child. The child is told to place his/her finger under the line of print and slide his/her finger below the words as they are spoken. The impress method involves the learner's visual, aural, oral and tactile senses. (See Figure 6:7.)

NEUROLOGICAL IMPRESS METHOD

FIGURE 6:7

351

The impress method, as the echoic approach, is a very slow, tedious technique and extremely time-consuming to use in the classroom. However, teacher aides, older students and parents can be trained to use the impress technique. There is as yet no overwhelming empirical evidence concerning which learners can benefit from the neurological impress method. However, the impress method has been reported to be effective with learners identified as learning disabled and reading disability cases.

Read Along (Book-Tape)

The most practical but less personal method of assisted reading in the classroom is involving learners in listening to tapes or records accompanied by books or stories. There are many publishers of books and tapes related to most children's interests. The teacher may also tape her own books for children to listen to and read along. Any procedure of assisted reading, e.g., echoic, impress or read along (book-tape) should be for fun and enjoyment and avoid teaching "skills." (See Figure 6:8.)

READ ALONG BOOK AND TAPE

FIGURE 6:8

There are several difficulties using book-tape read-along. First, the taped story should be paced at a rate that approximates individual fluency rates of listening-reading. The taped stories or books need to be somewhat close or possibly above the child's general "reading level." However, background experiences, interest, attention span, attitude and concept development related to story content are more important factors to consider than some hypothetical "reading level" of the material.

Chomsky (1976) related an interesting application of read along using stories and tapes with a group of children in a third grade who were reading one to two years below grade level. The children had experienced two years of drill in word analysis, long and short vowels, word endings, or blendings, etc.

The children listened individually to tape-recorded stories, simultaneously following along in the written text. Each child set his/her own pace, reading and listening to the same story until fluency in oral reading of the story was achieved. The children selected their own stories and books to listen and read. The program combined reading with writing. They wrote stories and answered questions, writing sentences using words from the stories. The children's eventual success in reading was attributed to the ability to learn how to read a book. Being able to read a whole book added motivation and success in reading. Initially, read along was used to memorize a book to get children having difficulty in reading to deal with large amounts of connected discourse. (See Figure 6:9 on page 354.)

Chomsky (1976) further advised that children need time to adjust to assisted reading to follow in text and listen at the same time without losing his/her place and to coordinate the eyes and ears. Chomsky also related that it will take varying times for children to achieve fluency in reading a book orally. She advises that teachers should have tape recorders available with collections of tapes/books for the child to take to a corner to listen to, undistracted. The children should be allowed to take tapes and books home to listen/read.

Chomsky (1976) emphasized that writing is an important part of the process of learning to read. Children can write stories related to stories read. Finally, Chomsky makes an important point. She stated, "Assisted reading provides the expectation of success.

353

ORGANIZATION AND MATERIALS FOR LISTENING / READING CENTER

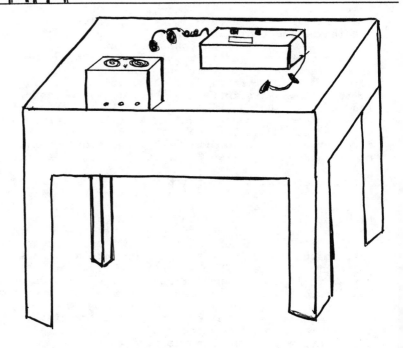

TAPES

BOOKS

A LISTENING CENTER

FIGURE 6:9

The child realizes that he/she will be able to read on his/her own without listening after awhile. The child cannot fail or be unsuccessful when listening to a story with a book to follow along."

According to Chomsky (1976) assisted reading is an effective reading method because it "bathes" or immerses the child with language to relate experience and the child's own linguistic ability. The child can process print and sound using the phonological, syntactic, and semantic input. The child's mind is actively focused on print material in a large context.

Given below are samples of lessons planned by teachers using assisted reading, including the echoic approach and read along (book-tape):

Sample Lessons Using Assisted Reading

Echoic Reading

Lesson 1

Assisted Reading

Purpose: To familiarize the children with graphic cues, to encourage a good feeling for stories and books.

Initiating: The children will all sit down quietly with me and we will do echoic reading of the story Mittens, by JoAnn Nelson.

Interaction: We will discuss our pets and how pets can and have helped people.

Expanding: We can listen to other story records about pets. We will bring any stories of pets that we might find in a magazine or paper. We can draw our pets or make a bulletin board with our pets' pictures. Write a story about your pet.

Evaluation: Discuss pet pictures and have the children share what the story meant to each of them.

<u>Echoic Reading</u>

Lesson 2

Purpose: To familiarize the child with <u>graphic</u> stimulus and instill <u>love of reading and books</u>.

Initiating: I have prepared a story on a transparency. It involves graphic-phonic stimulus, rhyming and a predicted redundancy that the children will anticipate and enjoy. The story is <u>Pierre</u>, by Maurice Sedak. We will use the overhead projector to read and follow the story.

Interacting: This may be done with one child or a group. I will begin the story by reading it line by line. There are two ways we may do the story.

1) The children will repeat the story line by line.

2) The children will predict the lines of the boy Pierre and say his lines for him, which are always, "I don't care."

    Ex.: One day
           his mother said
           when Pierre climbed out of bed,
           "Good morning darling boy,
           you are my only joy."
           Pierre said, "I don't care."

<u>Echoic Reading</u>

Lesson 3

Purpose: To familiarize the child with graphic stimulus, to instill love of stories and books.

Initiating: The child would sit down with me in a quiet area, and would follow the story with his eyes. I would read a line and the child would repeat it until we finished the whole story; the book being <u>Over in the Meadow</u>, by Olive A Wadsworth, illustrations by Ezra Jack Keats.

Interacting:	The child and I would read the story. We might then talk about how mother animals take care of their babies and teach them many things. We might discuss where each animal lived and why their homes were appropriate to them. We might discuss the child's experiences with any of the animals mentioned in the story.
Expanding:	The child may listen to a record that goes along with the book, and follow the words or pictures. The child may draw their favorite animal in its surroundings.
Evaluation:	Discuss the child's picture or pictures with him. The child may want to share the story orally with his classmates enabling you to measure comprehension.

Read Along

Lesson 1

Purpose:	To provide good language model for student, to provide enjoyable reading experience.
Organization:	I have a listening center set up in the corner with a desk, chair, tape recorder, earphones and a variety of books with both commercially prepared tapes and tapes I have prepared myself. I prefer to prepare my own because I feel many commercially prepared tapes are read at a rate unsuitable to the students' rate of reading, particularly in my classes. I also like to interact with the reader much as a parent and child interact when a story is read aloud. I do not use this as an opportunity to teach, but as an opportunity to stimulate, motivate, involve the reader in a pleasant reading experience.
Evaluation:	I've used this book and tape with first through fourth graders and it's evident by their desire to use it over and over again that it is very worthwhile.

357

The book is called "What's Inside?" After
listening, following along with the reading, the
students frequently want to spend time looking back
through the book, telling someone else to come and
look at it with them and many times I hear them responding during the tape.

LISTENING/READING AREA

FIGURE 6:10

Read Along

Lesson 2

Assisted Reading: Whose Mouse Are You?

Taped by Kelly Jackson

As a preface to this approach I had the class listen to a few stories I had taped using some of the books from the library shelf in my Title I room.

Then each student (only four in this class) chose a book he wanted to have taped as he read orally. After the first taping of the student reading, I taped myself reading the same story and had the student, using headsets, listen and follow along for three times (once daily). After three days the student was taped reading the story again.

The student evaluated his own performance, recognizing that in the second taping he sounded better and read faster, to use his own terminology.

Each of the four students was permitted to share his tape with the rest of the class at storytime. He held his book and turned the pages as the rest of the class listened.

Read Along

Lesson 3

These particular activities are centered on highly structured selections that will aid the beginning reader in predicting/confirming strategies. They were especially attractive to me because, as Bill Martin notes, (these) "selections have enough obvious repetitions in their underlying structures that children are propelled into anticipating the next line or episode."[1]

These selections would lend themselves particularly to echoic reading and the impress method, in that order. I feel it would not be long before the children would be reading these selections to themselves.

---

[1]Martin, Bill Jr. Sounds of Home. Holt, Rinehart and Winston, 1972.

Follow-up activities are aimed at getting reading material into the hands of the children to <u>stay</u>, as well as attempts to make these selections personalized possessions of each child. (Many of the children I see do not have good reading material at their disposal.)

Of course these activities would be planned periodically and the child would have the option of making choices to add to the collection of readings he was making.

These selections are from the Bill Martin, Sounds of Language Readers: "Sounds I Remember," "Sounds of home," and "Sounds of Numbers." These books are readily available to me with copies for each child. The other selections in these books would be excellent for reading aloud and other types of assisted reading, for example, book and tape.

Because the selections I have picked are interspersed throughout the previously mentioned books I would plan to have them done up on a form more conducive to individual selection or individual display.

Assisted Reading

Lesson 4

<u>Song of the Swallows by Leo Politis</u> - Tape and Book

Tape recorder with earphone is set up in a corner desk. Before beginning, show all the children how to operate the tape recorder and how to rewind it for the next person.

Children listen to tape and follow along in the book as they listen. They listen one at a time while the rest of the class continues other activities.

This activity is for enjoyment only, though teacher may ask casually which part the child liked best. There are no other required written or oral activities.

Purpose is to promote pleasure in reading. This is an especially good story with a song (La Golondrina) in it which the children might like to learn.

After all have listened one time, allow those who would like to hear the story again.

Language Experience Approach

The language experience approach is another whole language procedure related to socio-psycholinguistic theory. Language experiences can be interpreted broadly to include all language processes, e.g., listening, speaking, reading, and writing interrelated with experience. However, the language experience approach has been developed as a specific reading method. It has been narrowly identified as a beginning reading approach. The language experience approach will be described both as a broad, inclusive methodology and as a specific reading approach, although language-experience involves all communication transactions between language users. (See Figure 6:11.)

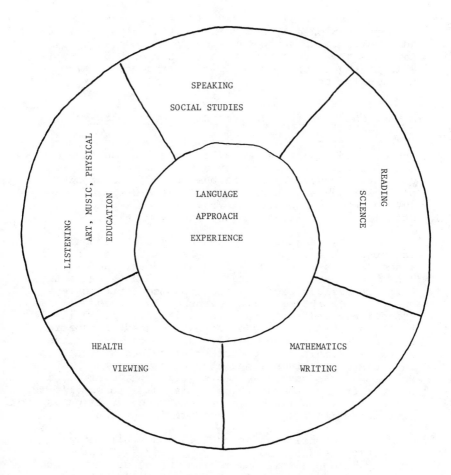

LANGUAGE-EXPERIENCE AND CONTENT

FIGURE 6:11

In this section a rationale for the language experience approach is given, followed by methods classroom teachers can plan and sample lessons illustrating language experience procedures and materials.

Nevertheless, it should be recognized that in a comprehension-centered communication classroom, language experience approach is but one, among other whole-language approaches described in this chapter, available to the teacher to facilitate students' communication abilities.

A Rationale for the Language Experience Approach

The child at the acquisition stage of learning to read and write needs to recognize and develop the concept that written language is a communication process. Previously it has been noted, the preschool child already has an understanding that print in the environment represents meaning. There is some understanding that written symbols convey meaning.

The language experience approach recognizes the young learner as a user of language. The child at school age is an effective language user. He/She knows the functions of oral language and is aware that print in various social situational contexts conveys meaning. The young child learns oral language very effectively and efficiently when language is available to the her/him in a given context related to experience. Over a period of time oral language facility is developed within meaningful, experiential-centered situations. The learner receives immediate and delayed feedback as she/he samples, selects, tests, predicts, confirms and/ or corrects hypotheses relating language to experience. Therefore, the child brings a background of language and experiences to the reading and writing processes.

The child has an oral language base upon which to develop reading and writing wtrategies. Reading and writing become natural extension and alternative language processes to communicate experiences with others. Reading and writing are learned easily and naturally when reading and writing are totally integrated. During early learning stages, the young child pretends to write by scribbling and copying print and pretends to read by imitating adults or significant others who have read aloud to him/her.

Reading and writing are learned naturally at the acquisition stage when print is related to the child's oral language patterns and are familiar written language patterns the child has had read to him/her. A logical beginning reading approach includes relating experiences to oral language which are dictated orally by the child and written down by someone, and read by the child. Another natural way to help the young child develop an "ear" for book learning is to read aloud poems and stories that have natural predictable language patterns. These approaches are described and illustrated in a later part of this section.

The language experience approach is an effective procedure because print is learned in meaningful language units. A child's dictated poem or story related to a real or vicarious experience provides a meaningful situational context. Written language is presented to the learner as a whole, integrated experience. Language units, including: graphemes, phonemes, syntax, morphemes, sentences, are available to the readers. There are no artificial, abstract, isolated letters, letter-sound relationships, words, or sentences out of context. The written language is related directly to the child's oral language, in a dictated story, and to context. The child learns to process print to construct meaning. Graphophonic cues, distinctive visual and sound features in written language, are learned within the context of meaning with the support of syntactic cues and semantic cues using the reader's own language patterns. The learner is able to apply predicting, confirming, correcting, and comprehending strategies naturally and meaningfully.

Finally, the language experience approach integrates speaking, listening, reading and writing into a total language approach. There is a close interdependence among all language processes. The learner develops awareness that each language process is useful for different communication functions. Written and oral language functions as means to communicate experiences. Oral language is used in face-to-face situations or through electronic media while written language is useful to communicate over time and space. There is no contrived barrier established in learning and using language to communicate information.

Various language experience methods are presented below which include all communication modes. (See Figure 6:12.)

READING

WRITING

SPEAKING

LISTENING

LANGUAGE   EXPERIENCE

APPROACH

TO   READING

LANGUAGE EXPERIENCE APPROACH

FIGURE 6:12

Methods of the Language Experience Approach

The language experience approach makes no clear
distinction among speaking, listening, reading and writing. Usually when teachers use a language experience
approach with children all language processes are

involved at one time or another. The language experience approach frequently is related to other comprehension-centered approaches described in this chapter.
For example, reading aloud to children a book or poem
may be followed by discussion, reaction, and writing by
children related to the language patterns and/or content
of the story or poem; self-selected reading and sustained silent reading, described in the following section, may involve various sharing activities based on
books read which may involve a child in writing a story,
doing further research on a topic related to the book
read, or writing a play based on the book and acting it
out. Various functional-type, everyday reading and
writing situations may involve reading a catalogue and
writing to order an item. There are other examples as
well in which a language experience approach can be integrated with other whole language activities.

Language experience methods are organized and
presented in three ways. First, learning to read
through listening, next, reading development through
speaking and third, reading through writing. There is
no arbitrary sequence in which teachers should plan and
provide various language experiences. The teacher must
take his/her cues from the children. It is vital that
the teacher knows each child's experiential background,
interests, and language development. This can most
effectively be accomplished by systematic observation
and listening to children as they are involved in planned
classroom learning activities. (See Chapter IV, Evaluation of Reading.)

Reading and Listening

The teacher can effectively relate listening
to language to reading written language by reading aloud
to children various stories, poems, jokes, riddles,
puns, limericks, and other written material. It is
essential that the material read to children is interesting and closely related to experiential background.
(See Reading Aloud to Children in a previous section
in this chapter.) (See Figure 6:13 on page 368.)

For children at the acquisition reading stage
one type of material to read aloud and written down to be
read by children is highly predictable language pattern
books. Lynn Rhodes has compiled a list of books and
stories from which teachers can select appropriate materials to read to children. This bibliography of highly
predictable language books can be seen in Appendix D.

READING STORIES AND POETRY

The Little Red Hen
The Three Billy Goats

A Song of Spring
The Shepard Boy

READING AND LISTENING TO STORIES AND POETRY

FIGURE 6:13

The teacher selects a story or poem which she/
he reads aloud to an individual child, a small group of
children or to the whole class, whichever grouping procedure is appropriate to the situation at the moment.

368

The children listen to the story and discuss and react
to the story if something is to be written down and
later read related to the story/poem read aloud. The
story or poem may be read aloud several times depending
on the age level of the children, the interest, and
attention to the material. Then invite the child(ren)
to suggest an alternative story that can be written down
based on the similar pattern in the story they heard.
With young children the teacher or aide will write down
the children's language patterns. Older children can
write their own story related to the language pattern
from the story. The dictated or written story may be
illustrated and is then read by the teacher to young
children and read to others by the older child. The
stories written by children (or the teacher if dictated)
may be bound into a book. (See a later section on making books by teachers, aides, children).

For example, a predictable trade book, I Know
an Old Lady, by Lady Rose Bonne, published by Rand-Mc
Nally, N.Y., 1961, may be selected by the teacher and
read aloud to a group of children. The pattern is predictable, identifiable, and repetitious. The teacher
may invite the children to join in on patterned portions
of the poem they have already identified. Following the
listening to the poem the teacher and children should
identify the elements of the poem to be imitated. Then
the teacher invites the children to dictate (or write)
a poem patterned after the poem.

The teacher may want to begin the poem by contributing the first two lines. The poem dictated should
be written on the chalkboard or on a large piece of
paper for all to see as the poem unfolds. It may be
necessary to edit the first draft by comparing the language pattern of the original with the imitated version.

The patterned story dictated by the children to
the teacher is given below:

I Know an Old Witch Who Swallowed a Bat

I know an old witch who swallowed a bat.
I don't know why she swallowed a bat.
I guess she'll get fat.

I know an old witch who swallowed a ghost.
That groaned and groaned and moaned inside her.
She swallowed the ghost to catch the bat.
I don't know why she swallowed the bat.
I guess she'll get fat

I know an old witch who swallowed a vampire.
How weird to swallow a vampire.
She swallowed the vampire to catch the ghost who groaned
    and groaned and moaned inside her. She swallowed
    the ghost to catch the bat.
I don't know why she swallowed the bat.
I guess she'll get fat.

Cramer and Cramer (1975) provide an excellent list of books teachers may select to use for patterned writing. See Appendix F.

Reading and Speaking

A highly effective material to help young readers relate print to meaning is wordless picture books. Wordless books provide the concrete referents the young child needs to tell the story through relating to pictures. The story plot, theme and events are conveyed through the pictures. Children also develop the context of story structure through wordless books. Some wordless books may be appropriate to use with older students and adults who have had extreme difficulty in reading.

There are a variety of procedures to apply with wordless books to provide a language experience approach. However, a few basic guidelines are suggested.

Generally, when using wordless books the teacher or aide will work with an individual child. The teacher or aide should briefly introduce the book to the child, say the title and browse through the pictures with the child. Encourage the child to talk about the pictures and make any appropriate comments about the topic of the book. The teacher should then suggest the child make up his/her own story. The teacher might comment that the author didn't write any story to go with the pictures but instead left it up to anyone to write/tell their own story about the pictures. The teacher should have available small sheets of paper to write down what the child says about each picture as the story unfolds. These pieces of paper can be paperclipped below each picture on the pages of the book. Of course, older children may compose and write their own story. Younger children will need to dictate their story for someone to write down for them. At the completion of telling and writing the story related to the pictures, the teacher may want to read back the story dictated by the child. Then, possibly the teacher (or aide) and child reads the story together, and finally, the child should try to read his/her story orally and silently. Some children may want to share their story by reading it aloud to others and showing the pictures.

A bibliography of wordless books from the Educational Research Council of America is given in Appendix G.

Various finger plays, songs, and jump rope rhymes, familiar to children can be told or sung and written down to be read. Young children easily and naturally relate to songs, rhymes, and finger plays that have been memorized. Children should see familiar jingles, poems, rhymes, and songs in print. These can be useful for reading material in the classroom.

Dorothy Watson (1979) used the example of children's jump rope rhymes and experiences at home and on the playground. The teacher can ask the children about jump rope rhyming patterns that they know and have the children recite the rhyme. The teacher writes down the rhyme for children to see the print. For example, the jump rope rhyme:

Teddy Bear, Teddy Bear turn around

Teddy Bear, Teddy Bear touch the ground. . .

The children and teacher read from the print. The teacher could duplicate the jump rope rhyme for the children to have a personal copy to read and take home to read. Children naturally get the idea that what they say can be represented in print. At the same time, children can learn various graphophonemic cues, such as, the "t" sound and letter correspondence in the rhyme, Teddy Bear, Teddy Bear. The "t" sound/letter relationship is repeated naturally throughout the rhyme. This is a more natural way to learn various graphophonemic relationships than in isolated, meaningless drill.

Older, ineffective readers may use popular song scripts which have repetitive, predictable language patterns for reading materials. Students may write or paraphrase contemporary music scripts to share with others. Various TV commercials may be written down and used for reading materials by older poor readers. These techniques help the reader relate everyday experience to print in meaningful context.

Reading and Writing

Besides integrating reading with listening and speaking, reading can be effectively correlated with the writing process. Obviously, writing is a component when a teacher reads to children and follow up with children's dictated ideas related to the listening experiences which are then recorded in print by the teacher. When the teacher, using wordless books, writes down the child's ideas related to the pictures, writing is involved. However, the teacher or another person is writing for the children.

At beginning first grade, children can begin to encode thoughts in print. During the time that a teacher acts as scribe to record ideas the children can be encouraged and given opportunities to write their own ideas. The writing process provides a natural integration and relationship to the reading process. A writer has to read and reread what he/she has encoded so reading is taking place during the writing process.

In addition, the writer is learning the graphophonemic system using written symbols to represent meaning. As children have opportunities to observe proficient writers encode ideas in print through dictated stories and poems, they are also begoming aware of the written orthography, e.g., the white spaces between letters, spelling patterns, the horizontal and vertical aspects of print and other orthographic features of print.

Many young children in Kindergarten and beginning first grade have a sense of print and can encode ideas into print using invented spelling. This is evident from the research done by Charles Read (1976). Even children who haven't had the advantage at home of scribbling or writing can be told to "play like you can write." There should be some free writing scheduled every day. There needs to be a purpose and audience for writing. Children at various age levels may write for different purposes. Children may write personal logs, diaries, stories, poems, letters, reports, recipes, rules for the classroom, record experiments, etc. (See Figure 6:14.)

THE BABY CHICKS

WE SAW BABY CHICKS.

THEY ARE WET CHICKS.

THE CHICKS WALKED.

THE CHICKS EAT.

WE LIKE CHICKS.

LANGUAGE EXPERIENCE:
VIEWING, TALKING, WRITING AND READING

FIGURE 6:14

To develop writing as a communication process
children should develop an early awareness of writing as
a means to communicate ideas to a reader. This means an
early and continuous focus on the function of writing
rather than the form of writing. Early opportunities

for writing should emphasize content and organizing ideas rather than a preoccupation with spelling, punctuation, capitalization, and handwriting. Any language process is learned by use in meaningful situations. Writing is learned by writing and reading is learned by practicing reading. An early emphasis on writing conventions inhibit the function of writing and get in the way of communicating meaning. (See Figure 6:15.)

PICK UP LITTER

WE WALKED AROUND THE SCHOOL.

WE SAW LITTER.

WE PICKED UP BOTTLES,

PAPER, ORANGE SKINS, AND

BROKEN PENCILS.

WE PLAN TO HAVE TRASH

CANS TO THROW LITTER IN.

LANGUAGE EXPERIENCE: FUNCTIONAL READING AND WRITING

FIGURE 6:15

Generally, teachers and parents are concerned about spelling and legibility when children first begin to write. However, recent research about the writing process, and in particular, spelling and children's knowledge of phonetics representation of letters, demonstrate a developmental pattern concerning what children know and learn about letter/sound relationships. There is evidence provided by Charles Read (1976) that spelling is developmental.

Young children progress through stages of invented spelling to the conventional spelling patterns of written language. At first, children use phonetic spelling to represent sounds in print. At an early stage children represent letters by the names of the letters. For example, in the word cherry, the "ch" is written as the letter "h" since the name of the letter "h" sounds like the "ch" at the beginning of cherry. The written word you is spelled "u"; "are" may be spelled "r", and so forth. Eventually, orthographic aspects and spelling patterns are learned developmentally.

The point is that children should begin to write early, even though they do not possess the conventional forms of written language. A classroom writing program will enhance and develop children's reading abilities.

There are a variety of activities teachers can plan to integrate writing and reading. The important thing is to have children at any level write something daily. Children can write letters, charts, poems, short stories, captions, posters, book, journals, and the like. There should be a silent writing time the same as silent reading time. After the writing time, those wanting to share their writing may read what they have written orally. A class post office provides a purpose for writing and reading between the class and teacher. Students can write and read letters from each other. The teacher can write notes to pupils.

In the next section, sample lessons and materials related to a language experience approach in a global sense and as a specific method are given. The lessons are examples of ways teachers can relate speaking and reading, listening and reading, and writing and reading in a total, whole language approach.

Sample Lessons

Using the Language Experience Approach

Lesson 1

Purpose
: To help students see relationships of their daily experiences to learning; also to help students participate by providing opportunities to contribute meaningfully.

Organization:
: The opportunity for this lesson happened one day this fall when one of my 3rd grade boys brought a praying mantis to school. Since his teacher permitted him to keep it with him throughout the day's work, it came to my class riding on Lamont's arm. Since these students are new to me this year and the school year had just begun, this gave a marvelous opportunity to build a good rapport with them. The students, I think, expected me to be alarmed, but instead became surprised when I was willing to let it walk on my hand. Many questions were asked by the students as well as myself about habits, behavior, needs, care of insect. We answered a few questions and the rest were recorded on chart paper. I produced the students' dictated story on chart paper and we discussed how we could find the answers to the questions that remained. Two students searched our bookshelves for the books on insects. Two others went to the library for other books. The next class meeting was spent in sharing and reading the information found in the library books. We added this to our experience story. Shortly after we finished our praying mantis story, Lamont brought a small rock snake to our class. We followed the same procedure as for the praying mantis and we will keep our story sheets permanently and add to them because we discovered Lamont has a special way with things in nature and he knows a lot about the ways of living things. He has a small boa at home which I'm hoping he keeps there.

Evaluation:
: I feel student participation and enthusiasm as well as interest in continuing the

Evaluation: procedure was the only indication that
(continued)   this lesson had been a success.

Experience Story

We Have a Visitor

Lamont brought a visitor to our class. He had
long skinny legs. His favorite food is insects. His
very favorite is bees. He does not make a noise. He
lives in Lamont's boot. He is a Praying Mantis.

Jeff had a Walking Stick in his hands. A girl
took a picture of it. It was green. It ran away.

Walking Sticks eat leaves.

Language Experience Approach

Lesson 2

Purpose: To develop thinking process, direction-
                ality, and humor in reading.

Initiating: The book being used is called The Chicken's
                Child, by Margaret A. Hartelius. The book
                has no words in it. It is a story about
                a chicken who for one reason or another
                acquires a baby alligator as her child.

Interacting: The child holds the book, turns the pages
                and makes up a story to go along with the
                pictures. The child may tell this to me,
                another child or a group of children. The
                child may want to tape the story to play
                to the other children also.

Expanding: The child may want to play the tape back
                and have other children act the story out.
                The child may want to tell other stories
                of mixed-up mothers and babies. The child
                may want to draw a sequential story of his
                own without words, and share that with the
                class.

Evaluation: By playing the story back I could note
                grammatical or pronunciation problems. I
                could note any problems in sequencing.

377

Language Experience Activity

Lesson 3

Ian and Terry have finished reading a story about camping in their reader "Hi-Ho Hortense" by Penny Platt. Under "things to think about and do" there are six pictures of things that could happen on a camping trip. The directions say to pick a picture and make up a story about the picture. Two people can write a story together.

Terry chose the picture of a bear chasing off campers, and Ian chose a picture of a boy about to fall into a lake. They wrote the story and dictated it to their teacher. They were really proud of what they wrote. Here it is:

On the Picnic

Ian and Terry went on a picnic in the woods. It was a sunny day. They had apples, corn, fish and pie to eat. They heard a noise in the woods, and a bear came out of the bushes. They ran as fast as they could go. The bear ate all the fish and apples. They came to the lake and Ian saw a boat. He decided to get in the boat to get away from the bear. He put one foot in the boat and one foot on the dock. Suddenly, the boat started to float away and Ian's legs stretched as far as they could. Then Ian fell into the water. It's a good thing Ian can swim. He swam to shore. Terry climbed a tree to get away from the bear. Later the boys went to see if the bear was gone. He was gone but so was all the food. The boys went home hungry. The next picnic will be in the backyard. There will be no bears there, only birds and rabbits and squirrels.

Language Experience Approach

Lesson 4

Purpose: Pupils will understand the association between oral and written language. They will learn that sequence is important to get where they want to go. They will use semantic cues, graphophonic cues and syntactic cues.

378

Initiating: We will plan a walking trip to the Public
                  Library. We will discuss the time we will
                  leave and the place to meet. The group of
                  six children will be informed that the
                  Librarian will take them for a tour of
                  the Library, there will be a puppet show
                  for them and she will show them a film.
                  The children will be able to choose two
                  books each to take with them to read.

Interacting: Do the above.

Applying: Let each child dictate his favorite part
                  of the trip, the journey, the books, the
                  puppet show or the film. I will write it
                  for them on paper that has room for them
                  to illustrate it.

Expanding: Some children may wish to draw a map of
                  the route they took to school. Although
                  the focus was on meaning, the children
                  had to use graphophonic and syntactic
                  cues heavily.

Evaluation: Observe individual children to see how
                  they made sense of what happened, how they
                  were able to relate what happened and if
                  they could read what they had dictated to
                  me.

Self-Selected and Sustained Silent Reading

        Any activity such as learning to ride a bicycle,
play a piano or ride a skateboard is learned by continued practice of the activity. Reading, or any of the
communication processes, is no different than other
physical or cognitive activities. The more one participates in doing the activity, all things considered
equal, the better one becomes at the activity.

        There has been a tendency when it comes to
learning to read to minimize opportunity to learn how
to read by simple reading. This is readily evident in
the history of reading instruction. Reading has been
thought to be learned by direct, planned instruction by
a teacher applying a sequence of reading skills. Then
after children are exposed to "reading skills" they are
permitted to begin to read stories which include the sequenced skills that have been taught to them. During the
time that stories are read by children, there is

continuous practice on isolated word identification and comprehension skills. "New" skills are constantly introduced and "old" skills are reviewed. And so it goes as children from the beginning and throughout the elementary years are directed in a piecemeal, sequenced approach through the maze of "reading skills."

When time permits, usually after children have had enough exposure and learning skills at the beginning level, the teacher provides "supplementary reading materials." These materials include library or trade books. The teacher directs the children to select and read library books when other work is completed. Possibly a "free" reading time is scheduled a certain period each day or during the week when time permits for everyone to read books they have chosen. A similar situation exists at levels in the elementary school beyond the early stage of learning to read. Frequently the teacher plans and directs the skills development and independent reading is a secondary consideration. Time for "real reading" is usually something that kids can do after the "important" business of skills learning has been done.

Fortunately a recent development in many schools has been known as uninterrupted sustained silent reading (USSR) or sustained silent reading. This trend has been a much needed step in the right direction to provide children an opportunity to practice and enjoy reading. The whole notion is nothing new. However, sustained silent reading or USSR, did mandate that everyone should read at a specific time in the school day or during the week. This usually included teachers and all personnel in the entire school. Sustained silent reading or "free," "independent" or "recreational" reading has had a long history in classrooms. The point is that in the past sustained reading was left up to the individual classroom teacher. Some teachers intuitively knew that planning and providing time for self-selection and the opportunity to read was necessary for children at any age level to develop reading ability and an enjoyment of reading. (See Figure 6:16, page 381.)

Self-selected reading, individualized reading, or personalized reading, as it has been known, is not novel. Olson (1952), developed the basic principles and concepts of seeking, self-selection, and pacing which was the basis of individualized reading. Seeking behavior is the notion that humans strive to satisfy their needs. Self-selection behavior is the principal that persons select from the environment those things

380

FIGURE 6:16

SELF-SELECTED READING

they need and for which they are ready. Self-pacing is
the belief that the individual learns tasks related to
his/her capacity and rate of learning. Prominent reading educators during the 1950's and 1960's, such as
Barbe (1961), Veatch (1959), Hunt (1975) and McCracken
(1971) and others, described elaborate individualized
or personalized reading programs for the classroom.

Some teachers planned and implemented a total
individualized reading program eliminating the basal
reader and conventional grouping practices. Other
teachers supplemented the basal reader program with
modified forms of individualized reading. Many individualized reading programs based on the principles
of seeking, self-selecting and pacing were eventually
discontinued. Possibly the primary reason was that
teachers would not teach the expected "reading skills"
and have complete or modified individualized reading
at the same time. Another reason that many individualized reading programs in classrooms disappeared was
the teacher's task in monitoring and keeping up with
large numbers of children on a daily and weekly basis.
The trend toward individualized reading programs in the

classroom appeared to have collapsed of its own weight. These were too many children, not enough materials, skills had to be taught, and teachers were ill-prepared to plan, organize and implement completely individualized reading programs or even some adapted form of individualized reading. Also, there has always been feelings of guilt among teachers that the "skills" were not being learned when children "only read." All segments of the public and school community have had a preoccupation with the belief that reading must be learned in a skill-by-skills approach.

Individualized or personalized reading reached its zenith during the 1960's and gradually diminished as a total reading approach. However, there are certainly vestiges of individualized, self-selected reading remaining in many classrooms. During the 1970's, individualized reading as a concept was extended to various forms of "individualized instruction," e.g., programmed reading, systems management, behavior objectives and criterion-referenced reading programs. Individualized reading as a self-selection of reading materials for sustained periods of time and for different purposes was minimized in many classrooms. Toward the end of the 1970's, the "Back to Basics" movement began with a renewed emphasis on "skills and drills" since reading scores of many children at various grade levels were far below what was expected. As a result, less time in classrooms was provided for real reading and more emphasis was given to directly teaching a vast array of sequenced skills.

The early, so-called individualized reading programs based on principles of seeking, self-selection and pacing, developed during a time when the reading process was understood as a "step-by-step, skills-by-skill approach," beginning with letter and word perception resulting in comprehension. The reading process was assumed to involve thinking, but the primary focus of reading instruction was on exact word pronunciation leading somehow to meaning. There was little consideration given to that application of linguistics and psychology to the reading process. Advances in socio-psycholinguistic research applied to the reading process has confirmed the belief that reading is learned by real reading in different reading situations and for different purposes.

Individualized reading or self-selected reading should be only one of different whole language approaches in the classroom at all levels in elementary,

382

junior, and high school. Self-selected reading with
sustained silent reading provides students with the
opportunity to interact with print as a whole language.
Psycholinguistic and socio-linguistic research has established language learning principles that language is
learned more effectively and efficiently in total language discourse and context.

SUSTAINED SILENT READING

FIGURE 6:17

The next section will describe the rationale
and principles of learning which form the basis for
self-selected/sustained silent reading as one among
other comprehension-centered language approaches described in this chapter to develop reading ability.

A Rationale for Self-Selected and Sustained Silent Reading

Self-selected reading (SSR) and sustained silent reading (SSR), are related components of one comprehension-centered reading appraoch. SSR/SSR will be described as a total approach which should be planned and implemented at every grade level.

The basis rationale underlying self-selected/ sustained reading is that people are different. People are different in their rate of learning, background experiences, interests and motivation. People learn at differing rates, perceive and conceptualize similar experiences in different perspectives, and experience different events in their lives, develop different interests related to experiences and possess varying degrees of motivation. No one set of reading materials or sequenced skills are appropriate for everyone.

Trusty (1971) described principles of learning and applies them to an individualized reading program (self-selected/sustained silent reading). She states the following principles of learning:

1) Children learn best when activities and materials are meaningful. Self-selection is meaningful to the individual.

2) Learning is more meaningful when pupils participate in goal-setting, planning and evaluation. This may take place when the teacher engages in a conference with a child.

3) Learning is more meaningful when the child has self-understanding and direction through an opportunity to explore a variety of interests and to make choices.

4) Children learn best when the situation provides satisfactory emotional content. Children need opportunities to talk about books, write stories and listen to stories.

5) Children learn more when they are permitted first-hand experiences. The language experience approach described in the preceding section of this chapter fits naturally into the self-selected and sustained silent reading approach. Teachers should capitalize on the foundation of experiences children bring to school.

6) Children learn more readily when many sensory approaches are used. For example, taped stories for children to read along with provides a visual and auditory input. Assisted reading or read-along as a comprehension-centered approach was described earlier in this chapter.

7) Children learn better when relieved of the pressure for competition and allowed the opportunity for cooperation. Grouping is flexible and temporary for different purposes.

8) Learning is more meaningful when failures are viewed constructively and appropriate measures of remediation are construed.

9) Children learn best when given opportunities to learn attitudes, feelings, values and appreciation through experiences, the same way they gain skills and knowledge.

10) Children learn best when their efforts are appreciated by the teachers and classmates. There should be opportunities to share reading experiences, dramatic presentations and creative writing with others.

Mork (1972) provided a basis for sustained silent reading in the classroom. He proposes that SSR (sustained silent reading) provides children the opportunity to practice their own reading skills, privately, without fear of mistakes. It allows them to react privately to ideas in print for extended periods of time.

Reed (1978) suggested that reading instruction is fragmented into isolated skill practice with little opportunity for "real life" reading experiences. If a student practices in bits and snatches of workbooks and worksheets, and never has the chance to apply the silent reading of a book of his/her own choosing, it cannot be assured that the student will ever become a skillful, voluntary reader.

Mork (1972) has stated that children and adults who read and enjoy it are often better readers. Enjoyment leads to more reading and more practice. Generally the child who gets other work done has more time to read. The unsuccessful reader has less time to read even if she/he chooses to read. Unsuccessful readers need as much, if not more, time for real reading practice.

Goodman and Watson (1977) have claimed that children learn to read by doing lots of silent reading in a variety of materials. They advocate a program in which time is scheduled for students to read silently every day. They have said, "that during silent reading students are encouraged to draw on their own experiences and to use their knowledge of language to help themselves become more efficient and proficient readers. When readers habitually depend on others for the next word, they stop developing their own reading strategies, and lose faith in their own ability to contribute to the reading process."

There is a growing body of knowledge and evidence that self-selected and sustained silent reading produces readers who can read and who enjoy and want to read. Next, consideration will be given to how a teacher may organize a self-selected/sustained silent reading approach as one approach together with other comprehension-based approaches.

Organizing Self-Selected and Sustained Silent Reading

The teacher must have an overall plan and structure for his/her total language program. Self selected/sustained reading (SSR/SSR) should be planned to fit into the overall schema of the total program. SSR/SSR will be one comprehension-centered approach discussed in this chapter and that can be implemented in the comprehension-centered classroom. Some teachers may prefer a regular time for children to participate in SSR/SSR. Other teachers may want to integrate SSR/SSR into the ongoing comprehension-centered, language-based program. For example, SSR/SSR fits nicely into the thematic unit approach within content areas. Thematic units are described in the next chapter related to a totally integrated whole language classroom. Whether SSR/SSR is organized and implemented for a specific time or integrated within the total language program, the teacher must have a plan if students are to benefit from extended reading.

The teacher must be aware of several organizational features to consider when planning and applying SSR/SSR in his/her classroom. First, the teacher must develop a general organizational schema including consideration of time and space. The physical environment will need to be planned; second, collecting materials appropriate for the children is a very significant concern; third, consideration should be given to when and how sustained silent reading will be scheduled; fourth, the teacher needs to think about holding conferences with children; fifth, various ways to have children share their reading should be part of the program; finally, the teacher must plan ways to evaluate pupil progress in reading, including techniques of keeping records, including teacher and children records. Each of these components of SSR/SSR will be described separately; however, they are closely interrelated in the ongoing SSR/SSR approach.

All aspects of scheduling time, utilization of classroom space, collection and availability of reading materials, scheduling sustained silent reading, holding individual and/or group conferences, sharing activities and evaluation, need to be considered in the teacher's overall plan. We will be concerned here primarily with use of time and space, or the physical classroom environment. Planning time and space will be an individual matter for the teacher. The consideration of use of time and space in the total language program will be more fully discussed later in Chapter VII. This topic will include not only SSR/SSR, but all other comprehension-centered language approaches described in this chapter. Several diagrams of organizing and utilizing classroom space and time are given which may be useful to refer to at this time. (See Chapter VII.)

The most direct method to organize a SSR/SSR approach is scheduling a specific time for all children to self-select reading materials and do sustained silent reading on a regular basis. The reading materials may be chosen from the school and classroom library or reading center. SSR/SSR is organized as a separate component within the total classroom. There may also be a specific period scheduled during the week for sharing books read or projects completed related to books read.

More complex organization of SSR/SSR might include differentiated times scheduling for certain children to engage in SSR/SSR at the same time as other children and the teacher are involved in other learning experiences; e.g., assisted reading, language experience, D.R.T.A., or other comprehension-centered activities. An even more differentiated SSR/SSR approach might be to arrange space in the classroom with a variety of learning centers integrating all language communication processes into content areas of social studies, science, mathematics, and health, e.g., thematic units. The children in various groups or individually would be participating in reading, writing, listening, speaking, art

387

projects related to a particular broad thematic unit of study. This may be scheduled for the whole day over a period of weeks, or several days a week for several weeks, or part of several days a week for a period of weeks until completion of the unit. The children would be able to self-select and read for sustained periods of time related to a large unit of study.

Teacher consideration and planning of time, space and children involved will influence the physical arrangement of the classroom. The placement of furniture including desks, tables, shelves and storage places for reading materials and easy accessibility of materials can be highly complex as SSR/SSR is integrated into a whole language classroom.

It seems logical for a teacher to begin a SSR/SSR approach on a simple level. For example, scheduling a specific time for self-selection of reading materials and a required time every day for sustained silent reading. Even this arrangement has its complications and problems. Later the teacher may wish to differentiate and apply a more flexible organization involving SSR/SSR within the total program. However, when beginning SSR/SSR it is essential to move forward in small steps, helping the children to understand their role and responsibilities as well as the role and responsibilities of the teacher. The next several steps a teacher should plan and organize to implement a SSR/SSR approach are important considerations whether the SSR/SSR is a separate schedule time apart from other classroom learning experiences or integrated naturally into a whole language classroom.

Collecting Reading Materials

An important factor in the successful implementation of a SSR/SSR approach is the amount and variety of reading materials available to children for sustained silent reading. Collecting reading materials by the teacher and children is an ongoing activity but especially significant when initiating a program as part of the total language program.

There are a variety of sources the teacher should consider to accumulate a vast amount of print material appropriate to different interests and reading abilities of all children in the classroom.

Margaret Lindberg (1979) has compiled: <u>Some</u>
<u>Resources for Developing Individualized Reading Pro-</u>
<u>grams and Thematic Units.</u> See Appendix H.

There should be a variety of different types of
literature available for children to self-select and read
during sustained reading time or at other appropriate
times, possibly related to thematic units or other purposes. Materials should include library and trade books
as the core of the SSR/SSR approach. The teacher should
obtain books of fiction, nonfiction, fairytales, adventure, mysteries, classics, biographies, poetry. Books
should range in difficulty of content and language structure related to the differences in the group of children.
Other reading materials available should include copies
of children's and popular magazines, newspapers, encyclopedias, various pamphlets and booklets related to
topical units studied, dictionairies, single concept
books, so-called "supplementary readers," how-to-do-
it manuals, and so forth.

Children and parents should be involved in contributing reading material to the program. Some teachers write to parents at the beginning of the year re-
questing any children's books around the home not being
used. Other sources of books include, having children
belong to paperback book clubs, such as Scholastic Book
Clubs (See Appendix H.) School book fairs are another
lucrative source for collecting paperback books for the
classroom. Teachers should be aware of inexpensive
books at flea markets and garage sales. The school and
public librarian are helpful people to know and to go
to for books. The school librarian may be asked to
locate and provide a collection of books on a thematic
unit or supply a variety of books to keep in the classroom for an extended period of time. Most public li-
braries permit teachers to check out a large collection
of books for several weeks. Also, old discarded readers, content books and workbooks with short stories can
be made into "Skinny Books" and added to the classroom
reading center. The children can design book covers
using construction paper for the skinny books. There
are good stories in old basal readers which are appeal-
ing to children as paperback books, especially "reluctant readers" or "poor readers who refuse to even touch
a whole book."

The teacher should be familiar with various
sources of literature for children. <u>Classroom Choices,</u>
books chosen by children, published by International
Reading Association in the October issue of <u>The Reading</u>

389

Teacher and Language Arts, published by the National
Council of Teachers of English (NCTE), are excellent
sources. Each source provides annotated descriptions
of children's literature currently available.

Teachers should be aware of sources for obtaining books free or at reduced prices. Federal and state
programs such as Reading is Fundamental (RIF) and Right
to Read are possible sources for obtaining a collection
of books. (See addresses to write to for these programs
in the list of resources by Lindberg (1979) in Appendix
H.)

Any and all sources of print material should
be explored to accumulate a variety of reading materials
which can be added to and changed throughout the year as
children's interests and needs change.

Self-Selecting Materials

An important aspect of individualized reading
and sustained silent reading is that children self-
select their own reading materials. This requires a
wide variety of choices from different types of print.
It also means the teacher must schedule and/or provide
time for self-selection of reading materials. This can
be accomplished in various ways depending on how extensive the SSR/SSR approach is used in the classroom.

The SSR/SSR approach may be scheduled at a
specific time each day for the whole class. Some time
will need to be provided for students to select what
they will read for the sustained silent reading time.
For example, if SSR is scheduled at a specific time
during the day, the teacher may schedule a certain number of children before the sustained reading period to
go to the school and classroom library to select the
books or other material they will read for SSR. However,
if SSR/SSR is scheduled flexibly within an integrated
classroom curriculum a certain period of time may be
scheduled for self-selection and several children may
sign up for the reading center in the classroom at different times during the day.

Each teacher will need to work out an
arrangement for self-selection of reading materials
which is effective. The arrangement of library, trade
books, magazines, newspapers, encyclopedias, pamphlets,
brochures and the like, should be planned and explained
to the students. The procedures for checking out

materials needs to be considered carefully. Library, trade books, magazines and newspapers can be displayed on shelves and tables in the reading center. The books can be arranged according to interest topics or by author with a card catalogue including subject, title and author. The teacher will need to explain procedures for browsing in the classroom reading center and how many children can self-select books at one time and when children can be scheduled to select materials for sustained silent reading. (See Chapter VII.)

Dorothy Watson (1978) explained a procedure for children to have reading material available for sustained silent reading. She suggests that children always have available three materials to read. She called this procedure: "Mine," Yours," and "Ours." The "Mine" is what the child always self-selects and decides to read. It may be anything within reason, such as, baseball cards, comic books, a magazine, and so forth. The child should be encouraged and allowed to read what he/she has chosen. The "Yours" is what the teacher has chosen for the child based on an understanding of the child's interests. The teacher recommends books to a child to expand interests as well as focus on current interests. (This may take place during a conference.) The "Ours" is a more difficult concept to apply; but is where the teacher or librarian and the child mutually decide on certain reading material. If this procedure is followed every student should have at least three different types of reading material available for sustained silent reading time at all times. This should minimize the problem of having nothing to read.

There are several problems that may occur using the SSR/SSR approach. One problem involves the beginning reader who has not developed much reading ability. A possible solution may be to encourage beginning readers to "pretend like you're reading." The teacher will need to make available a wide assortment of "easy-to-read" books and picture books with limited print. For other readers not reading independently read-along book/tape (assisted reading), reading couples, the use of paraprofessionals or aides to read along with the child, or older pupils serving as tutors may assist this type of reader during the SSR period. Another problem of concern during the self-selection of reading material is the child who can't or won't decide on what to choose to read. At time the teacher may need to select a book for the child; e.g., the "Yours" book. Still another problem is the child who selects a "status" book to read.

This is a book you know the child can't possibly read but the student wants to make others think he/she can; or, the child who can read very well but regularly selects easy books to read. Part of the solution to this problem may be to use the "Mine," "Yours," and "Ours" procedure, so the student always has at least other reading material, in addition to the "status book" or the very easy reading material available for the sustained silent reading period each day.

The teacher may have a great influence on the self-selection process of his/her students. The reading aloud aspect of a comprehension-centered program can assist children to broaden interests and expand their horizons. The teacher can carefully select a variety of different literature to read aloud. Only a part of a book or the whole book may be read to entice children to read it for themselves. After reading a book to children, the book may be placed in the reading center for self-selection. Frequently, other students will influence book selection. The teacher should provide time for children to share books they are reading. This will encourage other students to read similar books. More will be described later about sharing as an essential part of the SSR/SSR approach. Next, the sustained silent reading time will be described and procedures for implementing SSR suggested.

Sustained Silent Reading Methods

One of the most important approaches for teachers to plan for a whole language classroom is sustained silent reading time. All learners, beginning readers, developing readers and effective readers need time each day to read. There should be time for instruction in specific aspects of the reading process based on teacher identification of the reader's use of linguistic cues and learning strategy strengths and needs; however, more time needs to be provided for learners to do real reading.

The most direct way to organize SSR/SSR is scheduling a specific time during each day for everyone to read, including the teacher. Some teachers may prefer the first thing in the morning; others schedule SSR before children go to lunch; still others may schedule SSR after children come in from recess after lunch; or even before children go home at the end of the day. Usually, depending on the age of the children, SSR as a separate time period is implemented for a short

time to begin with and then the time is gradually increased as children become adjusted to reading silently
for longer periods of time. It has been recommended
that a timer be used to tell when SSR is over. Even
young children during first grade and older children
who appear to be "non-readers" should participate in SSR.
The teacher should accept and permit reading-like behavior. The student may be only leafing through the
pages in a book or looking at pictures, but it is similar to reading and should be accepted.

The SSR period should be free of any form of
teaching or working on worksheets, skill dittos and
other assignments. As mentioned previously, every
child should have at least three choices of reading
material; e.g., "Yours," "Mine," and "Ours." Reading is
the only behavior allowed during SSR time. The teacher
can effectively model reading behavior by also reading.
This means the teacher should read something for enjoyment or for information and not use the time for correcting papers or planning lessons.

Obviously, teachers and children unaccustomed
to SSR will need a transition period to adjust to this
approach. A few simple rules should suffice so that
SSR can be an enjoyable and rewarding time. For example, some basic rules during SSR might include:

1) Stay in your seat
2) No talking
3) Have reading materials available
4) READ-READ-READ

Some teachers hang a sign on their door an-
nouncing that it is SSR time so as not to be interrupted
by persons coming into the room.

It has become quite common for the whole school
to have SSR at the same time at least once a week as
a method of showing importance to reading. Everyone in
the school including the principal, secretary, custodian,
auxilary personnel, teachers and children all are expected to read. No interruptions are tolerated except
for emergency situations. However, SSR once a week on
a school-wide basis is not often enough for children to
have for reading. The classroom teacher should schedule
SSR on a daily basis in addition to school-wide SSR.

The goal of SSR along with other whole language
approaches described in this chapter is the development
of readers who can and do read. The long range objective

393

is to develop life-long readers. SSR is based on the premise according to Frank Smith and others, that, "reading is learned by reading." SSR provides readers the opportunity to develop efficiency and effectiveness in reading. Reading is a leisure time activity which can provide enjoyment and enrichment to one's life. The ability to read also gives the individual the opportunity to learn about the world and to expand horizons, to travel vicariously through time and space to places and events not always possible. Reading proficiency in varied printed material is developed through more practice. It seems true that persons who read a lot become even better readers. Those persons who seldom read are generally poor readers. In too many classroom situations the good readers have more time to practice reading than poor readers. The better readers usually get assigned work completed first and if they desire, may do independent reading. On the other hand, the poor readers need all the time to complete assigned work and seldom have time left to read even if they chose to read. The conclusion to be drawn seems to be: those who read become better readers while children who seldom read, do not improve as readers and, in fact, may become worse readers. Finally, the most devastating effect of not being able to read is that poor readers frequently never do like to read and avoid reading in their life as though it were the plague.

Yetta Goodman and Dorothy Watson (1978) advocated a program in which time is scheduled for stuents to read silently every day. They suggested during sustained silent reading that the teacher "encourage students to draw on their own experiences and to use their own knowledge of language to help themselves become more efficient and proficient readers." They further stated, "when readers habitually depend on others for "the next word," they stop developing their own reading strategies and lose faith in their own ability to contribute to the reading process."

Dorothy Watson (1978), has developed a procedure called Reader Selected Miscues (RSM) which is related to sustained silent reading. Briefly, when students are involved in SSR, they are to identify miscues or trouble spots in their reading. The procedure is for students to have several "2" x "8" bookmarks. The reader places a bookmark at any place where they encountered difficulty and continue reading. At the end of the SSR period, students examine their miscues and select three that caused major problems in meaning or caused distraction from their reading. The students

write a sentence containing a selected miscue on the
marker, underling the miscue, write their name, book
title and page number and return the three bookmarks to
the teacher.

The teacher may categorize the miscues to find
common problems and serve as a basis for group instruction. The last step involves discussion with students
who have similar reading problems. Reading problems may
include hard to pronounce names, dialect used by the
author, foreign terms, complex syntactic or wording
structures, different and unfamiliar concepts, and so
forth. Chapter V, Reading-Language Instruction, has
identified reading problems and strategies for dealing with various problems.

Watson (1978), described several important
attitudes about reading and about themselves as readers
as a result of the Reader Selected Miscue procedure.
She stated, "first, the reader, not the teacher or
other reading-circle mates, is in the driver's seat.
No one is on hand to call attention to errors or provide help. There are no interruptions from others
to intervene in the reading process. Second, the student realizes that everyone, even the most proficient
reader makes miscues. Third, the reader has autonomy
in selecting and rejecting material. The reader decides if the miscues cause loss of meaning or interest.
Fourth, readers become their own monitors; that is,
the students become actively involved in the meaning-
seeking process. Finally, a keep-going strategy is
legitimate. The student is asked not to break the flow
of reading by stopping to ask for help or to check the
dictionary."

Reader Selected Miscues is a highly workable
procedure to complement sustained silent reading. The
student becomes an active participant in her/his development as a reader. Students learn from each other
through discussion about similar and different miscues
they produce when they read. The Reader Selected Miscues method is a useful supplement to miscue analysis
done by the teacher as explained in Chapter IV, Evaluation of Reading.

The next aspect of a SSR/SSR approach is concerned with conferences held by the teacher with students.

Teacher-Student Conferences

The conference between teacher and student has long been recognized as an important part of a SSR/SSR approach. The difficulty has been for the classroom teacher to schedule time to meet regularly for a period of time with 25-30 students in a classroom. Obviously, it is quite impossible for one teacher to schedule time to monitor each student's individual reading progress. However, more time is available for conferences if basal reader oral reading groups and independent workbook/ditto skill papers are reduced considerably and/or eliminated completely, if possible. In a whole language classroom other whole language approaches are fused naturally with the SSR/SSR approach. If the teacher uses group basal reading and related workbook-type seatwork and supplements SSR/SSR with instruction, then it will be difficult to schedule individual conferences frequently. Nevertheless, the individual teacher-student conference should be part of the SSR/SSR approach.

The teacher will need to devise a scheduling procedure for conferences with students. This can be done by simply writing the student's name and time for the conference on the board or chart near the conference area. The conference can be conducted for various purposes and in different ways. Generally, the child is asked to bring the book or material she/he is currently reading or a book recently completed. The teacher should have the child read a few paragraphs or a brief part of the book orally. Some teachers do a spot check miscue analysis observing the miscues the reader makes. Also, the child should be asked to retell what the book is about and the teacher may ask open-ended questions. The teacher may occasionally use the conference time to administer a modified miscue analysis using a short, complete story for the child to read orally and retell. (See Chapter IV.) This information may be used to plan reading strategy lessons related to the interpretation of the student's miscues and retelling. The conference may also be useful to recommend reading materials to the student the "Yours" part of the "Mine," "Yours," "Ours" procedure for selecting reading materials. Another part of the conference may include teacher-pupil planning of follow-up activities or projects the student might do related to books read. This is related to the sharing part of the SSR/SSR approach described in the following section. (See Figure 6:18, page 397.)

- PUPILS SIGN-UP/SCHEDULED BY TEACHER
- CHILD BRINGS BOOK
    * READ A COUPLE OF PARAGRAPHS
    * EXAMINE MISCUES
    * CHECK COMPREHENSION
        OPEN-ENDED QUESTIONS
        RETELLING
    * SUGGEST READING MATERIALS
    * FOLLOW-UP ACTIVITIES

CONFERENCE PROCEDURES

FIGURE 6:18

397

Finally, the conference enables the teacher to
learn more about each child, his/her interests and experiences, and to monitor his/her reading performance
on an individual basis. The teacher will also have
opportunities to observe and evaluate each child's
language development in other whole language situations;
e.g., reading aloud, assisted reading, language experience, DRTA, functional reading activities, using
schema stories, ReQuest and whole language activities
in learning centers.

The next component of the SSR/SSR approach includes techniques for children to share with others what
they read.

Sharing Reading Experiences

An outgrowth or extension of SSR/SSR provides
the opportunity for students to share their reading
experiences with others. It is important that students
have many opportunities to describe reading experiences
to classmates in a variety of ways. Learning is enhanced for the individual when opportunity is given to
express experience. Other children learn and are influenced when students share reading experiences.
Students may share what they have read orally, in
writing, through art, or in a drama format.

The teacher may schedule a specific sharing
time once a week or sharing reading experiences may be
held more flexibly. If the SSR/SSR program is planned
for a certain time each day during the week, the teacher
may want to have sharing time at a certain time one day
a week. This method would probably be a good way to
begin a SSR/SSR program for the first time. However,
assuming a teacher has used SSR/SSR for some time in
his/her classroom, the teacher may schedule sharing of
reading experiences within a flexible program, including thematic units of study. There are no specific
procedures for planning and scheduling a time for students to share reading experiences with others. The
teacher will need to decide her/himself which arrangement is more effective given the individual situation.

Teachers should be familiar with a variety of
activities and permit students to select different
ways they can share what they have read with others in
the classroom. The teacher may elect to display various
ways students can share what they have read in the
classroom. Sharing activities may be displayed on a

398

chart in the reading center, writing center or drama center if centers are available in the classroom. The teacher may want to encourage students to select different sharing activities at individual conferences or at other times in the classroom. Sharing activities may be grouped in the following way: oral experiences, writing experiences, art experiences, and drama experiences. Examples of sharing experiences for each type is suggested below:

Oral Experiences

1. Dress up as a character in a book you are reading and describe the character you are portraying.

2. Read your favorite scene, incident or description.

3. Read part of the book and ask others to predict what will happen.

4. Play "Twenty Questions." If you have read a book with a well-known character, you may conduct the game. The other students ask questions which can only be answered with "yes" or "no." The class must guess the answer within 20 questions.

5. Play "What's My Line?" or "I've Got a Secret." You portray a character from the book you have read, and others try to guess his/her "line" or "secret."

6. Let children who have read poetry have choral reading. Sometimes an exciting narrative story is suitable for choral reading.

7. Have a student read an exciting story into a tape for others to listen to at a listening center.

8. Take part in a panel discussion with others who have read the book.

Writing Experiences

1. Write an autobiography from the point of view of the character in a book you are reading.

2. Write a review of a book, telling what it's about and why others should or shouldn't read it.

3. Write a short advertising blurb - an interest-arouser - about a book that might entice others to read it.

399

4. Design an advertisement for the book you read.

5. Design a book jacket, including your favorite scene.

6. If you've read a mystery book or one about treasure hunts, make a map or diagram.

7. Write a different ending for the story.

8. Write comments and a brief review of the book that will be available for a book jacket.

9. Write a letter to your school librarian telling her why she should buy the book.

10. If several have read the same book, divide into groups and let each group write the script for a scene or chapter.

11. Write a script for your favorite scene.

12. Write a comment, summary or impression of the book in the form of a limerick.

13. Write a poem describing a character, setting or incident in the book.

14. Keep a diary of one of the characters in the book.

15. Write a newspaper report, complete with headline, of an important event in the book.

16. Write a biography of the leading character using facts and details from the book.

17. Write a letter recommending the book to a friend.

Art Experiences

1. Draw a portrait of your favorite character.

2. Draw your favorite setting.

3. Make two drawings, comparing the setting of the book with your home, school or neighborhood.

4. Draw a series of pictures in sequence (a comic strip) showing the main parts of the story.

5. Design a book jacket.

6. Design a miniature billboard to advertise the book.

7. Design a poster publicizing the book.

8. Draw a series of scenes in sequence on a roll of paper to be shown on the TV.

9. Make a sketch of the setting that could be used on the stage.

10. Build a miniature stage set of a scene.

11. Draw a cartoon to represent a character or a scene.

12. Make a wall mural with several people drawing a favorite scene.

13. Make a model in soap, clay or wood to illustrate a setting, scene or incident. (A diorama could be useful here.)

14. Make a mobile with a coat hanger and pictures of scenes from the book (either original artwork or pictures from a magazine).

15. Display dolls dressed as characters in the book.

16. Make a scrapbook or collection on the subject of the book.

17. Collect pictures and things relating to the historical period (or nation) on the book.

18. Make a scrapbook of pictures that describes the characters (or scenes) in the book, giving each picture a descriptive title.

Drama Experiences

1. Dramatize an exciting or interesting incident from the book in which you--as the character--are involved.

2. Dramatize the book by using homemade hand puppets of cloth or paper bags.

3. Re-enact story action in the game of charades, asking children to guess which character is being pantomined.

4. Have children study the parts and act out scenes from the book. Practice reading dialogue over several times silently. Permit children to use books during play if needed. (Assume several children have read the same book.)

5. Simulate a radio play with sound effects based on the book.

6. Let children read only the dialogue in a scene from a book with each child reading a particular part. Let one child act as narrator to read any necessary description of the setting, etc. (Assume several children have read the same book.)

Evaluating Pupil Progress

The last component of the SSR/SSR approach described is that of evaluating students' reading development and progress. Both the teacher and students should be involved in monitoring progress in reading ability and other characteristics. There needs to be several kinds of record-keeping procedures that are effective and simple. In Chapter IV, Evaluation of Reading, various evaluative techniques were described to assess reading performance for the purpose of planning appropriate reading experiences for students. Several evaluative procedures identified in Chapter IV are useful to assess reading performance within the SSR/SSR approach. For example, the teacher will want to use miscue analysis of a child's oral reading as needed during teacher-pupil conferences. Also, record-keeping devices such as checklists, rating scales and anecdotal records, are effective procedures to record samples of individual reading behavior when the teacher is observing student's oral and silent reading as a part of the SSR/SSR approach.

Evaluation is a most important part of the curriculum area in the school program. Evaluation procedures are required by teachers to report the progress of his/her students to the students themselves, to parents and to the school authorities. However, even more essential than the above purposes for evaluation, is that evaluation of reading performance enables the teacher to plan and provide appropriate learning experiences for children. This is the practical, day-to-day, week-by-week purpose for carefully developing methods of evaluation related to the purposes of the evaluation.

Again, reference to Chapter IV will provide guidelines to assist teachers to develop observational skills to monitor the reading performances within a whole language program in the classroom, and in particular, as part of implementing a SSR/SSR approach.

First, teachers need to know which reading behaviors and characteristics of reading performances should be evaluated and then apply various evaluative techniques to keep records of these behaviors and characteristics.

Lyman Hunt (1975) has identified the following reading performances as a part of self-selected and sustained silent reading.

1. Increased Concentration during SSR time.
   Progress in sustained silent reading is usually quite obvious and reflects growing power in silent reading. This is basic. Watch for less response to distractions, or positively, to a greater degree of involvement and concentration during allotted SSR time.

2. Increased time span during SSR time.
   When the reader shows reluctance to stop, or asks to go beyond the allotted time, or wants to read rather than go to recess, you will be receiving an important signal.

3. Greater spontaneous reaction during silent reading.
   Uncontrolled reactions to particular parts of print should provide you with valuable cues. Stifle the boisterous laughter if you must; provide kleenex for the tears when needed; but note the depth of the reading experience while doing so. These spontaneous responses tell you a great deal.

4. Increased difficulty level in material selected and read.
   When over an ample span of time (6 weeks or more), you note an overall increase in the complexity, difficulty and depth of selections made by particular individuals, you have a measure of productive reading. Be prepared for some occasional regression on the part of some individuals. This is normal; in fact, it is desirable for some selections to be easy.

6. Greater impatience with disturbances.
When your program progresses as it should, there
will be a reduction in disturbances and internal
disruptions. More will be reading, fewer will be
disturbing. When some of the early offenders become
annoyed at others who are now bothering them, you
have a genuine sing of accomplishment, for the recently converted.

7. Increased effort in other subjects.
Watch for greater concentration and voluntary interest in study areas other than reading.

8. Increased voluntary activities.
Watch for evidence of more outside reading. This
will occur both in and out of school.

Hunt suggested that an observation check sheet
may be used based on the reading characteristics listed
above by the teacher as he/she observes students in the
SSR/SSR program.

Goodman and Watson (1978) suggested a simple
record-keeping system to be used by the teacher and
children to evaluate the individualized reading approach
(SSR/SSR). They recommend index cards on which students
can record necessary information that are easy to keep
and do not frustrate the reader. For example, the index
card used by the young reader to record what they read
would look like this:

Your Name
_____
Book Title
_____

On one side the card would have this information.

And on the other side:

Did you finish the book?

     yes [   ]   no [   ]

Did you like the book?

yes [   ]   some [   ]   no [   ]

A card for older readers might have on one side:

Name _____

Type of Material (book, magazine, newspaper, brochure, my own story, class
book, etc.) _____

_____

Title _____

And on the other side:

Did you finish the Material? _____

If not, why not? _____

_____

Would you recommend this book to anyone
else? _____

Who? (Name names) _____

What would you like to read (about) next?

_____

Record-keeping for evaluative purposes and
planning reading experiences for children should be
kept simple. The classroom teacher or the special
reading/disability teacher does not have the time to
keep elaborate, detailed records of each individual
student. Although systematic records are necessary,
record-keeping can become so cumbersome that it negates
the purpose for self-selection/sustained silent reading; the purpose being to develop student's ability in
reading and a love for reading. The best a teacher
and children can do to provide documentation for evaluation and to develop further reading progress is to
sample behavior over an extended period of time. Not
every book or print material read should be recorded.
Both teacher and student will need to be selective in
sampling reading performance from time to time.

There will be other reading situations in
which the teacher will have opportunities to observe
and record information for evaluative purposes and
to plan learning experiences related to the individual
needs. As children listen to books and stories, use
tapes and books, dictate or write individual stories,
are involved in other reading, writing and speaking
settings, the teacher will monitor language growth,
attitudes, interests and development in knowledge and
concepts about their world, self and others.

In conclusion, the SSR/SSR approach should be
an important part of every classroom language arts program. Students need the opportunity to do different

kinds of reading for their purposes and related to their
needs and interests. The teacher is the key person to
make this happen. SSR/SSR should not be "free reading"
as an afterthought or to simply fill in time, but read-
ind as an integral and worthwhile learning experience.
SSR/SSR requires much teacher planning and organization,
including collecting materials, procedures for self-
selecting materials, techniques for sustained silent
reading, holding conferences, planning sharing experiences and evaluating pupil progress. The benefits to
children and their reading progress is worth the effort.

Two examples of methods for organizing a SSR/
SSR approach within the classroom are given below:

Procedures for Sustained Silent Reading

Purpose: To enable a student an opportunity to select his or her own reading material
according to his or her own needs and
preferences. To provide time for reading
for no other reason than to read for the
enjoyment. To provide the opportunity to
practice reading strategies.

Organization: I have two purchased sets of reading materials in my room. One is the Bowmar Pri-
mary Reading series, the other is called
Pal Paperbacks. Each set is of high interest and are color-coded according to
level of difficulty. There are from 25 to
50 books in each set, each book is different in content. These books are always
displayed and available along with many
Scholastic paperbacks of varying degrees
of difficulty. I try to allow at least
one ½ hour class period a week for USSR.
However, I have found with my children,
many of whom are hesitant with proceeding
to choose and read on their own, that I
can encourage them to choose and read if
I limit them somewhat to level and choice;
for instance, "Today, try to find something which interests you from the yellow
and purple books." This also helps to
avoid the chances of a child's choosing
books which are so difficult that he re-
fuses to attempt to read. I do allow as
much leeway as I feel the students can
handle in making a choice. Some have no
problems at all in choosing. It helps to

407

know each child. Some days we choose
just the very easy books and read to see
how fast we can go (speedy reading day--
the students love it.) There are days
when I give them the entire choice of
reading materials and observe very carefully those children who frequently have
shown lack of confidence in choosing a
book. During USSR, the students are free
to read wherever they choose and are comfortable (rug, chairs, long table, carpet
squares in the corner or against the wall,
next to their friends, etc.) We are quite
limited to possibilities because of room
conditions. We have a few rules of respect which we all know and are expected
to observe while having "free reading"--
care of books, consideration for others'
need for quiet, etc. Sometimes I also
read silently while they are reading.
Sometimes I work on the reading center
or move among the class to observe.

Evaluation: I have always reminded my students that if
they find something they are excited about
and wish to share with me or the class or
a friend they are free to do so. We do
that on the following class period and
not during the "free reading" time. I
can tell by observing as they read and by
their responding to sharing that they
nearly all are using their free reading
time advantageously. I still have students
who will just look at pictures if left on
their own. I try to guide them somewhat
when making choices and then we frequently
share reading their book, alternately
reading the pages or paragraphs. I also
make sure that these students have many
opportunities with Assisted Reading approaches.

Individualized Reading Approach with SSR

Make a bulletin board with a reading tree. Tell
children how we can put leaves on our reading tree.
Each time we read a book we put a new leaf on a branch
with our name and the name of the book we read on it.

408

Explain that we are going to read silently and we get to choose any book from the library shelf and our reading shelf. Try to choose a book that you will enjoy reading. For example, if you like animals, read a book about animals. (Bookshelves should be stocked with books of many subjects and many reading levels.)

We will have one day a week when we will spend all our time reading. On other days, if we have time, we will read then, too. After you have finished your book, you will have a short conference with your teacher to tell a little about your book. Then you can add another leaf to our reading tree!

Directed-Reading-Thinking-Activity

Another whole language approach teachers should include in their classroom reading program is the Directed-Reading-Thinking-Activity (DRTA). The DRTA procedure has been developed by Russell Stauffer (1970).

Most teachers are familiar with the traditional Directed Reading Activity (DRA) which has been a method of teaching reading to elementary school children for many years. The DRA is closely related to the so-called basal reader approach. The DRA usually involves using a basal reader story with the teacher following the lesson in the teacher's manual and a group of children. The teacher has grouped the students according to similar "reading levels." The lesson format usually includes the following:

1. Preparation for Reading - motivating children to read the story. Providing background information about the story, etc.

2. Introduce "new words" (vocabulary) and review "old words." The teacher usually writes words in isolation or in sentences on the board or chart for children to pronounce.

3. Children read story orally and/or silently with teacher questionning to guide and direct the reading. Children usually take turns reading orally, particularly in primary grades but also in upper grades.

4. Follow-up activities usually include word attack skills, comprehension skills, vocabulary development in workbooks and ditto skill sheets.

5. Enrichment activities are suggested in the teacher's manual related to the story the children have read.

The Directed Reading Activity (DRA) has a long history and is directly associated with basal reader materials, ability groups and having children take turns reading orally with teacher questions at intervals during the oral reading. The DRA generally has not been comprehension-focused as implemented by some teachers although questions are asked about the story read. The emphasis frequently has been on having children pronounce isolated words, practice separate "sight words," phonic, structural analysis skills, context cues and dictionary skills. Also, DRA has promoted surface oral reading performance as an end and comprehension development has generally been treated superficially. Teacher questioning during the DRA lesson usually has included primarily recall of story details. Frequently, children do not focus attention on meaning, but rather on oral reading performance; e.g., word accuracy, and comprehension has been minimized.

DRTA, by contrast, is basically meaning-centered, as opposed to DRA, which has tended to reduce the reading process to oral reading performance, stressing isolated, separate reading skills, and treating comprehension as a by-product.

The description of DRTA considers several factors which teachers need to know to successfully implement this comprehension-centered approach within their reading program. First, a rationale or basis for DRTA is given; next, an explanation of what DRTA is; and third, procedures for doing DRTA.

A Rationale for DRTA

The basis for including DRTA as one procedure to develop children's reading ability involves teacher awareness of the reading process as a visual and cognitive task. The reader's thinking needs to interact actively with the author's message. The point has been made several times previously that the only purpose of reading is comprehension. The reading process involves more than the visual aspects of marks on paper recoded into sounds (pronunciation) which are possibly translated into meaning. The reader must bring his/her prior knowledge and experiences to the interaction with the author's ideas. The DRTA approach focuses the

410

reader's attention on an active participation with the
author to decode meaning. The orthographic features
provide the reader the symbolic linguistic system to decode the author's message. (See Figure 6:19 below.)

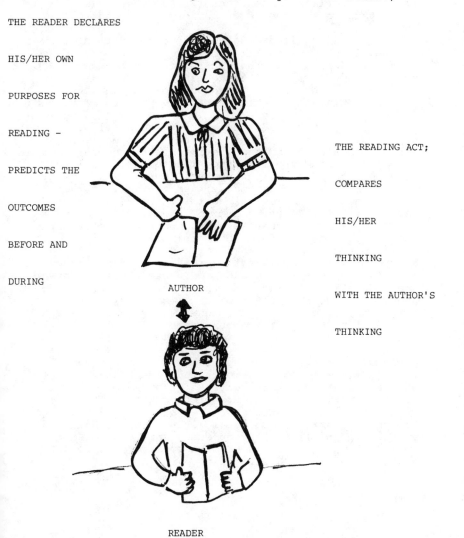

THE READER DECLARES

HIS/HER OWN

PURPOSES FOR

READING -

PREDICTS THE

OUTCOMES

BEFORE AND

DURING

THE READING ACT;

COMPARES

HIS/HER

THINKING

WITH THE AUTHOR'S

THINKING

AUTHOR

READER

DRTA PROCESS

FIGURE 6:19

411

Another reason for using DRTA is that reading should always be a purposeful experience. The reader's purposes are more important than the teacher's purposes or any purposes stated by publishers of reading program materials. The teacher should be available to facilitate to set their own purposes for reading.

Reading is asking questions and getting answers to questions. The most important questions are those of the reader; not another person or the teacher. The teacher may guide children to ask questions or model questions which children may want to find answers to as they are involved in the interactive process of reading.

Stauffer (1970) emphasized the development of pupil purposes in reading. The pupil's ideas, experiences, knowledge and ego are important concerns in developing reading proficiency. The teacher should direct reading experiences with the pupil purposes and questions in mind. Stauffer identified the role of the teacher as an intellectual agitator who asks--"What do you think? Why do you think so? Read the lines that prove it." Pupils must be given opportunities to state what they think, express their opinions and listen to ideas voiced by others in the group. Stauffer further stated, "pupils should not be reading to find answers to satisfy a teacher-asked question, but rather to answer their questions, related to their purposes. The teacher should free her/himself from the right answer and free children from parroting the answer they think the teacher will like and gain teacher approval."

Hoskinsson (1973) is in agreement when he explained, "The DRTA strategy is based on the assumption that pupils will be more motivated, interested, and will understand a story better if they set their own purposes for reading and practice making predictions regarding possible outcomes for a story." This may be somewhat akin to Goodman's (1970) notion that reading is a psycholinguistic guessing game and to Smith's view (1971) that readers predict their way through a text. (See Figure 6:20.)

PUPILS WILL BE MORE MOTIVATED, INTERESTED AND WILL UNDERSTAND

A STORY BETTER IF THEY SET THEIR OWN PURPOSES FOR READING

I THINK IT WAS
THE BUTLER WHO DID
IT BECAUSE.......

AND PRACTICE MAKING PREDICTIONS REGARDING POSSIBLE OUTCOMES

OF A STORY

PREDICTING IN DRTA

FIGURE 6:20

Finally, another basis for DRTA is the premise that reading involves the reader in predicting, confirming, rejecting and comprehending strategies. The reader, to construct the author's meaning, must bring his/her experiences to predict meaning, to confirm by comparing his/her conceptual knowledge and experiences with the author's, to reject or disconfirm meaning if there is a difference between the reader's and author's meaning, and to integrate prior knowledge/experiences with the author's message, arriving at a new construction of meaning, or an assimilation or accommodation of meaning.

Thus, DRTA is based upon an understanding of the reading process as a thinking task, involving readers setting their purposes and the reader actively participating in asking questions, finding the answers by applying their knowledge and attitudes to finding answers by applying their knowledge and attitudes to construct their interpretation of the author's meaning.

The following sections explain what DRTA is, procedures to implement DRTA with readers, and examples of DRTA lesson.

What is DRTA?

DRTA provides the learner, usually in a small group situation, the opportunity to declare his/her own purposes for reading. Essentially, the reader is involved in predicting outcomes before and during reading a story usually with teacher direction. The reader compares his/her thinking with the author's through processes. Each reader in the group accepts, rejects, or modifies his/her own speculations or the author's stated conclusions. The teacher's role is to assist each reader in the group by raising questions that help them set purposes, recognize inconsistencies, check assumptions, and find their own answers (Hoskinsson, 1973). (See Figure 6:21.)

THE READER ACCEPTS, REJECTS, EXTENDS OR

MODIFIES EITHER HIS/HER

OWN SPECULATIONS OR THE AUTHOR's
STATED CONCLUSIONS.

CONFIRMING OR DISCONFIRMING PREDICTIONS IN DRTA

FIGURE 6:21

Hoskinsson (1973) described three basic steps in DRTA approach:

1. <u>Predicting</u> - developing purposes for reading.

2. <u>Reasoning</u> - developing habits to check predictions, assumptions or speculations.

3. <u>Proving</u> - developing habits of testing predictions or finding evidence to back up conjectures.

Procedures for DRTA

The DRTA approach involves a small group of readers and the teacher. The children and teacher read the same story usually selected by the teacher. Stories selected for DRTA are mainly from a basal reader, although multiple copies of trade or library books may be used. It is important for the teacher to keep in mind that not all story material is appropriate for a DRTA lesson. Also, DRTA is applicable to informational or content material as well as story-type or fiction stories.

The reading in the group situation is primarily silent although oral reading may be included to confirm, reject or provide evidence to prove predictions. (See Figure 6:22.)

PARTICIPATION IN DRTA

FIGURE 6:22

416

The steps included in a DRTA are basically the following, although modification of procedures may be necessary depending upon the type of material and the "level" of reading ability of the children.

Step 1: The teacher may briefly introduce the story content to develop interest and experiences related to the plot of the story. The teacher may ask the children to share any experiences or other stories read related to the story plot, setting or theme.

Step 2: The teacher asks the children to read the title of the story and to speculate what a story with this title may be about. The teacher should direct the children's attention to the first picture and ask, "What do you think the story might be about now?" Using only the title and first picture the children make conjectures about the story related to their experiences. The teacher should accept all possible reasonable speculations and predictions. The teacher may write the predictions on the board.

Step 3: With the predictions in mind, the teacher has the children read the first page or two silently. After the silent reading the teacher asks the children to close their books. The teacher checks on comprehension by asking questions, such as, "What do you think now?"; "Were you right?"; :What do you think will happen next?" Oral reading might be needed to prove a point or to disprove a prediction. The teacher may cross out the predictions which were not appropriate, keeping those on the board that are still viable.

Step 4: The teacher asks the children to read silently two or three more pages and to examine any pictures, keeping in mind old conjectures still possible and new predictions based on new evidence from prior reading and illustrations. Almost all the facts may be in by now. After silent reading of the next part of the story the teacher develops comprehension by asking various open-ended questions, such as, "Now what do you think?"; "Were you right?"; "Can you prove it?";

"Find in the story and read orally to prove it." New conjectures may be written on the board and prior predictions eliminated as they prove inaccurate.

Step 5: Finally, the teacher asks the children to predict how the story will end. The teacher may ask, "How do you think the problem will be solved?"; or, "How do you think the story will end?" The teacher accepts all reasonable conjectures and asks the children to read silently to the end of the story. After the silent reading the children close their books and discuss the outcome of the story to prove or disprove predictions. Again, they may re-read orally to prove speculations. (See Figure 6:23, page 419.)

The parts in the story where the teacher has the children make predictions, read, stop reading to verify/confirm/disconfirm predictions will depend on the particular selection and/or group of children. There are variations of procedures that teachers can try. For example, some stories are appropriate to use the following procedures:

1. Read the entire story silently except the last page--then predict the outcome.

2. Examine the title, first and last pictures, make predictions--then read the entire story to confirm or disconfirm predictions.

3. Read half the story--make predictions--read remainder of the story--confirm or disconfirm predictions.

The DRTA procedure is one useful comprehension-centered approach to focus reader's attention of meaning. It is appropriate with certain types of narrative, fiction-type stories, especially mystery, adventure and other stories with a well-defined plot problem. DRTA is also useful with some informational or expository material. With content materials, or so-called "factual" or "memory-recall" questions, the teacher focuses on the content and guides readers to relate their knowledge of the topic to the author's message. This is accomplished by the teacher asking various open-ended questions being careful not to provide information in his/her questions. Also, the teacher guides readers to make predictions--having them read (or listen) the content--then

418

THE TEACHER'S ROLE IS TO ASSIST THE READER BY

RAISING QUESTIONS THAT HELP THEM SET PURPOSES,

RECOGNIZE INCONSISTENCIES, CHECK ASSUMPTIONS, AND

FIND THEIR OWN ANSWERS.

PROCEDURES IN DRTA

FIGURE 6:23

confirming or disconfirming speculations. The steps
for DRTA for narrative materials is similar for expository materials.

Through the process of teacher open-ended questioning and encouraging readers to make predictions
based on information (their own experiences and knowledge as well as the author's information) the teacher
enables readers to think beyond the so-called "literal
level," to interpretive, applicative, analytical and
evaluative thinking. At the same time the readers are
developing comprehension of skills identified as, "main
ideas," "supporting details," "sequence of events," and
so forth as they process content materials.

ReQuest

The ReQuest procedure is a technique to develop
comprehension described by Manzo (1968). It focuses on
students raising questions about what they read and
teacher modeling questioning behavior for students.
Dorothy Watson has added a retelling component to the
ReQuest procedure.

The ReQuest procedure and a diagram of the
technique is given below:

> Re-Reading
> Retelling
> Quest-Question
> Teacher Question - Student Response
> Student Question - Teacher Response
> Student Question - Student Response

The rationale, goals, procedures and examples
of lessons using ReQuest are described below.

Rationale for ReQuest

Reading is a communication process involving
reader and author interaction. The reader's task is to
construct, to some degree, the author's message. The
focus during the reading act should be on constructing
meaning.

ReQuest is a comprehension-centered approach
involving the interaction of the reader's experience with
the author's meaning. A third party, the teacher or
other student(s), participates with the reader and the

author. ReQuest is similar to DRTA in that teacher
(or student) questioning about the meaning is involved
in the method.

The basic premise underlying ReQuest is that
comprehension will be improved by the reader asking
questions and therefore, setting his/her reading purposes. The teacher also asks the student questions for
the purpose of modeling questioning behavior and to develop the reader's comprehension of the material being
read. (See Figure 6:24.)

RE QUEST

RATIONALE

*   READER COMPREHENSION IMPROVED BY READER ASKING QUESTIONS

*   TEACHER MODELS QUESTIONING BEHAVIOR FOR READER

*   READER SETS OWN PURPOSES FOR READING

TEACHER-STUDENT QUESTIONING

FIGURE 6:24

Goals of ReQuest

Manzo (1968) identified the goals of ReQuest, "as a method designed to improve students' reading comprehension by providing an active learning situation for the development of questioning behaviors. In addition, the verbal exchanges between students and teachers provide diagnostic information to teachers about specific learning difficulties or deficiencies of the students." Another goal of ReQuest is the direct, immediate feedback the student receives during the teacher-student interaction through questioning and retelling procedures.

Procedures for ReQuest

ReQuest can be used in an individual or group situation. It is usually most effective, as most methods are, in a one-to-one, teacher's student relationship. There is generally a combination of silent and oral reading, although silent reading by student and teacher is the most effective approach. At times assisted reading is useful when the student has demonstrated difficulty in oral reading a portion of the text, or when the student has not understood the meaning. Then the student and teacher can reread orally together the difficult segment of the text. (See Figure 6:25 on page 423.)

The ReQuest procedure begins with the teacher or student(s) selecting a whole story to read. The teacher explains the rules of the method to the student. Manzo (1968) suggested the teacher give the following information to the student: "The purpose of this lesson is to improve your understanding of what you read. We will each read silently the first sentence. Then we will take turns asking questions about the sentence and what it means. You will ask questions first, then I will ask questions. Try to ask the type of questions teachers might ask in a way teachers might ask them. You may ask as many questions as you wish. When you are asking questions, I will close my book (or pass the book to you if there is only one between us). When I ask questions, you close your book."

After the rules have been explained the student and teacher are ready to begin ReQuest procedure. The student and teacher read silently to a certain point in the story, (it may be more than one sentence, for example, the first paragraph). The teacher may ask the student to retell what has happened and follow-up with specific questions. Then the student asks the teacher

ORAL READING   SILENT READING

INDIVIDUAL SITUATION

OR

ORAL READING

SILENT READING

GROUP SITUATION

ReQuest

FIGURE 6:25

423

questions about the same portion of the story read. The teacher and student continue reading silently to another place in the story (or sentence by sentence, if this is the teacher's plan). The student may initiate the questioning followed by the teacher asking the student to retell the portion of the story read, including the teacher asking questions about what the student read.

The procedure continues in this manner through the story. At any point the teacher may ask the student to read orally a part of the selection, followed by teacher and/or student questions. If the student exhibits difficulty in oral reading the teacher may suggest they reread that portion together orally. Assisted reading can be a natural part of the ReQuest procedure to focus the students' attention on predicting and confirming strategies to make sense the reading.

The length of silent and/or oral reading selected may vary depending on the effectiveness and proficiency level of the student and the type of material read. The reading may be sentence-by-sentence as suggested by Manzo (1968), or larger language chunks, e.g., paragraph or page-by-page reading.

At a certain point, perhaps well into the story, the teacher may ask the reader to predict how the story will end. The teacher and student read silently to the end of the story to confirm or reject predictions regarding the outcome of the story. Thus, a modified DRTA may be injected into the ReQuest procedure to develop comprehension.

The teacher's modeling of questioning behavior should include a variety of questions. The teacher's questions during ReQuest should include characterization, plot development, theme and events. Teacher questions should involve so-called "literal," "interpretative," "evaluative" and other higher level thinking. The teacher might want to develop questions from a schema of the story, e.g., setting and episodic elements of story structures, such as, initiating events, internal responses, attempts, consequences, and resolution. As the teacher models "types" of questions, for the student she/he also provides an example of questioning techniques, such as, clarifying and focusing behavior.

In summary, the ReQuest procedure is particularly useful to use selectively with certain students because it focuses the reader's awareness on reading to construct meaning. The reader should be an active participant in the reading process. The reader deals with connected written discourse with the aid of a teacher in the ReQuest procedure. Reading becomes a purpose-setting activity as the reader formulates his or her own questions during the reading act. ReQuest would appear to be a useful method for students who have an intense preoccupation with the mechanics of reading (e.g., "sounding out," word-by-word reading, etc.), which results in low comprehension ability.

The following section provides examples of lessons using the ReQuest procedure:

Samples of ReQuest Lessons

Lesson 1

Purpose: To improve Robbin's reading comprehension by providing an active learning situation for the development of questioning behaviors and purpose setting.

Initiating: We will each read silently the first sentence from Witches Get Everything by Kaye M. Teall. Then we will take turns asking questions about the sentence and what it means, with Robbin being encouraged to ask the type of questions I might ask in a way that I might ask them. She will be encouraged to answer as fully as possible, and instructed that "I don't know" is not an acceptable answer.

Interacting: As Robbin and I alternate reading pages aloud to one another, I will ask thought provoking questions regarding what we have just read. Her questioning behavior should improve as a result of modeling mine.

Expanding: Our questioning will continue until Robbin is able to provide a reasonable response to the question "What do you think is going to happen in the rest of this selection? Why?" Robbin will need to tell what clues from the text led to her prediction. I'll then have her read to the end of the selection to see if her predictions were correct.

425

Evaluation: I'll evaluate Robbin's questions and
              answers throughout the exercise, praising
              good questioning strategies and those
              answers which show critical thinking and
              improved comprehension.

                        Lesson 2

         This lesson is planned for a reading group of
six. Likely to be termed a "low" group, it is composed
of two nearly-non-readers and four shaky beginning readers.

Purpose: To encourage the children to take respon-
              sibility for their own reading; to im-
              prove comprehension; to encourage respect
              for others reading.

Initiating: "Today we will each read a page silently.
              Then we will take turns asking questions
              about what we read. This will help you
              understand our story better."

              "When we ask each other a question we may
              not look at our books. We will turn them
              over when it is our turn to answer."

Interaction: We used the basal reader (Ginn's <u>Duck is a
              Duck</u>) for the text. For the silent reading,
              children were instructed to say 'blank' if
              they came to a word they did not remember.
              Each child silently read a page and asked
              a question, as did the teacher. We used
              only two books, one of which was passed
              along by the readers.

              As we went along, I reminded the others to
              pay close attention to the questions
              asked and answers given. I informed them
              that I would let someone retell the whole
              story at the end of the game.

Evaluation: These children are all very wiggly and
              talkative. Using the ReQuest method help-
              ed to keep their attention focused on
              their reading. They were quieter and more
              obliging toward others reading.

Evaluation:	Questions formed showed more thought from
(Continued)	some than I had hoped for. The non-readers still had difficulty because of lack of word memory.

Expansion:	We plan to try this with partners, using stories that we have read before. Hopefully, the non-readers will have better successes with familiar material.

Schema Stories

Dorothy Watson (1979) advocated a comprehension-focused technique called schema stories. The schema story procedure is an excellent approach to use in a teacher-directed small group activity. It is a novel way to replace traditional round-robin oral reading in achievement level groups. Schema stories redirect the reader's attention from surface oral reading performance for the teacher to reading to construct the author's meaning. Using schema stories involves readers in processing connected written text for a meaningful purpose. It demonstrates to readers there is more to reading a story than just pronunciation of words.

The rationale for schema stories, procedures and examples of applying the schema story technique is presented below.

Rationale for Schema Stories

The theoretical basis for schema stories, a comprehension-centered approach to learning to read, is related to research conducted concerning story grammar. (See Chapter V, Whole Language Reading Instruction.) A discourse analysis technique, story grammar, had discovered that even young children (ages 3-5) and certainly older children and adults possess a sense of story structure. The sense of story structure is developed at an early age through listening to stories and various experiences in life.

Schema stories help readers develop familiarity with a sense of story and the structure of stories. By listening to stories children become aware of beginnings of stories, ("Once upon a time . . ."), plot sequences leading to the climax, themes (good triumphs over evil), and endings (. . . and they lived happily ever after").

Such knowledge of story structure enables the reader to predict the course of the story structure enables the reader to predict the course of the story and to monitor their own reading (Watson, 1979).

Children who are read to frequently develop a schemata for certain types of stories, e.g., fairy tales, fables, folktales, etc.) and become familiar with different writing styles and written formats. In school, children need to learn and compare different and similar written schemata. For example, the schemata for a social studies text, science text, poetry, math problems, fiction stories and functional written material, such as, recipes, menus, how-to-do-it, etc., all have different written formats or schemata. Through listening, reading and writing activities children need to anticipate written information in a variety of formats. They need to have teacher guidance to learn to adjust to varying written structures. (See Figure 6:26, page 429.)

Finally, to become effective and efficient readers, learners need to develop understanding about the interrelationship of text, or how written text "hangs together." The teacher must help learners become familiar with the related parts of text which makes it comprehensible and meaningful and how the parts function together to form an organized whole written text. The teacher can read aloud different types of written formats, pointing out the structure and parts of the text to enable readers to build various written schematas into their cognitive structures. Also, teacher must provide a variety of written formats, or written structures for children to read, or listen to giving instruction to help learners attend to written landmarks to aid comprehension development.

Next, suggestions for procedures teachers can utilize for the schema stories approach are described.

Procedures for Schema Story Approach

The schema story method involves students at various times reading dis-similar texts (poetry, folktales, songs, math problems, science information, social studies, advertisements, menus, recipes, directions, etc.). The teachers should demonstrate different written schemata by reading various materials listed above to the children. At appropriate points the teacher may ask, "What will happen next? Does this remind you of anything else we've read? How is this similar?

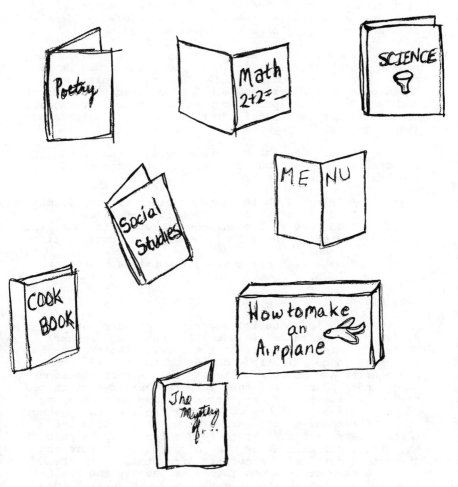

MATERIALS FOR SCHEMA STORIES

FIGURE 6:26

How is it different?" In effect, the teacher and students reconstruct and compare written schemata (Watson, 1979).

The schema stories approach based on research in story grammar lends itself primarily to prose stories. The approach can be used in small group situations with students who read at similar "levels" of proficiency. The method involves teacher selection of stories, usually narrative in form, with easily identifiable beginning, plot development and ending.

Some sources recommended by Watson (1979), for schema story materials, include: old, discarded basal readers, science, social studies and math books; weekly children's news magazines, e.g., Scholastic publications, such as, Scope and Sprint; copies of recipes, brochures, directions for games, and put-together print materials. (See Figure 6:27, page 431.)

After material for schema stories has been selected the teacher should construct the material. The basic procedures are:

* Select a whole story or other written format.
* Cut into substantial parts (3-6 parts).
* Be sure to include the title of the selection.
* Paste each part of the story on construction paper.
* Make multiple copies if possible. (Watson, 1979)

(See Figure 6:28, page 432.)

When the materials have been prepared and the students are assembled in a small group, the teacher gives each student a part of the story. Another approach is to have multiple copies of the parts of the whole story and have each student reconstruct the same story independently and then compare their reconstructed stories. However, if students each have only one part of the whole story, they would work together as a group with the teacher to reconstruct the story. Then the teacher asks each student to read silently their part of the story, thinking about what might happen before and after that particular excerpt. After this silent reading, the teacher asks who thinks he/she has the beginning and why. Then the student reads the section and the other students listen to decide: (1) if they agree that the beginning has been chosen; (2) if they have the

* OLD DISCARDED BASAL READERS, SCIENCE, SOCIAL STUDIES, MATH TEXTS

* STUDENT NEWS MAGAZINES, E.G., SCOPE, PRINT, WEEKLY READER, ETC...

* COPIES OF RECIPES, BROCHURES, DIRECTION FOR GAMES, PUT-TOGETHER, ETC...

SOURCES FOR SCHEMA STORIES

FIGURE 6:27

431

*   SELECT A WHOLE STORY OR PRINT
    MATERIAL

*   CUT INTO SUBSTANTIAL PARTS

 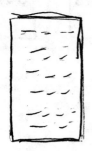  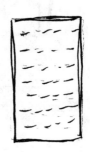

*   BE SURE TO INCLUDE TITLE OF SELECTION

*   PASTE EACH PART OF STORY ON CONSTRUCTION PAPER

*   MAKE MULTIPLE COPIES IF POSSIBLE

CONSTRUCTING SCHEMA STORIES

FIGURE 6:28

432

section of the story. The teacher and group proceed through the story in a similar manner, making and testing predictions, discussing decisions and listening to each other.

This procedure for group reading develops real purposes for oral reading and listening to others read orally compared to traditional directed-reading groups in which each student is expected to listen to another student read orally what he/she already can read for himself/herself. In addition, comprehension of the story is developed through the interaction of the group and the teacher, even though the teacher is not asking direct questions. Yet all "types and levels" of thinking and comprehension is going on as the group reconstructs the story so it makes sense

The following section illustrates examples applying schema stories with a group of children.

Samples of Schema Story Lessons

Story Schema

Lesson 1

Purpose: To recognize sequence and story line through the use of predicting strategy.

Initiating: Prior to beginning the activity, explain to the students, who will be working in groups of two, that there are many times in a story or book that the reader knows what is going to happen before he/she reads. This ability to predict makes reading easier and more enjoyable. Students are then given an envelope with a story cut into paragraphs (the story must be predictable), a piece of construction paper, and tape or glue. The first paragraph is marked in the envelope.

Interacting: Each group will reconstruct the story, based on predictable events, context clues, transitional devices, and any other clues. When the story has been put into correct order, it will then be glued onto the construction paper.

Interacting: (Continued)	It is impossible with a slower group of children to do this activity in a larger group where each group of two has the same story. Here you would begin with the first paragraph of a story such as "Snake in the Sleeping Bag" by Yvor Smitter from The Reader's Digest, October 1962. The first paragraph tells you that it is a very hot day and that everyone at the campsite is up and about. That is everyone except Al who is still in his sleeping bag. A closer look at Al lets everyone know that Al is not asleep; he mouths the words "snake" and it is evident that there is a snake in his sleeping bag and he cannot get up. The discussion begins here when the teacher says, "What would you do if you were there?" The students list the possibilities as to what the next step would be and decide which one is the most likely. This usually is to try smoking the snake out. The students then look at their paragraphs and find one that says just that. The discussion goes from there going step by step through what would actually be done by the students if a friend were in a sleeping bag with a snake (in this story, it is a very poisonous bushmaster).
Applying:	Students will then proceed to glue the parts of the story on their paper until they have a whole story in front of them to read intact.
Expanding:	Students could then become involved in a discussion about situations in which they were very afraid and had to act despite their fear. It can be brought out that fear makes people act unusual sometimes. It can also be discussed that when a family member or friend is involved, fear is often overcome by concern for the safety of the individual.

Students could then become involved in a little research of the bushmaster snake and the country in which it is found. Students could write their own stories about the most frightening or dangerous situation that they found themselves in. |

434

Evaluation: As the students are working, observe those
                who are having any difficulty coming up with
                the obvious. Circulate around the groups
                and ask specific questions of any such
                group of two.

Lesson 2

        The next example of a teacher using the schema
story approach is with a first grade teacher and a small
gtoup of children. They are reading the story, The
Gingerbread Man. The teacher has divided the story into
five parts. Each child is given one part of the story
to read. The children are asked to read their part
first silently and then orally to the group.

        The dialogue of the teacher and children as
they interact with the story is given below.

Teacher: Today we are going to read a story called,
                The Gingerbread Man. I have divided the
                story into parts and we're going to see if
                we can put the story back together. Each
                one will have a part of the story. Read
                your part of the story to yourself. Think
                where your part of the story belongs--the
                beginning, the middle, or the end. Then
                we'll each read the part of the story you
                have orally. Listen carefully to each one
                read their part. Then we'll see if we can
                put the story back together in the right
                order. (After silent reading the teacher
                continues.)

Teacher: OK, Larry, will you read your part of the
                story?

Larry: "He ran, and he ran, and he ran, and he
                ran, back to the little old woman and the
                little old man . . . . ."

Teacher: OK, that was Larry's part of the story.
                Each one think about where that part of the
                story goes.

Tanya: The last part.

Teacher: OK, let's put it here and see.

435

Teacher:	Tanya, will you read your part?
Tanya:	"Stop, stop!" cried the little old woman and the little old man. But the gingerbread man shouted, "Run, run as fast as you can. You can't catch me. I'm the gingerbread man"..
Teacher:	What part of the story do you think this is? Where does this go?
Kim:	At the beginning?
Lonnie:	The beginning.
Teacher:	The beginning? The very beginning of the story?
Larry:	No, almost the beginning.
Teacher:	Alright, let's place the part Tanya read here and read another part. Sherrie will you read your part?
Sherrie:	Once upon a time a little old woman said to a little old man, "I will make a ginger-bread boy to keep us company." . . . . .
Teacher:	Where do you think the part Sherrie read goes?
Lonnie:	At the very beginning.
Teacher:	Where do you think, Sherrie?
Sherrie:	The beginning.
Teacher:	Does everybody think this part is the very beginning? Why?
Kim:	Yes, lots of stories begin, Once upon a time.
Teacher:	Alright we've read three parts--we think we have the beginning of the story. We need two more parts of the story don't we?
Teacher:	Lonnie, let's see where your part of the story goes.

Lonnie:	The gingerbread man met a fox. "Poor gingerbread boy," said that foxy old fox. "I will not chase you. Why don't you sit down and rest for awhile?" The gingerbread man sat down and snap! That foxy old fox just missed . . . . .
Teacher:	OK Lonnie, where do you think this goes?
Lonnie:	At the end . . . the end.
Teacher:	Do you think that's the very end?
Larry:	I don't think so--the part I read was the very end because the gingerbread man got home safe and he was put in a cookie jar.
Teacher:	What do the rest of you think?
Sherrie:	Yes, Larry had the very last part.
Teacher:	Well, let's have Kim read her part and maybe it will be easier to figure out where Lonnie's part fits.
Kim:	The gingerbread man met a mooley cow. "Wow!" said the mooley cow. "A gingerbread boy would taste mighty good to my baby calf." But the gingerbread man just laughed. "I've run away from a little old woman and a little old man, and a frisky puppy, and I can run away from you too, I can . . . .
Teacher:	Good Kim. Now, where does this part of the story go?
Tanya:	It is the middle--after the part I read about the puppy and the goat.
Teacher:	Do you think Tanya is right?
Sherrie:	Yes, then the gingerbread man met the fox after the cow, goat.
Teacher:	Alright, good. We have put the story back into the right order.
Tanya:	Once upon a time.

Teacher:	Yes, stories sometimes begin that way don't they?
Teacher:	Then all the other things happened in the middle, didn't they?
Children:	Yes!
Teacher:	How did we know the end of the story?
Lonnie:	And they lived happily ever after.
Teacher:	You all did a good job putting the story in the order it happened.

Written Conversation

Carolyn Burke of the University of Indiana has developed a procedure called written conversation. It is a type of assisted writing. The teacher and child sit down together and carry on a conversation only in a written form. Neither one is allowed to talk. Written conversation provides a real audience for communication. Any written expression needs an audience and a purpose for communicating. Written conversation is a fun-type learning experience which provides practice in reading writing. Also, the teacher may learn more about his/her students by occasionally doing written conversation. (See Figure 6:29, page 439.)

The procedure for written conversation is very simple. The teacher begins by writing a sentence for the child to read and asks him/her to reply in writing. The child responds in writing and the conversation continues as the teacher and child write to each other asking questions and writing statements similar to an ordinary oral conversation. Children can also have written conversations with each other. After the teacher demonstrates written conversation with a few children, they can do it in pairs. During written conversation both parties try to "converse" silently, but if a reading problem occurs, the message may be read aloud for the reader. For example:

Teacher:	My name is Ms. Jones.
Child:	My name is Sue.
Teacher:	I have a cat.
Child:	I have a dog.
Teacher:	What is your dog's name?

438

WRITTEN CONVERSATION

PROCEDURES

*   TEACHER AND CHILD SIT TOGETHER

*   TEACHER WRITES SENTENCE FOR CHILD TO READ
*   CHILD WRITES A RESPONSE TO THE TEACHER

WRITTEN CONVERSATION

FIGURE 6:29

```
Child:     Sam
Teacher:   My cat is black and white.
Child:     My dog is brown with white stripes.
Teacher:   My cat like milk.
Child:     My dog likes bones.
```

Written conversation is a useful method to develop writing and reading abilities because the focus is
on meaning. The child has a purpose to read what someone else has written in order to respond meaningfully
with his/her own message. Written conversation can be
an additional whole language approach in the classroom.

Functional Reading and Writing Activities

All language processes, e.g., speaking, listening, reading and writing, are tools used by human beings
to communicate meaning. Language serves a useful purpose in most human interaction. The young child learns
the linguistic systems of language and the uses or functions of language simultaneously. Halliday (1975) has
documented evidence that children develop several
"models" of language. Halliday's language "models" or
functions of language learned by children were described
in Chapter II, Oral Language Development. Language is
learned because it has uses or purposes the child perceives as necessary to participate in the normal human
events that take place in the environment. The young
child learns to use language because he/she is exposed
to language related to meaningful experiences. The form
or mechanics of the linguistic systems do not need to be
presented in a formal manner to learn language and to
use language. Language is learned naturally when the
learner perceives the purposes, uses or functions of
language. Language is learned easily in meaningful,
contextualized situations in interaction with other proficient language users who provide support feedback and
interaction. Therefore, meaning or function is more
significant in language learning than form, mechanics,
or metalinguistic, language used to talk about language,
e.g. sounds, letters, phonics, parts of speech, punctuation, grammar, definitions, etc.

Page and Pinnell (1979) stated that children's
concept of the uses of language and purposes for language enable them to learn language easily and naturally
without direct teaching. Children have learned and used
language for their own purposes. After children enter
school they are asked to use language for purposes they

do not understand. Instruction in language learning
in school, particularly reading and writing, emphasize
practice in making sounds, saying words and phrases
usually out of meaningful context. The purpose of
this practice often is clear to the teacher but not to
students. Even in the middle grades students often have
no clear notion of purposes of reading and writing.

Halliday (1974), Doughty, Pearce, and Thornton (1977), and Tough (1977), stressed the need that
teachers should continue to help students develop and
expand the functions for which they use oral language,
building reading and writing skills on purposes which
are valid and meaningful to students.

Page and Pinnell (1979) have developed a conceptual framework focused on problem solving for which
use of written language is a solution. They identified
the problems humans seek to solve by using written language which falls into several major categories: (1)
communicating over space; (2) communicating over time;
(3) coping with complexity (see Figure 6:30, page 442);
(4) representing and making sense of life experiences;
(5) seeking pleasure and enjoyment (see Figure 6:31,
page 443); (6) coping with leisure time; (7) filling
rules in the culture (See Figure 6:32, page 444).

Reading and writing skills need to be learned
as students perceive the need to use written language
for their own purposes. Written language is useful
when language needs to be preserved over time and
referred back to, e.g., notes to oneself, written
records, documents, minutes of meetings, contracts,
and the like; or, when language needs to be studied because of its complexity, e.g., reading a story; and,
written language is used to solve problems related to
occupational roles in society. (See Figure 6:33 below.)

FUNCTIONAL READING

FIGURE 6:33

441

* COMMUNICATING OVER SPACE:

    LETTERS

    BOOKS

    STORIES

* COMMUNICATING OVER TIME:

    SCIENCE FICTION

    NOTES TO ONESELF

    MINUTES OF MEETING

    HISTORY

* COPING WITH COMPLEXITY:

    INSURANCE POLICIES

    TAX RETURNS

    WILLS

    LAWS

    DIRECTIONS

PURPOSE OF WRITTEN LANGUAGE

FIGURE 6:30

PURPOSE OF WRITTEN LANGUAGE

FIGURE 6:31

PURPOSES OF WRITTEN LANGUAGE

FIGURE 6:32

444

Page and Pinnell (1979) reported interesting findings from teacher and student responses to why people read for what purposes do you read.

First, a group of teachers were asked to give reasons why people read. The list of reasons for reading included:

to get information
for pleasure
to learn things
to learn what's going on
    in the world

to know what they are
    buying
to communicate with others
to escape from reality

Teachers were asked what do you read and to list all the reasons they read for the previous week. One teacher's list is as follows:

the grocery list
the TV schedule
labels on cans
my teacher's manual
a program at a concert
the faculty bulletin

several recipes
a letter from my mother
the newspaper
name tags
a menu to order food

Middle grade students were asked, "Why do people read?" The students' answers, in part, included the following reasons:

So they can do stuff better
To learn how to read
If they don't read, they don't know the words, if
    someone asks them to spell a question.

So that people can read street signs, car instru-
    ments, stuff at work, how to get to places, and
    how to build things with Dad.

So you aren't dumb.
I really don't know.
To get a job.

The similarities and differences between the teachers and student's responses to the question, "Why do you read?", provide insight concerning the purposes that deal with real life situations, while students' perceptions are general and/or related to instruction they've had in reading. The point is that often students don't connect the writing instruction in school with any relevant real life experiences.

445

Functional reading and writing experiences are those activities that are life-centered and related to "read-life" needs. As much as possible, reading and writing should take place in socially situational contexts. Teachers must provide opportunities for learners to develop and set their own purposes. Functional reading activities frequently can be integrated within the total reading program. Print materials such as TV guides, newspapers, magazines, "how-to" manuals, telephone books, comic books, cookbooks, science experiments, catalogues, travel brochures, pamphlets, posters, food product labels, signs, maps, tour books, greeting cards, menus, baseball cards, and many others, can be utilized for reading material related to thematic units in literature study, social studies, science, health, mathematics, art, music and physical education. Using "real-life" print materials enable learners to make the connection between purposes for reading and writing in school and outside school. (See Figure 6:34, page 447.)

The following section will suggest procedures teachers can use to plan functional type written language experiences at various grade levels. Obviously, the teacher has to be selective in using certain activities related to the age/grade level of the children.

Procedures for Functional Reading and Writing Experiences

Functional reading and writing experiences should not necessarily be planned separately from other on-going comprehension-centered approaches described in this chapter. The teacher should be aware of opportunities to include so-called, "real-life" materials within other comprehension-centered approaches and as a part of thematic units in "content areas." For example, print materials, such as, baseball cards, comic books, newspapers, magazines and "how-to-do-it books may be a part of the SSR/SSR approach. Students should have opportunities to self-select and read materials related to their own purposes and interests, or the "Mine," part of the "Mine," "Yours," and "Ours" techniques suggested by Dorothy Watson for sustained silent reading time. Also, a variety of different print materials including, recipes, directions for playing a game, putting together a model, a newspaper or magazine article may be used as schema stories to develop students' familiarity with different schemata of print organization. (See preceding section on Schema Stories). Menus, recipes, and food labels are appropriate "real-life" print materials

FUNCTIONAL PRINT MATERIALS

FIGURE 6:34

for children to read when learning about nutrition as part of a unit in health or when studying fools of different cultures. As much as possible functional print materials should be naturally integrated within the total curriculum, along with traditional school textbooks.

Applying Halliday's "models" of oral language development to learning written language, reading and writing, Kenneth and Yetta Goodman (1976) have related language functions to experiences and activities teachers can apply in the classroom.

Examples of Functional Reading and Writing Lessons

There are many types of functional language experiences that teachers may integrate in some manner related to pupil purposes. Functional activities have been described in materials by: Adams, Coble, and Houndshelf (1977); Breyfogle, Nelson, Pitts and Santich (1976); Kohn (1973); and Herr (1977). Teachers should consult these sources and others for additional kinds of "real-life" language experiences. When teachers select functional print materials one basic criteria to keep in mind is that materials should be whole language in nature and in a social situation if possible, especially for very young children, e.g., primary level.

Lesson 1

Purpose: To develop the need for reading, to follow directions, and develop sequence.

Introduction: This activity would be done in the fall. We might have picked our own apples, or the children might bring Appleseed and the book Rain Makes Applesauce. We would discuss the things you can make from apples and safety rules of cooking.

Interacting: If I was working with a large group of children, each group would be responsible for a different activity associated with making applesauce. First group of children, wash the apples. The second group cores the apples. The third group cut the apples into pieces. Then we put the apples in a covered skillet and let them cook. When they are mushy each child

448

Interacting: (Continued)	takes a turn mashing the apples through the strainer. We follow the directions for the rest of the recipe, eat and enjoy.
Expanding:	Each child has a copy of the recipe, and with help at home may make up their own recipes of favorite foods, and we can make a cookbook.
Evaluation:	Observe children in activities, reinforce functional uses of reading.

Activity Sheet - A recipe for Applesauce

You will need:

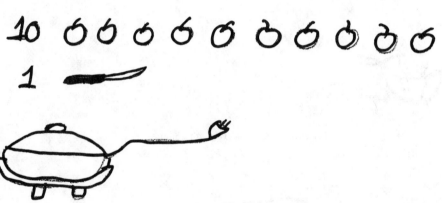

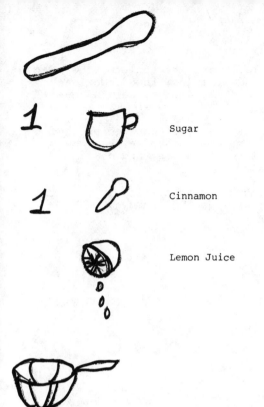

1   Sugar

1   Cinnamon

Lemon Juice

Directions for Making Applesause

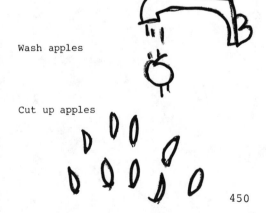

Wash apples

Cut up apples

450

Cook in frying pan until mushy

Mash through strainer with a spoon

Put apples in a bowl

Add 1 cup sugar

Add 1 spoon cinnamon

Add some lemon juice

Stir

Eat and enjoy

Lesson 2

Functional Reading Techniques

1. Each year as a functional activity, we take a walk around the school neighborhood and "get acquainted" with all the signs to be read. I usually like to do this right at the beginning of school, and then once or twice again during the school year. The children love to do it, and it allows them an opportunity to be familiar with all the "reading material" that surrounds them.

2. Another functional activity that I find to be effective is to have each child think about his favorite meal, and then share with me the ingredients mom uses, and how she makes it. I then print these on stencils and run them off--enough that every child has an entire set. After we enjoy sharing our recipes with each other (each child reads his/her own) we decorate the cover, and give them to Mom for Mother's Day.

Sample page of our cookbook:

Busketti

Ingredients: Half package long noodles
              1 can tomato sauce
              1 bowl mushed-up tomatoes

Cook the long noodles until they are soft and don't break. Open the can of sauce and pour it with the mushed-up tomatoes. Squeeze your hands around in it for a little while, but wash your hands first. Pour the sauce on top of the cooked noodles, but take the water off them first. Put the dish in the oven until it is time to eat. Set the table, and then watch TV for a while. Bake at 150 for about 30 minutes, then call everybody for supper.

        You can imagine about twenty-five of these. Some of them are simply darling, but this is the only one I recall right now. This is always one of my favorite projects of the school year!

Lesson 3

Functional Reading

Purpose: To help children understand the need to
              read, follow and understand directions.

452

Introduction: On game day a child brought the game
Finder's Keeper's to class. I discovered
that he did not know how to play it.
Everyone was enthusiastic and wanted to
learn. An interesting discussion was held
about games they have at home that they
have never been able to play because of
the difficult instructions.

Interaction: Together we read the instructions and I
placed the unknown words on the board. We
redesigned each sentence to fit the
child's vocabulary and I transferred
these to a chart. Each child read the
charts. When play of the game started
each child knew exactly what to do.

Expanding: One child suggested we write a letter to
Milton Bradley and ask them to make the
instructions easier to read.

Some children needed visual memory exercises and others needed practice counting
money. Other games were suggested to
improve these skills.

Evaluation: As the children played the game in later
sessions, I observed how well they remembered the sequence of play. I also observed improvement in money counting
skills and visual memory skills. A cloze
test was constructed to see how well the
directions were understood and remembered.
The enthusiasm and expressed desire to do
this again with other games was a good
indication as to how successful this reading experience had been.

Instructions for Finders Keepers as Written on the Box

Twenty-four cups of different shapes are placed
on the game board, as shown on the cover. At the beginning of the game, each cup covers a COIN of unknown
value. In his turn, a player spons the dial, lifts up
one cup, FINDS A COIN under it, and becomes a KEEPER.
He replaces the COIN with one of his MARKERS. He
should try to remember which cups still cover COINS,
because if he lifts a cup with a MARKER under it, he
pays a penalty. THE OBJECT OF THE GAME is to win the
most money. This is usually done by remembering which
cups cover COINS.........not MARKERS.

Setting Up the Game

1. The playing board shows 24 spots in a random design and 4 black corners.

2. The tray contains a spinner and 48 punch-out COINS which are markers 5...10...25...or "0." The COINS marked "5" are called "Nickels." The "10's" are "Dimes." The "25's" are "Quarters" and the "0's" are called "Zonks."

3. Each player is given 5 dimes.

4. 24 COINS: 3 Quarters, 9 Nickels, 10 Dimes, and 2 Zonks are turned FACE DOWN, mixed and placed on the board, (face down) one on each Spot.

5. The plastic cups are carefully broken from their runners and placed on the board, each cup covering a COIN. The different shapes should be placed at random, similar to that shown on the cover of the box.

6. The colored plastic MARKERS are used as follows:
   a. Four Players: Each is given 6 MARKERS of a color. Red, White, Blue and Yellow

   b. Three Players: Each is given 8 MARKERS, using Red, White, and Blue.

   c. Two Players: One player uses twelve light colored MARKERS - Yellow and White. The other player uses twelve dark colored MARKERS - Red and Blue.

Playing the Game

1. The first one to _____ a triangle goes _____.

2. You _____ again and _____ up the cup that is the same _____.

3. If a coin is under it you get to _____ it. If someone else's _____ is _____ the cup I pay him a _____. If my _____ is there I _____ everybody a dime.

4. Put the _____ back on top of the marker.

5. The first person to use up all of his _____ gets to keep the rest of the _____ under the cups.

6. Everybody _____ their money.

7. The one with the _____ _____ WINS!

454

Setting Up the Game

1. Each _____ gets:

   _____ dimes

   _____ markers

2. Put:

   _____ quarters

   _____ nickels

   _____ dimes

   _____ zonks

   Face _____ on the squares of the playing

   _____.

3. _____ them up and _____ them with a

   plastic _____.

Possible Answers:

Setting up the Game

1.	Player	3.	Mix
	5		cover
	6		cup

2.	3
	10
	2
	down
	board

Playing the Game

1.	spin	3.	keep	4.	cup
	first		marker	5.	markers
			under		coins
2.	spin		dime	6.	counts
	pick		marker	7.	most money
	shape		pay		

455

Lesson 4

Functional Reading Activity

In this activity students will order from a Christmas catalog. They will order gifts for all members of their immediate family, as well as those living with them under the same roof.

The following will be included:

1. Setting up a budget based on the number of presents to be purchased, and a maximum and minimum for each.

2. Comparing two similar items for price, available sizes, quality, accessories, etc.

3. Keeping notes on alternate choices

4. Deciding on gifts.

5. Placing an order using the order form attached.

6. In some cases items will be marked "out of stock" by the "store"; at that time second choices will be ordered by the student.

Using the order form will expose the student to an additional form of written communication.

The effectiveness of the reading lesson will be evaluated by the degree to which the students' orders parallel their meaning.

NAME _____

Last   First   Initial

ADDRESS _____

Street   City   State   Zip

CHARGE ACCOUNT # ☒☒☒   DATE

catalog #	description	color code	quantity	weight	price	size	page number

457

Lesson 5

Functional Reading Activity

Purpose: To encourage my group of 3 fourth grade boys that reading is necessary and the results also can be fun. (Something they really haven't totally accepted.)

Introduction: Today we are going to make some cookies-- you are to be the bakers.

Initiating: The recipe was read first in order to find out that they were going to make M&M Cookies! They were hooked already. Second, the ingredients were read, the utensils assembled and finally the step by step process of putting it all together.

Expanding: The boys want to make things once a week now and surprise their Mothers with their goodies on Mother's Day.

Evaluation: The boys discovered working together was fun and co-operation was very necessary. They learned that reading recipes was not such a mystery after all and the end results were delicious. It was very hard to wait a day though because we didn't have enough time to put it all together and bake all in one 30 minute period. I told them, who knows; maybe some day I might read about them being famous chefs all because they learned how to read recipes in my class.

The recipe was taken from The St. Paul's Kids' Cookbook which the boys enjoyed looking through because it was put together and illustrated by some of my former students when we lived in Kansas City, Missouri.

M & M Cookies

1 cup butter   2¼ cups sifted flour
1 cup brown sugar   1 teaspoon soda
1 cup granulated sugar   1 teaspoon salt
2 teaspoons vanilla   1 cup M & M's
2 eggs

458

Blend butter and sugars, beat in vanilla and eggs. Sift
remaining dry ingredients together. Add to sugar mix-
ture. Mix well with the M & M's. Grease the cooking
sheets, bake at 375 10-12 minutes. Makes 3 to 5 dozen
cookies depending on how big you make the cookies and
how much dough you eat before you bake them. The extra
M & M's are good to eat just plain.

Lesson 6

Functional Reading Center

Purpose: To encourage reluctant readers using
practical applications of comprehension-
centered approaches. To practice total
reading experience using semantic and
syntactic cues. To combine reading and
writing. To use and extend vocabularies
used in students' everyday lives. Language experience (Functional reading) for
older students. Students draw on their
own experience and see the necessity of
gaining meaning from print.

Organization: The functional reading center is a three-
sided visual on a table for the necessary
materials. The center consists of nine
activities of which the student must complete any five. Students may select
activities which they find interesting.
When completed, written work is placed in
the proper folder for evaluation.

Materials for Center:

Better Homes and Gardens <u>Cooking For Two</u>
and <u>Snacks and Refreshments</u>

Cookbooks of any type
grocery mailers
department store catalogs
letters to the editor from newspaper
hard candy
newspaper insert "Spring Car Care"
deck of cards
white paper
menu from fast food restaurant (Cassano
   is good for exercise)

Introduction: Discuss some of the useful applications for reading and writing. "When do you read and write during the day?"

Interacting: Focus on uses of reading and writing highlighted in the center. Discuss the activities in the center and explain its organization for use in the class curriculum.

Application: Students work in center until five activities are completed.

Expanding: Written exercises which accompany each activity. Motivation to read other materials for the class Individualized Reading Program.

Evaluation: Collect written work from folders.

The school language program needs to be related to childrens' real experiences, interests, purposes and problems. Teachers need to capitalize on the intuitive knowledge children have about the uses of language. Language, reading and writing, will be learned as naturally and easily as children learn oral language if meaning, not form or mechanics of language is kept in proper focus. Functional reading experiences need to be a natural part of the school curriculum and coordinated with other oral and written language activities.

Whole Language Learning Center Activities

Learning Centers or stations in the classroom are another way for teachers to organize and provide learning experiences for children. Learning centers have become popular with many teachers over the past decade. The learning center concept began many years ago with the reading corner or library in the classroom. Generally, reading corners or centers were unstructured and usually contained shelves of books for children to select for independent or "free reading time." Over the past decade or more, learning centers have become more structured related to specific skill objectives, activities related to the specific objectives, and methods to evaluate the child's achievement of the objectives.

Learning centers have developed in classrooms for the purpose of providing individualized instruction. Each child may be scheduled at a specific time to work in a learning center to provide enrichment. Teachers have designed and developed a variety of learning centers, including reading, writing, math, listening centers, drama, and centers related to science and social studies. However, reading centers have tended to be most popular with teachers, especially at the primary level.

The organization and design of whole language learning centers as one organizational plan will be described in detail in Chapter VII.

Next, a rationale, examples of whole language activities for learning centers and sample lessons for whole language activities are presented.

Rationale for Whole Language Learning Center Activities

Whole language activities for learning centers are based on the premise that language learning is more natural and easier in connected discourse, or whole text. Whole language means that the learner strives to construct meaning when given language that has unity. There is a certain relationship between propositions and concepts represented symbolically in oral and written language. The language is not broken apart into its separate systems, e.g., graphophonemic, syntactic and semantic. The learner always has access to interrelated language cues and strategies that exist naturally as a part of language. The psycho-sociolinguistic nature of language learning involves the learner as an active participant searching for and constructing meaning. Whole language activities are always comprehension-centered.

Learning centers, particularly for reading, have traditionally emphasized separate, isolated graphophonemic cues, or letters and sounds, letter-sound relationships, isolated words, phrases, and sentences. Not always have learning center activities included comprehension of whole text. If comprehension is dealt with it is usually at the sentence and paragraph level. Seldom are whole stories, books or texts included in reading center activities. Most learning centers in classrooms are based on a "skills-model" of the reading process. The materials in skills center activities usually include ditto skill sheets, workbook pages, worksheets, isolated letter-sound, syllable, word and

461

sentence games. These activities and materials reinforce the learner's concept of the reading process as
basically a word recognition task rather than a comprehension process.

Whole language activities designed and organized by teachers can be a useful component in the whole
language classroom. They provide a supplement to other
approaches described in the preceding sections of this
chapter.

The learning center concept can effectively
develop children's independent learning and help to
individualize learning. Learning centers can also promote social interaction and group participation as children work and learn together. However, for learning
centers to develop children's language abilities the
activities planned and designed by teachers must focus
on meaning.

Teachers may want to have a "game center" in
their room which includes popular letter and word games,
such as Concentration, Scrabble, word puzzles, and even
some ditto skill sheet materials. However, this type of
center should be used by children if they choose to for
a recreational and fun-type activity, not as a requirement. The learning activities in reading, writing,
listening, and content centers the teacher assigns children to do should focus on the constructing meaning.

Whole language learning activities in centers
may be used in relationship to on-going learning experiences in the curriculum, e.g., thematic units on any
topic; personal interests and purposes of the children
(functional-type language experiences); and, to provide
new experiences to expand and develop interests, experiential background related to the curriculum objectives
or to personal interests and problems.

Whole language learning center activities can
be designed to provide expanding or enriching experiences after various comprehension-centered approaches.
For example, after reading aloud a story to children,
a writing center activity may be based on the book, Can
I Keep Him? by Steven Kellog. After the children have
listened to the book the written assignment is: "Pretend
that you found an animal on the way to school this morning. Write a letter and ask me if you can bring that
animal to reading. You are going to have to give me
some good reasons for bringing it." The children write

their letter to the teacher and the teacher should write a letter back to the child.

Various activities, writing, drawing pictures and so forth, may be available in the listening center after children have participated in assisted reading with a book or story and the taped version of the story to read along.

Written and oral activities and projects may be included in various centers in the room to share books read as part of self-selected and sustained silent reading (SSR/SSR). Various projects were described using the SSR/SSR approach earlier in this chapter for ways children can share books they have read.

Children can be assigned or volunteer to use schema stories and written conversation in learning centers. The teacher will need to prepare short stories which are cut up into whole sections for children, individually or in groups, to reconstruct into a meaningful sequence. (See procedures in the previous section on Schema Stories).

Finally, functional reading and writing activities are a natural way to include whole language activities in learning centers. In fact, the entire classroom environment may be organized on the basis of Halliday's functions of language, or "models" of Language (see Chapter VII).

Next, whole language activities are presented. Teachers may want to use the examples in their own classrooms or better yet, use the examples as models for designing their own whole language activities related to the children's age/grade level, interests and curriculum.

Activities for Whole Language Learning Centers

Harste, Burke and DeFord (1975) described how a reading methods class developed gaming techniques for children to utilize their intuitive knowledge of how language works as a strategy for unlocking print. The teacher identifies a book and develops a game for it which specifically gives the child practice on the strategies he/she most needs to have reinforced. Games based on whole stories can be placed in the classroom reading center.

The following is a brief listing of whole language activities that teachers may incorporate into learning centers at different age/grade levels:

1. To bring the child's real world to the classroom, have them bring food and household products to set up a play store. They can make shopping lists, receipts, commercials and stories about their store.

2. Have children tape stories they have created for other children to listen to.

3. Have a class post office, letting students mail letters anytime; also write a special note to each child once a week.

4. Provide a set of sequence pictures having the children write a caption describing the pictures.

5. Have objects for children to touch, taste, smell before writing about them:

Examples: an apple, an old hat, a doll, a toy car, etc.

6. Have a pet center which may include: a hamster, acquarium, etc. Have rules and charts to determine food and feeing schedule. Keep records of animal behavior.

7. Have a weather station or center, particularly when doing a unit on weather. Make homemade weather instruments; e.g., wind direction and speed, temperature, humidity, rainfall, etc. Keep records of weather on charts. Compare weather over a period of time.

8. Have a science center with books and equipment for children to do simple experiments. Students can read directions about how to do experiments, perform experiments and write results of experiments. Correlate experiments in science center with science unit topic.

Or the book may be made up of pages that are illustrations on one page and stories on the opposite page.

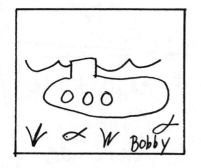

On Saturday we went to Disneyland. My favorite ride was on the submarine. I thought it was real.

Bobby

After the stories and pictures are complete, they are bound into books which the teacher reads to the total class and then puts them on the library table for the children to enjoy. Some classes exchange books. Others invite first and second grade classes to their room for a story time when the teacher reads books which have been "authored" by kindergarten children.

Making Individual Books

The making of books is culminated in the making of individual books. Each child should have the opportunity to author one or two books during the year. These books need not be more than three or four pages in length, but an individual binding should set the story apart as the work of an individual. The teacher should be sensitive as to the development of stories that deserve special recognition--stories that are complete

within themselves. These books are developed at any
time during the year and should never be an assigned
activity.

As children have the experiences of individual
authorship, their appreciation for others is deepened
and their desire to read what other authors have
written is heightened.

The following are sample lessons of whole
language learning experiences appropriate for learning
centers in the classroom:

Lesson 1

Purpose: To use students' everyday experiences as
                  bases for story writing and sharing.

Introduction: Present "Everything Went Wrong" folder

Interacting: Let students read directions, talk about
                  days when everything went wrong, and read
                  one of the enclosed books. Some books that
                  could be included are "One Day Everything
                  Went Wrong," "Alexander and the Terrible,
                  Horrible, No Good, Very Bad Day," and
                  Tales of a Fourth Grade Nothing.

Expanding: Have students, following directions,
                  write their own language experience story
                  about a day when everything went wrong.

Evaluating: Read student-written stories and see how
                  well they convey the feeling of how every-
                  thing went wrong and also whether the

student included items suggested on folder cover.

Lesson 2

Whole-Language Game: Roll-a-Story

Purpose: To develop concept of story elements as well as sequencing through a writing activity.

Introduction: Ask student to recall reading stories with distinct characteristics: a main character, a plot, problem, solution, other characters, etc. One that may be brought to mind is TOO MUCH NOISE by Ann McGovern, the focus of a previous DRTA.

Interacting: Discuss the story elements and how an author uses those elements to make an interesting story. Ask students to suggest other examples of how stories could be made, giving random story elements and collectively working them into a short story a few paragraphs long.

Expanding: Present the folder game "Roll-a-Story," an adaptation of "Strange Stories." Tell students to follow directions and then to put their completed work into the folder.

Evaluating: Read the student-authored stories to see how successfully story elements were integrated, as well as to evaluate the degree of semantic present in the story.

Lesson 3

Reading Aloud Activity

Purpose: To develop language models as an intro-duction to poetry. (This could be used with the whole class or as an individual center activity on tape.)

Introduction: Read a selection from Mary O'Neill's, Hailstones and Halibut Bones.

Interacting: Discuss how colors feel and what colors we use to express certain feelings.

Expanding: Together with the students, develop a similar poem about a color, answering the question "What is -----?" and modeling the language after that of Mary O'Neill's book.

Evaluation: Observe the responses of the children to the reading and their acuity in developing their own color poem.

Lesson 4

Freckle Juice Game

Purpose: With this activity, the teacher can:

468

Purpose: (Continued)	1. acquaint children with the works of a contemporary author 2. experience enjoyment through reading 3. reinforce comprehension by playing a game 4. introduce students to condensed forms of a story
Introduction	Discuss the author--Judy Blume. Present the full length copy of Freckle Juice. Read the first few pages of the book and then allow children to finish the book on their own.
Interaction:	After students complete reading the book, explain the game Freckle Juice. They can play this game in groups of two, three, or four.
Expansion:	At this time read to the group a condensed version of Freckle Juice. Hopefully they will notice the differences between the full length and condensed versions. Explain the technique of condensation and its purpose. The students could work in groups to list portions that had been omitted in the condensed version and discuss their importance to the story. This is also an opportune time to introduce a bibliography of Judy Blume books appropriate for your grade level. Her latest novels, Forever and Wifey are not written for young readers. They are both sexually explicit and are intended for adults.
Evaluation:	Observe the ease and enjoyment with which students can play Freckle Juice. Also, determine if students were encouraged to read other books by this same author.

Lesson 5

Biography

| Purpose: | The purpose of this activity is threefold:
1. to arouse an interest in biographies
2. to enjoy reading this literary form
3. to create a biography |

Introduction: Read biographies to the class during literature enjoyment. Discuss the characteristics of a biography.

Interaction: After the discussion of biographies, a visit to the library to be certain students can locate these books is suggested. Develop a classroom biography center where books of this type can be borrowed.

Expansion: Encourage children to bring biographies from home and the local library when possible.

Assist students as they prepare to develop a biography of a friend or admired person.

Parents could be invited to assist by working with students as they edit their work, typing the manuscript and helping students to bind their biographies.

Evaluation: Observe the enjoyment and knowledge gained as students author, illustrate and edit biographies.

Lesson 6

Graph It

Purpose: 1. to correlate reading with math
2. to follow directions
3. to make a graph

Introduction: We have been studying graphs in math. In this center, you will have a chance to make a graph. Your graph will show where different animals live.

Interacting: Children will read and follow directions.

1. Look at the animal pictures on the bulletin board.
2. Get a piece of paper and some small strips from the envelope.
3. Glue a strip in the column that shows where each animal lives.
4. Put your name on your graph and put it in the box.

470

Expanding: Provide other opportunities for making
                 and reading graphs.

Evaluation: Check papers turned in.

Materials: ditto (in graph form), small strips,
                 glue, large envelope for paper and strips,
                 box for completed graphs

WHERE DO I LIVE?

in the city	on the farm	in the woods

Lesson 7

Check Yourself Center

Purpose: To develop comprehension strategies

Introduction: This center will be introduced by review-
                ing the care and handling of books.
                There will also be an explanation on the
                use of the center.

Directions

1. Choose a story and read it.
2. Look on the back inside cover and
    take the cards out of the pocket.
3. Read the statement on the care and
    choose the answer you think is
    correct.

4. Look at the color at the top of the card. Now lay the card on the "computer" color card. Find the answer which shows the same color as the color at the top of the card. This is the correct answer. Now you can check your own answers on all of the other cards in the same way.

5. Make a picture of your favorite part of the book. Put the name of the book on your picture. Don't forget to color your picture. Now put your name on the picture and put it in the folder on the table.

Interacting: Child reads story, answers questions, checks his own answers, and illustrates favorite part of book.

Expanding: A puppet show or play about the child's favorite book may be performed.

Evaluation: Teacher observation of the child in the center and of drawings made.

Materials: Library books or stories not being used for instruction, "computer" or some type of self-checking device, folder for completed pictures, drawing paper, crayons, pencils.

Summary

An overview of reading from a socio-psycholinguistic perspective was described. The reading process was viewed as an interaction between an author and reader involving an interrelationship of several elements: linguistic cues, thought patterns, strategies and context. Whole language reading approaches were described consistent with the theoretical construct of socio-psycholinguistic principles.

Current reading practices were described that reduce reading to a collection of skills, practice on isolated skills and application of skills to reading.

Whole language approaches were presented involving students in real reading. Methods, materials and activities were described for teachers to select from, that are literature-based, student-centered and focused on meaning. The selection of methods include the following: reading aloud, assisted reading, language experience, self-selected and sustained silent reading, directed-reading, thinking-activity (DRTA), ReQuest, schema stories, written conversation, functional reading and writing and whole language activities for learning centers.

Whole language approaches included: a rationale, procedures, materials and examples of lessons.

Whole language approaches were suggested as the primary methodology for developing proficiency and effectiveness at all levels of reading development. The approaches were based on socio-psycholinguistic theory that reading is learned by reading.

Teaching Competencies

1. Design/plan a reading experience involving a child/ children in an <u>Assisted Reading</u> activity. In planning an assisted reading activity, consider the following: (1) interests of child (children); (2) background experiences; (3) conceptual development; (4) language cues and strategies strengths/ needs; (5) comprehension strengths/needs; (6) organizing for time, place, number of children who can benefit; (7) type of material/equipment; i.e., audio tape, record, person reading with child/ children, etc.; (8) diagnosis/evaluation of child/ children's performance if necessary; (9) determine diagnostic/evaluative techniques, i.e., observation with record-keeping or other. Write a brief plan before implementing. Keep in Resource Notebook.

2. Design/plan a reading experience involving a child/ children in a <u>Reading Aloud</u> activity. Consider factors listed in Number One above. Write a brief plan of the activity before implementing. Keep in Resource Notebook.

3. Design/plan a reading experience involving children in a <u>Directed-Reading-Thinking-Activity</u> (DRTA). Consider appropriate factors identified in <u>Number One</u> above. Write a brief plan before implementing. Keep in Resource Notebook.

4. Design/plan reading experiences involving a child (children) in Reading Strategy Lessons. Plan certain types of Reading Strategy Lessons only for a child or children who have been diagnosed as needing a specific lesson (See Chapter VI on Diagnosis/ Evaluation) related to oral miscue analysis. In planning a specific Reading Strategy Lesson, consider the following factors as listed in Number One. Write a brief plan of the lesson before applying. Write in Resource Notebook.

5. Design/plan reading experiences involving a Language Experience Approach activity. Consider factors identified in Number One. Write a brief plan before applying. Write in Resource Notebook.

6. Design/plan reading experiences involving a child/ children in an Individualized Reading Program accompanied by Sustained Silent Reading (SSR). Consider factors listed in Number One before and during the planning and application of your plan. Write a brief plan of your organization before applying. Keep in Resource Notebook.

7. Design/plan reading experiences involving a child/ children in Functional Reading activities. When planning consider factors identified as in Number One. Write a brief plan before applying. Write in Resource Notebook.

8. Plan/design a whole language reading center for use in a classroom. Consider various factors identified in Number One. Write a plan and design in a diagram before implementing. Keep in Resource Notebook.

Questions to Investigate

1) Explain how reading aloud to students and assisted reading are methods/approaches to learn to read which are compatible and related to a psycholinguistic view of the reading process. Relate the reading aloud/assisted reading method to purposes and types of materials.

2) You have just been appointed to a special primary-grade reading committee. Your task is to acquaint the teachers with the language-experience approach to reading. How would you do this so that teachers would want to incorporate this type of approach into their reading program?

3) You have just been told that you will be responsible for developing an individualized reading
   program (self-selected/sustained silent reading -
   SSR) for your school. How do you feel about this?
   How would you go about doing this? What kinds of
   information would you need?

4) Explain how the schema story approach and Directed-
   Reading-Thinking-Activity (DRTA) are reflected and
   related to a psycholinguistic view of the reading
   process. Discuss purposes, types of materials and
   grouping procedures to use with schema stories and
   DRTA.

5) List as many types of functional reading. Type
   activities as you can that could be included within
   a total reading program. Identify kinds of
   materials that would need to be available in the
   classroom for use by students.

Whole Language Reading Approaches

References

Adams, Anne H.; Coble, Charles R. and Hounshell, Paul
    B. Mainstreaming Language Arts and Social Studies.
    Santa Monica, California: Goodyear Publishing
    Co., 1977.

Allington, Richard. "Sustained Approaches to Reading
    and Writing." Language Arts. Vol. 52, September
    1975, pp. 813-815.

Barbe, Walter B. Educator's Guide to Personalized
    Reading. Englewood Cliffs, New Jersey: Prentice-
    Hall, Inc., 1961

Berstein, Margery. "Relationship Between Interest and
    Reading Comprehension." Journal of Educational Re-
    search, December 1955.

Betts, Emmett A. "What Is Individualized Reading?"
    The Reading Teacher. Vol. 26, April 1973, pp. 678-
    679.

Bissett, Donald. "Bibliography of Literature." Presen-
    tation at Kettering Council of IRA, Kettering, Ohio,
    1978.

Boyd, Gertrude A. and Jones, Daisy M. Teaching Communication Skills in the Elementary School. New York: D. Van Nostrand Co., 1977.

Breyfogle, Ethel; Nelson, Sue; Pitts, Carol and Santich, Pamela. Creating a Learning Environment: A Learning Center Handbook. Santa Monica, California: 1976.

Burke, Carolyn L. "Analysis of Oral Reading Miscues: Applied Psycholinguistics." Help for the Reading Teacher: New Directions in Reading. Urbana, Illinois: National Council of Teachers of English, 1975.

Burke, Carolyn L. "Strategies for Reading." In Videotape Series, The Language Base for Reading. Indiana University, Bloomington, Indiana, 1976.

Chomsky, Carol. "After Decoding: What?" Language Arts, Vol. 53, March 1976, pp. 288-296.

Cramer, Ronald L. "Reading to Children: Why and How." The Reading Teacher. Vol. 28, February 1975, pp. 460-463.

Cramer, Ronald L. and Cramer, Barbara B. "Writing by Imitating Language Models." Language Arts.

Doughty, Peter S.; Pearce, John J., and Thornton, Geoffrey, M. Exploring Language. London: Edw and Arnold, 1972

Eastland, Patricia Ann. "'Read-Aloud' Stories in the Primary Literature Program." The Reading Teacher. Vol. 22, December 1968, pp. 216-222.

Estes, Thomas H. and Vaughn, Joseph L. "Reading Interest and Comprehension: Implications." The Reading Teacher. Vol. 27, November 1973.

Evans, Howard M. and Townes, John C. "Sustained Silent Reading: Does It Increase Skills?" The Reading Teacher. Vol. 29, November 1975, pp. 155-156.

Fox, Sharon E. "Assisting Children's Language Development." The Reading Teacher. Vol. 29, April 1976, pp. 666-670.

Goodman, Yetta and Burke, Carolyn L. Reading Strategies: Focus on Comprehension. Holt, Rinehart and Winston, 1980.

Goodman, Yetta and Watson, Dorothy. "A Reading Program to Live With: Focus on Comprehension." _Language Arts_. Vol. 54, November/December 1977, pp. 868-879

Hall, Maryanne. "Linguistically Speaking, Why Language Experience?" _The Reading Teacher_. Vol. 25, January 1972, pp. 328-331.

Harste, Jerome; Burke, Carolyn C. and DeFord, Diane. "An Instructional Development Activity for Teachers: Making Whole Language Reading Games." In Mainstreaming, The Special Child and The Reading Process. Instructional Packet by Jerome C. Harste, Darryl Strickler and Carolyn Burke, Indiana University, 1975.

Henderson, Edmund H. "Group Instruction in a Language Experience Approach." _The Reading Teacher_. Vol. 26, March 1973, pp. 589-597.

Herr, Selma E. _Learning Activities for Reading_. Dubuque, Iowa: Wm. C. Brown Publishers, 1977.

Hollingsworth, Paul M. "An Experiment with the Impress Method of teaching Reading." _The Reading Teacher_. Vol. 24, November 1970, pp. 112-114.

Hoskinsson, Kenneth; Sherman, Thomas and Smith, Linda A. "Assisted Reading and Parent Involvement." _The Reading Teacher_. Vol. 27, April 1974, pp. 710-715.

Hoskinsson, Kenneth and Krohm, Bernadette. "Reading by Immersion: Assisted Reading." _Elementary English_. Vol. 51, September 1974, pp. 833-836.

Hoskinsson, Kenneth. "The Many Facets of Assisted Reading." Elementary English. Vol. 52, March 1975, pp. 312-315.

Hunt, L'yman C. "The Challenge of Individualized Reading Instruction." 1975.

Kohl, Herbert. _Reading, How To_. Bantam Books, New York: E. P. Dutton and Company, Inc. 1974.

Lamme, Linda Leonard. "Reading Aloud to Young Children." _Language Arts_. Vol. 53, November/December 1976, pp. 886-888.

Lindberg, Margaret. "Comprehension-Centered Reading Program." Presented at a Psycholinguistics and Reading Workshop. University of Dayton, Dayton, Ohio, July 1979.

Manzo, A.V. "Improving Reading Comprehension Through Reciprocal Questioning." Unpublished doctoral dissertation. Syracuse University, 1968.

McCormick, Sandra. "Should You Read Aloud to Your Children?" Language Arts. Vol. 54, February 1977, pp. 139-143.

McCracken, Robert. "Initiating Sustained Silent Reading." Journal of Reading. May 1971, pp. 521-524.

McDonell, Gloria M. "Relating Language to Early Reading Experiences." The Reading Teacher. Vol. 28, February 1975, pp. 438-444.

Odom, Sterling C. "Individualizing a Reading Program." The Reading Teacher. Vol. 24, February 1971, pp. 403-410.

Olson, Willard C. "Seeking, Self-Selecting and Pacing in Use of Books by Children." The Packet. Boston: D.C. Heath and Co., Spring 1952.

Page, William and Pinnell, Gay Su. Teaching Reading Comprehension. ERIC Clearinghouse on Reading and Communication Skills. National Institute of Education. Urbana, Illinois: National Council of Teachers of English, 1979.

Personke, Carl R. "A Listening Post in Beginning Reading." The Reading Teacher. Vol. 22, November 1968, pp. 130-135.

Read, Charles. Children's Categorizations of Speech Sounds. Urbana-Champaign, Illinois: National Council of Teachers of English, 1976.

Reed, Kathleen. "An Investigation of the Effects of Sustained Silent Reading on Reading Comprehension Skills and Attitudes Toward Reading of Urban Secondary School Students." ERIC Document EDI66665, July 1979.

Rhodes, Lynn K. "I Can Read! Predictable Books as Resources for Reading and Writing Instruction." The Reading Teacher. Vol. 34, February 1981, pp. 5-22.

Schnecberg, Helen. "Listening While Reading - A Four Year Study." The Reading Teacher. Vol. 30, March 1977, pp. 629-635.

Stauffer, Russell G. and Harrell, Max M. "Individualized Reading Thinking Activities." The Reading Teacher. Vol 28, May 1975, pp. 765-769.

Stauffer, Russell G. Teaching Reading as a Thinking Process. New York: Harper and Row, Publishers, 1969.

Thorn, Elizabeth A. "Language Experience Approach to Reading." The Reading Teacher. Vol. 23, October 1969, pp. 3-8.

Tough, Joan. The Development of Meaning: A Study of Children's Use of Language. New York: John Wiley and Sons, 1977.

Trusty, Kay. "Principles of Learning and Individualized Reading." The Reading Teacher. Vol. 24, May 1971, pp. 730-736.

Veatch, Jeannette. Individualizing Your Reading Programs. New York: G.P. Putnam's Sons, 1959.

Watson, Dorothy. "Reader Selected Miscues: Getting More From Sustained Silent Reading." English Education. Vol. 10, December 1979, pp. 75-85.

Watson, Dorothy. "A Comprehension-Centered Reading Program." Presented at a Psycholinguistics and Reading Workshop, University of Dayton, Dayton, Ohio, June 1979.

Watson, Dorothy. "Strategies for a Comprehension-Centered Classroom." In Reading Comprehension: An Instructional Videotape Series. Beverly P. Farr and Darryl J. Strickler (Eds.). Indiana University, Bloomington, Indiana: Indiana University Printing, 1979.

CHAPTER VII

ORGANIZING A WHOLE LANGUAGE CLASSROOM

Knowledge Competencies

1. What goals and objectives are important for a whole
   language curriculum?
2. What are the characteristics of each school-wide
   organizational plan: graded school, nongraded,
   team teaching, open classroom?
3. What are the characteristics of various classroom
   grouping organization?
4. How can an integrated whole language curriculum be
   implemented and what organizational components need
   to be considered?
5. What are the factors involved in organizing whole
   language learning centers?
6. How do thematic units relate to the philosophy and
   organization of the whole language curriculum?

        The classroom teacher or special teacher out-
side the classroom, e.g. slow learning class, learning
disabilities room, remedial reading, etc., has the complex task on a daily basis of bringing together the
theory of language learning and putting it into practice. The teacher must plan, organize and implement
the language and content curriculum related to the
learners' needs. The curriculum includes learning objectives (knowledge, skills, attitudes and values) and
learning experiences developmentally related to a particular group of children and the learner within a
group. Obviously, this is no easy task.

        The whole language curriculum is predicated on
socio-psycholinguistic principles of language learning.
The theoretical foundation for organizing a whole language classroom was described in Chapters I, II, and
III. The theories or oral and written language learning developed by Goodman (1972), Smith (1979) and
Halliday (1975), are the foundation for a language and
content curricular organization in the classroom that
is language-centered, child-centered and meaning-
centered.

        There are four interrelated criteria teachers
should consider when planning and organizing the classroom program. The criteria are: (1) Language **learning**
should include meaningful, natural language pat**terns;**
(2) Language learning should include whole language not

fragmented elements of language; (3) Language learning should be functional or purposeful; and (4) Language should be learned in a meaningful context. The point has been made that language processes, e.g. speaking, listening, reading and writing, should be integrated and learned as means, not ends. Language is used to learn about self, others, feelings, the environment and the world. The whole language approaches described in Chapter VI, reading strategy instruction present in Chapter V, and evaluation techniques identified in Chapter IV, are synthesized into an integrated language and content curriculum.

Teachers who want to move from a more traditional skills-oriented classroom to a whole language classroom must understand the socio-psycholinguistic nature of language learning. They need to be committed to learning about children's needs, their growth characteristics and be able to locate materials and plan language experiences appropriate to natural language learning principles.

This chapter will describe several aspects of organizing a whole language learning from a focus on skills to meaning. In this chapter the components of organization described include: (1) Goals of a comprehension-centered language program; (2) School-wide and Classroom Organizational plans and grouping procedures; (3) the Integrated Whole Language Classroom; (4) Stages of teacher development toward an integrated comprension-centered program; (5) Organizing learning centers; and (6) Thematic units.

Goals of a Whole Language Classroom

The whole language school setting focuses attention on the individual child within the larger group situation. The emphasis is on linguistic and cognitive abilities, strengths and experiential background each child brings at any given time to learning situations. The teacher committed to developing a whole language program views the child according to the Peace Corp adage: "If you want to join the Peace Corp you should see the glass as half-full, not half-empty." The whole language teacher has a positive attitude toward every child's learning ability and possesses knowledge about language learning. The attitude and values of the teacher make a significant difference in determining whether each child at a given developmental stage will progress in language and content learning according to his/her cognitive, social, emotional and physical growth patterns.

The teacher lacking a knowledge base about language learning principles, but who is positive and truly interested in helping children learn, will not be as effective a teacher as he/she could be. The "skills-oriented" teacher will place too many obstacles in the way of children learning language. This is an unfortunate situation for children. The really sad part is that many teachers and administrators are oblivious to socio-psycholinguistic learning principles and the practical application of organizing whole language experiences. They go on their way teaching skill-after-skill-after-skill, rationalizing that most of the children at a particular grade level by the end of the year are reading at or above the grade level. Never mind that possibly as many as one-half or one-third of the children are not progressing in language learning, particularly reading. It may be an overgeneralization, but most "skill-oriented" teachers are unaware of the number of children who can read but who dislike reading and therefore, do not read as much as they could. Skills reading instruction and purposeless oral reading in groups have frequently dulled children's interest in reading and produced negative attitudes toward reading.

The whole language classroom has goals which provide a structure, direction and purpose for the children and the teacher. The learning experiences planned and applied by the teacher with student participation is not dictated by curriculum guides, courses of study, textbook manuals, although these materials are useful as reference resources in planning the language and content curriculum. Rather, the teacher applies her/his knowledge of human growth and development; socio-psycholinguistic principles, observation of each child, understanding of materials and providing appropriate learning experiences, and makes decisions concerning children's learning activities in the classroom.

The goals which provide the structure and direction for a whole language classroom are as follows:

1. Each child increases independence in learning.

Children need opportunities to self-select and participate in language activities of their own choosing. They need to assume increasing responsibility for their own planning, doing and evaluating language activities. For example, selecting their own reading materials and writing topics, self-correcting while reading and writing, evaluating their own performance, and selecting and creating their own activities. The teacher must practice minimal intervention in student's reading, writing, listening, and speaking. She/He should provide appropriate feedback to the child's language. The teacher should not disrupt the langugae process and should encourage and promote student independence. The teacher can have a positive influence upon children's language and content learning by modeling uses of speaking, listening, reading, and writing.

2. Each child increases understanding of self and the world

Learning activities should be functional to meet student's present needs. The teacher should provide learning experiences that emerge from the lives of the students. As much as possible students should use their own language and experiences in language activities. Language activities should be natural, involving the whole person, integrating language into all content areas. Language learning activities should be integrated with different events and topics and expand student's learning by exposing them to new experiences.

3. Each child increases self-esteem

The happiness and well-being of each child is essential. Each child must progress in learning to his/her capacity. The teacher encourages self-initiative and self-reliance in an atmosphere of self-controlled freedom. The classroom includes children's art, language and constructions to promote self-respect, feelings of self-worth and importance. The teacher listens attentively to children, informally and in instructional situations. He/She converses informally with children demonstrating a real interest in their lives.

4. Each child increases in a sense of purpose

Language learning activities involve functional language appropriate to each age level, interest and needs. The teacher maintains a major focus on meaning and enjoyment in all language activities (speaking, listening, reading, and writing). All activities use whole meaningful language. Language and content is learned because it is useful. Students perceive the need to learn because activities are self-selected or chosen by the teacher who relates learning to interests, needs,

484

experiences and provides new experiences to expand
learning.

The ultimate goal of the whole language classroom is to provide learning experiences that make sense
to children and that enable them to learn language and
content that builds upon what they already know. Then
children will develop independence, understand self and
the world, increase in self-esteem and have a sense of
purpose in their lives.

Organizational Patterns in the School and Classroom

The teacher needs to be familiar with various
school-wide and classroom organizational structures and
develop his/her language and content curriculum within
the existing framework or change the organizational
structure to conform to whole language learning experiences.

The whole language curriculum can fit into almost any current school-wide and classroom organizational structure. The overall organizational plan does not
have to change, however, administrator's, teacher's,
children's, and parent's philosophy of language learning
and attitudes and values toward learning need to change.
There are some school-wide and classroom organization
schemata that may be more conducive to a whole language
and content program. For example, the graded or nongraded self-contained classroom as a school-wide plan
and the integrated or open classroom seems to provide
more support and facilitate a whole language approach
than other organizational structures. However, it
should be recognized that many schools and classrooms
are organized in various ways. Teachers have to operate within existing organizational structures that frequently are difficult to change.

In this section a description is given for
different school-wide and classroom organizational plans.
The self-contained school organization and the integrated or open classroom will be described in more detail in a later section.

School-Wide Organization for Reading

Self-Contained Graded School

Most elementary schools traditionally have been
organized as self-contained graded classrooms. The
children and teachers are grouped by grade levels,

e.g., Kindergarten, first grade, second grade, . . .
sixth grade. The children are grouped heterogeneously
in terms of ability, achievement, social and emotional
growth. Each self-contained graded classroom has one
teacher and usually 20-30 children at approximately the
same age leve.

The traditional self-contained school organization has certain characteristics. Each classroom
teacher is responsible for the language and content
curriculum at a particular grade level. The language
ares curriculum, particularly at primary levels.

Children are grouped by reading achievement
levels as early as first grade into two, three or more
groups in the classroom. The published basal reader
generally determines the reading curriculum in the classroom. Content areas, science, social studies, mathematics, and health are scheduled separately from language arts. Spelling, handwriting and English are
usually scheduled at specific times. However, some
teachers in self-contained classrooms have scheduled a
language arts block of time, e.g., reading, writing,
language study and spelling and a content block of time,
e.g., science, social studies, health and mathematics.
Nevertheless, even within block scheduling, each language art and content subject frequently is scheduled
separately.

The self-contained classroom, graded or nongraded, has many advantages considered from a psycho-
sociolinguistic and whole language perspective. The
teacher has the opportunity to naturally integrate and
coordinate language learning and content learning. All
language processes can be developed within the context
of learning about the world. There need be no separate
periods scheduled for specific language skills and content. Language development becomes the means, not the
end, to learn information and use language. Each child
is simultaneously developing greater language facility
within a purposeful context as he/she is developing
knowledge, attitudes, values and skills.

The thematic unit approach, with language
learning and use as the core, is an effective method
related to the graded self-contained school organization. Teachers at each grade level within his/her
classroom may schedule large blocks of time for children
to read, write, listen and talk and learn about a common
theme. Unit study can be planned for flexible time

486

periods. Thematic units will be described in a later section of this chapter.

Nongraded School Organization

The nongraded school concept became popular during the 1960's. This concept organizes instruction based on different rates at which children learned. Grade labels, first grade, second grade, and so on, are eliminated and generally replaced with labels designating levels of learning. The non-graded concept has been applied mainly to reorganizing the primary graded school and the reading program. In theory, each child is evaluated and placed at a certain level in reading and allowed to progress as fast or as slowly as he/she is able. Each teacher is assigned responsibility for several levels within the primary reading program (K-3) or (1-3). For example, a school with six primary classes, two first grades, two second grades and two third grade classrooms, is divided into six teachers with 180 children. The reading program is divided into 20 levels, beginning with readiness level through possibly sixth grade level. One teacher is assigned children reading at readiness, pre-primer and primer level; another teacher is assigned children reading at easy first reader level (Transitional between primer and 1^1 level). 1^1 reader level and 1^2 reader level. Another teacher is assigned: easy second reader level (Transitional between 1^2 and 2^1; 2^1 and 2^2 reader level; and so on through reader level 6^1 or 6^2. (See Figure 7:1 on page 488.)

Most nongraded school reading programs are organized with published basal reader materials. These materials are the core of the reading program. The children may be in a self-contained classroom for all other subjects but move to another teacher according to their identified reading level. During the year children move ahead in reading levels at their own rate of progress. Some children progress through six or more levels equivalent to gaining two or more years in reading achievement; other children progress through 3 or 4 levels, equal to one year's growth in reading achievement; while still other children may only progress one or two levels during a whole year.

The nongraded school organizational scheme basically groups children by reading level. As a result there is usually multiage grouping within a classroom. There may be younger children with older children.

487

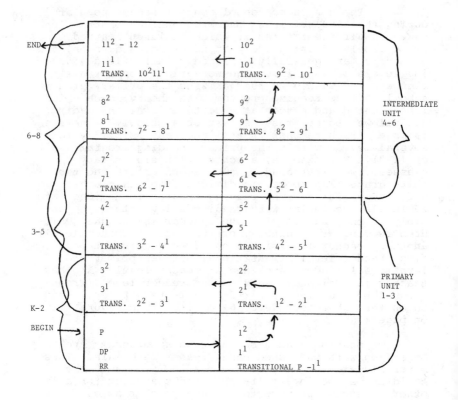

CLASSROOM   CLASSROOM

1 TEACHER   1 TEACHER

NONGRADED SCHOOL ORGANIZATION FOR READING K-8

FIGURE 7:1

However, the whole child's physical, emotional, social and mental growth, is considered when moving a child from one level to another. The difficulty with the nongraded school concept is that it artificially separated reading from other language processes, e.g., writing, spelling and from content areas. Also, children are grouped primarily on the basis of a "reading level." This is a very narrow way to group children for language learning. Although teachers use different material, the basic material for reading is a set of basal readers. Another disadvantage is that organizing children into sequential "reading levels" tend to focus instruction on isolated skills and drills in the particular published program. Teachers often use isolated word recognition and comprehension checklist or tests of skills to make decisions about the child's progress and when the child is ready to move to another level within the group, or to another teacher with a higher range of reading levels. As a result, the reading program in a nongraded school often becomes a fragmented, skills-oriented, level-by-level approach. The nongraded organization is an attempt to provide for individual differences in rate of learn-ing, which in effect, reinforces learning to read as an isolated skills approach. However, at the time the nongraded school was proposed and implemented during the 1960's as an alternative to the traditional graded school, socio-psycholinguistic research and language development research was only beginning. The dominate theory of language learning, and in particular, reading, was the sequential, isolated skills approach.

The original intent and purpose of the nongraded school was positive. The purpose was to individualize learning of children. The concept of nongradedness, or not labelling children by grade levels, is a useful concept for a comprehension-centered school and classroom. However, it is only one component of the total language and content curriculum in a school. Allowing a child to learn and develop at his/her own rate is a worthy goal and should be continued. However, the simplistic notion of "levels of reading" as the criteria for organizing language programs needs to be re-examined in the light of research findings in language learning.

Team Teaching

During the 1960's team teaching was proposed as a school-wide organizational plan. Team teaching can be implemented within a graded or nongraded school. Team teaching, known also as cooperative teaching,

489

involves organizing two or more teachers to function as a team. Teachers of adjoining classrooms or open space large areas act as a team and plan reading and/or other content areas cooperatively. The children assigned to each teacher on the team may have two or more teachers. Team teaching is proposed as an organizational structure to provide for advantages of departmentalization, e.g., each teacher teaches one or two "subjects," as well as retain advantages of the self-contained classroom organization.

The teachers on the team plan flexible reading groups, observing, discussing, monitoring pupil progress and sharing instructional methods. The teaching strengths of each teacher may be utilized effectively, e.g., one teacher may be strong in creative writing, art, music, and so forth, and could share ideas with other teachers and flexibly regroup children to teach in his/her strong area. The team teaching organization can be an effective approach if teachers on the team are compatible. However, team teaching can evolve into nothing more than departmentalization if team planning time is not a part of the program.

The advantages of team teaching should be exploited in the development of a whole language schoolwide and classroom program. The sharing of ideas, methods and materials can be beneficial to teacher and children. Also, children's learning may be enhanced through interaction with two or more teachers rather than one. (See Figure 7:2 on page 491.)

Classroom Organization Plans

The nature of school-wide organization in a building will definitely influence the teacher's organization of learning in the classroom. However, within any school-wide organizational schema, e.g., graded, nongraded or team teaching, the teacher has a certain degree of freedom and flexibility. How much flexibility a teacher has within his/her own classroom, remedial reading room, LD resource room, or other setting will depend in part on the expectations of the principal, other teachers and parents. Generally, unless the reading-language program is so highly skill-structured and/or a skills management system is imposed upon teachers, most teachers are free to schedule and organize learning independently. However, a teacher may still need to conform in part to a specific set of reading-language materials.

TEAM TEACHING

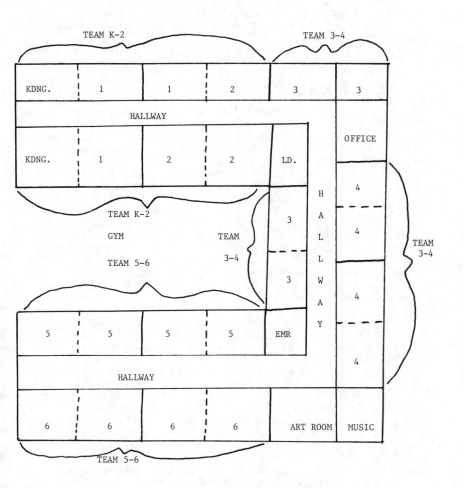

TEAM TEACHING ORGANIZATION

FIGURE 7:2

491

This section will review and present various grouping patterns teachers should be familiar with as they plan and schedule language and content learning experiences. The teacher should keep in mind the goals of a whole language program, the socio-psycholinguistic nature of language learning and various whole language instruction (Chapter V) and reading approaches (Chapter VI) when selecting grouping patterns as they plan, organize and monitor children's learning experiences and achievement. The grouping patterns described briefly include: (1) interest groups; (2) research groups; (3) reading strategy groups; (4) tutorial groups; (5) friendship or social groups; and (6) achievement level groups.

Interest Groups

Interest grouping involves the teacher grouping certain children according to identified interests in reading, or two or more children group themselves related to a common interest. The teacher may suggest an interest group based on his/her records from the self-selected/sustained silent reading (SSR/SSR) component of the whole language classroom. Several children who have read books on a similar topic, e.g., biographies of football players, mystery books, adventure, humorous fiction, etc., may be grouped together in the reading center to share different books on the same general topic. Children who have read books by the same author may meet together informally to compare ideas. The teacher should make interest groups available to children on a voluntary basis in addition to other grouping patterns and learning experiences.

The teacher's use of grouping by interests is a natural part of the SSR/SSR approach. As the teacher observes and records a sampling of books read by each child and/or examines the records of books read kept by children, she/he can suggest interest groups, or encourage children to organize their own interest group. The groups are flexible and temporary. The interest group may disband as soon as it has served its purpose. Interest grouping is advantageous because the children in a particular interest group are not labeled by achievement levels. It is natural that there may be a mix of proficient and ineffective readers in the group. The only criteria for inclusion in the group is that each child is reading or has read a book on a similar topic or by the same author and have common interests.

Organizing groups by interests does take considerable planning and some monitoring by the teacher.

It does not happen automatically. The teacher must make
it possible. The teacher must know the interest and experience of each child to organize interest groups. She/
He needs to keep up with the current reading materials
and topics of each child. The procedures for self-
selected reading/sustained silent reading (SSR/SSR) are
important for the teacher to know when organizing interest groups. These procedures were described in
Chapter VI.

Interest gtouping may develop from individual
teacher-pupil conferences as the teacher identifies
children's common interests, experiences and books being
read. The teacher may suggest certain children meet together to plan ways of sharing their reading experiences
with each other and with the whole class. For example,
a group of children who have read the same book may plan
a dramatization such as a puppet show, a skit, paint a
mural of significant happenings in the book, or present
a panel discussion about the story before the class. A
sampling of different projects interest goups can do
were presented in Chapter VI.

Interest groups are only one organizational
procedure available to teachers in the whole language
program. This type of grouping may be scheduled regularly during any given day for one or more groups of
children. The children in the group need to be scheduled by the teacher for a specific time at a specific
place in the classroom. The groups need to become self-
directive, freeing the teacher to work with other children in different whole language approaches and types
of grouping patterns. However, at times the teacher,
teacher aide or another adult in the program, may monitor the interest group when necessary to keep the children in the group on the task.

The organizational procedures for interest
groups, as well as other types of grouping described
below, are explained in a later section on the integrated whole language program.

Research Groups

Research grouping involves the teacher in
planning, organizing and monitoring small groups of
students according to teacher-selected and pupil-
selected topics. The research group's purpose is to
locate and prepare information which is usually shared
with the whole group. Research groups, as other grouping patterns, are temporary and include students at

493

different rates of learning and ability levels. However, research groups generally function for a longer time than other grouping patterns, e.g., interest, friendship.

Social studies, science, health, and mathematics, the content areas, usually should involve research groups. An effective approach to learning, described later in this chapter, thematic units, utilize research groups as one way to develop and apply all language processes to learn and present information.

The procedures and organization of research groups involves considerable teacher planning and monitoring of activities. Briefly, a theme is identified from the curriculum for social studies, science, mathematics, health, literature, or includes an interdisciplinary approach. Next, the teacher and students identify sub-topics related to the theme and raise questions to investigate. Materials, print and non-print, need to be gathered and available for pupils to research the sub-topics. Then research groups are organized by the teacher and students. Usually a chairperson and recording secretary are identified for each group. The group size should be 4-6 students. Each group meets regularly to plan projects assigned to individual group members. Work is assigned, reference material and various media are collected and the research work begins. The teacher, and hopefully an aide or student teacher is available to assist the groups in planning, assigning work loads to members of the group, locating materials, taking notes, outlining material, and planning how to share information. The teacher needs to plan the time, space and materials for research groups to function over a period of time. Finally, there should be a culminating activity in which each group reports information in a variety of formats, e.g., skits, murals, panel discussion, individual oral and written reports, dioramas, and so forth. During research grouping, students participate in purposeful reading, writing, listening and speaking activities. Students learn to use language functions, identified by Halliday (1975), including uses of language for heuristic and informational purposes, e.g., to find information to questions and to inform others about ideas and events.

Also, as students research ideas they are involved in using and learning language to interact with each other, e.g., the interactional use of language. Research grouping is a complex but very rewarding

494

grouping pattern, along with other types of classroom grouping patterns.

Reading Strategy Grouping

Teachers in traditional classroom reading programs frequently organize special "skills groups" as a part of the instructional program. "Special needs" or "skills grouping" involves a child or a group of children working on specific isolated word analysis, comprehension and study skills. The teacher usually has children grouped according to reading achievement levels within the classroom and specific skills are presented and practiced by children using workbooks, ditto skill sheets, letter/sound, word games, flashcards and other traditional materials. The children in skills groups work on specific skills after the group has read a particular story in the reader. This work is frequently referred to as "seatwork" or "independent activities." Most skills are isolated and separate from real reading, although the skills are usually imbedded within the context of the story the reading group has read in the commercial reading materials.

Reading strategy groups, on the other hand, are organized by the teacher based on systematic observation of children as they read in various oral and silent reading situations. Students also are involved in Reader Selected Miscues (RSM) as described by Dorothy Watson (1979) and presented in Chapter VI as part of the SSR/SSR approach.

Grouping children for strategy groups is done on the basis of a formal, informal, or modified Reading Miscue Inventory administered by the teacher as a child reads orally and retells what he/she has read. Reading strategy groups should be flexible and for temporary purposes. Children in reading strategy groups may be at different stages of reading development but have similar linguistic and strategy strengths and needs. As a child develops strength in certain linguistic cueing systems that previously were observed as weak, and as certain strategies, e.g., predicting, confirming, correcting, integrating information, improve, the child should be removed from a reading strategy group. Reading strategy grouping should be flexible and on a temporary basis.

In Chapter V, reading strategy lessons were described and examples of strategy lessons related to

495

specific linguistic cues, e.g., graphophonemic, syntactic, semantic and learning strategies were presented. First, the teacher should be knowledgeable about the psycholinguistic nature of the reading process and develop competence in using the Burke and Goodman's Reading Miscue Inventory (1972). (See Chapter IV.) The classroom teacher will need to apply a modified miscue analysis procedure to monitor reading performance of more children on a regular basis.

Various whole language approaches described in Chapter VI will provide opportunities for the teacher to systematically observe oral reading behavior and keep simple records of pupil's oral reading miscues and comprehension. For example, the teacher can observe and note miscues a child makes as he/she reads language experience stories; during teacher-pupil conferences as part of SSR/SSR when a child reads aloud a portion of a book she/he is currently reading; as children reread orally during the DRTA or Story Schema activity; and, during a ReQuest activity, to only mention a few whole language reading situations.

The teacher needs to plan the time to observe children in oral reading settings and develop a simple record-keeping device to record miscue behavior. After a certain miscue pattern has been established from a sampling of a student's oral reading, the teacher can begin to organize reading strategy lessons for children having similar strengths and needs. Reading strategy lessons in Chapter V can be designed and used with children in a small group who have common needs. Reading strategy groups may be organized based on teacher observation of pupil's oral reading within whole language approaches. For example, the expanding part of a reading strategy lesson may involve assisted reading (book and tape), a language experience activity, self-selected and sustained silent reading, or writing. (See Chapter V, reading strategy lesson format.)

Grouping children by strategies involves the teacher identifying commercially-prepared materials, or designing her/his own materials related to different reader's needs in the classroom. Next, the teacher has to organize and plan the time and use of space to group children who will benefit from instruction. This is a demanding task for the teacher with many children. Fortunately most children at any grade level do not require planned reading strategy lessons most of the time. Many children will learn to read by actually reading and writing. They will naturally develop reading profiency by being read to, participating in language experience activities, self-selecting their own reading materials and doing lots of sustained silent reading and writing, and by participating in other whole language approaches. The poor and ineffective readers at any developmental stage will need periodic reading strategy lessons. The teacher must believe and trust that most children develop reading ability without direct instruction, particularly if reading involves children in dealing with whole language. Another possible way for teachers to overcome grouping problems related to planned reading strategy groups is to include strategy lessons within whole language activities in learning centers. This approach still requires teacher planning, collecting and designing reading or writing materials for the center activities. However, it occasionally frees the teacher from directing reading strategy groups. (See Whole Language Center Activities in Chapter VI.)

It should be clear that reading strategy groups are only one among other grouping procedures that are ways for teachers to organize the whole language and content curriculum.

Tutorial Grouping

It has been known for a long time that children learn from other children. Pupil tutors can positively influence learning. The teacher needs to provide and plan opportunities for children to learn together. Children who can read or write more effectively can assist children who experience difficulty within the classroom. Some teachers have arranged for older children in higher grades to tutor younger children in reading. Children frequently "talk the same language" and sometimes are more effective in "teaching" than the teacher.

Tutorial grouping should be informal and temporary. The teacher needs to know each child well before assigning pupils as tutors to help other pupils. The tutor and tutee should be compatible and get along well with each other. At times a better reader may tutor a poor reader. Other times, children may be similar in reading or writing ability. Pupil tutors should not be expected to do "formal teaching." Rather, pupil tutors may have the child being tutored read aloud a story and possibly discuss the story. This is effective when older students help younger children.

The teacher should consider each child's needs
when assigning a pupil tutor. The grouping should be
flexible and various children should learn together for
short periods of time. Each child at some time may help
another child so that the same children are not always
in the role of tutor. The teacher will need to monitor
pupil tutoring to some extent.

Friendship Grouping

Friendship groups are similar to interest
groups. Usually children choose to read together or
discuss books they are currently reading or have read
on the same general topic or by the same author. However, children may read together or talk about books
only on the basis of friendship toward one another.

The teacher may make friendship grouping available at certain times. Children may sign up at a
specific time and place in the classroom to read with
best friends. Naturally, this should be an informal
setting with no restrictions. Friendship grouping relates to the SSR/SSR approach. Children should have
opportunities occasionally to share their readings without direct teaching or intervention by the teacher.
Children will look forward to the particular time during
any school day when they can read with friends.

Achievement Grouping

Achievement level grouping is the most common,
frequently used grouping pattern in all grades in the
traditional classroom. However, in the integrated whole
language classroom achievement grouping should have the
lowest priority. There are many negative factors and
psychological side-effects that result from achievement
grouping. This type of grouping, used excessively, does
not meet the wide range of abilities of individuals in
the group for the following reasons: interests are
varied; individual reading strategies strengths and
needs are not considered; self-fulfilling expectations
which are either too low, too high, or "average" are
realized; and, children are placed in rigid groups once
they are placed at achievement levels.

The teacher may occasionally group children who
consistently read at a similar stage or difficulty of
reading development. DRTA and schema story approaches

are appropriate for grouping children reading the same story. However, these procedures should not be utilized excessively within the total language program. Rather, other approaches, e.g., reading aloud, assisted reading, language experience, SSR/SSR, functional reading activities, whole language activities in learning centers, and so forth, can be provided to minimize grouping by reading achievement level. Children are still learning at their own rate and differences in progress are not emphasized when other types of grouping are used.

Other grouping patterns described previously are more effective organizational techniques to meet individual learning differences and to promote positive self-concepts and achievement. Grouping children by interests, research topics, reading strategy needs, tutorial groups, and friendship groups, enable each child to achieve the goals of a whole language classroom.

The Integrated Whole Language-Centered Classroom

The integrated language classroom is recommended as the organizational structure enabling students to achieve the previously stated goals of the whole language program. An integrated whole language classroom relates and coordinates all language and content learning. Teaching and learning occurs naturally. This does not suggest there is little structure or planning required by the teacher. In fact, an integrated whole language and content classroom necessitates more planning and structure. The teacher must be more knowledgeable about language learning principles, child growth and developmental characteristics, content, methods, materials, evaluation and organization. There is no one teacher's manual, course of study or curriculum guide that tells the teacher what to do. The teacher makes educational decisions on the basis of a comprehension-centered theoretical orientation and continuous perception and understanding about each student and the group.

The rationale and philosophical basis for an integrated whole language classroom in the following sections are discussed and characteristics of the integrated classroom are compared with traditional classroom. Next, several practices and problems are described when teachers attempt to change from a traditional to an integrated language-centered classroom. Finally, the teacher and pupil roles are explored in an integrated whole language-content classroom.

The concept of an integrated whole language classroom has developed over a period of time. Its recent antecedent is the British infant school model, the informal classroom or, integrated day, and American models of the informal classroom, or the open classroom. During the 1960's and early 1970's, some schools experimented with the open classroom. However, the open classroom concept never really emerged on a wide scale and most American classrooms continue to be organized along traditional lines. The philosophy expressed for the open classroom is generally agreed upon by schools, as stated in school philosophies in terms of pupil outcomes. However, the practices and means for achieving the goals are seldom realized in practice in traditionally organized schools.

The integrated whole language classroom philosophy is the belief that all children are predisposed to learn and want to learn. All children are able to learn language as easily and naturally as they are able to breathe. Children are naturally curious and need to explore their environment and to organize experiences. It is further believed that children are motivated to learn what they developmentally need to learn, are interested in learning and have a purpose in learning. Human beings are problem solvers, asking questions, testing hypotheses, collecting evidence, sorting information, analyzing information and drawing conclusions related to questions and hypotheses. There is a natural inclination to learn whatever there is to be learned that will fulfill and nourish the human condition.

The basic rationale for an integrated whole language classroom is the belief that all learning must be comprehension-centered. All learning must make sense to the learner. Not all learning will be achieved at once, but by presenting the learner with learning experiences that are predictable and related to prior experiences, learning will be comprehensible. In addition, and related to comprehension-centered learning, is the belief that all learning must be child-centered. Learning must focus on where the child is in terms of language and experiences and construct new learning according to the learner's development. Finally, the belief is that learning is language-based, related to thinking and experiences. The child learns language and uses language to learn. Language is used to represent and communicate thinking and experiences and to act upon ideas with others in a communication process.

500

Teachers need to develop an understanding and acceptance of the philosophy and rationale underlying the integrated whole language classroom and know the characteristics common to a language-centered classroom. The next section explains the differences between a traditional and integrated whole language classroom.

Characteristics of the Integrated Whole Language Classroom

There is no one blueprint or model for one monolithic integrated language-centered classroom. Neither is there one traditional classroom. The teacher variable and other factors influence how teaching and learning occur in any classroom. However, there are certain characteristics that contrast an integrated language-centered classroom with a traditional classroom. The integrated classroom tends to be organized and conducted in distinctly different ways according to the teacher's and school's acceptance and implementation of the philosophy and goals described previously in this chapter. The traditional classroom also has a philosophical orientation and implements learning in various procedures which are consistent with the rationale concerning teaching and learning.

Verna Southgate (1973) identified the contrasts between traditional and informal classrooms as follows:

Traditional Classroom

1. The emphasis is on teaching.
2. The classroom is curriculum-centered.
3. The classroom has separate subjects.
4. Knowledge and skills are learned in discrete and separate ways.
5. Time is divided into separate parts for each subject.
6. Learning experiences are limited to one classroom. Other areas in school are usually quite regulated and scheduled.
7. The teacher is the authority figure above the children. There is usually little interaction among children. The teachers seldom interact or plan with other teachers. The school and parents are separated and the school is apart from the community.

501

Informal Classroom

1. The emphasis is on learning.
2. The classroom is child-centered.
3. There is a removal of subject barriers. Know-ledge is regarded as a whole. One line of dis-covery can spring from or lead to another.
4. Time barriers are removed. Scheduling time is flexible.
5. Remove-barriers of walls. Children work in all areas of the school and beyond the school.
6. Barriers between the teacher, pupils and people in the community are decreased. There is more social interaction.

The integrated whole language and content classroom is organized to focus on the child as learner. There is flexibility organizing the time, space and materials. The teacher and learners interact within necessary agreed upon rights and responsibilities. Lan-guage learning, e.g., speaking, listening, reading, writing, and content are integrated. Language processes are learned within content and content is learned through language abilities. Language processes and con-tent are learned in meaningful situations with whole, connected language discourse so learners can made sense of both language learning and content.

The language and content curriculum begins with where the child is and expands upon the learner's pre-vious knowledge and functions of language and content. The integrated whole language and content classroom teacher monitors student's language used and the back-ground experiences, interest and attitudes the learner brings to learning experiences. There can be no one set of materials, use of space or organizational plan to fit each learner's developmental learning pattern, and rate of learning. The teacher in the integrated class-room accepts the uniqueness of each child's language and experiences and adapting language, content and cur-riculum to the child, groups of children and the whole class.

There are various practices and problems as teachers attempt to modify and change from a traditional classroom to an integrated language-centered classroom. These practices and problems are briefly described in the following section. A more detailed procedure for gradually moving from a traditional to an integrated classroom is described later in the chapter under the subheading, "Stages of Teacher Development Toward an Integrated Classroom."

Practices and Problems of the Integrated Whole Language Classroom

The decision on the part of any teacher to adapt, modify, and eventually change from a traditionally organized classroom to an integrated whole language-centered classroom must be a personal one. It should be a voluntary decision. No teacher should be forced to change. There must be in-service training and staff development programs for a lengthy period of time before, during and after the teacher changes his/her program. Also, the change must be gradual. The teacher, with the support of the principal and parents, needs to develop an understanding of the psycho-sociolinguistic nature of language learning theory and develop knowledge of evaluation techniques, use of whole language, materials and approaches and organizational procedures consistent with a child-centered, language-centered and comprehension-centered classroom curriculum. The knowledge of children, understanding the language learning process, selection of materials and learning approaches and implementation using various organizational grouping patterns will take time. The teacher will need constant encouragement, support and patience from others as she/he is involved in learning and implementing an integrated language-centered classroom.

Some teachers naturally are more receptive to change or modify their classroom practices than other teachers. This may be a result of the individual differences among teachers, including: personality and style of teaching, philosophy about teaching reading and other factors. Experienced teachers generally are more receptive to change than inexperienced or beginning teachers. They seem to know intuitively and through experience in teaching language that children become effective language users when they provide language experiences that make sense. They have observed children struggle to read when instruction is preoccupied with isolated drill and practice on letters, sounds, words and sentences, apart from meaningful print material. The inexperienced teacher, though exposed to psycholinguistic theory and practice in language learning, is still generally influenced by the way they were taught and traditional reading practices and procedures.

There are a variety of practices and suggestions offered to teachers and administrators interested
in moving from a traditional classroom to an integrated
language-centered classroom. Many practical suggestions
come from teachers and other educators who have some
experience in making the transition.

Bretz (1973) recommended the following suggestion for teachers considering the transition from a formal to an open classroom. Teachers might choose to
change slowly to establish a feeling of security for all
involved. She suggested the teacher should select areas
of greatest strength, e.g., math, language arts, etc.
Language arts is an appropriate area to informalize because it incorporates fundamental skills necessary to
succeed in all other areas. She recommends using a
block of time each day and develop and plan a focal
point of study from a list of language arts activities.
The teacher would teach all other subjects the rest of
the day in a conventional way. Ninety minutes is suggested each day for a language arts block. The teacher
organizes each area of language arts, e.g., reading,
spelling, handwriting, writing, language skills and research work, and list materials and activities to use.
Bretz identified procedures to use for each language
art area and materials and activities to individualize
instruction for the children. Finally, the open concept
is expanded to other subjects to become an integrated
day.

Morgan (1973) emphasized organizing learning
centers to provide open and integrated learning experiences for children. She describes how the teacher can
organize writing, social studies, science, math, art
centers in the classroom. She describes a hypothetical
example of an integrated day in which the children and
teacher are involved in planning and participating in
the classroom. The teacher guides the children to establish rules of behavior, materials, and traffic pattern in the room. The teacher provides directions and
guidelines for each learning center in the room. Morgan
described a typical day's activities beginning with a
morning planning meeting, children's use of learning
centers and proceeding to children choosing activities
to do in centers and the teacher monitoring children's
activities and meeting with small groups to teach skills
and reading with another group. Through the planned
learning center activities children are involved in
speaking, reading, listening and writing experiences.
She stresses that children are guided in how to learn
and that the process takes time to develop on the part

504

of the teacher. Finally, she identified how the role of the teacher changes in the open or informal classroom, including that of organizer, manager, diagnostician, guide, facilitator, poser of questions, resource person and much more.

The actual practice of implementing an integrated language-centered classroom involves a very gradual transition from traditional organizational procedures. There are three areas of concern:

(1) grouping of children
(2) training children in use of materials and learning experiences
(3) establishing discipline and control.

At the beginning the teacher must think through these three areas very carefully. The teacher may want to begin with only part of the children during a language arts block of time rather than the whole class at one time. Another alternative is to begin with only a short period of time during the language arts block with all the children.

Using the former plan for organizing, part of the children during the whole language arts time in the morning may include adding a learning center, e.g., listening or writing center. Some teachers recommend beginning with the more effective readers in the class while keeping other groups intact. Then gradually as the effective readers gain independence, involve another group of children, and finally, the remainder of the children are participating in the whole language program. The teacher will need to try out various whole language learning experiences with the effective readers, such as, sustained silent reading/self-selection (SSR/SSR), whole language learning center activities, including writing, listening and speaking (drama) experiences, schema stories, self-directed DRTA and projects, e.g., written reports. The teacher needs to train the children to develop responsibility for selecting activities and materials from learning centers and completing tasks. Also, the children need to learn responsibility and self-discipline as they learn more independently. However, the teacher will meet regularly with the group to plan and monitor progress, and teach specific strategy lessons as necessary from information collected from samples of each child's oral and silent reading (self-selected miscues). At this early stage in the teacher's and group's transition, the teacher still teaches traditional reading groups, utilizing conventional grouping

505

practices, e.g., achievement groups ("average" and "slow" groups) and uses conventional materials, e.g., basal readers, workbooks, and so forth. Gradually, the rest of the children are assimilated by small groups into the whole language program.

The second plan, using all the children for a shorter time during the language arts block, or only the conventional reading period, may be an effective transition for other teachers. The teacher gradually moves away from the traditional three or four achievement groups with basal readers to other whole language experiences. The grouping is flexible, including some achievement level groups for DRTA, reading strategy grouping based on individual miscue analysis of children as they meet with the teacher for conferences. Time is scheduled for SSR/SSR, at the same time each day. Learning centers are added to the existing reading center in the room. The teacher develops whole language activities for the centers involving all language processes to relate reading to writing, speaking, and listening. Other whole language approaches such as assisted reading, reading aloud, the language experience approach and ReQuest are scheduled with selected individuals or groups of children. This plan of transition would be more difficult possibly than beginning with only part of the children.

In the next section, Stages of Teacher Development Toward an Integrated Classroom, a more complete description of stages will be given, concerning complex interrelated components the teacher must cope with during the process of change.

There are problems and concerns which teachers need to be aware of and deal with before and during the transition from a traditionally organized classroom to an integrated language and content classroom. Vera Southgate (1973) identified several problems teachers may experience. At first teachers may feel uneasy about not doing much direct teaching. The emphasis on learning and providing a stimulating environment may not result in children wanting to learn to read. There will be children who are not always motivated to read even though materials and experiences are meaningful. Teachers may feel apprehensive that he/she cannot help the children at the time they need help when he/she is monitoring or teaching other children. The teacher may not feel she/he has an adequate knowledge of each child and the language learning process despite inservice programs to build this background experience.

The teacher has to develop organizational skills to plan and monitor each child's learning. Record-keeping becomes a problem.

There may be a conflict between developing reading strategies, creativity and learning content. Reading and writing strategies must be given priority as well as creative activities and learning in content areas. It is difficult for teachers to balance creativity and content learning. Teachers may feel distressed about the lack of isolated skills, instruction. The resolution of this conflict is that skills are learned within a meaningful context in which the child has an interest. Traditionally sequenced reading and writing skills are developed as children perceive the need to read and write for real purposes. The separate skills if they need to be taught are presented within the purposes for reading and writing, not apart from the purposes.

Next, is a consideration of the teacher's and pupil's role and responsibilities in an integrated whole language classroom.

Teacher and Pupil Role in the Integrated Whole Language Classroom

The teacher and pupils need to develop different behaviors in an integrated language classroom. The responsibilities of the teacher are similar to the traditional classroom, yet the means and behaviors to accomplishing the responsibilities are different. The teacher in the integrated classroom needs to know about children, e.g., monitor their experiences, development and progress in learning, plan and select appropriate learning experiences and materials, and provide an environment consistent with the goals, philosophy and characteristics of a whole language classroom. The students need to behave in different ways in the integrated whole language classroom. They need to develop responsibility for their own learning and selection of learning experiences in addition to activities planned and made available by the teacher. With teacher guidance the students need to increase in ability to develop self-purpose for learning.

The teacher naturally plays a crucial role in organizing and maintaining the learning environment and learning atmosphere. All learning experiences involving materials and children are focused on comprehension and making sense through communication processes. The teacher must plan, organize and implement learning experiences and materials for large group, small group, and individual situations. The materials, learning activities and groups are planned and arranged so the teacher observes children in meaningful communication and content settings.

The learning environment and room atmosphere involves the children's own language in print (language experiences) or on tape (oral reading for miscue analysis). Language is used which is familiar to children (predictable language books, poetry, jump rope rhymes, songs). Spoken and written language appropriate to the age level is functional language related to interests and experiences (recipes, directions to construct things, rules to follow in learning centers, etc.). There is a wide variety and number of printed materials (books, brochures, magazines, newspapers, signs, cookbooks, catalogues, etc.). There is a variety of media other than print (tapes, records, filmstrips, pictures, etc.). The teacher arranges the classroom so it is comfortable and pleasant for children to select and enjoy print materials (sustained silent reading). The language environment is changed by the teacher and children to maintain currency, interest and variety. Displays of children's written work are seen and current to topics of interest and study. There is time available for children to talk, for student-teacher talk, and student reading and writing. Space is available for various groups, e.g., whole class, small group and individual work.

The teacher interacts with children to facilitate learning, to observe children as they read, write, speak and listen, and to plan and provide feedback when necessary. The teacher listens attentively to children and talks with children. All learning experiences are whole language in which communication is meaningful. The teacher does not intervene when children are reading, writing, or listening. The teacher encourages independence in learning and self-correction. The teacher acts as a model for children to read, write, listen and speak. The children have many opportunities to see the teacher reading and writing for his or her purposes when they are involved in reading and writing.

The child's role in the whole language classroom includes responsibility for his/her own learning and respect for others. The child has increasing opportunities for independent learning and selection of learning experiences. The child will be expected to increase responsibility for his/her own planning, doing and

508

evaluating learning. The child should increasingly select his/her own reading and writing materials, self-correct while reading and writing, evaluates his/her own performances and selects from a variety of learning experiences.

Since most school experiences for children beyond first grade are traditional, teachers in higher grades will need to provide a gradual phasing-in period to implement an integrated whole language classroom. Since teaching experiences have been influenced by traditional methods, teachers will need time to adjust and modify their philosophy, the classroom environment, and methods and materials in the integrated language classroom.

The next section will explore stages by which teachers can make the transition from a traditional to an integrated, whole language and content classroom.

Stages of Teacher Development Toward an Integrated Whole Language Classroom

The goal of language learning in school is to enable children to communicate meaning (speaking and writing) and to interpret and comprehend messages (listening and reading). Meaning conveyed and received is communicated to relate on an interpersonal basis and to inform and receive information in textual situations (Halliday, 1973).

In many classrooms oral and written language functions frequently as ends rather than means to communicate meaning. Reading and writing skills are practiced in isolation, unrelated to any real communicative function. Separate periods of time are scheduled apart from real purposes to inform, become informed, or to interact using language to communicate meaning. Sub-skills of reading and writing are arranged in a hierarchial sequence and presented separated from use. Language learning should be perceived as the means to the end, the end being comprehension of the world, understand self and relating to others through the use of language. (See Figure 7:3, page 510.)

Furthermore, current classroom organization and management practices reflect language learning as an end rather than a means to communicate meaning and content. First, there is limited classroom personnel. Generally, one teacher is assigned with 25-30 children

509

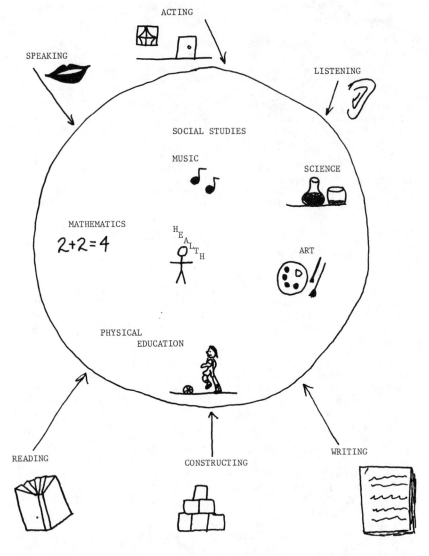

AN INTEGRATED WHOLE LANGUAGE CURRICULUM

FIGURE 7:3

510

who have different backgrounds, abilities, interests and needs. Second, classroom space is used inflexibly. Third, language learning is compartmentalized into rigid periods apart from use. Fourth, evaluation and instructional techniques fractionate language learning into bits and pieces. Finally, the grouping of children is usually fixed and based on different abilities.

During the decades of the 60's and early 70's considerable experimentation in language learning, classroom organization and instructional approaches was evident. Psycholinguists, such as Goodman and Smith, developed theories and models of the reading process. Open classrooms, team teaching and differentiated staffing and systems management were tried as organizational procedures. I.T.A. "linguistic readers," programmed reading and "new basal reading systems" were developed and implemented in classroom reading programs. Despite organizational and various reading programs innovations, there was little significant improvement in the reading of many children. Basically, the innovations were implemented on an inaccurate understanding of the reading process. Generally, reading and writing were taught as isolated subjects apart from content and as fragmented isolated skills.

Several promising organizational innovations of the 1960's included the open classroom concept, differentiated staffing, and flexible use of personnel, time, space, and to some degree, instructional approaches. However, there was little progress made in applying open classroom concepts in many classrooms. In fact, the past several years has witnessed a "back to basics" syndrome. A rigid, isolated and skills-oriented language curriculum is evident in most classrooms today. However, since the 60's and early 70's socio-psycholinguistic research, conducted by Goodman (1976), Smith (1978), and Halliday (1975) has provided new insight into language learning, particularly reading. There is now a sound understanding about the reading process upon which to build and develop a meaningful whole language-content curriculum. Teachers have available greater knowledge concerning how and why language is learned and what methods and materials are effective in developing language processes.

The time is appropriate for applying socio-psycholinguistic principles to language learning in classrooms. Teachers, knowledgeable about socio-psycholinguistic principles of language learning, can develop teaching behaviors to progress in stages from a

traditional, isolated, skills-centered language program
to an integrated whole language curriculum. Teachers
need to develop competency in several interrelated
organizational behaviors over a period of time. These
organizational factors include: (1) Use of time; (2)
Use of space; (3) Use of personnel; (4) Evaluation;
(5) Instructional approaches; (6) Grouping procedures;
(7) Scheduling time and instructional approaches.

Four stages are identified and described to
help teachers develop their teaching from an isolated,
fragmented, skills-oriented language classroom to an
integrated, whole language classroom. The stages are:
(1) Traditional; (2) Modified Traditional; (3) Transitional Integrated; and (4) Integrated. (See Figure 7:4,
page 513.)

Teachers need to change gradually from a
basically traditional to an integrated whole language
curriculum. It will more than likely take several years
for most teachers to successfully implement an integrated whole language curriculum in the classroom. However, some teachers have already made significant progress toward an integrated language curriculum.

Each of the four stages is described below and
characteristics of several interrelated organizational
components are given. These characteristics are generalizations and teachers will need to adapt the generalizations to unique classroom situations and grade levels.

The Traditional Stage

Personnel: The typical classroom in the elementary school generally has one teacher assigned to
25-30 children. The teacher is responsible for teaching reading and other language arts and content areas,
e.g., social studies, science and mathematics. She/he
may also teach art, music and physical education. The
teacher's role is to meet children's needs, teach and
manage all the components of the classroom.

Space: Classroom space is usually used inflexibly with children seated in rows, clusters of
desks, a U-shape, or some other variation. The teacher
generally has a fixed place for his/her desk. Shelves
of books usually line one or more walls. There may be

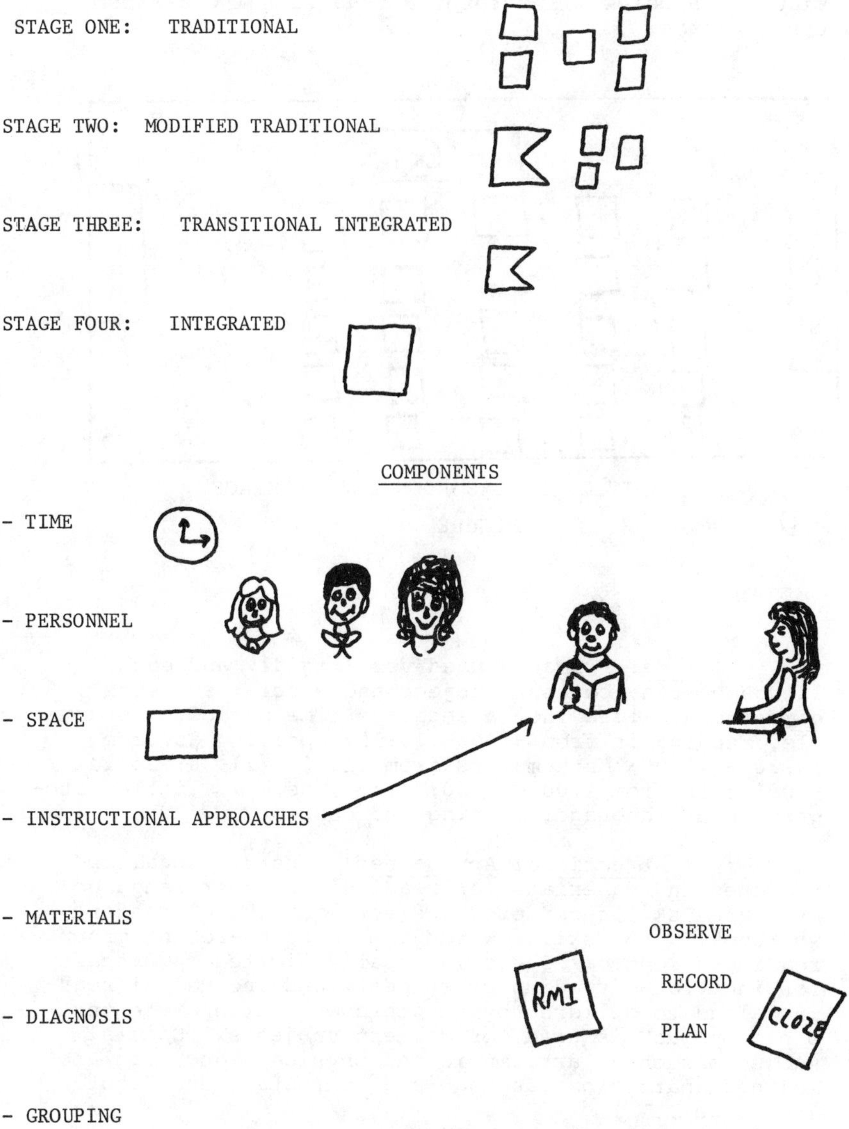

STAGE ONE: TRADITIONAL

STAGE TWO: MODIFIED TRADITIONAL

STAGE THREE: TRANSITIONAL INTEGRATED

STAGE FOUR: INTEGRATED

COMPONENTS

- TIME

- PERSONNEL

- SPACE

- INSTRUCTIONAL APPROACHES

- MATERIALS

- DIAGNOSIS

- GROUPING

OBSERVE

RECORD

PLAN

RMI

CLOZE

STAGES OF CLASSROOM DEVELOPMENT
AND COMPONENTS OF ORGANIZATION

FIGURE 7:4
513

a reading center and/or possibly a listening center.
Figure 7:5 below illustrates a traditional classroom
use of space:

TRADITIONAL CLASSROOM USE OF SPACE

Ⓧ Teacher   FIGURE 7:5

Time: Time is used very rigidly and each
language arts, content subject and special subjects is
compartmentalized into a separate time period. For example, reading is from 9:00 - 10:15; Spelling is from
10:30 - 11:00; Mathematics from 11:00 - 11:30; Social
Studies is from 1:00 - 1:30; etc. There is little integration of language learning and content.

Instructional Approaches: Instructional approaches and materials for reading and other language
arts are "skills-centered and textbook (basal reader),
workbook, ditto skill, word games, "round-robin" group
reading-oriented. There is usually limited opportunity
for individual reading by students and incidental reading aloud to children by the teacher. A separate textbook approach is used for content subjects. Special
subjects such as art, music and physical education are
learned apart from language and content. (See Figure
7:6, page 515 .)

STAGE ONE:

TRADITIONAL

BASAL READER

WORKBOOKS

DITTO SKILLS SHEETS

LETTER/SOUND-WORD

GAMES

SOME BOOK READING (INCIDENTAL)

SOME READING ALOUD (INCIDENTAL)

TEXT CENTERED SOCIAL STUDIES,
    MATH, SCIENCE

STAGE TWO:

MODIFIED TRADITIONAL

BASAL READER

WORKBOOKS

DITTO SKILLS

LANGUAGE CENTERS

MORE BOOK READING*

MORE WRITING*

LANGUAGE EXPERIENCE*

SEPARATE TEXT-CENTERED SOCIAL STUDIES,
    SCIENCE, MATH, ART, MUSIC

INSTRUCTIONAL APPROACHES AND MATERIALS

FIGURE 7:6

515

Evaluation: The basic evaluative procedure includes: standardized reading tests used as pre-post tests from year to year; basal reader tests; isolated skill checklists; word tests; workbook; wordsheet pages and incidental teacher observation with minimum record keeping. Reading performance is assessed by breaking up language into small units.

Grouping: Grouping is predominantely two or three ability and/or achievement levels for oral reading groups, including independent seatwork usually on isolated bits of language, e.g., letter, sounds, words, sentences and paragraphs. There may be some individual reading from library books when other work is completed. The teacher may read to the whole class on a regular and/ or incidental basis. Spelling is taught at a separate time usually to the whole class. Written composition is scheduled, if at all, on a limited basis and generally with the whole class. There is a reading center in the classroom where children may select books to read. Children are found in fixed patterns of grouping with only one basic grouping procedure used, achievement level groups in reading, which includes the fast, middle, and slow group. See Figure 7:7.

Scheduling Time and Instructional Approaches: The daily schedule in a traditional classroom may look like this, as shown below:

TIME	GROUP A	GROUP B	GROUP C
9:00-9:25	⊗ Directed Reading	Seatwork	Individual Reading
9:25-9:50	Seatwork	Individual Reading	Directed Reading ⊗
9:50-10:15	Individual Reading	Directed Reading ⊗	Seatwork
10:30-11:00	←———————— Spelling ————————→		
11:00-11:30	←———————— Mathematics ————————→		
12:30-2:30	Social Studies and Science Separate periods Art, Music, Physical Education Separate periods		

TIME SCHEDULE AND INSTRUCTIONAL APPROACHES
FOR TRADITIONAL STAGE

⊗ Teacher   FIGURE 7:7

The overall use of time in all four stages of
teacher development from a traditional to an integrated
whole language classroom is given below in Figure 7:8.

STAGE ONE: STAGE TWO:

TRADITIONAL   MODIFIED TRANSITIONAL

9:00-10:15   READING   9:00-11:00   READING, WRITING,
10:15-10:30   RECESS   SPELLING BLOCK
10:30-11:00   SPELLING   11:00-11:45   MATH
11:00-11:45   MATH   1:00-1:30   SOCIAL STUDIES
1:00-1:30   SOCIAL STUDIES   1:30-2:00   ART/MUSIC/P.E.
1:30-2:00   ART/MUSIC/P.E.   2:00-2:30   SCIENCE
2:00-2:30   SCIENCE   2:30-3:00   FINISH UP
2:30-3:00   FINISH UP

STAGE THREE: STAGE FOUR:

TRANSITIONAL INTEGRATED   INTEGRATED

9:00-11:45   LANGUAGE BLOCK   9:00-3:00   ALL CONTENT
                (READING, WRITING,   (SOCIAL STUDIES,
                SPELLING, LISTENING,   MATH, SCINECE, ART,
                ART, MUSIC)   MUSIC, P.E.)
1:00-3:00   CONTENT BLOCK   WITH LANGUAGE
                (SOCIAL STUDIES,   (READ, WRITE, LISTEN,
                MATH, SCIENCE)   SPEAK)
                ART/MUSIC/P.E.   THEMATIC APPROACH

USE OF TIME

FIGURE 7:8

517

Modified Traditional Stage

Personnel: There is one teacher and one paraprofessional or teacher aide at this stage. The aide
may be a paid paraprofessional, volunteer parents or a
student teacher. The ratio of adults to pupils is reduced by half from 1:25 to approximately 1:13 compared
to the Traditional Stage. The teacher would, of course,
be responsible for scheduling duties for the aide. Additional personnel permits more individual evaluation
and individual and small group interaction.

Time: A language arts block of time is scheduled for the morning, coordinating reading, writing, and
spelling, to some degree, from 9:00 a.m. to 11:00 a.m.
Mathematics, content areas and special subjects are
scheduled at separate times in the afternoon. (See
Figure 7:7.)

Space: The classroom space is beginning to
open up. Space is used more flexibly. Pupil's desks
are clustered for more interaction and a writing center
and/or listening center is added. The classroom arrangement may resemble this:

MODIFIED TRADITIONAL USE OF SPACE
TEACHER, PARAPROFESSIONAL, AIDE OR STUDENT TEACHER

FIGURE 7:9

Instructional Approaches: Basal readers, workbooks, ditto skill workpages and isolated letter-word
games are still emphasized. However, these activities
are supplemented with more comprehension-centered approaches, including language experience stories, teacher
reading aloud to pupils and independent language activities in reading, writing and/or listening centers.
There is more self-selected, individual reading and
creative writing evident. There are separate textbooks
and periods for content and special subjects. (See
Figure 7:6.)

Evaluative Techniques: Standardized reading
tests, basal reader tests, workbook worksheets, and the
like, continue to be used to assess pupil needs and progress. Most techniques emphasize isolated language
units to test reading performance. However, modified
forms of miscue analysis and systematic teacher observation of pupils in connected language discourse is
possible to supplement traditional skills-centered
tests. (See Figure 7:10.).

STAGE ONE :   STAGE TWO :

TRADITIONAL   MODIFIED TRADITIONAL

BASAL READER TESTS   BASAL READER TESTS

STANDARDIZED TESTS   STANDARDIZED TESTS

ISOLATED SKILLS CHECKLISTS   WORKBOOK WORKSHEET

ISOLATED WORD LISTS   ➡   MODIFIED RMI *

WORKBOOK / WORKSHEET   MORE PLANNED TEACHER OBSERVATION *

INCIDENTAL TEACHER   MORE SAMPLES OF READING AND WRITING *

OBSERVATION

TEACHER-MADE TESTS

EVALUATION TECHNIQUES

FIGURE 7:10

519

Grouping: Fixed achievement groups for reading
and independent, isolated skills seatwork is emphasized
less. The addition of learning centers with more whole
language learning experiences, such as, self-selected
reading, creative writing, language experience stories
will, in part, replace or supplement reading achievement
groups. A teacher and an aide are able to use miscue
analysis with pupils and organize reading strategy
lessons related to identified strengths and needs in
whole language context. Children with similar needs
are grouped on the basis of miscue assessment. Spelling
is integrated with writing, although still taught separately. Pupils have more opportunities for creative
and practical writing as an outgrowth of real reading
approaches and with the addition of a writing center.

Scheduling Time: Although the language arts
are scheduled for a block of time in the morning, there
is still specific time periods for groups of pupils as
in the Traditional Stage. However, within the time
periods for group reading more time is provided for
whole language activities such as reading strategy
lessons based on miscue analysis. Also, instead of an
emphasis on isolated skills, workbooks, and ditto worksheets, time is scheduled for learning experiences in
the reading, writing and/or listening center. Content
and special subjects are still scheduled at a separate
time in the afternoon. (See Figure 7:11, page 521.)

The Transitional Integrated Stage

Personnel: Additional personnel is particularly helpful at this stage so that pupils have the
benefit of adult assistance in very small groups and
on an individual basis. This is especially true at
the beginning and primary years of learning to read and
write. During this stage there is a teacher, a paid
paraprofessional or volunteer aide and a student teacher.
In a typical classroom of 25 to 30 children this would
provide an adult to pupil ration of approximately 1:8,
one teacher to every eight children.

Time: The morning is scheduled as a coordinated language arts block of time including the integration of art and music. The afternoon is scheduled as a
content block, including social studies, science, and
mathematics. Art, music and physical education are still
scheduled for separate periods with special teachers.
(See Figure 7:15.)

The following figure is illustrative of
scheduling time and activities during this stage:

TIME	GROUP A	GROUP B	GROUP C
9:00–9:40	Directed Reading Reading Strategy Lesson ⊗	Reading Center Individual Reading Assisted Reading	Writing Center Language Experi- ence Spelling ●
9:40–10:20	Writing Center Language Experi- ence Spelling ●	Directed Reading Reading Strategy Lesson ⊗	Reading Center Individual Read- ing Assisted Reading
10:20–11:00	Reading Center Individual Reading Assisted Reading	Writing Center Language Experi- ence Spelling ●	Directed Reading Reading Strategy Lesson ⊗
	FORMAL SPELLING		
11:00–11:30		MATHEMATICS	
12:30–2:30	Separate Periods for Social Studies, Science, Art, Music, Physical Education		

⊗ Teacher   ● Aide

TIME SCHEDULE AND INSTRUCTIONAL APPROACHES
FOR MODIFIED TRADITIONAL STAGE

FIGURE 7:11

521

Space: In the morning communication block,
classroom space is used flexibly. The pupils are
arranged in clusters at work tables or desks in small
groups. The work tables or clusters of desks are useful for projects in art related to reading-writing
activities, book reading, etc. At least three learning
centers are in operation, reading, listening and writing,
for individual and small group whole language approaches,
such as, reading aloud by the teacher (or aide, student
teacher), assisted reading, language experience stories,
etc. The classroom space may be organized as shown below in Figure 7:12.

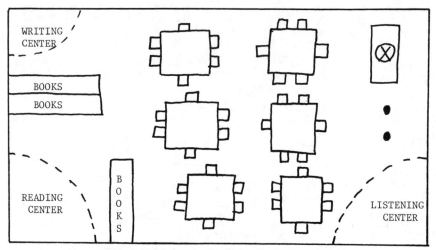

TRANSITIONAL INTEGRATED USE OF SPACE

⊗ Teacher   ● Paraprofessional   ● Student Teacher

FIGURE 7:12

Instructional Approaches: At this stage basal
readers, workbooks and ditto worksheets are greatly
minimized. The teacher and/or aides will use a basal
reader for Directed-Reading-Thinking-Activities (DRTA).
Three learning centers, reading, writing and listening,
provide opportunities for pupils to learn using whole
language approaches, including: teacher (aide) reading
aloud in small groups and/or on a one-to-one basis as
necessary; assisted reading (book-tape, echoic, impress);

language experience stories (dictated); self-selected
reading with sustained silent reading, reading strategy
lessons (based on miscue analysis) and creative writing.
Content areas will be coordinated in the afternoon using
multi-level print and multi-media materials. (See
Figure 7:13 below.)

STAGE THREE: STAGE FOUR:

TRANSITIONAL INTEGRATED   INTEGRATED

LESS BASAL READER, WORKBOOK ETC.   FOCUS ON WHOLE LANGUAGE

ADD MORE LANGUAGE CENTERS   CONCEPT DEVELOPMENT

MORE COMPREHENSION - CENTERED   SMALL GROUP DISCUSSION

    APPROACHES: DICTATION

        READING ALOUD   SHARING

        ASSISTED READING   DRAMA, PUPPETS

        WRITING   ORAL REPORTING

CONTENT INTEGRATED   READ ALOUD   (TEACH)

ART, MUSIC, P.E. RELATED   BOOK READING

RE QUEST   WRITING

                                          ASSISTED READING

                                          RE QUEST

                                          SCHEMA STORIES

                                          WRITTEN CONVERSATION

                                          WHOLE LANGUAGE CONTENT

                                          DRTA

                                          LANGUAGE EXPERIENCE

INSTRUCTIONAL MATERIALS AND APPROACHES

FIGURE 7:13

Evaluative Procedures: Evaluation techniques
are more individualized and whole language-centered with
an increase in personnel which includes teacher, paraprofessional and student teacher. Although basal readers and workbooks are still used minimally at this stage,
whole language approaches identified above are more
apparent. Evaluation involves teacher observation with
systematic record keeping of language performance in
real connected reading, writing, speaking and listening
experiences. The teacher and other aides may give complete and modified miscue analysis to identify strengths
and needs. Reading strategy lessons are planned for
groups or for an individual child based on common needs.
The cloze test, another whole language test, is available to assess reading levels and reading strategy needs.
(See Figure 7:14.)

STAGE THREE: STAGE FOUR:

TRADITIONAL INTEGRATED   INTEGRATED

LESS BASAL READER TESTS   TEACHER PLANNED OBSERVATION
                                               IN REAL READING, WRITING,
TEACHER OBSERVATION IN   LISTENING, TALKING SITUATIONS
   REAL READING AND WRITING   RELATED TO CONTENT

SITUATIONS - INDIVIDUAL AND   RMI
   GROUP

RMI - COMPLETE / MODIFIED   IMI

CLOZE TESTS   CLOZE

INTERESTS INVENTORIES   INTEREST INVENTORY

                                            CONTINUOUS RECORD KEEPING

                                            PUPIL SAMPLES

                                            GROUP TEXTBOOK SURVEY - CONTENT

EVALUATION TECHNIQUES IN TRADITIONAL INTEGRATED
AND INTEGRATED STAGES

FIGURE 7:14
524

Grouping: The flexible use of space, time, personnel and instructional approaches enables the teacher to plan and organize small group and individual learning experiences. Reading, writing, and listening centers are available for self-selected and sustained reading, creative and practical writing, language experience (dictated stories and assisted reading along with book and tape.) Groups are organized for DRTA and reading strategy lessons. Spelling becomes more individualized as writing opportunities increase. Social studies, science and math are organized as a content unit study in the afternoon. There is some integration of the morning communication block with content. The teacher, paraprofessional or aide and student teacher are available to work closely and flexibly with an individual child and small groups as needed.

Scheduling Time and Instructional Approaches: The morning language block is almost totally integrated with no separate periods for reading, writing and spelling. Each language process is closely related and reinforcing to the others. Various whole language approaches are planned related to assessed needs and age level of the children. An example of the daily morning schedule is given below:

TIME	Read Aloud	Self-Selected Reading SSR	Wrt. Center, Lang. Exp., Spelling	Lst. Center, Asstd. Reading
9:00-11:30	Writing Cnt. Language Exp. Spelling	Reading Strategy Lesson	SSR	Read Aloud
9:00-11:30	Listening Cnt. Asstd. Reading	Wrt. Center Lan. Exp. Spelling	Rd. Strategy Lesson	SSR
9:00-11:30	Rd. Strategy Lesson	DRTA	List. Cnt. Asstd. Rdng.	Writing Cnt. Lan. Exp./Sp.
1:00-3:00	Unit Study - Social Studies - Science - Math - Art - Music - Physical Education			

Teacher Paraprofessional/Student Teacher

TIME SCHEDULE AND INSTRUCTIONAL APPROACHES
FOR TRANSITIONAL INTEGRATED STAGE

FIGURE 7:15

The Integrated Stage

Personnel: At the integrated stage it is useful to have at least four adults, a teacher, paraprofessional (paid aide), volunteer aides and a student
teacher. In addition, older pupils from higher grades
may be available to help younger children. The ratio of
adults to children is 1:6. This creates many possibilities for direct assistance when needed to children individually and in small groups. This is particularly
advantageous at beginning and primary grades as children
are developing written language abilities. Children who
need more attention and feedback will have it available.
More whole language approaches such as, reading aloud by
the teacher (aide or student teacher), language experience dictated stories, and the like, are possible with
more adults able to provide direct assistance.

Time: There are no separate periods during the
day for language arts and content learning. A thematic
unit approach is used in which reading, writing, speaking and listening are learned and function as means
rather than isolated skills to be learned in and of
themselves. Language functions for pupils do develop
ideas about the world, their environment and to interact with others in real communication situations related to planned general and specific themes. Themes
for content learning are identified which are appropriate for developmental cognitive levels. There is no
distinct demarcation during a typical day for specific
language skill learning. Reading and writing are
learned as they function naturally within any content.
The thematic unit approach will be described in a later
section in the chapter. (See Figure 7:16, page 527.)

Space: Classroom space is used flexibly with
various learning centers to develop language abilities
through a thematic unit approach. Certain classroom
areas are organized for social studies, science and math
centers. There are different variations possible for
arranging a classroom to integrate language abilities
within content experiences. An example of the use of
classroom space to facilitate language learning similar
to how children learn oral language is given below.
M.A.K. Halliday (1973), has identified several functions
of language which the child learns and applies to the
use of language. They include: instrumental (I want);
regulatory (Do this); interactional (Me and you); personal (Here I come); Heuristic (Tell my why); imaginative (Let's pretend); and informative (I've got something to tell you). According to Halliday, these

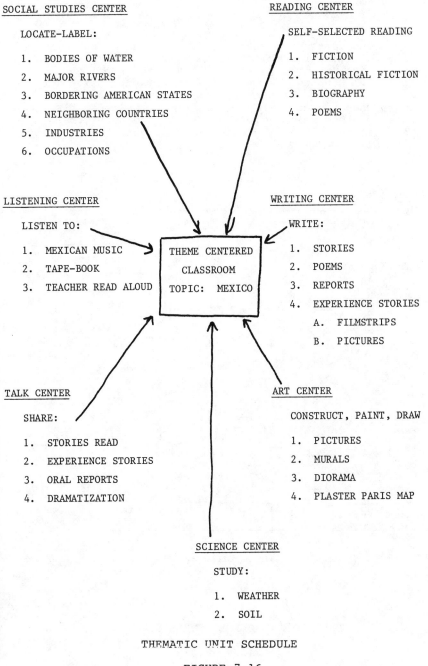

SOCIAL STUDIES CENTER

LOCATE-LABEL:

1. BODIES OF WATER
2. MAJOR RIVERS
3. BORDERING AMERICAN STATES
4. NEIGHBORING COUNTRIES
5. INDUSTRIES
6. OCCUPATIONS

READING CENTER

SELF-SELECTED READING

1. FICTION
2. HISTORICAL FICTION
3. BIOGRAPHY
4. POEMS

LISTENING CENTER

LISTEN TO:

1. MEXICAN MUSIC
2. TAPE-BOOK
3. TEACHER READ ALOUD

THEME CENTERED
CLASSROOM
TOPIC: MEXICO

WRITING CENTER

WRITE:

1. STORIES
2. POEMS
3. REPORTS
4. EXPERIENCE STORIES
   A. FILMSTRIPS
   B. PICTURES

TALK CENTER

SHARE:

1. STORIES READ
2. EXPERIENCE STORIES
3. ORAL REPORTS
4. DRAMATIZATION

ART CENTER

CONSTRUCT, PAINT, DRAW

1. PICTURES
2. MURALS
3. DIORAMA
4. PLASTER PARIS MAP

SCIENCE CENTER

STUDY:

1. WEATHER
2. SOIL

THEMATIC UNIT SCHEDULE

FIGURE 7:16

527

functions merge into macrofunctions as children develop a lexicogrammar, or syntactic structure. The
macrofunctions are: Ideational, interpersonal and
textual. Language is used to express and receive ideas
with others in a situational context. Instructional
approaches and use of space are organized to enable
children to develop written language processes, reading
and writing, similarly to how oral language was learned
naturally. (See Figure 7:17.)

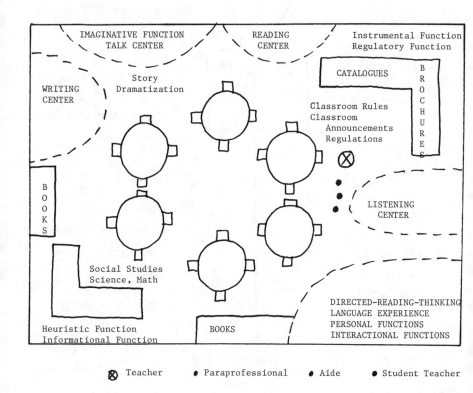

INTEGRATED WHOLE LANGUAGE CLASSROOM

FIGURE 7:17

Instructional Approaches: General themes are identified for specific grade levels. The school year is organized around themes in social studies, science, and mathematics. Art, music and physical education are integrated within thematic units. Language learning, reading, writing, speaking and listening, develops within the context of content. Instructional materials such as books, newspapers, magazines, filmstrips, tapes, records, exhibits, and the like are available related to themes. Concept development is a major concern. Instructional approaches focus on whole language materials. Instructional approaches to develop language abilities function as means to the end, e.g., learning about the world, self and others include: teacher, reading aloud, assisted reading, language experiences, self-selected reading with sustained silent reading, Directed-Reading-Thinking-Activity, Reading Strategy Lessons (related to miscue analysis) and functional reading activities. (See Figure 7:13.)

Evaluative Techniques: Evaluation of language abilities and content learning involves observation in real, meaningful settings as children interact with whole language. Reading development is assessed using miscue analysis for planning and organizing reading strategy lessons, cloze tests, interest inventories, anecdotal records and pupil samples of reading, writing, speaking and listening. Several teaching personnel available at one time in the classroom permits continuous individual evaluation. (See Figure 7:14.)

Grouping: Learning experiences are organized using language centers and content area centers with whole language activities related to life-centered thematic units. Grouping is on an individual and small group basis, flexible and temporary, with a minimum of fixed, achievement level groups. The classroom curriculum may be organized for functional purposes for which language is learned, namely, to satisfy wants, to interact with others, to discover, to imagine and create and to inform. (See Figure 7:18, page 530.)

Scheduling Time: The integrated whole language classroom has no specific time barriers or artificial periods to separate language and content. The whole day is related and integrated. For example, a specific thematic unit, the study of Mexico, is scheduled for two or three weeks. The differentiated staff (ie.e., teacher aide, volunteer aide and student teacher) plan and organize the classroom language and content centers around the central theme. The reading center includes

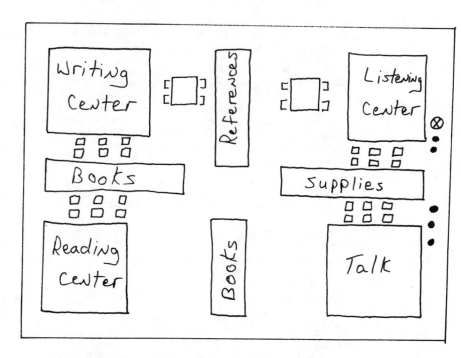

USE OF SPACE IN INTEGRATED CLASSROOM

FIGURE 7:18

fiction, historical fiction, biography and poetry for
self-selection about Mexico. In the writing center,
activities are scheduled for pupils to write stories,
poems and reports about Mexican history and culture.
Filmstrips and pictures are available for viewing, discussing and writing language experience stories. At the
listening center, tapes, books, and records are available to listen to Mexican literature and music. In the
talk center, pupils share books read, experience stories
dictated or written, oral reports prepared in research

530

groups in the social studies center, and present
dramatizations. (See Figure 7:16.)

The social studies center includes map study
to read and write about Mexican history and culture, to
locate geographical facts, e.g., bodies of water, major
rivers, neighboring countries, and the like. Finally,
art and music is integrated in which pupils construct
crafts of Mexican culture, paint and draw pictures,
paint murals and construct dioramas, maps, etc.

The teacher and aides organize the time, use
of space, evaluate, plan instructional approaches and
materials, plan grouping patterns as they interact with
pupils individually, in small groups, and on a whole
class basis for sharing projects and findings. Planning, organizing and application is continuous on a
flexible basis.

Conclusion

Traditional and current classroom language
curriculum programs separate and fragment language
learning and meaning. Oral and written language learning become an end rather than means to the end which is
the production (speaking and writing) and reception
(listening and reading) or meaning.

Classroom management and organizational innovations popular in the 1960's and 1970's, fell short of
the mark, due in part to an inadequate understanding of
the reading-language learning process. So-called inno-
vative instructional programs, e.g., I.T.A., programmed
reading, "linguistic readers," were based on an un-
realistic knowledge of the reading process.

Psycholinguistic research into language learning has provided new insight about how language is
learned. Language is learned more easily when language
is perceived by learners as functional and related to
real needs and meaningful content.

The teacher needs to know how language is
learned and gradually develop an integrated whole language-content curriculum in the classroom. The teacher,
with additional personnel available needs to develop new
behaviors to manage and organize several complex, interrelated components which operate simultaneously in the
classroom. Four developmental stages have been identified including various components. Most teachers with

training can move away from a traditional skills-oriented language program to an integrated whole language curriculum in which children's language abilities are developed through a life-centered, comprehension-centered, whole language experience approach.

The four developmental stages identified are: Traditional, Modified Traditional, Transitional Integrated, and Integrated. During each stage the teachers behavior undergoes change regarding the planning and management of several interrelated components including: personnel, use of time and space, evaluative techniques, instructional approaches, grouping procedures and the interaction of scheduling time and instructional approaches.

Additional personnel, with differentiated staffing, is necessary to conduct individual evaluation using whole language techniques, e.g., miscue analysis and systematic observation with record keeping, and to provide natural, whole language learning experiences; time and space is gradually planned and used more flexibly, opening up the classroom with whole language learning centers and language arts learning is integrated within thematic units.

The integrated whole language curriculum is a life-centered, child-centered environment in which written language (reading and writing) is learned as naturally as oral language (speaking and listening) was learned. Communication abilities are learned as they are required to function normally in contestualized meaningful content. There is no sharp distinction or artificial distinction between skills and content.

Teaching will be challenging and exciting in new ways in the integrated whole language classroom. Children will experience excitement and joy in learning because reading and writing will function as normally as speaking and listening in learning about ideas and in interacting interpersonally with others.

A Case Study of a Teacher's Development Toward an Integrated Whole Language Classroom

An integrated whole language classroom involves the teacher and the children at any grade/level in numerous, complex variables. A "typical" classroom setting usually has an enrollment of 25 children with similar and different experience backgrounds, interests, strengths,

needs and developmental growth patterns. The teacher
needs to consider several factors in planning and providing for each child's unique development. These
factors include: <u>personnel</u>, <u>time</u>, <u>use of space</u>, <u>learn-
ing experiences</u>, and <u>activities</u> (instruction), materials,
<u>evaluation</u> (assessment), <u>grouping</u>, <u>scheduling time</u>, and
<u>management</u> technique with each other on a minute-by-
minute, hour-by-hour, day-by-day, and week-by-week
basis.

Using a hypothetical example, a description is
given of how a classroom teacher can organize and manage
an integrated whole language classroom program.

Over a period of time most teachers can progress from a "traditional" to an integrated whole language classroom in which most learning is coordinated.
Previously, we have identified and described stages of
teacher growth and development. Most beginning and
experienced teachers organize learning in the classroom
in a traditional way during their early years of teaching. The characteristics of the traditional classroom
are well known, accepted and perpetuated. Such classrooms are labeled: Stage 1: <u>Traditional</u>. There are
two intermediary stages most teachers may go through before achieving a totally integrated whole classroom.
Stage 2: is referred to as <u>Modified Traditional</u> and
Stage 3: <u>Transitional Integrated</u>. Many teachers organize their classrooms with several characteristics of
the <u>Modified Traditional</u> and <u>Transitional Integrated</u>
classroom. However, more teachers are able, with assistance and support, to organize and manage all the complex
components in a whole language classroom.

The components for each stage of teacher development are the same. The difference is the teacher's
knowledge of the socio-psycholinguistic nature of the
reading-language process, knowing how children learn,
and planning and implementation of <u>time</u>, <u>personnel</u>,
<u>space</u>, <u>materials</u>, <u>learning experiences</u>, <u>assessment pro-
cedures</u>, <u>grouping</u>, and <u>management techniques</u>.

The focus here is on Stage 4: <u>The Integrated
Whole Language Classroom</u>. Our hypothetical classroom
involves, Ms. Brown, a third grade teacher and 25 children. Ms. Brown has taught in a self-contained classroom for two years. She is in her third year of teaching and began teaching the third grade in a traditional
manner. She scheduled separate language arts and content subjects, the classroom space was organized with
traditional rows of desks, bookshelves, and a reading

corner with library books. The instructional materials included basal readers, workbooks, skill sheets, and word recognition games as the basic materials. Library and trade books were in limited use. The evaluation of children's reading levels and needs included basal reader tests, standardized tests, workbooks, and skill worksheets. She grouped children for reading primarily by achievement groups--high, middle and low, received 25-30 minutes in the morning of teacher-directed reading, followed by 25-30 minutes of seatwork and, if there was time, children could do independent reading, or play word recognition games. Spelling, writing, mathematics and content areas were scheduled in separate periods each day.

Ms. Brown had a part-time teacher aide, one hour each morning, however, she usually had the aide running off ditto skill sheets, working with one child with word flash cards or practicing words on a list.

After her first year of teaching in a traditionally organized classroom, Ms. Brown developed a sense of uneasiness and frustration about the lack of progress many children made in reading, writing, spelling and content areas. Also, only a few children in the class really liked or chose to read. Oh, yes, the standardized achievement test given in May showed the average mean scores of the class at grade level - 3.8; thirteen children scored at or above 3.8 and twelve children scored 3.7 or below. This was almost the normal curve with the children evenly distributed at all stanines from 1 to 9, in reading, spelling, mathematics, social studies, reference skills and English mechanics. Still, Ms. Brown knew that she was not satisfied with the progress of most children in language arts and content areas. Something was missing! She felt the children showed little excitement for learning and they saw little purpose in language and content learning. The textbooks had dictated the program and she didn't feel satisfaction about her teaching.

Subsequently, Ms. Brown heard about a term called, "Psycholinguistics." She began reading books and articles about psycholinguistics, language learning, "Whole language" activities and the "Comprehension-Centered" classroom. She attended graduate courses and workshops to learn more about psycholinguistic theories related to language learning application in the classroom.

534

During Ms. Brown's second year of teaching she began to change from a traditional classroom to characteristics of a Modified Traditional and Transitional Integrated Classroom.

First, she realized the need for more <u>personnel</u> in the classroom. She felt she could have "gone it alone," but decided additional personnel in the classroom would help to reach each child as an individual. She had her teacher aide one hour each morning as in previous years. However, she also requested a university practicum student in teacher education from the nearby undersity. The student was available in her classroom three mornings a week. The last half of the year Ms. Brown organized several parents as volunteer aides, scheduled for an hour a day.

Ms. Brown also reorganized her use of <u>time</u> on a daily basis. She changed from separate reading, spelling, writing, math and social studies/science periods to a language arts block of time all morning and a content block of time during the afternoon. She still had some separate periods for the language arts and social studies, math and sciences. She also changed the use of <u>space</u>. The children's desks were placed in clusters for more small group interactions and projects. She added a writing and listening center in the corners of the room to her existing reading corner.

She gradually phased out teacher-directed oral reading in achievement groups with basal readers, accompaning workbooks and skill ditto sheets. She replaced these materials with books, stories and tapes in the listening center, a large collection of books in the reading center and writing activities in the writing center. The social studies and science textbooks were used as reference books to identify general topics for thematic study. Ms. Brown collected single concept books, constructed "skinny books" from old social studies and science books related to unit topics and used filmstrips and other visual aids.

During her third year she included more whole language approaches. The change from dependence on the basal reader, workbooks and dittos required different <u>materials and approaches</u>. At first she still had three reading groups with basal readers/workbooks. However, as the year went on, less time was scheduled for these activities. As listening and writing centers were added, Ms. Brown planned for children to do assisted reading with book/tape. She planned more

self-selected reading and sustained silent reading.
There was more writing by children. She read aloud to
children frequently and language experience approaches
were included with some children.

Ms. Brown's paid aide, a university education
student and volunteer parent aides assisted small groups
and individuals by reading aloud to children and writing
dictated experience stories with children who needed
these activities.

The additional personnel helped Ms. Brown to
organize other types of grouping patterns. The children
grouped flexibly for different purposes. For example,
some children were scheduled for the writing center,
others for assisted reading in the listening center, and
several children were scheduled for sustained silent
reading in the reading center. The teacher, paid aide,
volunteer parents and university student were available
to work with an individual child or small group on
reading strategy lessons related to oral reading miscue
analysis.

As Ms. Brown moved into the Transitional Integrated stage her assessment techniques changed. She
began using more whole language procedures such as the
modified RMI, Cloze tests and syntematic observation
with record-keeping as the children were involved in
read reading, writing, speaking, listening situations.
Workbook, ditto skill sheets and basal reader tests were
gradually phased out as children were participating in
whole language learning experiences. Also, the language arts were integrated with science and social
studies units. The children were involved in reading
and writing reports on problems related to the
thematic units. However, content subjects were still
scheduled at a different time than the language arts.

The flexible use of time, e.g., language arts
block and content areas and space, or more open use of
space created the need for different management techniques. Ms. Brown and her co-workers planned together
for each day related to children's interests, background
experiences and language development. More classroom
structure was necessary because there was a variety of
materials, grouping patterns and learning experiences
going on during the day and from day to day. Ms. Brown
planned with the co-workers who would be involved with
an individual child and groups of children during the
day. At times Ms. Brown would read aloud a story to a
small group of children interested in a particular topic

536

The paid aide would work with a small group in the writing center doing a language experience story based on an experience from the previous day. The university student or volunteer parents would be in the listening center with a small group or listening to a child read orally for a miscue analysis. Next, one of the aides would follow up the reading aloud session with a writing activity related to the story in the writing center. At the same time some children were in the reading center doing self-selected sustained silent reading. During this time Ms. Brown would work with a small group on a strategy lesson based on a previous oral reading session with these children. As the morning went on other children were in the reading center doing sustained silent reading. Finally, Ms. Brown would meet with a group for a Directed-Reading-Thinking-Activity, ReQuest or Schema Story. The classrom aides may work with a child on a language experience story or do written conversation. In the writing center, children could work on their personal daily journals, write letters to classmates for the classroom post office, or write reports related to a social studies or science thematic unit.

Class rules needed to be posted in each area of the room so that children know the rules for using the centers, such as, when to use them and for how long. A whole class planning session was initiated beginning each day, checking briefly to see that each child knew what he/she was expected to do. Materials needed to be set up and accessible at the end of the day in preparation for the following day. Traffic pattern in the room needed to be planned by Ms. Brown, aides and children. A few basic behavior rules needed to be understood and developed. For example, talking with others is allowed, but in a quiet manner. No running or interfering with others when they are working is permitted.

With children, teachers and helpers involved in different learning experiences at the same time, it is essential that a cooperative spirit and climate develop. The classroom in the Transitional Integrated stage of a teacher's development becomes an active and exciting classroom in which all are involved in meaningful language and learning experiences. When children realize this they also become more interested learners. Misbehavior problems are reduced, but not completely eliminated. There is structure and routine, but also an excitement of learning.

Ms. Brown is well on the way to achieving an integrated whole language curriculum in her classroom.

Organizing Whole Language Learning Centers

Whole language learning centers are an effective organizational procedure to open up the classroom and provide children with integrated learning experiences. In Chapter VI, Whole Language Reading Approaches, examples of various whole language learning activities for learning centers were described. In preceding sections in this chapter, The Integrated Whole Language Classroom and Stages of Teacher Development Toward an Integrated Whole Language Classroom, learning centers were emphasized as one organizational technique to enable each student to achieve goals of the whole language classroom. Learning centers also are consistent with the rationale and philosophy of an integrated whole language classroom. Namely, that all children want to learn, all children are curious, children are motivated to learn, and all learning must be whole language-centered, child-centered and experienced-base.

The teacher, of course, is the key to successful planning and implementation of whole language learning centers as one organizational feature in his/her classroom. The teacher needs to understand the purposes of centers, types of centers, how to organize the room, organize time, keep records, individualize student participation in certain activities, his/her role, the students' roles, types of activities and evaluation of children and whole language learning center activities available in the centers. Each aspect of implementing whole language learning centers is described below.

Purpose of Whole Language Learning Centers

Whole language learning centers are different from traditional "skills"/centers of stations. The learning center activities never isolate or fragment oral or written language processes. Speaking, listening, reading and writing experiences are presented to children in meaningful, whole context. There is no differentiation or hierarchy of skills at different "levels." The sequence of learning experiences is within the materials and the child involved in the activity. The child's language developmental stage, his/her experiences and rate of learning are factors the teacher needs to consider when designing and applying language activities for learning centers.

Whole language learning centers are organized to provide independent learning experiences on an individual and/or small group basis. There is no differentiation between introduction to "skills," "reinforcement of 'skills,'" or "enrichment" activities. The purpose of whole language learning centers will depend upon the type of center. Generally, there will be overlapping language processes used in each center. However, a center may emphasize speaking, listening, reading or writing, but still involve other language abilities. The function of language centers may depend on a particular thematic unit the class is studying. The teacher may want to eventually organize social studies, science, math and art centers, involving all language processes. Purposes for centers relate to the language processes and the content to be learned.

Types of Whole Language Learning Centers

There are a variety of types of whole language learning centers a teacher may want to organize in the classroom. The basic types of centers include: reading, writing, speaking and listening centers. In the beginning, the teacher may want to gradually add whole language centers that focus learning experiences on one specific language process, for example, reading. However, language activities included in the center (see Whole Language Learning Activities in Chapter VI) usually involve other language processes. A teacher beginning to change from a traditional classroom organization to a modified traditional classroom may need to experiment with adding only one learning center, e.g., a writing center to an existing reading center in the classroom. Then as she/he has developed center activities and the center is functioning the teacher may add another center. It should be remembered that other organizational procedures are used by the teacher, e.g., interest grouping, strategy lesson grouping, and research grouping.

As the teacher and students are successful using whole language learning centers, other content centers may be organized. Science, social studies and math centers may be developed related to a thematic unit approach. It would be advisable for the teacher to try one content center at a time since he/she will already have to keep the language centers operating.

There are alternative ways for teachers to organize and implement whole language-content centers in the classroom. One method is to integrate content learning activities within the language centers, e.g., speaking, listening, reading and writing. The other option is to organize separate language centers but integrate language processes within the content centers. A third alternative might be to integrate the separate language centers into a language arts center and organize separate content centers that are closely related to a thematic unit. The individual teacher will need to decide which alternative is most appropriate at a given time.

Organization of the Room

Each teacher will need to survey the space and furniture available to him/her in the classroom. There can be no one blueprint for organizing the room. Yet there are common principles and factors to consider when designing, planning and implementing whole language-content learning centers in a given classroom. Guidelines to help in organizing the room, include the following:

1. Consider the types of whole language-content learning centers to organize.

2. Identify the space necessary for the center.

3. Consider how many children can use the center at a given time.

4. Think about the type of furniture needed for the center, e.g., table, chairs, etc.

5. Consider how children will move to the center from where they sit in the classroom. Plan the most direct traffic pattern. This becomes more complex as more centers are added.

6. Plan storage areas close by for children to have easy access to supplies needed for the center.

7. Plan learning centers which involve noice or talking away from quiet activities in the classroom. Plan using dividers for centers that may be distracting to other students in the room.

540

8. Think about using all space in the classroom,
    including ceilings, floors, walls and, of
    course, corners.

   An example of a whole language classroom design
with learning centers is given in Figure 7:19, page 542.

Organizing a Time Schedule

   The teacher will need to decide when and how
much time a center will be used. This will be an individual matter for a teacher to decide. Generally,
the inexperienced teacher in a traditional setting
should schedule limited time for children to work in
centers. As teachers gain more confidence and experience in opening up the classroom and allowing children
more independence, more time during a given day may be
planned for center learning. Each teacher should decide
for herself/himself when to schedule more time. This
will depend on the number of whole language-content
centers available in the classroom. As the teacher
moves away from the traditional reading achievement
groups and independent workbook/ditto skill sheets activities to more whole language approaches, learning
centers are useful for children to develop their own
purposes and to self-selecting materials to read,
choosing topics to write about, planning projects and
listening/viewing stories and poetry. The teachers
will direct and guide children in flexible groups using
strategy lessons with children with similar needs, use
DRTA, schema stories, language experiences, read aloud
stories and poems to children and engage in other approaches.

   The teacher will need to carefully schedule
the children who will work in whole language-content
learning centers, who she/he will have direct contact
with and which children will work in other areas of the
classroom at the same time. Examples of a time schedule
for a teacher at a certain stage of classroom development, e.g., traditional, modified traditional, transitional integrated, and integrated, was given in a previous section of this chapter. (See Stages of Teacher
Development Toward an Integrated Whole Language Classroom.)

Record Keeping

   The teacher and students should have ways to
record continuous progress and identify activities

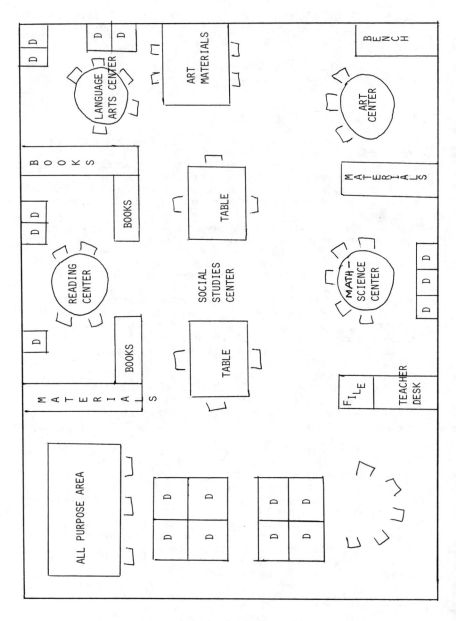

WHOLE LANGUAGE LEARNING CENTER CLASSROOM
FIGURE 7:19
542

completed. Record keeping should be simple and not time-consuming. Some records should be kept by students and other records by the teacher.

Each student can keep a personal record of learning activities completed and hand it in to the teacher periodically as the teacher meets with each student at a conference. Some whole language games may have self-checking procedures so the child can keep a record of his/her progress. The child can also keep a personal folder of samples of books read and stories, poems, reports and experiments written. The student does not have to keep samples of everything.

The teacher might devise a chart system with students' names and activities in the centers. She/He could check the completion of activities. Also, the teacher may want to have a personal folder to keep writing and reading samples.

The reader is referred to Chapter IV, Evaluation of Reading for observing and record keeping devices.

Individualizing Student Participation in Center Activities

Whole language-content learning centers provide an opportunity for the teacher to individualize learning and develop student independence by providing choices for children. Center activities can be planned which consider children's interests, experiences, language strengths and needs. As the teacher observes children in various strategy lessons, identifying miscues, she/he can devise "activities" to fit strengths and weaknesses in using language cueing systems and strategies as the child constructs meaning. (See Types of Strategy Lessons in Chapter V.) Various environmental print materials can be available for children to read and write related to interests, e.g., writing to complete an application form to send for something, writing a grocery list to purchase items from the classroom supermarket, reading a recipe book to prepare something for a class party or special occasion. There should be choices for students to select to read, write, listen, talk, view, construct and dramatize.

The Role of the Teacher

The role of the teacher will vary depending on the extent to which learning centers are used in the classroom. If whole language centers and content centers are used on a limited basis with other grouping patterns, e.g., interest, research, tutorial, strategy grouping and self-selected reading, the teacher will still need to develop, plan and implement centers, although other organizational procedures are used as well. However, if a teacher has reached the integrated language-content classroom stage, learning centers may be a total program. Whichever, the plan, the teacher will need to consider his/her role and responsibility within the structure of the classroom organization.

The teacher's responsibilities include the following:

1. Design whole language-content activities.

2. Organize space and time for center activities.

3. Evaluate/observe children as they work in centers and the products of the children.

4. Change center activities.

5. Keep records of pupil progress and work samples.

6. Guide students to responsible behavior to learn individually and in groups.

The Student's Role

The teacher needs to guide children gradually to assume more responsibility for their own learning. Students need to learn independently, to set their own purposes for learning within the framework of choices available. They need to learn to work with others, respecting the right of others and to help other students. Students have a responsibility to self-evaluate their progress and to keep records of work completed. Finally, children are responsible in center activities for using their time wisely.

Evaluation

Evaluation includes teacher evaluation and student self-evaluation of whole language-content learning center activities. The teacher should evaluate each child's process of learning while engaged in

544

center activities, what the child produces or accomplishes and the center activities. Evaluation of learning involve record keeping techniques devised by the teacher. (See Chapter IV, Evaluation of Reading, the section on Systematic Record Keeping.)

The student needs to monitor his/her behavior, progress and participation as well as the product of learning. Self-checking and pre-determined criteria can be used by the child to receive immediate feedback. The child should keep samples of work to see progress in reading, writing and learning over a period of time. The samples of oral reading, writing and projects produced by students will be useful to the teacher in reporting pupil progress to parents.

Organizing and implementing whole language-content learning centers are time-consuming and require extra effort on the part of the teacher. However, whole language centers are another organizational procedure which are rewarding learning experiences for children. They can enable the teacher to observe and guide other children while some children are engaged in center activities. The whole language learning center concept is consistent with the philosophy, rationale and goals of an integrated whole language-content classroom.

Thematic Units: A Language-Centered Approach

The thematic unit approach is an organizational procedure which incorporates learning around a broad theme or topic. Language, thinking and content are integrated. Language is used and functions naturally as means to the end--learning content, learning about self and others. Learning is purposeful and involves a search to construct meaning and to solve problems. There is no artificial separation of language learning, thinking and content in learning. All learning is integrated within common, broad themes. The themes are expanded into objectives or purposes (sub-problems or questions), then related to selected learning experiences and materials, organized in such a way that purposes are achieved, objectives are evaluated, and learning is shared.

The thematic unit approach includes all aspects of language development, methods, evaluation, and organizational procedures described previously in this book. In effect, the teacher achieves a true integration

545

of language and content learning when using thematic
units. This is the highest level of teacher development and proficiency and student learning. All language
processes, e.g., reading, writing, speaking and listening are integrated, learned and used to learn a body of
knowledge. Young children learning oral language and
written language already have internalized and know
that language is used to learn. They have learned language and how to use it because it works for them.
Thematic units are a vehicle to enable students to use
and learn language naturally and for real purposes to
communicate meaning. There is no other purpose for
communication.

In this section, consideration will be given to
the following: (1) planning broad thematic units; (2)
planning and organizing specific thematic units; and
(3) an example demonstrating the application of a
thematic unit in a classroom.

Planning Broad Thematic Units

Generally thematic units are planned from subjects such as social studies, science, mathematics and
literature. Frequently units integrate knowledge from
several disciplines including language and other forms
of expression, e.g., art, music, dance, and drama.
The teacher should consider the possible integration of
all language processes, other forms of communication and
the integration of various disciplines. The diagram in
Figure 7:20 below illustrates the concept of thematic
units.

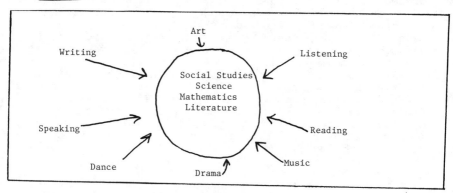

CONCEPTUAL MODEL OF THEMATIC UNITS

FIGURE 7:20

546

The most effective utilization of thematic units is in the totally integrated whole language-content classroom. The whole year at specific age-grade levels is planned around general, broad themes. Each theme is planned for a time period during the year. Each day, week, and month is planned as an integrated whole.

A spiral curriculum for grades K-3; 4-6; 7-9; 10-12 may be planned with increasing conceptual difficulty from lower grade levels to higher grade levels. The spiral curriculum integrates all disciplines, e.g., science, social studies, mathematics and literature, as much as possible. Broad themes may include the following:

Grades	Broad Themes Across Grade Levels	
12	1.) Production and Consumption of Food, Clothing, Shelter	
11	2.) Safety, Survival, and Health	
10	3.) Education	
9	4.) Government	
8	5.) Air, Earth, and Space - Environment and Ecology	
7	6.) Transportation	World ↑
6	7.) Work and Careers	Nation ↕
5	8.) Values, Feeling, and Culture	Region ↑
4	9.) Recreation	State ↕
3	10.) Technology	Community ↕
2		Home
1		
K		

Each broad theme may be planned and applied at successive grade levels. The broad themes are sub-divided into topics or problems according to the developmental levels of students. The curriculum at all levels develops major concepts, knowledge, skills, attitudes and values from concrete and general experiences at lower grade levels and specific experiences at higher levels. Problems for study are related to past human experiences, present and immediate topics and future experiences.

The ten broad themes listed above are planned for a year's study at each grade level. At the elementary/middle school level, subjects, such as: science, social studies, mathematics, English and literature are integrated within the themes. At the primary level (K-2), the focus is on home and community; at intermediate level (3-5), the focus is on state and countries; at middle grades (6-8), the emphasis is on nations and the world. However, at all levels, there is a relationship between home, community, state, country and the world.

Separate thematic units are planned for each of the ten themes, although there is integration across and within broad themes. For example, the study of home and community at the primary level includes all ten broad themes during a year. The focus at a given time may be concerned with production and consumption of food, clothing, and shelter but include related themes, such as: safety, survival and health, air, earth and space and values and culture. At the intermediate level (3-5) the emphasis is on the state and national level, however, the relationship of the home and community to the state and national level is evident. Each broad thematic unit is integrated at the intermediate level focusing on past, present and future development of production and consumption of basic needs (e.g., food, clothing and shelter), safety, survival and health, education, government . . . recreation. Again each broad theme is a focus during the year, however, other themes are integrated as they relate to the central broad theme.

Planning and Organizing Specific Thematic Units

Specific thematic units planned by the teacher for a given level should consider the following related aspects according to Lynn Rhodes (1979):

1. Who are you planning for? (grade, proficiency levels, interests, pupil experiences).

2. What time line do you have in mind? (How long will the unit last? What part of the day will it consume?, etc.)

3. What is the theme around which you want to plan the unit?

4. Are you adapting an already prepared unit? If so, what adaptions must you make?

5. What are the concepts, content you want the students to learn?

6. What language (reading, writing, speaking, listening) expressions, strategies, perceptions, attitudes do you want to develop further?

7. What activities, lessons have you planned to teach what you have outlined in #5, #6. (Specify grouping, resources, follow-up when necessary, information necessary to understand activity or lesson, etc.)

8. What resources do you intend to utilize? (Think about trade books, films, filmstrips, pictures, textbooks, community people and places, magazines, children's own work, records, professional references, etc.)

Rhodes also adds suggested organizational strategies for thematic units:

1. Introductory section which discusses theme, children for whom the unit was developed, time line, adaptation of already existing unit (if appropriate), etc.

2. List concepts you want students to learn (#5 above in planning).

3. List language learning you want to occur (#6 above in planning).

4. Activities, Lessons

    a) Introduction of theme to group.
    b) Activities, lessons to develop theme.
    c) Tying the unit together and ending it.

5. List resources in categories.

Examples of a Thematic Unit

The following thematic unit was planned and implemented by Cheryl Reichel (1980). She provides an overview of her philosophy of the language process, selection of materials, teaching techniques and procedures and instructional materials. The following thematic unit relates to the suggestions for organizing a unit given above by Lynn Rhodes:

Unit of Democracy

Cheryl Reichel (1980)

The Setting: Departmental Self-contained Junior High,
              5 sections of Social Studies.

Broad Theme: Types of Government

Specific
  Theme: Democracy

Philosophy:

The process of reading is extremely complex. When a child reads for enjoyment, she must be able to perceive the words as having a meaning by the experiences she has had in her life. This is also true when a child reads content material from a textbook. She must be able to associate what she has read with the experiences she has had or else the child will not remember the reading. There are eight processes that must be in good working order before the child can fully comprehend what she has read and quite often one or more of these processes are weaknesses. The reading process includes: 1) sensory, 2) perceptual, 3) sequential, 4) experiential, 5) thinking, 6) learning, 7) association, and 8) affective. For this reason, a teacher must be on guard against giving reading assignments indiscriminately and without direction or additional materials.

Readability of Materials:

A teacher should determine whether the reading
material is the same grade level in which she is teaching. A good way to determine if the children are capable of comprehending the material and at the same time
to assess the readability of the text is to give a
Cloze test from different parts of the text. This
should not include facts that the children would not
have had before, but rather a general passage of terms
that are throughout the book.

Once the teacher has determined a reading span for
the class, a group of complementary materials for the
subject should be gathered and kept in the room. Additional materials could be added as new subjects would
arise. Good outside sources are: magazines, newspapers, library centers, book loans from children's
homes, encyclopedias, filmstrips, movies, "Skinny books,"
manilla folders with picture and short story, tape
recordings of short books. These materials would cover
a wide enough span to reach all of the children.

Components, strategies, teaching techniques, procedures:

This unit is designed for four to five weeks.
Throughout this time, the children should be able to
develop a good solid concept of what democracy means in
America. To achieve this the children will develop individual contracts from the chart (see Figure 7:21, page
552). The children will be divided into groups of between 3-5 (25-30 in classroom).

I will discuss each child's interests and help
each of them write a contract of items they should complete for a certain grade. Each child must do at
least three of each of the items.

After groups have been decided, give a name or number to each and assign the bulletin board to any group
that wants it. The bulletin board should be done after
school or during recess. It can be changed every few
days, once a week, or just as often as there are groups
wanting this task. It is IMPORTANT that no task be
used as a reward or a punishment. They are tasks to be
done and all are needed (a little Montessorri here!).

The entire class will be compiling a Civics Handbook and it should be discussed at this point. They
will need to gather information from many sources
throughout the room. Specific instruction sheets will

	EDITOR	SENATOR	CONGRESS-MAN	PRESI-DENT	LOCAL T.V. STATION	RADIO STATION	
BULLETIN BOARD							
CIVICS HANDBOOK							
LETTERS	EDITOR	SENATOR	CONGRESS-MAN	PRESI-DENT	LOCAL T.V. STATION	RADIO STATION	
STUDY GUIDES AND FILMSTRIPS							
BOOK REPORT (ORAL OR WRITTEN-A PLAY WOULD BE ACCEPTABLE)							
CURRENT EVENTS (tapes presented as radio report)							
ART PROJECT	CLAY	POSTER	DRAWING	MURAL	FRIEZE	T.V.	
GROUP PROJECTS	PLAY	CLASS ELECT-IONS	DEBATES	NEWS-PAPER	CIVIC HAND-BOOK		

DEMOCRACY UNIT - JOBSHEET
FIGURE 7:21

be posted in the Research Center. (See room map, center #6.) A structured overview of what is expected in the Civics Handbook will help in clarification.

The filmstrips are without tapes and the children need to read the information on them. Study guides will be appropriate here to be sure they get all they can from the filmstrip.

552

A whole class lesson on locating information in books (index, table of contents, glossaries, etc.) and how to use encyclopedias should be given before this unit begins. Locating information in the newspaper might be discussed here also.

For better reports a general study guide could be made to help the children develop good book reports. They should know who is telling the story, what the plot of the story is, how the climax builds, etc. A general outline of a good report could be made up by one of the groups. It should include: 1) Introductory paragraph, 2) Setting, 3) Characterization, 4) Climax, 5) Summary and opinion. Each of these topics should be developed into a paragraph. An annotated bibliography of many available books will be given to the children and their first assignment is to decide on a book that deals with some aspect of democracy. They can choose books that are not found on the bibliography, but they need to get the book approved.

Each learning station should be discussed with the whole class. I will work with one group at a time, setting them up at a station while the others are beginning their books in silent reading.

Instructional Materials:

For a specific resource list, please turn to the last page of the Unit on Democarcy that is attached. The materials include library books, numerous film-strips, charts, tape recorders, movies, newspapers, encyclopedias, "Skinny books," picture file and art supplies.

Centers for Democracy Unit:

1. Current Events
   - Newspapers, News Magazines
   - Tape Recorder for making daily radio announce-ments and presentations

2. Library Center
   - Annotated Bibliographies
   - Assortment of books about a) history
     a) history
     b) people
     c) democracy in other countries
     d) other forms of government
     e) etc.

3. Art Center (supplies at end of lockers)

4. Bulletin Board and Display table

5. "Letters" Center
   - barriers between desks with information posted on them:
     a) letterhead
     b) addresses of politicians, editors, famous historians, etc.
     c) "how to" do specific letters

6. Research Center
   - construction and gathering of materials for Civics Handbooks that will be given to parents
   - use art table for some construction of books

7. Filmstrip Viewing - individuals

8. Filmstrip Viewing - small groups
   - study guides aid the children in viewing

See Figure 7:22, page 555, illustrating the classroom organization of space.

UNIT OF DEMOCRACY

THEME - A careful study of the privileges Americans enjoy and their accompanying responsibilities provides young people with an opportunity to gain: 1) a fuller understanding of what it means to live in a free nation; 2) a deeper appreciation of our rich American heritage; and 3) a greater awareness of their opportunities and responsibilities.

The goal is to help young people actively support democratic principles and to prepare them for full participation in democratic processes.

INTRODUCTION - Democracy is an abstract concept that is somewhat difficult for intermediate children to comprehend, therefore, it must be presented by sensory, concrete means to facilitate the learning experience. The children live in a democracy and their very lifestyles are the way they are because of democratic principles. Rudolf Dreikurs (noted social psychiatrist and author of Children: the Challenge) notes that, "It is largely the impact of democracy that has transformed our social

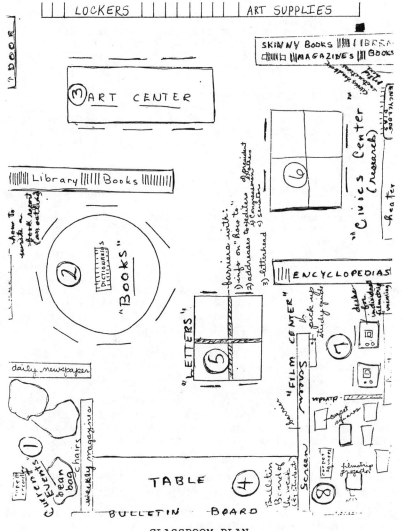

CLASSROOM PLAN

FIGURE 7:22

atmosphere and made the traditional methods of child rearing obsolete . . . In a society of equals we cannot rule over another." I believe that, even if a child cannot define democracy, he has a conceptual opinion of what it is and it is used whenever the child mentions his/her rights.

At the conclusion of this unit, the children should have a greater respect of the word "rights" and have a fuller understanding of how a democratic society affects their lives.

LEARNING AND RESOURCE CENTER (An explanation) - I have constructed a four part learning center to aid the individual child to work towards a fuller understanding of democracy. This method of learning is especially valuable when the topic of study is rights, freedom, and democracy.

The four parts of the Learning Center are: 1) "Democracy in the Classroom" (class election results are listed, class "bill of rights" posted, suggestion box for future amendments awaits, a copy of the U. S. Constitution is posted, and the three branches of government are shown). 2) "Reading Center (work sheets are posted, library and reference books are here, and a project section is posted). 3) "Freedom of the Press" (newspaper articles are listed, newspaper games are posted). 4) "Freedom of Speech" (important addresses of public officials are posted, letters and replies are posted, and incentive for petitions are awaiting-- letterhead from the school is available).

I will have motivations to get the children started on the learning centers (free periods, use of the center in lieu of a quiz, etc.) One thing that each child in the class must do is write a letter to the editor of the local paper, or a letter to any political figure. No motivation will be given for this, but the reward will be either having their letters published or receiving an answer from an important political figure.

If learning stations are particularly attractive to the class, I will set up more than one.

BROAD GOAL A - A concept of what democracy means should be developed in the children.

Objective I: The children will have a sound idea of the meaning of democracy.

556

ACTIVITIES:

1.   As an opening activity the children will be
asked what their concept of democracy is in one word--
they should call out anything they think of. I will
list their ideas on the board.

2.   The filmstrip "Your American Citizenship" will
be shown.

3.   A discussion will be held comparing the
students' ideas with the filmmakers.

4.   The Learning Center I have constructed will be
introduced.

5.   Discuss freedoms and responsibilities that are
connected to democracy. Have a bulletin board with
Roosevelt's "four freedoms" listed. (freedom of speech,
freedom from want, freedom of worship, freedom from
fear).

6.   After Activity 5, have the children relate
other freedoms they feel are important.

BROAD GOAL B - The students will be able to trace the
development of American Democracy.

Objective I: The children will know the basic documents
that were developed while our democratic system was
being formed.

ACTIVITIES:

1.   Short one act plays that depict famous historical events should be assigned to small groups of children (involving the entire class). Use Bicentennial
Plays and Programs, by Aileen Fisher.

2.   Using the posters from "Symbols of Freedom,"
the children will be able to trace "democracy in the
making" during the pioneer days.

3.   The children shall be divided into groups to
read and report on:

        a. The Declaration of Independence
        b. The constitution
        c. The Bill of Rights
        d. The Three Branches of Government

557

The conclusion can be done as an oral report by the group leader, or it could be dramatized.

4. Art Activity: The children should draw posters depicting the major ideas of the Bill of Rights.

5. Develop, on the board, an outline comparing the Articles of Confederation with the Constitution.

6. Discussion: Why has the Constitution been amended but never rewritten?

Objective II: The children will know that certain people were most influentital in putting together the important works of our early government.

ACTIVITIES:

1. The children should read and report on one of the founders of American democracy.

2. After Activity 1, I will announce the intention of forming a "Civics Handbook" of our reports, pictures, any interviews, and a special dictionary section of government terms.

3. Invite a local--well thought of--politician to discuss his feelings of the famous people of our rich heritage.

Objective III: The children will understand the basic working structure of our government; i.e.: the Three Branches of Government.

ACTIVITIES:

1. Bulletin Board: The children will gather newspaper and magazine articles that tell about the three branches of government, (Congress, Supreme Court, and the President).

2. After Activity 1, the class shall be divided into three groups to look up and list powers specifically granted and those forbidden to each of the three branches of government.

BROAD GOAL C

The children will understand the importance of knowing our heritage in America.

558

Objective I: The children will understand important steps in the developing of American democracy and will appreciate the rich background they have inherited.

ACTIVITIES:

   1. Show the film "America the Beautiful."

   2. Art Activity: In mural fashion, children will make a time line showing important steps in the development of American democracy.

Objective II: The children will understand the basic functions of our political system.

ACTIVITIES: Have children plan questions for the following speakers.)

   1. Have a local politician discuss freedom of speech and his job.

   2. Have local clergy discuss freedom of religion.

   3. Have local editor discuss freedom of the press.

   4. Divide the class into groups to research the following: the Electoral College, primary elections, registration, Presidential Nominating Committee, checks and balances, power of veto, or impeachment. All that the children find should be listed on the board as points of interest. A spokesperson for each, relates the facts found.

   5. Each child should make a chart showing the growth of political parties in the U.S. to be added to their Civic Handbooks.

   6. Show the filmstrips: "The President," "Congress," and "Federal Courts."

   7. Each child should review the newspaper daily to find a topic that interests them, so that they can write a letter to the editor of the paper or to a politician that can be beneficial to them.

Objective III: The children will enjoy knowing the symbols of our Democratic system.

ACTIVITIES:

1. Use "Symbols of Freedom" posters to discuss symbols of American Democracy.

2. List on board all symbols or sayings the children can think of. (Examples: Liberty bell, U. S. Capital, flag, Uncle Sam, American eagle, etc.)

3. Art Projects: Divide the class into two parts of American symbols project:

      a) One group will make a frieze for the symbols.
      b) The other group will make clay figures of the symbols.

4. As children come across difficult political or governmental words, be sure and add them to the Government Dictionary for their Civics Handbook.

5. Show filmstrip of "Light of Liberty."

BROAD GOAL D

The children will develop knowledge of what it takes to be a responsible citizen.

Objective I: The children will develop knowledge of what is involved with voting rights.

ACTIVITIES:

1. Field Trip: Visit a local council meeting, school board, or local court.

2. Arrange with local Board of Elections for class to see how a voting machine works.

3. Board work: Get state manuals that list qualifications for voting and have children skim the manual while calling out qualifications that I will list on the board.

4. Learn the voting procedure by living it. Representatives will be nominated and the children will vote on two candidates to represent them to handle the suggestion box from the Learning Center

5. The class will be set up to handle all facets of voting; i.e.: Registration, Ballots, Voting Booths, Casting, Official Supervisor.

560

6. Recite the poem, "The Poor Voter on Election Day" by John Greenleaf Whittier. Perhaps place on bulletin board.

> (The proudest now is but my peer.
> The highest not more high.
> Today of all the weary year.
> A king of mean am I.
> Today alike are great and small.
> The nameless and the known.
> My place is the people's hall.
> The ballot box my throne.)

7. Show the filmstrip, "Your State Government."

Objective II: The children will develop an interest in current events.

ACTIVITIES:

1. Prepare on the board a brief "Who's, Who?" of persons prominent in our country today; who you think are making significant contributions to the democratic way of life.

2. After Activity 1, have the children choose a person from the board and do a report to be given in class.

3. Invite a member of the state or local legislature, an attorney or some other well-informed citizen to talk to the class about proposed legislature (have children have questions ready).

4. Start a petition that the class feels would benefit the community. Example: Have the animal lovers from SICSA take over the duties of animal shelter rather than leaving this up to inhumane bureaucrats.

5. Show filmstrip, "The Meaning of Democracy."

6. Responsibility comes with taxing and the work force--show filmstrip, "Everyone Uses Money."

CONCLUSION: Discussion Questions:

1. Do you feel there should be a voting age-limit?

2. In what way is good citizenship similar to good sportsmanship and observing the "rules of the game?"

561

3. What can we do to make our school community a more democratic society? How can we help?

4. What qualities do you think democratic leaders should have? What qualities are necessary for intelligent following?

5. Why is trial by jury of one's peers important in the effective functioning of a democratic society.

CULMINATION OF UNIT:

1. Prepare Civics Handbooks
   a) Have children create cover.
   b) Type all pages on ditto sheets (have children transfer drawings) and runn off copies for everyone.
   c) Hand out copies on parent's day in class.

2. Parent's Day
   a) The skits that we worked on at the beginning of this unit should be performed for parents. The students should have time to go over these to do them well. All students should be involved.
   b) All posters, drawings, reports, clay figures, murals, friezes, etc., should be on display.

INSTRUCTIONAL RESOURCES - BOOKS

Curriculum Materials Center:

Cause of War, by Kenyon Cramer

Golden Book of American Revolution, by Fred Cook

Bicentennial Plays and Programs, by Aileen Fisher

The First Book of Elections, by Edmund Lindop

Thomas Jefferson, by John Dos Passo

The Picture Story and Biography of John Adams, by Regina Z. Kelly

The Story of George Washington, by May McNeer

What's the Big Idea Ben Franklin, by Jean Fritz

Public Library:

Know Your Government, by George E. Ross

Electing A President, by Duane Bradley

The Congress, by Gerald W. Johnson

We are the Government, by Mary Elting

All about Courts and the Law, by Ruth Brindze

The First Book of the Constitution, by Richard B. Morris

Home Library:

National Geographic, "Women of the Revolution: Patriots in Petticoats" page 475, October 1975.

Kids' America, by Steven Caney, pp. 354-402, "Land of Opportunity"

We, the People, the Story of the United States Capitol, distributed by the National Geographic, 1973.

Our Presidents, by Barbara Barclay

FILMSTRIPS

Meaning of Democracy   The President
Making Democracy Work   The Congress
Light of Liberty   Federal Courts
Everyone Uses Money
Your American Citizenship
United Nations
America the Beautiful

CHARTS

Symbols of Freedom

DITTO WORK SHEETS

Democracy in Action, packet

Summary

     The organization of the whole language class-
room involves an interrelationship of several components described in each previous chapter. The
teacher needs to be knowledgeable concerning the socio-
psycholinguistic nature of language learning. She/He
needs insight about how oral and written language are
learned. Evaluation procedures must be consistent with
the nature of the process and learning experiences and
materials need to be carefully selected to provide a
supportive learning environment.

     This chapter has attempted to bring together the
complex components that are involved in teaching and
learning in the classroom. First, the whole language
classroom is based on a philosophy which views children as active learners constructing meaning. The
goals of the whole language classroom are child-
centered. Each learner achieves independence, understanding of self, other and his/her world, self-exteem
and a sense of purpose.

     The whole language school and classroom has
available several school-wide and classroom organizational patterns. Several school-wide, i.e., graded,
nongraded, self-contained, departmentalized and team
teaching, were described, within the school-wide organization, the whole language teacher should be familiar
with alternative classroom grouping patterns. She/He
should use a variety of grouping plans related to the
students, methods of evaluation, materials and approaches that are appropriate to the whole language curriculum
It was recommended that achievement level grouping be
minimized if not eliminated as a grouping method. Alternate grouping patterns, consistent with the philosophy and goals of the whole language classroom include:
interest, friendship research, strategy, tutorial,
and the like.

     The integrated, whole language-content class-
room was described providing a rationale and contrasting the characteristics of a whole language classroom
with a traditional skill-centered classroom. Problems
and practices were identified in implementing a whole
language-content classroom. The most important problem may be that the teacher's decision to change from a
traditional classroom to a whole language should be a
personal and voluntary choice. The teaching and learning practices during the process of change allows different ways of making the transition from a traditional to

564

an integrated whole language classroom. Factors involved in change include: numbers of students; content areas or language areas to begin with, scheduling time, including how many students and areas of instruction; and the use of space related to how many students involved, areas of instruction and time. Special consideration needs to be given to training children in use of materials, activities, use of time and discipline or classroom management techniques. Moreover, the role of the teacher and students has to change. The classroom environment and learning atmosphere changes from teacher-centered to child-centered. The environment is rich with student products. There is a cooperative atmosphere in which students and the teacher help one another. The teacher's role is more of an observer, monitor, encourager, and model. The student's role changes from passive follower to active learner. The student learns to make choices, assumes responsibility for his/her learning, respects others and evaluates his/her learning.

Whole language learning centers were advocated as an organizational component consistent with the philosophy and goals of the integrated whole language-content classroom. Whole language centers provide independence in learning. Centers include language and content centers. The teacher needs to consider several procedures when planning and implementing whole language centers. First, the children who will use the centers must be evaluated related to the kinds of activities they will do. Second, the use of space in the classroom and the use of time must be planned. Third, how to keep records and monitor learning should be considered. Fourth, the teacher must carefully consider her role and the role of the students. Of course, the teacher will be responsible for designing and selecting the activities in the centers. The students' role involves independent learning, making choices, helping others, self-evaluating and using time wisely. Finally, both teacher and students have responsibility to evaluate learning in whole language center activities.

Not every teacher is ready or should change from a traditional classroom to an integrated whole language classroom. Moreover, not every teacher who wants to change will change in the same way or at the same time. Stages of teacher development to change from traditional to integrated classroom were described in four levels. Characteristics of the traditions, modified traditional, transitional integrated and fully integrated were described. The characteristics included components that need to be organized by any classroom teacher. The components included: personnel, time, space, evaluation of students, methods and materials (instruction) and grouping. The ultimate integrated whole language classroom includes: language processes, i.e., reading, writing, speaking and listening learned, used, and integrated with content areas, i.e., social studies, mathematics, science and literature, with art, music, dramatization and physical education, as part of thematic unit organization.

Thematic units should be organized across the grade levels and integrated to language and content curriculum. It was proposed that broad themes be identified in a spiral curriculum from separate disciplines and that language, art, music, drama, dance and physical activities should be the means to learn content (the world, self, and others). The broad themes related to each grade level were subdivided into specific themes including major concepts, generalization, and specific facts and effective areas to learn. At successive grade/age levels learning about the broad/ specific themes would proceed from concrete, general, and real experiences at lower grade level to more abstract, specific, and vicarious experiences at higher age/grade levels. The procedures in planning thematic units were given and an example of a specific theme at an appropriate grade level was described.

In conclusion, language learning and content learning should be integrated as much as possible. The organization of the whole language classroom requires hard work and challenge for the teacher. Published materials i.e., basal readers, content textbooks, course of studies and curriculum guides provide the framework but must not dictate the same progress for learners. The teacher, knowledgeable about language learning, whole language evaluation procedures, whole language materials and organizational structures, will be the key variable whether each student achieves success in learning.

Teaching Competencies

1. Design/plan reading experiences related to various
   whole language reading approaches described in
   Chapter VI and identified as Teaching Competencies
   in Chapter VI: Apply at least <u>one</u> type of grouping,
   i.e., interest, strategy group, research, tutorial,
   research, etc. When planning a grouping procedure
   consider the following factors when appropriate to
   a certain type of grouping of children: (1) interests; (2) background experiences; (3) conceptual development; (4) language cues and strategies,
   strengths and weaknesses; (5) time; (6) classroom
   setting; (7) size of group; (8) types of materials,
   learning activities; (9) evaluation procedures,
   i.e., observing with some type of record keeping.
   Write a plan before implementing.

2. Plan/design a whole language reading center for use
   in the classroom. Consider various factors identified in number one above under Teaching Competencies.
   Write a plan to explain the center and draw a diagram of the center before implementing the center.

Questions to Investigate

1. Explain advantages and disadvantages of one school-
   wide organizational procedure, i.e., graded school,
   non-graded school, team teaching, Individually
   Guided Education (IGE), open or integrated school.

2. Compare advantages and disadvantages of two types of
   classroom grouping procedures to enhance and promote
   student learning, i.e., interest groups, strategy
   (skill) groups, peer tutoring, research groups,
   friendship groups, achievement level groups.

3. Discuss and explain the advantages and disadvantages
   of an integrated language/content classroom in terms
   of student learning compared to a more traditional or
   conventional classroom.

4. Explain the differences between language "skills"
   centers and "whole" language centers. Identify
   basic differences in types of learning activities,
   materials and purposes/philosophy as the basis for
   "skills" and "whole" language centers.

5. State and describe the steps involved in preparing
   a learning center.

6. Explain the theoretical/philosophical background for organzing thematic units in the language-content curriculum in the classroom.

References

Bretz, Carol. "Language Arts: A Vehicle to Open Education." The Reading Teacher. March 1973.

Goodman, Kenneth S. "Behind the Eye: What Happens in Reading." In Reading: Process and Programs. (Eds) Kenneth Goodman and Olive Niles. Urbana, IL: NCTE, 1972.

Goodman, Kenneth S. "The Reading Process." In Proceedings of Western Learning Symposium. Billingham, WA., 1974.

Goodman, Yetta M. and Burke, Carolyn L. Reading Miscue Inventory: Proudness for Diagnosis and Evaluation. New York: Macmillan Co., 1972.

Halliday, M.A.K. Explorations in the Functions of Language. New York: Elseview, 1973.

Halliday, M.A.K. Learning How to Mean: Explorations in the Development of Language. New York: Elseview, 1975.

Morgan, Lorraine. "Role of the Teacher in the Informal Classroom." The Reading Teacher. March 1973.

Reichel, Cheryl. "A Thematic Unit on Democracy." Paper presented at University, Dayton, Dayton, OH, Apr. 1980.

Rhodes, Lynn. "A Comprehension-Centered Classroom." Speech at Psycholinguistic and Reading Workshop: University of Dayton, Dayton, Ohio, July 1979.

Smith, Frank. Comprehension and Learning. New York: H.H.,Rinehart and Winston, 1979.

Smith, Frank. Understanding Reading. New York: Holt, Rinehart and Winston, 1978.

Southgate, Verna. "The Language Arts in Informal British Infant Schools." The Reading Teacher. January 1973.

Watson, Dorothy. "Reader Selected Miscues: Getting More From Sustained Silent Reading." English Education. Vol. 10, December 1978, pp. 75-85.

BIBLIOGRAPHY OF LITERATURE
Special "Language" Books

Recognizing Rhyme

Fritz Eichenberg. APE IN A CAPE. Harcourt, 1952.

Fritz Eichenberg. DANCING ON THE MOON. Harcourt, 1955.

Walter Einsel. DID YOU EVER SEE. Wm. R. Scott, 1962 or Scholastic.

Dennis Nolan. BIG PIG. Prentice-Hall, 1976.

Polly Cameron. I CAN'T SAID THE ANT. Coward McCann, 1961 or Scholastic.

Charlotte Pomerantz. THE PIGGY IN THE PUDDLE. Macmillan, 1974.

Introducing Playing with Vocabulary

Muriel Batherman. BIG AND SMALL, SHORT AND TALL. Scholastic, 1972.

Elizabeth Hulbert. OUT AND IN. Scholastic, 1970.

Mary Sue White. WORD TWINS. Abingdon, 1961.

Cynthia Basil. NAILHEADS AND POTATO EYES. Wm. Morrow, 1976.

Betsy and Giulio Maestro. WHERE TO MY FRIENDS? Crown, 1976.

Tana Hoban. OVER, UNDER AND THROUGH. Macmillan, 1973.

Tana Hoban. BIG ONES, LITTLE ONES. Greenwillow, 1976.

John Graham. A CROWD OF COWS. Harcourt Brace, 1968

* Charles Keller. DAFFYNITIONS. Prentice-Hall, 1976.

Karla Kuskin. SQUARE AS A HOUSE. Harper, 1960.

* Bernice Hunt. THE WHATCHAMACALLIT BOOK. Putnam, 1976.

* Virgil Partch. VIP QUOTES. Windmill, 1975.

Ann and Paul Rand. SPARKLE AND SPIN. Harcourt, Brace, 1957.

* William Steig. C.D.B! Windmill, 1968.

* Suitable for children in grades 4-8, the other titles are for younger children.

Sampling Different Types of Books in Picturebook Format

Traditional Literature Myths, Fales, Folktales, Folksongs, and Nursery Rhymes).

THE NORTH WIND AND THE SUN illustrated by Brian Wildsmith, F. Watts, 1964.

ONCE A MOUSE A Fable Cut in Wood by Marcia Brown. Scribner's, 1961.

THE ELVES AND THE SHOEMAKER Pictures by Katrin Brandt. Follett, 1967.

THE THREE BEARS by Paul Galdone. Seabury, 1975.

THE GINGERBREAD BOY by Paul Galdone. Seabury, 1975.

THE COOL RIDE IN THE SKY - Told by Diane Wolkstein, Paul Galdone drew the pictures. A. Knopf, 1973.

THE THREE BILLY GOATS GRUFF by Paul Galdone, Seabury, 1973.

HUMPTY DUMPTY illustrated by Rodney Pepper. Viking, 1975.

HUSH, LITTLE BABY illustrated by Margon Zemach. Dutton,

OLD MOTHER HUBBARD AND HER DOG drawings by IB Spang Olsen. Coward, McCann, 1976.

THE FOX WENT OUT ON A CHILLY NIGHT by Peter Spier. Doubleday, 1961. Fold song for 4th and 5th graders.

Contemporary Realism

BREAD AND JAM FOR FRANCES by Russel Hoban. Harper, 1964.

THE AWFUL MESS by Anne Rockwell. Parents' Magazine Press, 1973.

THE ANTEATER NAMED AUTHOR by Bernard Waber. Houghton Mifflin, 1967.

DON'T YOU REMEMBER? by Lucille Clifton. Illustrated by E. Ness. Dutton, 1973.

OF COURSE POLLY CAN RIDE A BIKE by Astrid Lindgren. Follett, 1972.

WILLIAM'S DOLL by Charlotte Zolotow. Harper, 1972.

THE TERRIBLE THING THAT HAPPENED AT OUR HOUSE by Marge Blaine. Parent's Magazine Press, 1975.

TIME FOR JODY by Wendy Kesselman. Pictures by Gerald Dumas. Harper, 1975.

SHE COME BRINGING ME THAT LITTLE BABY GIRL by Eloise Greenfield.

IRA SLEEPS OVER by Bernard Waber. Houghton Mifflin, 1972.

Experience "Stories"

THIS IS BETSY by Gunilla Wolde. Random House, 1975.

TOMMY GOES TO THE DOCTOR by Gunilla Wolde. Houghton Mifflin, 1972.

GOOD MORNING HANNAH AND GOOD MORNING DANNY by Dale and Al Carson, Atheneum, 1972.

A DAY OFF by Toni Tobias. Pictures by Ray Cruz. Putnam, 1973.

HE'S MY BROTHER by Joe Lasker. Albert WHITMAN & Co., 1974.

Fantasy

THE THING IN DELORES' PIANO by Robert Tallon. Bobbs-Merril, 1970.

SIX RAGS APIECE by Marcia Newfield. Warne, 1976.

HAMBUG RABBIT by Lornia Balian. Abington, 1974.

Informational

MY DOCTOR by Harlow Rockwell. Macmillan, 1973.

STRAIGHT HAIR, CURLY HAIR by Augusta Goldin. T.Y. Crowell, 1976.

Concept

NUMBERS a book by John J. Reiss. Bradbury, 1971.

PAINT ALL KINDS OF NUMBERS by Arnold Spilka. Walck, 1963.

HOW A HOUSE HAPPENS by Jan Adkins. Walker, 1972.

100 HAMBURGERS - THE GETTING THIN BOOK by Mary Lynn Solot. Pictures by Paul Galdone. Lothrop, 1972.

OUR ANIMAL FRIENDS AT MAPLE HILL FARM by Alice & Martin Provensen. Random House, 1974.

Poetry

EVERETT ANDERSON'S YEAR by Lucille Clifton. Holt, Rinehart & Winston, 1974.

A LITTLE BOOK OF LITTLE BEASTS by Mary Ann Hoberman. Pictures by Peter Parnall. Simon and Schuster, 1973.

THE ROSE ON MY CAKE by Carla Ruskin. Harper and Rowe, 1964.

Sampling Different Types of Books
for Older Children

In Picture Book Format

TIN LIZZIE written and illustrated by Peter Spier. Doubleday, 1975.

THE DRAGON TAKES A WIFE by William Dean Myers. Illustrated by Ann Geifale. Bobbs-Merril, 1972.

MAURICE SENDAK'S REALLY ROSIE: Starring the Nutshell Kids. Scenario, Lyrics and Pictures by Maurice Sendak. Music by Carol King, Harper, 1975.

MERRY EVER AFTER written and illustrated by Joe Lasker. Viking, 1976.

WHAT EVER HAPPENED TO THE BAXTER PLACE? by Pat Ross. Pantheon, 1976.

TOOLCHEST by Jane Adkins. Walker, 1973.

ASCHANTI TO ZULU: African Traditions by Margaret Musgrove. Dial, 1976.

Folklore

THE BATTLE OF REUBEN ROBIN AND KITE UNCLE JOHN by Mary Calhoun. Morrow, 1978.

THE MERMAID AND THE WHALE by Georgess McHargue. Pictures by Robert Andrew Parker. Holt, Rinehart & Winston, 1973.

KIVIOK'S MAGIC JOURNEY - An Eskimo legend. Written and illustrated by James Houston. A Margaret K. McElderry Book. Athenum, 1973.

THE FIRE BRINGER - A Paiute Indian Legend. Retold by Margaret Hodges and illustrated by Peter Parnall. Little, Brown and Co., 1972.

THE DAY WHEN THE ANIMALS TALKED by William J. Faulkner. Follett, 1977.

Comtemporary Realism

Humor

THE HOBOKEN CHICKEN EMERGENCY by Marcus Pinkwater.
Prentice-Hall, 1977.

TALES OF A FOURTH GRADE NOTHING by Judy Blume. Dutton,
1972.

HOW TO EAT FRIED WORMS by Thomas Rockwill. Franklin
Watts, 1973.

FAST SAM, COOL CLYDE, AND STUFF by Walter Dean Myers.
Viking, 1975.

DEAR LOVEY HART, I AM DESPERATE by Ellen Conford.
Little, Brown, 1975.

Growing Panes

HOW I WENT SHOPPING AND WHAT I GOT by Eleanor Clymer,
Illustrated by Trina Shart Hyman. Holt, Rinehard and
Winston, 1972.

FELICIA THE CRITIC by Ellen Conford. Little, Brown, 1973.

MATT GARGAN'S BOY by Alfred Slote. Lippincott, 1975.

PETER AND VERONICA by Marilyn Sachs. Doubleday, 1969.

FROM THE MIXED-UP FILES OF MRS. BASIL E. FRANKWEILER.
Written and illustrated by E. L. Konigsburg. Atheneum,
1968.

SISTER by Eloise Greenfield. T.Y. Crowell, 1974.

SHAPE UP, BRUKE by Richard Shaw. Nelson, 1976.

Surprising Subject Matter

Death

ANNIE AND THE OLD ONE by Miska Miles. Illustrated by
Peter Parnall. Atlantic-Little, Brown, 1971.

A TASTE OF BLACKBERRIES by Doris Buchanan Smith. Illustrated by Charles Robinson. Crowell, 1973.

THERE ARE TWO KINDS OF TERRIBLE by Peggy Mann. Doubleday, 1977.

BRIDGE TO TERABITHIA by Katherine Preston. T.Y. Crowell, 1977.

BEAT THE TURTLE DRUM by Constance Green. Viking, 1976.

A SUMMER TO DIE by Lois Lowry. Houghton Mifflin, 1977.

MAY I CROSS YOUR GOLDEN RIVER? by Paige Dixon. Atheneum, 1975.

A FIGURE OF SPEECH A novel by Norma Fox Mazer. Delacorte, 1973.

Divorce

A BOOK FOR JODEN by Marcia Newfield. Atheneum, 1975.

A MONTH OF SUNDAYS by Rose Blue. Franklin Watts, 1972.

MY DAD LIVES IN A DOWNTOWN HOTEL by Peggy Mann. Doubleday, 1972.

IT'S NOT THE END OF THE WORLD by Judy Blume. Bradbury Press, 1972.

Feminism

PHILLIP HALL LIKES ME. I RECKON MAYBE by Betty Green. Dial, 1974.

MATT GARGAN'S BOY by Alfred Slote. Lippincott, 1975.

KICK A STONE HOME by Doris Buchanan Smith. T.Y. Crowell, 1974.

THE REAL ME by Betty Miles. Knopf, 1974.

FIRST SREVE by Mary Towne. Drawings by Ruth Sanderson. Atheneum, 1976.

Sexuality

CONFESSIONS OF AN ONLY CHILD by Norma Klein. Patheon, 1974.

ARE YOU THERE GOD? IT'S ME MARGARET by Judy Blume.
Bradbury Press, 1970.

MOM THE WOLF MAN AND ME by Norma Klein. A novel that
speaks to today. Pantheon, 1972.

I'LL GET THERE. IT BETTER BE WORTH THE TRIP by John
Donovan. Harper, 1969.

A NICE ITALIAN GIRL by Elizabeth Cristman. Dodd Mead,
1976.

GAY: WHAT YOU SHOULD KNOW ABOUT HOMOSEXUALITY by Morton
Hunt. Farrar/Strauss, 1977.

Fantasy and Science Fiction

DAR TELLUM: STRANGER FROM A DISTANT PLANET by James
E. Berry. Illustrated by Enrico Schull. Walker and
Co., 1973.

THE PREPOSTEROUS ADVENTURES OF SWIMMER by Alexander Key.
Westminister, 1973.

CHILDREN OF MORROW by H. M. Hoover. Four Winds Press,
1973.

THE DARK IS RISING by Susan Cooper. Illustrations by
Alan E. Cober. A Margaret K. McElderry Book. Athenum,
1973.

THE MISSING PERSON'S LEAGE by Frank Bonham. Dutton,
1976.

CRISIS ON CONSHELF TEN by Monica Lewis. Atheneum, 1977.

Historical Fiction

WHAT'S THE BIG IDEA, BEN FRANKLIN? by Jean Fritz.
Illustrated by Margot Tomes. Coward, McCann & Geoghe-
gan, 1976.

POOR RICHARD IN FRANCE by F. N. Monjo. Pictures by
Brinton Turkle. Holt, Rinehart, and Winston, 1973.

THE STONES by Janet Hickman. Illustrated by Richard
Cuffari. Macmillan, 1976.

SAN DOMINGO: THE MEDICINE HAT STALLION by Marguerite Henry. Rand McNally, 1972.

NAVAJO SLAVE by Lynne Gessner. Harvey House, 1976.

TO SPOIL THE SUN by Joyce Rockwood. Holt, Rinehart, and Winston, 1976.

Biography

THE CURTAIN RISES - The Story of Ossie Davis by Lewis Funke. Grosset and Dunlap, 1971.

FROM LEW ALCINDOR TO KAREEM ABDUL JABBAR by James Haskins. Illustrated with photographs. Lothrop, Lee, and Shepard Co., 1972.

MARIA TALLCHIEF by Tobi Tobias. Illustrated by Michael Hampshire. Crowell, 1970.

Informational Books

JUDO: A Gentle Beginning by Jeannette Bruce. Illustrated by Don Madden. Crowell, 1976.

THE CODE AND CIPHER BOOK by Jane Sarnoff and Reynold Ruffins. Scribner's, 1975.

FRACTIONS ARE PARTS OF THINGS - A Young Math Book by J. Richard Dennis. Illustrated by Donal Crews. T. Y. Crowell, 1971.

THE METRIC SYSTEM -MEASURE FOR ALL MANKIND by Frank Ross, Jr. Illustrated by Robert Galster. S. G. Phillips, 1974.

FROM IDEA INTO HOUSE by Rolf Myller. Atheneum, 1974.

AND THEN THERE WERE NONE - America's vanishing wildlife by Nina Leen, with commentary by Joseph A. Davis. Holt, 1973.

WATCHING THE NEW BABY by Joan Samson. Photographs by Gary Gladstone. Atheneum, 1974.

APPENDIX B

WHAT'S NEW AND NOT SO NEW IN

CHILDREN'S LITERATURE

Alike. AT MARY BLOOM'S. New York: Wm. Morrow, 1973.

Amery, Heather and Angela Littler. FUNCRAFT BOOK OF MAGNETS & BATTERIES. New York, Scholastic, 1976.

Arkhurst, Joyce Cooper. THE ADVENTURES OF SPIDER. New York: Scholastic, 1964.

Arkin, Alan. THE LEMMING CONDITION. New York: Bantam, 1977.

Babbit, Natalie. THE EYES OF THE AMARYLLIS. New York: Farrar, Straus & Giroux, 1977.

Baylor, Byrd. EVERYBODY NEEDS A ROCK. New York; Scribner, 1974.

Baylor, Byrd. GUESS WHO MY FAVORITE PERSON IS. New York: Scribner & Sons, 1975.

Burningham, John. WOULD YOU RATHER . . . New York: Thomas Y. Crowell, 1978.

Carini, Edward. TAKE ANOTHER LOOK. Englewood Cliffs, New Jersey: Prentice-Hall, 1970.

Carle, Eric. THE GROUCHY LADYBUG. New York: Thomas Y. Crowell, 1977.

Carle, Eric. THE SECRET BIRTHDAY MESSAGE. New York: Thomas Y. Crowell, 1972.

Carle, Eric. THE VERY HUNGRY CATEPILLER. New York: Scholastic.

Chase, Catherine (retold by). THE NIGHTINGALE AND THE FOOL. New York: Dandelion Press, 1979.

Chew, Ruth. EARTHSTAR MAGIC. New York: Scholastic, 1979.

Cleaver, Vera and Bill. DELPHA GREEN & CO. New York: J.B. Lippincott, 1977.

Conford, Ellen. ME AND THE TERRIBLE TWO. New York: Simon & Schuster, 1974.

Craig, M. Jean (retold by). THE DONKEY PRINCE. New York: Doubleday & Co., 1977.

Cunningham, Julia. COME TO THE EDGE. New York: Avon Books, 1977.

dePaola, Tomie. CHARLIE NEEDS A CLOAK. New York: Scholastic, 1973.

dePaola, Tomie. THE CLOWN OF GOD. New York: Harcourt Brace Jovanovich, 1978.

dePaola, Tomie. THE CLOUD BOOK. New York: Scholastic, 1975.

dePaola, Tomie. NANA UPSTAIRS AND NANA DOWNSTAIRS. New York: G. P. Putnam's Sons, 1973.

dePaola, Tomie. OLIVER BUTTON IS A SISSY. Harcourt Brace Jovanovich, 1979.

dePaola, Tomie. THE POPCORN BOOK. New York: Scholastic, 1978.

dePaola, Tomie. STREGA NONA. Englewood Cliffs, New Jersey: Prentice-Hall, 1975.

dePaola, Tomie. WHEN EVERYONE WAS FAST ASLEEP. New York: Penguin Books, 1979.

DeVries, John. IN MY BACKYARD. Ontario, Canada: Scholastic-Tab Publications, 1975.

Dunning, Stephen; Lueders, E.; Smith, H. (Compilers). SOME HAYSTACKS DON'T EVEN HAVE ANY NEEDLES. Chicago: Scott, Foresman, 1969.

Edwards, Julie. MANDY. New York: Bantam, 1973.

Emberley, Ed. ED EMBERLEY'S ABC. Boston: Little, Brown & Co., 1978.

Emberley, Barbara (adapted by). ONE WIDE RIVER TO CROSS. New York: Scholastic, 1966.

Froman, Robert. HOT AND COLD AND IN BETWEEN. New York: Young Reader's Press, 1971.

Galdone, Joanna. THE TAILYPO. New York: Seabury Press, 1977.

George, Jean Craighead. THE SUMMER OF THE FALCON. New York: Harper & Rowe, 1962.

Goodal, John S. CREEPY CASTLE. Atheneum, 1974.

Goodal, John S. THE STORY OF AN ENGLISH VILLAGE. New York: Atheneum, 1978.

Greene, Constance C. BEAT THE TURTLE DRUM. New York: Viking, 1976.

Hickman, Janet. THE STONES. New York: Macmillan, 1976.

Hickman, Janet. VALLEY OF THE SHADOW. New York: Macmillan, 1974.

Hickman, Janet. ZOAR BLUE. New York: Macmillan, 1978.

Hoban, Tana. WHERE IS IT? New York: Windmill Books, 1978.

Hoberman, Mary Ann. A HOUSE IS A HOUSE FOR ME. New York: Viking Press, 1978.

Hopkins, Lee Bennet and Misha Arenstein (editors). POTATO CHIPS AND A SLICE OF MOON. New York: Scholastic, 1976.

Jonson, George (retold by). FAVORITE TALES OF MONSTERS AND TROLLS. New York: Random House, 1977.

Keats, Ezra Jack. THE TRIP. New York: Scholastic Books, 1978.

Kohn, Bernice. THE ORGANIC LIVING BOOK. New York: Viking, 1973.

Konigsburg, E.L. FATHER'S ARCANE DAUGHTER. New York: Atheneum, 1976.

Krasilovsky, Phyllis. THE VERY LITTLE GIRL. New York: Doubleday & Co., 1953.

Le Cain, Errol (illustrator). THORN ROSE. New York: Penguin Books, 1977.

L'Engle, Madeleine. A SWIFTLY TILTING PLANET. New York: Farrar, Straus & Giroux, 1978.

LeGuin, Ursula K. VERY FAR AWAY FROM ANYWHERE ELSE. New York: Bantam, 1978.

Lipsyte, Robert. ONE FAT SUMMER. New York: Harper & Rowe, 1977.

Littledale, Freya (retold by). THE SNOW CHILD. New York: Scholastic, 1978.

Mahy, Margaret. ULTRA-VIOLET CATASTROPHE. New York: Parent's Magazine, 1975.

Mayer, Mercer. HICCUPS. New York: Dial Press, 1976.

Mayer, Mercer. OOPS. New York: Dial Press, 1977.

Miller, Donna. EGG CARTON CRITTERS. New York: Scholastic, 1978.

McDermott, Beverly Brodsky. THE CRYSTAL APPLE. New York: Viking Press, 1974.

McGovern, Ann. BLACK IS BEAUTIFUL. New York: Scholastic, 1970.

Parish, Peggy. TEACH US, AMELIA BEDELIA. New York: Scholastic, 1977.

Paterson, Katherine. BRIDGE TO TERABITHIA. New York: Thomas Y. Crowell, 1977.

Prelutsky, Jack. CIRCUS. New York: Collier Books, 1974.

Preston, Edna Mitchell. SQUAWK TO THE MOON, LITTLE GOOSE. New York: Viking Press, 1974.

Raskin, Ellen. THE WESTING GAME. New York. E.P. Dutton, 1978.

Raynor, Mary. MR. & MRS. PIG'S EVENING OUT. New York: Atheneum, 1976.

Rockwell, Thomas. HOW TO EAT FRIED WORMS. New York: Dell, 1973.

Rose, Anne. AKIMBA AND THE MAGIC CROW. New York: Scholastic, 1976.

Ross, Jessica. MS. KLONDIKE. New York: Viking Press, 1977.

Seuling, Barbara. THE TEENY TINE WOMAN. New York: Penguin, 1976.

Shulevitz, Uri. DAWN. New York: Farrar, Straus & Giroux, 1974..

Simon, Seymour. LOOK TO THE NIGHT SKY. New York: Puffin, 1977.

Simon, Seymour. THE PAPER AIRPLANE BOOK. New York: Viking Press, 1971.

Simon, Seymour. PETS IN A JAR. New York: Viking Press, 1975.

Singer, Isaac Bashevis. WHY NOAH CHOSE THE DOVE. New York: Farrar, Straus & Giroux, 1976.

Slote, Alfred. MY FATHER, THE COACH. New York: J.B. Lippincott, 1972.

Spier, Peter (illustrator). THE ERIE CANAL. New York: Doubleday, 1970.

Steig, William. THE AMAZING BONE. New York: Farrar, Straus & Giroux, 1976.

Steig, William. AMOS AND BORIS. New York: Farrar, Straus & Giroux, 1971.

Steig, William. CALEB AND KATE. New York: Scholastic, 1977.

Steig, William. FATHER PALMER'S WAGON RIDE. New York: Farrar, Straus & Giroux, 1974.

Steig, William. TIFFKY DOOFKY. New York: Farrar, Straus & Giroux, 1978.

Stevenson, James. COULD BE WORSE! New York: Penguin Books, 1977.

Stewig, John. SENDING MESSAGES. Boston: Houghton Mifflin, 1978.

Stobbs, William (illustrator). JOHNY-CAKE. New York: Viking Press, 1972.

Stolz, Mary. CAT IN THE MIRROR. New York: Harper & Row, 1975.

Tallon, Robert. ZOOPHABETS. New York: Scholastic, 1979.

Tarcov, Edith H. (retold by). THE FROG PRINCE. New York: Scholastic, 1974.

Turkle, Brinton. IT'S ONLY ARNOLD. New York: The Viking Press, 1973.

Viorst, Judith. ALEXANDER WHO USED TO BE RICH LAST SUNDAY. New York: Atheneum, 1978.

Ward, Lynd. THE SILVER PONEY. Boston: Houghton Mifflin, 1973.

Weisman, Joan. HOW OLD IS OLD? Detroit, Michigan: Program Resources, Inc., 1978.

LITERATURE FOR PRIMARY GRADES

A TREE FOR PETER* Kate Serendy

THE LEMONADE TRICK* Scott Corbett

THE HATEFUL PLATEFUL TRICK* Scott Corbett

THE CASE OF THE FUGITIVE FIREBUG* Scott Corbett

THE TRUMPET OF THE SWAN* E.B. White

TALES OF A FOURTH GRADE NOTHING Judy Blume

OTHERWISE KNOWN AS SHEILA THE GREAT* Judy Blume

LITTLE EDDIE* Carolyn Haywood

MY FRIEND CHARLIE James Flora

CHICKEN SOUP WITH RICE Maurice Sendak

AMELIA BEDELIA BOOKS Peggy Parish

CLIFFORD BOOKS Norman Bridwell

DID YOU CARRY THE FLAG TODAY, CHARLIE? Rebecca Caudill

TIKKI TIKKI TEABO Arlene Nosel

RAMONA AND HER FATHER Beverly Cleary

MISHSASH Molly Cone

THE BOXCAR CHILDREN Gertrude Warner

MRS. PIGGLE WIGGLE Betsy McDonald

OWLS IN THE FAMILY Fawley Mowat

STEVE AND THE SEVEN ORPHANS Mirian Maron

GETTING SOMETHING ON MAGGIE MARMELSTEIN* Marjorie
Sharnel

Seasonal Books:

WHICH WITCH   Robert Lasson

A CERTAIN SMALL SHEPARD   Rebecca Caudil

THE STORY OF HOLLY AND IVY   Rumer Godden

LOTTIE'S VALENTINE

ALEXANDER AND THE TERRIBLE, HORRIBLE, NO GOOD, VERY
BAD DAY   Judith Viorst

BIBLIOGRAPHY OF PREDICTABLE BOOKS

Alain. ONE TWO THREE GOING TO SEA. New York: Scholastic Book Services, 1964.

Aliki. MY FIVE SENSES. New York: Thomas Y. Crowell Co., 1962.

Balian, Lorna. WHERE IN THE WORLD IS HENRY? Scarsdale, New York: Bradbury Press, 1972.

Barchas, Sarah E. I WAS WALKING DOWN THE ROAD. New York: Scholastic Book Services, 1975. Illustrated by Jack Kent.

Baum, Arline and Joseph. ONE BRIGHT MONDAY MORNING. New York: Random House, 1962.

Becker, John. SEVEN LITTLE RABBITS. New York: Scholastic Book Services, 1973. Illustrated by Barbara Cooney.

Beckman, Kaj. LISA CANNOT SLEEP. New York: Franklin Watts, 1969. Ill. by Per Beckman.

Boone, Rose and Mills, Alan. I KNOW AN OLD LADY. New York: Rand McNally. Ill. by Abner Graboff.

Brand, Oscar. WHEN I FIRST CAME TO THIS LAND, New York: Putnam's Sons, 1974. Ill. by Doria Burn.

Brandenburg, Franz. A ROBBER, A ROBBER. New York: Greenwillow Books, 1976. Ill. by Aliki.

Brandenburg, Franz. I ONCE KNEW A MAN. New York: Macmillan, 1970. Ill. by Aliki.

Brooke, L. Leslie. JONNY CROW'S GARDEN. New York: Frederick Warne & Co., 1903.

Brown, Marcia. (Ill.) THE THREE BILLY GOATS GRUFF. New York: Harcourt, Brace and World, 1975.

Brown, Margaret Wise. FOUR FUR FEET. New York: William R. Scott, undated. Ill. by Remy Charlip.

Brown, Margaret Wise. GOODNIGHT MOON. New York: Harper & Row, 1947. Ill. by Clement Hurd.

Brown, Margaret Wise. WHERE HAVE YOU BEEN? New York: Scholastic Book Services, 1952. Ill. by Barbara Cooney.

Carle, Eric. THE VERY HUNGRY CATERPILLAR. Cleveland, Ohio: Collins World, No date.

Charlip, Remy. FORTUNATELY. New York: Parents' Magazine Press, 1964.

_____. WHAT GOOD LUCK! WHAT BAD LUCK! New York: Scholastic Book Services, 1969.

deRegniers, Beartice Schenk. CATCH A LITTLE FOX. New York: Seabury Press, 1970. Ill. by Brinton Turkle.

_____. MAY I BRING A FRIEND? New York: Atheneum, 1972, Ill. by Beni Montressor.

_____. THE DAY EVERYBODY CRIED. New York: The Viking Press, 1967. Ill. by Nonny Hogrogian.

_____. WILLY O'DWYER JUMPED IN THE FIRE. New York: Atheneum, 1968. Ill. by Beni Montressro.

_____. HOW JOE THE BEAR AND SAM THE MOUSE GOT TOGETHER. New York: Parents' Magazine Press, 1965.

_____. THE LITTLE BOOK. New York: Henry Z. Walck, 1961.

Domanska, Janina. DIN,DAN, DON, IT'S CHRISTMAS. New York: Greenwillow Books, 1975.

_____. IF ALL THE SEAS WERE ONE SEA. New York: Macmillan, 1971.

Einsel, Walter. DID YOU EVER SEE? New York: Scholastic Book Services, 1962.

Emberly, Barbara & Ed. ONE WIDE RIVER TO CROSS. Englewood Cliffs, N.J., Prentice-Hall, 1966.

_____. DRUMMER HOFF. Englewood Cliffs, N.J.: Prentice-Hall, 1967.

Emberly, Ed. KLIPPITY KLOP. Boston: Little Brown & Co., 1974.

Ets, Mary Hall. PLAY WITH ME. New York: Viking Press, 1955.

Flack, Marjorie. ASK MR. BEAR. New York: Macmillan, 1932.

Galdone, Paul. HENNY PENNY. New York: Scholastic Book Services, 1968.

_____. THE LITTLE RED HEN. New York: Scholastic Book Services, 1973.

_____. THE THREE BEARS. New York: Scholastic Book Services, 1972.

_____. THE THREE BILLY GOATS GRUFF. New York: Seabury Press, 1970.

_____. THE THREE LITTLE PIGS. New York: Seabury Press, 1970.

Graham, John. A CROWD OF COWS. New York: Scholastic Book Services, 1968. Ill. by Foedor Rojankovsky.

_____. I LOVE YOU, MOUSE. New York: Harcourt Brace Jovanovich, 1976. Ill. by Tomie dePaola.

Greenberg, Polly. OH LORD, I WISH I WAS A BUZZARD. New York: Macmillan, 1968. Ill. by Aliki.

Hoffman, Hilde. THE GREEN GRASS GROWS ALL AROUND. New York: Macmillan, 1968.

Hogrogian, Nonny. ONE FINE DAY. New York: Macmillan, 1971.

Hutchins, Pat. GOOD-NIGHT OWL. New York: Macmillan, 1972.

_____. THE SURPRISE PARTY. New York: Collier Books, 1969.

_____. ROSIE'S WALK. New York: Macmillan, 1968.

Hutchins, Pat. TITCH. New York. Collier Books, 1971.

Keats, Ezra Jack. OVER IN THE MEADOW. New York: Scholastic Book Services, 1971.

Kent, Jack. THE FAT CAT. New York: Scholastic Book Services, 1971.

Klein, Lenore. BRAVE DANIEL. New York: Scholastic Book Services, 1958. Ill. by John Fischetti.

Kraus, Robert. WHOSE MOUSE ARE YOU? New York:
Colier Books, 1970.

Kraus, Ruth. BEARS. New York: Scholastic Book Services, 1948. Ill. by Phyllis Rowland. Also New York:
Harper & Row, 1948.

_____. WHAT A FINE DAY FOR . . . New York:
Parents' Magazine Press, 1967. Ill. by Remy Charlip,
music Al Carmines.

_____. THE HAPPY DAY. New York: Harper & Row,
1949. I.. by Marc Simont.

Langstaff, John. THE GOLDEN VANITY. New York:
Harcourt Brace Jovanovich, 1972. Ill. by David Gentle-
man.

_____. OH, A-HUNTING WE WILL GO. New York:
Atheneum, 1974. Ill. by Nancy Winslow Parker.

_____. OVER IN THE MEADOW. New York: Harcourt
Brace and World, 1957. Ill. by Feodor Rojandovsky.

Langstaff, John. SOLDIER, SOLDIER, WON'T YOU MARRY ME?
Garden City, N.Y.: Doubleday and co., 1972. Ill. by
Anita Lobel.

Langstaff, John. GATHER MY GOLD TOGETHER: FOUR SONGS
FOR FOUR SEASONS. Garden City, N.Y.: Doubleday & Co.,
1971. Ill. by Julia Noonan.

Lexau, Joan. CROCODILE AND HEN. New York: Harper &
Row, 1969. Ill. by Joan Sandlin.

Lobel, Anita. KING ROOSTER, QUEEN HEN. New York:
Greenwillow Books, 1975.

Mack, Stan. 10 BEARS IN MY BED. New York: Pantheon
Books, 1974.

Mayer, Mercer. IF I HAD. . . New York: Dial Press,
1968.

_____. JUST FOR YOU. New York: Golden Press, 1975.

McGovern, Ann. TOO MUCH NOISE. New York: Scholastic
Book Service, 1967. Ill. by Simms Taback.

Memling, Carl. TEN LITTLE INDIANS. Racine, Wisconsin:
    Golden Press, 1961. Ill. by Feodor Rojankovsky.

Merriam, Eve. DO YOU WANT TO SEE SOMETHING? New
York: Scholastic Book Services, 1965. Ill. by Abner
Graboff.

Moffet, Martha. A FLOWER POT IS NOT A HAT. New York:
E. P. Dutton & Co., 1972. Ill. by Susan Perl.

Patrick, Gloria. A BUG IN A JUG AND OTHER FUNNY RHYMES.
New York: Scholastic Book Services, 1970. Ill. by Joan
Hanson.

Peppe, Rodney. (Ill.) THE HOUSE THAT JACK BUILT. New
York: Delacorte Press, 1970. (Another version by
Seymour Chwast, Random House).

Quackenbush, Robert. SHE'LL BE COMIN' ROUND THE MOUN-
TAIN. New York: J. B. Lippincott, 1973.

_____. TOO MANY LOLLIPOPS. New York: Scholastic
Book Services, 1975.

Rokoff, Sandra. HERE IS A CAT. Singapore: Hallmark
Children's Editions, undated. Ill. by Michael Rokoff.

Scheer, Julian and Bilwck, Marvin. RAIN MAKES APPLE-
SAUCE. New York: Holiday House, 1964.

_____. UPSIDE DOWN HAY. New York: Holliday House,
1968. Ill. by Kelly Oechsli.

Sendak. Maurice. WHERE THE WILD THINGS ARE. New York:
Scholastic Book Services, 1963.

Shaw, Charles B. IT LOOKED LIKE SPILT MILK. New York:
Harper & Row, 1947.

Shulevitz, Uri. ONE MONDAY MORNING. New York: Charles
Scribner's Sons, 1967.

Skaar, Grace. WHAT DO THE ANIMALS SAY? New York:
Scholastic Book Services, 1972.

Spier, Peter. THE FOX WENT OUT ON A CHILLY NIGHT.
Garden City, N.Y.: Doubleday & Co., 1961.

Stover, Joann. IF EVERYBODY DID. New York: David
McKay, 1960.

Tolstoy, Alexei. THE GREAT BIG ENORMOUS TURNIP. New
York: Franklin Watts, 1968. Ill. by Helen Oxenbury.

Welber, Robert. GOODBYE, HELLO. New York: Pantheon Books, 1974. Ill. by Cyndy Szekeres.

Wondriska, William. ALL THE ANIMALS WERE ANGRY. New York: Holt, Rinehart and Winston, 1970.

Zaid, Barry. Chicken Little. New York: Random House, no date.

Zolotow, Charlotte. DO YOU KNOW WHAT I'LL DO? New York: Harper & Row, 1958.

_____. IT'S NOT FAIR. New York: Random House, 1976. Ill. by William Pene duBois.

Predictable Stories Found in Instructional Materials

CATS AND KITTENS. Glenview, Ill.: Scott Foresman & Co., 1971 Level 2.

Domjan, Joseph. I WENT TO THE MARKET. New York: Holt, Rinehart & Winston, 1970 (Instant Reader, Bill Martin, Jr.).

HEAD TO FEET. Glenview, Ill.: Scott Foresman, 1971. Ill. by John Miles, Level 2.

Hollander, Shiela K. SAMMY'S SUPPER. Glenview, ILL.: Scott Foresman & Co., 1971. Ill. Level 3.

_____. BABY MONKEY. Glenview, Ill.: Scott Foresman & Co., 1971. Ill. by Cecile Webster. Level 4.

THE LION'S TAIL. Glenview, Ill. Scott Foresman, 1971. Ill. by Joe Szegy. Level 2.

Madden, Don. (Ill.) THE THREE LITTLE PIGS. Glenview, Ill.: Scott Foresman, 1971. Level 3.

THE MAN AND THE DONKEY. Glenview, Ill.: Scott Foresman, 1971, by Mae Gerhard.

Martin, Bill, Jr. BROWN BEAR, BROWN BEAR, WHAT DO YOU SEE? New York: Holt, Rinehart & Winston, 1970. Ill. by Eric Carle. (Instant Reader).

_____. A GHOST STORY. New York: Holt, Rinehart & Winston, 1970. Ill. by Eric Carle. (Instant Reader).

Martin, Bill, Jr. THE HAUNTED HOUSE. New York: Holt,
Rinehart & Winston, 1970. Ill. by Peter Lippman.
(Instant Reader).

_____. TATTY MAE AND CATTY MAE. New York: Holt,
Rinehart & Winston, 1970. Ill. by Aldren A. Watson
(Instant Reader).

_____. (Adapted) TEN LITTLE SQUIRRELS. New York:
Holt, Rinehart & Winston, 1970. Ill. by Bernard
Martin (Instant Reader).

_____. WELCOME HOME, HENRY. New York: Holt,
Rinehart & Winston. Ill. by Emanuele Luzzati (Instant
Reader).

_____. WHEN IT RAINS . . . IT RAINS. New York:
Holt, Rinehart & Winston, 1970. Ill. by Emanuele
Luzzati (Instant Reader).

THE MISSING NECKLACE. Glenview, Ill.: Scott Foresman,
1971. Ill. by Phoebe Moore. Level 3.

BOOKS KIDS LOVE

FOR WHOLE LANGUAGE ACTIVITIES

Benton, Robert. DON'T EVER WISH FOR A 7-FOOT BEAR. Alfred A. Knopf, 1972.

Berenstain, Stan and Jan. THE SPOOKY OLD TREE. Random House, 1978.

Carle, Eric. THE VERY HUNGRY CATERPILLAR. Collins/World.

Cosgrove, Stephen. LEO THE LION. Price/Stern/Sloan, 1979.

Deck, Mary Celeste. THE BOOK ABOUT KITTENS. Price/Stern/Sloan, 1979.

DeRegniers, Beatrice Schank. MAY I BRING A FRIEND? Atheneum, 1964.

Gynne, Fred. THE KING WHO RAINED. Windmill Books, 1970.

Hamberger, John. A SLEEPLESS DAY. Scholastic, 1975. (Wordless Book).

Hanson, Joan. I'M GOING TO RUN AWAY. Platt and Munk, 1977.

Hazen, Barbara Shook. THE GORILLA DID IT. Atheneum, 1974.

Heide, Florence Parry. SOME THINGS ARE SCARY. Scholastics, 1969.

_____. THAT'S WHAT FRIENDS ARE FOR. Scholastic, 1968.

Kellog, Steven. CAN I KEEP HIM? Dial, 1971.

_____. THE ISLAND OF SKOG. Dial, 1973.

_____. THE MYSTERIOUS TADPOLE. Dial, 1977.

_____. WON'T SOMEBODY PLAY WITH ME? Dial, 1972.

Klein, Suzanne. AN ELEPHANT IN MY BED. Follet, 1974.

Kwitz, Mary De Ball. LITTLE CHICK'S STORY. Scholastic, 1978.

Martin, Bill. INSTANT READERS. Holt, Rinehart and Winston, Inc.

Mayer, Mercer. FROG GOES TO DINNER. Dial, 1974 (Wordless Book).

_____. IF I HAD . . . Dial, 1968.

_____. JUST FOR YOU. Golden Press, 1975.

_____. OOPS. Dial, 1977 (Wordless Book).

Mayer, Mercer and Mayer, Marianna. A BOY, A DOG, A FROG, AND A FRIEND. Dial (Wordless Book).

_____. ONE FROG TOO MANY. Dial (Wordless Book).

Mack, Stan. 10 BEARS IN MY BED. Pantheon Books, 1974.

O'Neill, Mary. HAILSTONES AND HALIBUT BONES. Doubleday, 1961.

Sendak, Maurice. CHICKEN SOUP WITH RICE. Scholastic, 1962. (Has an accompanying record that is terrific).

Silverstein, Stan. WHERE THE SIDEWALK ENDS. Harper and Row, 1974.

Stamaty, Mark Alan. WHERE'S MY HIPPOPOTAMUS? Dial, 1977.

Viorst, Judith. ALEXANDER AND THE TERRIBLE, HORRIBLE, NO GOOD, VERY BAD DAY. Atheneum, 1973.

_____. SUNDAY MORNING. Atheneum, 1968.

_____. THE TENTH GOOD THING ABOUT BARNEY. Atheneum, 1971.

APPENDIX F

LIST I - PATTERN BOOKS

Anglund, Joan Walsh, A FRIEND IS SOMEONE WHO LIKES YOU.

Blossom, Budney, A KISS IS ROUND, WILSON.

Bonne, Lady Rose, I KNOW AN OLD LADY.

Brod, Ruth & Stan, HOW WOULD YOU ACT?

Barry, Katharina, A BUG IS TO HUG, Harcourt.

Browne, Margaret Wise, WHERE HAVE YOU BEEN? Harper.

Cameron, Polly, "I CAN'T" SAID THE ANT, Scholastic, 1969.

Charlip, Remy, WHAT GOOD LUCK! WHAT BAD LUCK!, Scholastic, 1970.

DeRegniers, Beatrice Schenk, MAY I BRING A FRIEND? Atheneum.

Einsel, Walter, DID YOU EVER SEE? Scholastic.

Emberly, Barbara, DRUMMER HOFF, Prentice.

Emberly, Ed., THE WING ON A FLEA, Little.

Hampson, Denman, WHAT IS THAT?

Heide, Florence, SOME THINGS ARE SCARY, Scholastic.

Heilbtoner, Joan, THIS IS THE HOUSE WHERE JACK LIVES, Harper.

Joslin, Susyle, WHAT DO YOU SAY, DEAR? Scholastic.

Karp, Laura, OPPOSITES, World Publishing.

Klein, Lenore, BRAVE DANIEL, Scholastic.

Krauss, Ruth, A HOLE IS TO DIG, Harper.

Krauss, Ruth, MAMA, I WISH I WAS SNOW, Scholastic.

Krauss, Ruth and Johnson, Crockett, IS THIS YOU? Scholastic.

Longman, Harold, WOULD YOU PUT YOUR MONEY IN A SAND BANK?

MacPherson, Elizabeth, A TALE OF TAILS.

Martin, Bill Jr., BROWN BEAR, BROWN BEAR, Holt.

_____. DAVID WAS MAD, Holt.

_____. INSTANT READERS SERIES, Holt.

_____. OWL SERIES, Holt.

_____. SOUNDS OF LANGUAGE SERIES, Holt.

_____. TEN LITTLE CATERPILLARS, Holt.

Memling, Carl, HI, ALL YOU RABBITS, Parents.

O'Neil, Mary, HAILSTONES AND HALIBUT BONES, Scholastic.

Raskin, Ellen, NOTHING EVER HAPPENS ON MY BLOCK, Atheneum.

Schultz, Charles, "HAPPINESS IS . . . " Determined Productions.

_____. "SECURITY IS . . . " Determined Productions.

_____. "LOVE IS . . . " Determined Productions.

Sendak, Maurice, CHICKEN SOUP WITH RICE, Scholastic.

Seuss, Dr. ONE FISH, TWO FISH, Random House.

Sullivan, Joan, ROUND IS A PANCAKE, Holt.

Udry, Janice, A TREE IS NICE, Harper.

Walter, Barbara, I PACKED MY TRUNK, Follett.

Wright, H. R., A MAKER OF BONES, Holt.

LIST II: STORY STARTER BOOKS

DeRegniers, Beatrice & Schenk, Irene, SOMETHING SPECIAL, Harcourt, Collection of Rhymes.

Fortunata, CATCH A LITTLE FOX, Lucky Books.

Holland, Ruth, A BAD DAY, David McKay, 1964.

Krauss, Robert, WHOSE MOUSE ARE YOU? Macmillan, 1970.

Lansing, Jane K., ALPHABET ZOO.

Lenski, Louis, I LIKE WINTER, Walck.

Rison, Old, I AM A BUNNY.

Kaufman, Joe, BIG AND LITTLE, Golden, 1968.

Hampson, Deman, WHAT IS THAT?

Simon, Mina & Howard, IF YOU WERE AN EEL, HOW WOULD YOU
FEEL? Follett, 1963.

Slepian, Jan & Seidler, Ann, THE HUNGRY THING, Follett,
1967.

Smith, Dorothy Hall, THE BIG LITTLE BOOK, Harper.

Rees, Ennis, GILLYGALOOS AND GALLY WHOPPERS, Abelard
Schuman, 1969.

Hoban, Russ, NOTHING TO DO.

Jacobs, Leland & Johnson, Elinor, SEE SAW, I WISH I WERE
A RABBIT, Chas. Merrill.

Raskin, Ellen, NOTHING EVER HAPPENS ON MY BLOCK.

Longman, Harold, WATCH OUT! HOW TO BE SAFE AND NOT SORRY,
Parents.

Tresselt, Alvin, WHITE SNOW, BRIGHT SNOW, Lathrup.

_____. A THOUSAND LIGHTS AND FIREFLIES, Parents.

Buton, Virginia Lee, THE LITTLE HOUSE, Houghton.

Emberly, Barbara (adapted by). ONE WIDE RIVER TO CROSS.
Prentice.

Gaeddert, Lou Ann, NOISY NANCY NORRIS, Doubleday.

Lionni, Leo, INCH BY INCH, Astor-Honor.

Domanska, Janina, IF ALL THE SEAS WERE ONE SEA.
Macmillan.

APPENDIX G

BIBLIOGRAPHY OF WORDLESS BOOKS

Alexander, Martha. BOBO'S DREAM. New York: Dial Press, 1970.

_____. OUT, OUT, OUT. New York: Dial Press, 1970.

Alika. GO TELL AUNT RHODY. New York: Parents' Magazine Press, 1969.

Anderson, Laurie. THE PACKAGE. Indianapolis, Inc.: Bobbs-Merrill, 1977.

Anno, Mitsumasa. ANNO'S COUNTING BOOK. Cleveland: Collins-World, 1978.

_____. ANNO'S JOURNEY. Cleveland: Collins-World, 1978.

_____. DR. ANNO'S MAGICAL MIDNIGHT CIRCUS. New York: John Weatherhill, 1972.

_____. TOPSEY TURVIES. New York: John Weatherhill, 1970,

Ardizzone, Edward. THE WRONG SIDE OF THE BED. New York: Doubleday Publishing, 1970.

Arnosky, Jim. MUD TIME AND MORE. Reading, Mass.: Addison-Wesley, 1978.

Arguego, Jose. LOOK WHAT I CAN DO. New York: Charles Scribner's Sons, 1971.

Asch, Frank. THE BLUE BALLOON. New York: McGraw-Hill Co., 1972.

_____. IN THE EYE OF THE TEDDY. New York: McGraw-Hill Co., 1972.

Barton, Byron. ELEPHANT. New York: Seabury, 1971.

Baum, Will. BIRDS OF A FEATHER. Reading, Mass.: Addison-Wesley, 1969.

Billout, Guy. THE NUMBER 24. New York: Dial Press, 1973.

601

Bollinger-Savelli, Antinella. THE KNITTED CAT.
New York: Macmillan, 1972.

Briggs, Raymond. THE SNOWMAN. New York: Random
House, 1978.

Burton, Marilee Robin. THE ELEPHANT'S NEST. New York:
Harper & Row, 1979.

Cannon, Beth. A CAT HAD A FISH ABOUT A DREAM. New York:
Pantheon Books, 1976.

Carle, Eric. DO YOU WANT TO BE MY FRIEND. New York:
Thomas Y. Crowell, 1971.

_____. I SEE A SONG. New York: Thomas Y. Crowell,
1973.

_____. THE VERY LONG TAIL. New York: Thomas Y.
Crowell, 1972.

_____. THE VERY LONG TRAIN. New York: Thomas Y.
Crowell, 1972.

Carrick, Donald. DRIP DROP. New York: Thomas Y. Crowell, 1972.

Carroll, Ruth. THE CHIMP AND THE CLOWN. New York:
Henry Z. Walck, 1968.

_____. THE CHRISTMAS KITTEN. New York: Henry Z.
Walck, 1973.

_____. ROLLING DOWN HILL. New York: Henry Z.
Walck, 1973.

_____. WHAT WISKERS DID. New York: Henry Z.
Walck, 1965.

_____. THE WITCH KITTEN. New York: Henry Z.
Walck, 1973.

Chamberlin, Bob, and Bergman, Donna. I'M NOT LITTLE,
I'M BIG. Puppet Press, 1973.

Degen, Bruce. AUNT POSSUM AND THE PUMPKIN MAN. New
York: Crown Publishers, 1977.

DeGroat, Diane. ALLIGATOR'S TOOTHACHE. New York:
Crown Publishers, 1977.

DePaola, Thomas Anthony. PANCAKES FOR BREAKFAST. New York: Harcourt Brace Jovanovich, 1978.

Emberly, Ed. A BIRTHDAY WISH. Boston: Little, Brown, 1977.

Espenscheid, Gertrude. THE OH BALL. New York: Harper & Row, 1966.

Fromm, Lilo. MUFFEL AND PLUMS. New York: Macmillan, 1973.

Fuchs, Erick. JOURNEY TO THE MOON. New York: Delcorte Press, 1969.

Goodall, John S. THE ADVENTURES OF PADDY PORK. New York: Harcourt Brace Jovanovich, 1968.

_____. THE BALLOONING ADVENTURES OF PADDY PORK. New York: Harcourt Brace Jovanovich, 1969.

_____. CREEPY CASTLE. New York: Atheneum Publishers, 1975.

_____. AN EDWARDIAN SUMMER. New York: Atheneum Publishers, 1976.

_____. JACKO. New York: Harcourt Brace Jovanovich, 1971.

_____. THE MIDNIGHT ADVENTURES OF KELLY, DOT, AND ESMERELDA. New York: Atheneum Publishers, 1972.

_____. PADDY'S EVENING OUT. New York: Atheneum Publishers, 1973.

_____. PADDY PORK'S HOLIDAY. New York: Atheneum Publishers, 1976.

_____. SHREWBETTINA'S BIRTHDAY. New York: Harcourt Brace Jovanovich, 1970.

_____. THE SURPRISE PICNIC. New York: Harcourt Brace Jovanovich, 1970.

Hamburger, John. A SLEEPING DAY. New York: Four Winds (Scholastic), 1973.

Hartelius, Margaret A. THE BIRTHDAY TROMBONE. Garden City, N.Y.: Doubleday, 1977.

Hartelius, Margaret A. THE CHICKEN'S CHILD. Garden City, N.Y.: Doubleday, 1975.

Heller, Linda. LILI AT THE TABLE. New York: Macmillan, 1979.

Hoban, Tanna. LOOK AGAIN. New York: Macmillan, 1971.

_____. SHAPES AND THINGS. New York: Macmillan, 1970.

Hogrogian, Nonny. APPLES. New York: Macmillan, 1972.

Hutchins, Pat. CHANGES, CHANGES. New York: Macmillan, 1971.

Knobler, Susan. THE TADPOLE AND THE FROG. New York: Harvey House, (E.M. Hale), 1975.

Krahn, Fernando. THE BIGGEST CHRISTMAS TREE ON EARTH. Boston: Little, Brown, 1978.

_____. CATCH THAT CAT! New York: E.P. Dutton, 1978.

_____. A FLYING SAUCER FULL OF SPAGETTI. New York: E.P. Dutton, 1970.

_____. THE GREAT APE. New York: Viking Press, 1978.

_____. HOW SANTA CLAUS HAD A LONG AND DIFFICULT JOURNEY DELIVERING HIS PRESENTS. New York: Delcorte Press, 1970.

_____. JOURNEY OF SEBASTIAN. New York: Delcorte Press, 1976.

_____. LITTLE LOVE STORY. Philadelphia: J. B. Lippincott, 1976.

_____. THE MYSTERY OF THE GIANT FOOTPRINTS. New York: E.P. Dutton, 1977.

_____. ROBOT-BOT-BOT. New York: E.P. Dutton, 1979.

Lisker, Sonia. THE ATTIC WITCH. New York: Four Winds (Scholastic), 1973.

_____. LOST. New York: Harcourt Brace Jovanovich, 1975.

McTrusty, Ron. DANDELION YEAR. New York: Harvey House (E.M. Hale), 1979.

Mari, Iela. THE APPLE AND THE MOTH. New York: Pantheon Books, 1970.

_____. THE CHICKEN AND THE EGG. New York: Pantheon Books, 1970.

_____. THE MAGIC BALLOON. New York: S. G. Phillips, 1969.

Mayer, Mercer. AH-CHOO. New York: Dial Press, 1976.

_____. BUBBLE, BUBBLE. New York: Parents' Magazine Press, 1973.

_____. A BOY, A DOG, AND A FROG. New York: Dial Press, 1967.

Mayer, Mercer. A BOY, A DOG, A FROG, AND A FRIEND. New York: Dial Press, 1971.

_____. A FROG GOES TO DINNER. New York: Dial Press, 1974.

_____. FROG ON HIS OWN. New York: Dial Press, 1973.

_____. FROG WHERE ARE YOU. New York: Dial Press, 1969.

_____. THE GREAT CAT CHASE. New York: Four Winds (Scholastic), 1975.

_____. HICCUP. New York: Four Winds (Scholastic), 1976.

_____. ONE FROG TOO MANY. New York: Four Winds (Scholastic), 1975.

_____. OOPS. New York: Four Winds (Scholastic), 1977.

_____. TWO MORE MORAL TALES. New York: Four Winds (Scholastic), 1974.

Mayer, Remate. HIDE AND SEEK. Scarsdale, N.Y.: Bradbury Press, 1972.

_____. VICKI. New York: Atheneum Publishers, 1969.

Miller, Barry. ALPHABET WORLD. New York: Macmillan, 1971.

Mitgutsch, Ali. IN THE BUSY TOWN. New York: Golden (Western Publishing), 1973.

Mordillo, Guillermo. DAMP AND DAFFY DOINGS OF A DARING PIRATE SHIP. New York: Harlin Quist, 1971.

Olschewski, Alfred. WINTERBIRD. Boston: Houghton Mifflin, 1969.

Ramage, Corinne. THE JONESES. Philadelphia: J.B. Lippincott, 1975.

Reich, Hanns. ANIMALS OF MANY LANDS. New York: Hill & Wang, 1966.

_____. DOGS. New York: Hill & Wang, 1973.

_____. LAUGHING CAMERA. New York: Hill & Wang, 1967.

_____. LAUGHING CAMERA II. New York: Hill & Wang, 1970.

_____. LOVERS. New York: Hill & Wang, 1968.

Rice, Brian and Evans, Tony. ENGLISH SURPRISE. New York: Flash (Music Sales Corp., Div. of Quick Fox, Inc.), 1973.

Ringi, Kjili. THE MAGIC STICK. New York: Harper & Row, 1968.

_____. THE WINNER. New York: Harper & Row, 1969.

Rockwell, Anne F. ALBERT E. CUB AND ZEBRA: AN ALPHABET STORYBOOK. New York: Thomas Y. Crowell, 1977.

Schnick, Eleanor. MAKING FRIENDS. New York: Macmillan, 1969.

Shimin, Symeon. A SPECIAL BIRTHDAY. New York: McGraw-Hill, 1976.

Simmons, Ellie. CAT. New York: David McKay, 1968.

_____. DOG. New York: David McKay, 1967.

_____. FAMILY. New York: David McKay, 1970.

Simmons, Ellie. WHEELS. New York: David McKay, 1969.

Steiner, Charlotte. I AM ANDY. New York: Alfred A. Knopf, 1961.

Sugano, Yoshikatsu. THE KITTENS ADVENTURE. New York: McGraw-Hill, 1971.

Sugita, Yutaka. GOODNIGHT 1, 2, 3. New York: Scroll Press, 1971.

_____. MY FRIEND LITTLE JOHN AND ME. New York: E.P. Dutton, 1976.

Turkle, Brinton. DEEP IN THE FOREST. New York: E.P. Dutton, 1976.

Ueno, Noriko. ELEPHANT BUTTONS. New York: Harper & Row, 1973.

Ungerer, Tomi. ONE, TWO, THREE. New York: Harper & Row, 1964.

_____. ONE, TWO, WHERE'S MY SHOE? New York: Harper & Row, 1964.

_____. SNAIL, WHERE ARE YOU? New York: Harper & Row, 1962.

Vasiliu, Mircea. WHAT'S HAPPENING? Binghamton, N.Y.: John Day (c/o Conklin Book Ctr., Inc.), 1970.

Ward, Lynd. THE SILVER PONY. Boston: Houghton Mifflin, 1973.

Wezel, Peter. GOOD BIRD. New York: Harper & Row, 1966.

Winter, Paula. THE BEAR AND THE FLY. New York: Crown Publishers, 1976.

Wondriska, William. A LONG PIECE OF STRING. New York: Holt, Rinehart & Winston, 1963.

APPENDIX H

SOME RESOURCES FOR DEVELOPING INDIVIDUALIZED

READING PROGRAMS AND THEMATIC UNITS

I. 1. Collecting Books

    a. Paperback book clubs, esp.:

       1. Scholastic Book Clubs
         (Arrow, Tab, Etc.)
         904 Sylvan Avenue.
         Englewood Cliffs, N.J. 07632

       2. Read Book Club
         (Jr. Hi., H.S.)
         Xerox Co.
         Columbus, Ohio 43216

2. Annotated Book Lists

    a. Publisher's Catalogs, esp.:

       1. Garrard Books (Ele)
         Champaign, Ill. 61820

       2. Dell Paperbacks (Ele)
         245 East 47th Street
         New York, N.Y. 10017

       3. Bowmar Publications (Ele-H.S.)
         4563 Colorado Blvd.
         Los Angeles, CA 90039

       4. Scholastic Publishing Co.
         (Ele-H.S.)

    b. "Classroom Choices" Books chosen by children and adults (beginning reading-older readers), International Reading Association, published in The Reading Teacher journal each October.

3. Kits

    a. Individualized Reading Program (Scholastic Publishers) Composed of books, teaching

guides, conference forms, activity cards and
games.

    1. "Reaching Out" (Ele)
    2. "Reaching Forward" (middle grades)

b. Read Alongs: Books, filmstrips, cassettes,
records

    1. "Monster Books," Bill Martin Books,
       (Bowmar Pub. Co., early Ele.)
    2. Little Golden Books, box of books
       plus tapes (early Ele.)
    3. "Troll Read-Alongs," older kids,
       science materials, etc. Educational
       Reading Service, Mahwah, N.J.

4. Reluctant Reader Materials

a. "Pacemaker Bestsellers," 40 books per unit,
4 books for each title
Interest Level: Mid-grades - H.S.
Reading Level: 2-3 grade
Fearon-Pitman Publishers, Inc., 6 David Dr.
Belmont, CA 94002

b. "Pal Paperbacks," short selections, adven-
ture, mysteries, etc.
Interest Level: Mid-grade - H.S.
Reading Level: 3-5 grade, also

c. "Radlauer Sports Language Lab," similar set-
up, grade range and interests
Bowmar Publishing Co.

d. Scholastic Publishing Co.

    1. SPRINT Libraries, 5 titles per lib.,
       4 books per title, teaching guides with
       plot summaries, discussion questions,
       etc.
       Interest Level: middle grades
       Reading Levels: 5 libraries at
       second gr., 4 at third.

    2. Reluctant Reader Libraries, teacher
       guides, etc.,
       Interest Level: 7-12 grades
       Reading Level: 4-10 grades

3. Action Reading System, Units for 10 to 20 students, books or short stories, plays, cassettes, and teacher guides.
Interest Level: 7-12 grades
Reading Level: second grade and above

4. "Action Magazine:" Hi interest stories, features, same ranges and reading levels as the Action Reading System.

II. Thematic Units

1. Reading Ladders for Human Relations (p.b. book) Annotated books grouped by age range, on 4 themes each with various subthemes. Editor: Virginia Reid, 1972 public. American Council on Education, One DuPont Circle, Washington, D.C. 20036.

2. SPIRAL Program, 12 titles, 6 major teenage themes, teachers' guides, etc.
Interest Level: 7-12 grades
Reading Level: 2-3 grades
Continental Press, Elizabethtown, PA 17022

3. Read Paperback Book Club (listed above, p. 131) of interest to Jr. Hi. and H.S.; teachers' guide for each book: summary of story, identification of themes, questions, multimedia projects. National Council of Teachers of English, 1111 Kenyon Road, Urbana, Ill. 61801, Order No. 40866A.

III. Collecting Funds for Books

1. Reading is Fundamental (RIF) Program, grades K-12, provides up to 50% of cost of books for projects meeting RIF criteria. RIF, L'enfant 2500, Smithsonian Institution, Washington, DC 20560.

2. Federal Funds for paperbacks are also provided by Right to Read and Title IV-B. Info. in Reading Teacher Journal, Jan. 1978, pp. 432-33.

3. Collecting community funds to pay for various book purchases can be done by asking businesses, merchants, etc. to donate monies to schools, classroom. PTA groups, Library Groups, individuals can be involved in the solicitations.

611

GLOSSARY

Assisted Reading: A form of reading which involves listening as a reader processes the print in a whole story context.

Cloze Test (Procedure): Any of several ways of measuring a person's ability to restore omitted portions of an oral or written message from its remaining context. Note: W. Taylor coined the term CLOZE in 1953 to reflect the gestalt principle of 'closure,' the ability to complete an incomplete stimulus. In reading practice, a standardized procedure and set of scores have been developed to differentiate frustration/instructional reading levels and instructional/independent reading levels.

Comprehension: 1) the process of getting the meaning of a communication, as in personal letter, speech, sign language. 2) the knowledge or understanding that is the result of such a process.

DRTA: A further step in the directed reading activity. The Directed Reading Thinking Activity's chief elements are prediction and verification. Students in the pre-reading stage set their own purposes for reading by making predictions; in the reading stage they verify their predictions and in the discussion stage they check their verification.

Echoic Reading: Oral reading in which students imitate or repeat another's reading.

Graphophonemic: The relationship between the visual graphic print and the sound system of language.

Informal Reading Inventory: (IRI) The use of a graded series of passages of increasing difficulty, usually taken from basal readers, to make an informal diagnosis of one or more levels or reading performance. Note: This technique was first described at some length by E. Betts in a 1946 publication as a way of identifying several levels of student functioning in reading: independent, instructional, and frustration levels. The technique is adaptable to the rough assessment of oral reading skills and comprehension, as well as of silent reading. In addition, if passages are read to the student, some indication of level of listening comprehension may be gained.

Language Experience Approach: 1) An approach to learning to read in which the student's or group's own words or oral compositions are written down and used as materials of instruction for reading, writing, and spelling, speaking, and listening. 2) A curriculum program which emphasizes the interrelationship of various types of language experience.

Language Process: Speaking, listening, reading and writing are verbal processes of communication.

Language Systems: The English language includes the graphophonemic, syntactic and semantic systems.

Linguistics: 1) The study of the nature and the structure of language and languages. 2) The study of the nature of language communication. Note: linguistic study includes several areas of specialized interests, as biolinguistics, sociolinguistics, historical linguistics, etc.

Miscue: An oral reading response that differs from the expected response to the written text. Note: Miscues are the interaction between the reader's grammatical system, experience and the printed page just as are accurate reading responses. For this reason, Kenneth Goodman and his associates believe miscues reflect the strengths and weaknesses of the reading strategy of the reader. Thus an analysis of the miscues of individuals may provide information for planning reading instruction.

Morphological: Adjective of morphology. 1) The patterns of word-formation in a language, including deviation, inflection, and compounding. 2) The study of such patterns.

Neurological Impress Remedial Technique: A method designed to improve fluency in reading. Note: The teacher sits slightly behind the student and orally reads the text while one of them points out the part of the text being read. The student attempts to read along as quickly and accurately as possible. In beginning sessions, the teacher reads louder and slightly faster than the student. Later, the teacher decreases in volume and speed so that the student will be in the lead.

Phonological: The sound system of a language.

Propositional Analysis: A procedure to formally represent meaning in a text with the primary emphasis on semantics. Analysis of idea units represented by the sentence comprised of one or more propositions.

Psycholinguistics: The interdisciplinary field of psychology and linguistics in which language behavior is examined.

Reading Strategy Lesson: Lessons that highlight or focus on specific language cues and strategies in a meaningful context.

Schema Theory: Knowledge stored in memory which can be activated to relate to experiences.

Semantics: 1) The study of meaning, especially the study of relations between referents and names, and between concepts and names. 2) The formal study of the meaning of meaning; especially the relationship of signs to verbal referents or objects. 3) The study of meaning in artificial language systems, rather than in natural language; pure semantics.

Sociolinguistics: The study of the relationships between linguistic behavior and other aspects of social behavior. Note: Sociolinguistics examine such relationships as those between an individual's speech and that of other in a speech community; the effects of travel and media on language; and effects of political, social and economical power structures on the perception of language differences.

Story Grammar: In text analysis, a grammar designed to specify relations among episodes in a story and to formulate rules for generating other stories.

Syntactic: Referring to the grammatical relations and functions of sentence components.

Vocabulary: 1) A list of words, as in a dictionary, glossary; lexicon. 2) Those words known or used by a person or a group. 3) All the words of a language. 4) Nonverbal forms of expression, as the vocabulary of the painter, dancer, etc. 5) (Cap) A subtest of several intelligence and reading tests. Note: Special types of vocabulary, as meaning vocabulary are given under the describing term.

<u>Whole Language</u>: Written and oral language in connected
discourse in a meaningful contextual setting.

<u>Word Attack</u>: In common usage, word analysis or word
identification. Note: Word attack is frequently limited to the act of 'sounding it out.'

372.41
an 546

119 109

$ 35.00